Global public goods
for health

Disclaimer

The authors alone are responsible for the views expressed in this book.

Global public goods for health

Health economic and public health perspectives

Edited by

Richard D. Smith

School of Medicine, Health Policy and Practice,
University of East Anglia

Robert Beaglehole

Department of Health Services Provision,
World Health Organization, Geneva

David Woodward

Independent Development Economist, Geneva

and

Nick Drager

Strategy Unit, Office of the Director General,
World Health Organization, Geneva

OXFORD
UNIVERSITY PRESS

OXFORD

UNIVERSITY PRESS

Great Clarendon Street, Oxford OX2 6DP

Oxford University Press is a department of the University of Oxford.
It furthers the University's objective of excellence in research, scholarship,
and education by publishing worldwide in

Oxford New York

Auckland Bangkok Buenos Aires Cape Town Chennai
Dar es Salaam Delhi Hong Kong Istanbul Karachi Kolkata
Kuala Lumpur Madrid Melbourne Mexico City Mumbai
Nairobi São Paulo Shanghai Taipei Tokyo Toronto

Oxford is a registered trade mark of Oxford University Press
in the UK and in certain other countries

Published in the United States
by Oxford University Press Inc., New York

© World Health Organization, 2003

British Library Cataloguing in Publication Data
Data available

Library of Congress Cataloging in Publication Data
Data available

ISBN 0–19–852544–3 (Hbk)
ISBN 0–19–852798–5 (Pbk)

10 9 8 7 6 5 4 3 2

Typeset by Newgen Imaging Systems (P) Ltd., Chennai, India
Printed in Great Britain
on acid-free paper by
Biddles Ltd, King's Lynn, Norfolk

Dedication

To global health improvement.

Foreword

Globalization presents us an unprecedented opportunity to deliver better health for the world's poorest. It is becoming ever clearer that our increasingly interdependent and interconnected world means that domestic action alone is not sufficient to secure better health, but that collective action at the global level is essential to address the increasing cross border risks to public health security.

Looking through the lens of the 'Global Public Goods' concept, this book helps us to better construct an agenda that will advance the health of poor populations. The concept of global public goods *for health* is shown to be extremely useful in identifying which health interventions require such international collective action, and suggesting how they may be better produced and financed.

Improved health for the poor cannot be reached without a fundamental change in the way we work together. This means shared agenda's, new partnerships and funding mechanisms—such as the global alliance on vaccines and immunization and the global fund to fight HIV/AIDS, TB, and malaria. It also means developing new ways of conceptualizing and thinking about how to address current and future health challenges. This book, with its in-depth, rigorous analysis of global public goods for health, takes us along a key new path—a path that will be essential for us to follow to meet our common goal: better health for all.

April 2003

Gro Harlem Brundtland
Director General of WHO

Preface

Health is firmly on the global development agenda. There is a growing awareness of cross-border issues in health and trade that require new policy responses and financing mechanisms, including international patent régimes and pharmaceutical prices, the global spread of antimicrobial resistance, and the Framework Convention on Tobacco Control. The recent establishment of the Global Health Fund to fight HIV/AIDS, Tuberculosis, and Malaria is raising the profile of international assistance for health, and provides an important new global funding mechanism.

This expanding importance of health as an international issue, and the growth in attention given to health by nonhealth sector bodies, such as the World Bank and United Nations, has brought to prominence the concept of global public goods (GPGs) as applied to health. The GPG concept, as detailed in Chapter 1, considers the production of "goods" (encompassing a range of physical commodities, services, technologies, and information) that are in the interest of the world as a whole, such as controlling global climate change and preventing infectious disease pandemics. These goods often demonstrate "public good" attributes: once they are provided, no one can readily be excluded from their consumption, and one person's consumption does not prevent anyone else from consuming them. These attributes mean that there is often a lack of incentive to produce these goods—a situation exacerbated on the international stage as there is no "global government" to regulate or enforce production. Thus, the central issue of concern within the concept of GPGs becomes one of *ensuring collective action at the international level.*

The publication of "Global Public Goods: International Cooperation in the 21st Century" by Kaul *et al.* (1999) brought the concept of GPGs in to the international spotlight. This publication explored the application of the GPG concept across many sectors of international concern, such as trade agreements, the environment, and international security. "Health" was considered as one of a number of specific sectors to which the GPG concept may be applied, and Kaul has written separately on the subject of GPG and health (Kaul and Faust 2001).

Other organizations have recently begun to explore the relevance of the GPG concept to their activities. For example, the Swedish Ministry of Foreign Affairs commissioned a report entitled "Financing and Providing Global Public Goods: Expectations and Prospects." This developed a conceptual framework for examining the provision and financing of GPGs, applied, for illustrative purposes, to biodiversity, climate change, AIDS research, peace and security, and financial stability (Sagasti and Bezanson 2001). There has also been consideration of the concept with respect to health more specifically. For example, the World Health Organization's recent "Commission on Macroeconomics and Health"(CMH) took a particular interest in the use of the GPG concept in the improvement of health for poorer nations, and discussed several aspects of health as possible GPGs in its Working Group 2 (CMH 2001). This work primarily focused on different aspects of health research, such as investment in R&D orphan drug legislation, patent laws, and genomics, but also included communicable disease control, antimicrobial resistance, the role of international agencies, and methods of financing GPGH.

However, most writing on GPGs has been broad-based and multisectoral, with only brief consideration of GPGs with respect to health; most discussion within the health sector (including that of the CMH) has focused on medical technologies. This has raised more questions than answers, including, for example: the need to identify the international collective action problem that is to be addressed in health; whether health itself may be classed as a GPG; whether there are specific GPGs that affect health; whether and how best the GPG concept will enable health advancement among poor populations in poor countries; how the production and delivery of appropriate GPGs for health may be strengthened; how concepts of international collective action and GPGs for health relate to those of equity and human rights; and how the GPG concept interacts with national activities and priorities in health.

With questions such as these in mind, the Department of Health and Development of WHO began to explore the appropriateness and usefulness of the concept of GPG *for health* (GPGH) in more detail than previously. This volume provides the first large-scale unisectoral application of the GPG concept. The book is written from a nontechnical perspective, and is suitable for a wide range of readers, including policymakers, advisers, researchers, consultants, practitioners, and students in domestic and international public health, economics, and development, in both developed and developing countries.

The main focus of analysis of the GPGH concept in this book is whether, and how best, it can be used to advance the health of poor populations, especially those in poor countries. To this end, a series of papers were commissioned to explore the applicability of the GPGH concept in several key areas. These "case studies" form the core of this volume. Specifically, we seek to: establish whether health *per se* can validly be considered as a GPG, and what elements of health may be considered as GPGs *for* health; clarify whether the topics covered as case studies can be classified as a GPGH, or have GPG aspects; consider the usefulness of the GPG concept in improving health within the topics presented as case studies; and present a policy and research agenda for the implementation and development of the GPGH concept so as to optimize its health effects.

The first section of the book outlines the conceptual background of GPGH. The first chapter outlines the economic foundations of the GPG paradigm, explores key issues and implications arising from this paradigm, and examines how it may appropriately be applied to health. Critically, this chapter explores whether health *per se* may be considered as a GPG, and formulates a definition for GPGH—different to that used by Kaul *et al.* (1999)—which is used in subsequent chapters.

Section 2 follows with a series of case studies of possible GPGH; covering a series of important issues in communicable disease and environmental changes that affect health. Chapter 2 provides a case study of an existing GPGH: polio eradication. The history of polio eradication provides several important lessons for the future production of the other GPGH identified within this section, in both economic and political terms. Chapter 3 on the control of tuberculosis and Chapter 4 on the containment of antimicrobial resistance, explore the usefulness of the GPGH concept for the advancement of these specific topic areas. These chapters highlight several key respects in which the GPGH concept may assist in the establishment and financing of programs in these areas, as well as several limitations. Chapter 5 departs from the theme of communicable disease and considers the GPG concept as applied to aspects of environmental degradation that affect health. In many ways, the environment is a fundamental GPGH, as our health ultimately depends upon the air we breath, the water we drink, and the food we eat. The analysis of this important area from the GPG perspective is therefore especially illuminating of the usefulness and limitations of this approach.

The book then moves on from these "vertical" themes to a series of more "horizontal" issues. In Section 3 these concern the archetypal global public good of "knowledge." Here, aspects that militate against knowledge being a GPGH, as well as factors which are required to release its full potential as a GPGH, are explored in three areas. First, Chapter 6 considers "medical knowledge," providing a panoramic view of the broad issues involved in the production, dissemination, and use of knowledge embodied in medicines, both commercial and traditional. Chapter 7 considers knowledge more specifically in the application of the GPGH concept to genomics knowledge. Chapter 8 takes another angle, considering aspects of public health infrastructure as "access goods," identifying public health knowledge as a key element of that infrastructure.

Section 4 continues to consider the "horizontal" issue of legislation. Although this book is considering *global* public goods, it is clear from the previous chapters that both international *and national* law will be fundamental to securing the production of any GPGH. Agreements, for example, on the financing of GPGs, the role of nations in their production, and changes to patent regimes to generate wider dissemination and use of knowledge, all require various forms of national and international legislation to ensure cooperation. This is outlined in a broad sense in Chapter 9, which focuses on international law. Chapters 10 and 11 present more specific case studies of international law "in action," through the International Health Regulations and the WHO Framework Convention on Tobacco Control, respectively, contributing to the production of the GPGH of epidemic containment and tobacco control.

Section 5 reflects on the usefulness of the GPG concept within the context of health. Chapter 12 takes a somewhat critical view of the GPGH concept, and proposes an alternative paradigm that may achieve more for global health. Chapter 13 considers the common themes that result from the previous chapters, specifically the value that the GPG concept adds to aspects of health, and the limitations of that concept. This chapter concludes with an assessment of the appropriateness and usefulness of the GPG concept in the pursuit of increased global health, and in particular the health of the poor.

In Section 6, Chapter 14, the editors return to the initial purpose of the book outlined in this foreword, and conclude with a series of priorities for research and policy with respect to further use of the GPGH concept.

Overall, the GPG concept has much to offer the financing and provision of global health programs. For example, it is a framework focused on the problems of, and possible solutions to, collective action at the global level. As such, it can unify often-disparate disciplinary approaches, such as the legal, economic, and medical. It also allows the presentation of a coherent argument to complement "traditional" aid, and as such may be a powerful tool for advocacy. It provides further rationale for the funding of developing country infrastructure and systems by the developed world. However, it is of utmost importance that the limitations of the concept are recognized. If not, it will be in danger of becoming overexposed and devalued, and may even be detrimental to the health of those in greatest need.

This book will assist greatly in progressing the debate concerning the use of the GPG concept in health. However, the debate needs to be built upon and developed to secure a niche for the GPG concept within the wider array of international approaches to the funding and provision of health for the benefit of all. We hope that readers will feel prompted to engage in that debate, and look forward to the next steps.

Richard D Smith
Robert Beaglehole
David Woodward
Nick Drager
Geneva, April 2003

References

CMH. *Macroeconomics and Health: Investing in Health for Economic Development*. Geneva: World Health Organization, http://www.cmhealth.org/, 2001.

Kaul I, Grunberg I, Stern MA. *Global Public Goods: International Cooperation in the 21st Century*. New York: Oxford University Press, 1999.

Kaul I, Faust M. Global public goods and health: Taking the agenda forward. *Bull World Health Organ* 2001; **79**: 869–74.

Sagasti F, Bezanson. *Financing and Providing Global Public Goods: Expectations and Prospects*. Developing Financing 2000, Study 2001:2. Prepared for the Ministry for Foreign Affairs, Sweden: www.utrikes.regeringen.se/inenglish/policy/devcoop/financing.htm, 2001.

Contents

Contributors

Arnab Acharya trained in theoretical economics at the Universtity of Illinois and in public health at Harvard University. He is a research fellow at Institute of Development Studies where he conducts research on public health and poverty. He has published both on theoretical economics and on public health. His current fields of research are poverty and health, cost-effectiveness analysis of public health measures, and ethical issues in economic development.

Mary Agocs is a United States physician who trained in epidemiology and public health at the US Centers for Disease Control and Prevention and the London School of Hygiene and Tropical Medicine. She has worked and written on the epidemiology of air pollution-associated diseases, has taught epidemiology in Eastern Europe, and provided guidance for policymakers at the United States Senate and United Nations Foundation. Since 2000, she has worked in the area of polio eradication, currently at the World Health Organization in Cairo, Egypt.

Michael J Ahern trained in geography at the School of Oriental and African Studies (University of London) and in infectious disease control at the London School of Hygiene and Tropical Medicine where he is a Research Fellow in the Centre on Global Change and Health. His current research focuses on the health effects of global change in general, and in particular the effects on communities in lower-income countries.

R Bruce Aylward is a Canadian physician who trained in epidemiology and public health at the Johns Hopkins School of Public Health and the London School of Hygiene and Tropical Medicine. He has worked and written on the epidemiology and control of a number infectious diseases, focusing primarily on the area of vaccines and immunization. Since 1998 he has been the head of the Global Polio Eradication Initiative at the World Health Organization in Geneva, Switzerland.

Robert Beaglehole trained in medicine in New Zealand and in epidemiology and public health at the London School of Hygiene and Tropical Medicine and the University of North Carolina at Chapel Hill. He is on leave from his position as Professor of Community Health at the University of Auckland, New Zealand and working as a public health adviser in the Department of Health Service Provision at WHO, Geneva on strengthening the public health workforce in developing countries. He has published over 200 scientific papers, several books co-authored with Ruth Bonita on epidemiology and public health, and is co-editor of the *Oxford Textbook of Public Health*, fourth edition.

Douglas W Bettcher is the Coordinator of the Framework Convention on Tobacco Control team, Tobacco Free Initiative at the World Health Organization in Geneva. He holds a PhD in International Relations and also a Graduate Diploma in World Politics both from the London School of Economics and Political Science; a Master's of Public Health from the London School of Hygiene and Tropical Medicine; and a Doctor of Medicine degree from the University of Alberta, Canada. Dr Bettcher sits on the Editorial Boards of the *Bulletin of the World Health Organization* and *Global Governance*, and is a Vice-Chair of the public health interest group of the American Society of International Law. He has written widely on several topics, including globalization and health, foreign policy and health security, international law and public health, tobacco control, and trade and health policy issues.

Colin D Butler is a post doctoral fellow at the National Centre for Epidemiology and Population Health, at The Australian National University, Canberra. When a medical student he was arrested during the campaign to save Tasmania's Franklin River from inundation, and in 1989 he co-founded a nongovernmental organization, called BODHI, which continues to support health, education, and environmental projects in India and Tibet. His main research interests concern global environmental change and human health, global income distribution, and the influence of economically dominant populations upon ideology, science, and the health of disadvantaged people.

Arachu Castro is Instructor in Medical Anthropology in the Department of Social Medicine, Harvard Medical School, and member of the research team at Partners In Health. She has worked in the areas of infectious disease, reproductive health, and nutrition, mostly in Mexico, Haiti, Cuba, Peru, and Argentina. Dr. Castro obtained her PhD in Anthropology at the École des Hautes Etudes en Sciences Sociales in Paris, France, her PhD in Sociology at the University of Barcelona, Spain, and her Master of Public Health at Harvard School of Public Health. She was one of the editors and co-authors of *The Global Plan to Stop TB*.

Joanna Coast (BA (Econ), MSc, PhD) is a Senior Lecturer in Health Economics at the University of Bristol. Her research contributions are in the area of health economics applied within the context of social medicine and she has published extensively on the economics of antimicrobial resistance, health-care rationing, and the organization of care.

Flavio Comim is a Research Associate at the Von Hugel Institute, St Edmund's College, Cambridge. He teaches at Universidade Federal do Rio Grande do Sul in Brazil. He received his PhD from the University of Cambridge in 1999. His areas of research comprise development economics, poverty, inequality and, social capital theories with particular emphasis on the capability approach. He has published papers in History of Political Economy, Review of Political Economy and Structural Change and Economic Dynamics.

Abdallah S Daar is at the University of Toronto, where he is Professor of Public Health Sciences and Surgery as well as Director of the Program in Applied Ethics and Biotechnology at the Joint Centre for Bioethics. He is a member of the International Ethics Committee of the Human Genome Organization, Fellow of the New York Academy of Sciences and a member of the Institute Advisory Board of the Institute of Infection and Immunity of the Canadian Institutes of Health Research. He has published two books and has over 200 publications, including the WHO report (with J-F Mattei) entitled Medical Genetics and Biotechnology: Implications for Public Health.

Nick Drager is Coordinator in the Strategy Unit in the Office of the Director General of the World Health Organization. He has extensive experience working with senior government officials in developing countries worldwide and their major development partners in: sector analysis, health policy development, strategic planning, and resource allocation decisions. His current work focuses on emerging global public health issues related to globalization and trade. The policy-related, research, and training activities of the work program are designed to contribute to enabling public health practitioners to analyze and act on the broader determinants of health development, as well as to place public health interests higher on the international development agenda to improve health outcomes for the poor. He has an MD from McGill University and a PhD. in Economics from Hautes Etudes Internationales, University of Geneva.

Janet Dzator has a Doctorate in Economics from the University of Queensland. She has been researching and teaching in Economics in Ghana and Australia for the last 10 years. She is one of the two founding members of the Health Statistics Course in the Institute of Statistics, Social and Economics Research, University of Ghana and an invited speaker on "Economic arguments for the cancellation of developing countries debt" at the University of Queensland in 1999. Currently, she is a Research Fellow in Health Economics at Curtin University, Perth, Australia. She has published in peer reviewed journals such as *Social Science and Medicine, Social Indicators Research, Economic Analysis and Policy* and the *Ugandan Health Bulletin.*

Sarah England is a Task Manager in the Stop TB partnership secretariat at the World Health Organization. She holds a doctorate in clinical medicine from Oxford and an MBA and BSc from Simon Fraser University and the University of Toronto. Dr England has extensive field experience in South-East Asia as a Fellow of Harvard University, as a consultant for CIDA and the World Bank and as WHO field staff. She designed the structure of the Vaccine Fund of the Global Alliance for Vaccines and Immunization and co-wrote the proposal that resulted in US$ 750 million in support from Bill and Melinda Gates. Her current work concerns financing the global effort to Stop TB.

Paul Farmer is a physician–anthropologist who has worked for 20 years in Haiti, where he serves as medical director of a hospital serving the rural poor. Among his books are "AIDS and Accusation" (University of California), winner of the Wellcome Medal of the Royal Anthropological Society of Great Britain and

Ireland; "Infections and Inequalities" (University of California), winner of the Margaret Mead Award; and the forthcoming "Pathologies of Power" (University of California). He is also the editor of "Women, Poverty, and AIDS" (Common Courage), which was awarded the Eileen Basker Prize of the American Anthropological Association. He is a Professor at Harvard Medical School, and founding director of Partners In Health, which supports medical and public health projects in Latin America.

David P Fidler is professor of law at Indiana University School of Law, Bloomington, Indiana. He is a leading expert on international law and public health. He has published widely in both international legal and public health periodicals. His books include "International Law and Infectious Diseases" (Clarendon Press, 1999) and "International Law and Public Health: Materials on and Analysis of Global Health Jurisprudence" (Transnational Publishers, 2000). He has served as an international legal consultant on global public health issues to the World Health Organization, US Centers for Disease Control and Prevention, and numerous nongovernmental organizations. He earned degrees at the University of Kansas, Harvard Law School, and the University of Oxford.

Jayati Ghosh received her PhD from the University of Cambridge in 1983. She is currently Professor of Economics at Jawaharlal Nehru University, New Delhi. In addition to more than 70 published articles, she has co-authored (with CP Chandrasekhar) two books, "Crisis as Conquest: Learning from East Asia" (Orient Longman, 2001) and "The Market that Failed: A Decade of Neoliberal Economic Reforms in India" (Leftword Books, 2002). She also writes several regular columns on economics and current affairs in the press. She is currently the Executive Secretary of International Development Economics Associates, an international network of heterodox South-based economists (www.networkideas.org).

Johan Giesecke is State Epidemiologist for Sweden at the Swedish Institute for Infectious Disease Control, and Professor of Infectious Disease Epidemiology at the Karolinska Institute Medical University, Stockholm, Sweden. He graduated as MD from that university and worked for 10 years as an infectious disease clinician before taking an MSc in epidemiology at the London School of Hygiene and Tropical Medicine. He has been active in the efforts to harmonize infectious disease surveillance and control within the European Union, and on a one-year sabbatical to WHO Geneva in 1999/2000 he led the work on the revision of the International Health Regulations. He has published some 150 scientific papers, and has written a textbook on infectious disease epidemiology.

Jim Yong Kim is a physician-anthropologist, assistant professor of medical anthropology at Harvard Medical School and chief of the Division of Social Medicine and Health Inequalities at Brigham and Women's Hospital. He was a lead editor for *The Global Plan to Stop TB* and is co-editor of *Dying for Growth: Global Inequality and the Health of the Poor*. He is a co-founder of Partners In Health and he works closely with the World Health Organization as chair of a working group focused on appropriate care and drug access for patients with drug-resistant TB.

Jennifer Linkins has a background in business and finance, with an MBA from INSEAD in Fontainebleau France. She worked as an information systems consultant for several years before joining the World Health Organization in 1996. Since 1999, she has worked as a Technical Officer with the Global Polio Eradication Initiative.

Anthony J McMichael is Director of the National Centre for Epidemiology and Population Health, at The Australian National University, Canberra. He was, from 1994 until 2001, Professor of Epidemiology at the London School of Hygiene and Tropical Medicine. His research interests over three decades have spanned occupational diseases, dietary influences on chronic diseases, social epidemiological research and, more recently, the population health consequences of global environmental change. Since 1993 he has coordinated the assessment of health impacts for the UN's Intergovernmental Panel on Climate Change. His recent book, *Human Frontiers, Environments and Disease: Past Patterns, Uncertain Futures*, was published in 2001 by Cambridge University Press.

Gavin Mooney is Professor of Health Economics and Director of the Social and Public Health Economics Research Group (SPHERe) at Curtin University in Perth, Australia. He also holds a Visiting position at Aarhus University in Denmark. He has written over 200 papers in health economics and written or edited 16 books. He has worked on many occasions as an adviser to WHO. He is the director of a web-based course in health economics up to Masters level. His main research interests are in the economics of aboriginal health, of equity and of ethics.

Richard Peck received his PhD from Princeton University in 1983 under the supervision of Hugo Sonnenschein. He also worked at Princeton as Joe Stiglitz's research assistant. Richard Peck undertaken research in the areas of public finance, regulation and substance abuse and has published in numerous journals including *Econometrica and Journal of Public Economics*. He was the senior author of "A Welfare Analysis of Tobacco Consumption" that appeared in the *Tobacco Control in Developing Countries* edited by Jha and Chaloupka. The Robert Wood Johnson Foundation, The National Cancer Institute, The Rockefeller Foundation and the World Bank have supported his research. He has been at the University of Illinois at Chicago since 1982.

John Powles is a graduate of Sydney University medical school. After spending 4 years in the UK in the early 1970s he spent 16 years at Monash Univesity in Melbourne before taking up his current post in 1991—in what is now the Department of Public Health and Primary Care in Cambridge. He has been heavily involved in public health education and research in Bulgaria, recently concentrating on the reasons for the very high risks of stroke. He has a long-standing interest in the determinants of health levels in populations and related policy issues.

Aaron Shakow is a research affiliate at the Program in Infectious Disease and Social Change, Harvard Medical School. A historian by training, his work has focused on the transnational spread of health and development policy as sociopolitical phenomena, with special emphasis on Latin America and the Middle East. Since 1997, he has worked with the medical non-profit Partners In Health as a grantwriter and public relations specialist. He is currently a doctoral candidate in the Department of History at Harvard University, focusing on the practice and political iconography of European and Ottoman medicine in eighteenth-century Istanbul.

Peter A Singer is Sun Life Financial Chair and Director of the University of Toronto Joint Center for Bioethics, Program Leader of the Canadian Program on Genomics and Global Health, Director of the University of Toronto PAHO/WHO Collaborating Center for Bioethics, and Professor of Medicine at the University of Toronto. He completed medical school at the University of Toronto, and postgraduate studies at the University of Chicago and Yale University. A Canadian Institutes of Health Research Investigator, he has published over 150 peer-reviewed articles on bioethics. He holds major research grants from US National Institutes of Health, Ontario Research and Development Challenge Fund, and Genome Canada. His current research focus is global health ethics.

Richard D Smith is a Senior Lecturer in Health Economics at the University of East Anglia, having held positions previously in Sydney, Cambridge, Bristol, and Melbourne, and is an Honorary Associate Professor at the University of Hong Kong. His research interests and experience range across many facets of health economics, most recently focusing on the monetary and nonmonetary assessment of health benefits, the economics of antimicrobial resistance, primary care reform, and the impact of globalization on health and health services. Richard has also taught widely, and is currently Director of Postgraduate Taught Programs within the School of Medicine, Health Policy and Practice.

Allyn L Taylor is a health policy adviser at the World Health Organization and an adjunct professor at the University of Maryland School of Law and the Johns Hopkins Bloomberg School of Hygiene and Public Health Department of Health Policy and Management. She has written numerous articles and book chapters on international health law concerns, including global governance and international public health law, health and human rights, tobacco control, women's health, biotechnology and cloning, and communicable disease control. She currently serves as the chair of the International Health Law Interest Group of the American Society of International Law.

Halla Thorsteinsdóttir is a Senior Research Associate in the Program in Applied Ethics and Biotechnology and the Canadian Program on Genomics and Global Health at the University of Toronto Joint Centre for Bioethics. She completed her doctoral studies in 1998 at the Science Policy Research Unit (SPRU), University of Sussex, Britain. Prior to that she completed a masters degree in Development Economics from Carleton University, Canada. She has worked in science policy research in Canada, Iceland and in Britain. Her research has spanned wide topics from analysing research collaboration in small science systems, to examining the factors which encourage the development of health biotechnologies in developing countries.

Chris Vanderwarker served as a research assistant at the Program in Infectious Disease and Social Change, Harvard Medical School from 2000 to 2002. In this capacity he assisted in the analysis and formulation of development policy focusing on pragmatic interventions to control epidemics of drug-resistant tuberculosis. Currently, he is working on the implementation of the Botswana National Antiretroviral Program in conjunction with the Botswana–Harvard Partnership. In 2003 he will begin a dual doctoral degree program in medicine and anthropology at the University of Pennsylvania.

David Woodward is an independent development economist. At the time of writing he was working for the Stragegy Unit of the World Health Organization. He was previously an economic adviser in the British Foreign and Commonwealth Office, and a technical assistant to the British Executive Director at the IMF and World Bank, and has worked on a wide range of development issues for non-governmental organizations, UNDP, UNCTAD, and the Institute of Child Health (University of London). He is the author of *Debt, Adjustment and Poverty in Developing Countries* (London: Pinter Publishers/Save the Children (UK), 1992), and *The Next Crisis? Direct and Equity Investment in Developing Countries* (London: Zed Books, 2001).

Abbreviations

AFP	acute flaccid paralysis
AHSG	Assembly of Heads of States and Governments
AIDS	acquired immuno deficiency syndrome
AMR	antimicrobial resistance
APUA	Alliance for the Prudent Use of Antibiotics
ARI	acute respiratory infection
CARE	Cooperative for American Relief to Everywhere
CDC	Centers for Disease Control
CDM	clean development mechanism
CFCS	chlorofluoro carbons
CIA	Central Intelligence Agency
CMH	Committee on Macroeconomics and Health
CNN	Cable News Network
CIL	Customary International Law
CORE	Congress of Racial Equality
DALY	disability-adjusted life year
DNA	deoxyribonucleic acid
DOT	directly observed therapy
DOTS	Directly Observed Treatment with Short-course Chemotherapy
EC	European Commission
EEA	European Environmental Agency
EPI	Expanded Program on Immunization
ESTs	expressed sequence tags
FCTC	Framework Convention on Tobacco Control
GCC	Global Climate Coalition
GDP	gross domestic product
GFA AIDS	Global Fund Against AIDS
GFATM	Global Fund to Fight AIDS, TB, and Malaria
GHG	greenhouse gas
GNP	gross national product
GPEI	Global Polio Eradication Initiative
GPG	global public good
GPGH	global public good for health
GPH	global public health
IAEN	International AIDS Economic Network

IATA	International Air Travel Association
ICCs	Interagency Coordinating Committees
IGOs	intergovernmental organizations
IHR	International Health Regulations
IMF	International Monetary Fund
IOM	Institute of Medicine
IP	intellectual property
IPCC	Intergovernmental Panel on Climate Change
IPV	inactivated polio vaccine
IRT	international relations theory
IUATLD	International Union Against TB and Lung Disease
MNCs	Multinational Corporations
MSF	Médecins Sans Frontières
MRSA	methicillin resistant staphylococcus aureus
NGOs	nongovernmental organizations
NIDs	national immunization days
OAU	Organization of African Unity
ODA	overseas development assistance
OECD	Organization for Economic Cooperation and Development
OPV	oral polio vaccine
PAHO	Pan-American Health Organization
PEI	polio eradication initiative
R&D	Research and Development
RNA	ribonucleic acid
SAARC	South Asian Association for Regional Cooperation
SDRs	Special Drawing Rights
SNPs	single nucleotide polymorphisms
SOL	stratospheric ozone layer
TB	tuberculosis
TBT	Technical Barriers to Trade
TCGs	Technical Consultative Groups
TNCs	transnational corporations
TRIPs	Trade-Related Aspects of Intellectual Property Rights
UN	United Nations
UNDP	United Nations Development Program
UNEP	United Nations Environment Program
UNESCO	United Nations Educational, Scientific, and Cultural Organization
UNFCC	UN Framework Convention on Climate Change
UNHCR	United Nations High Commission for Refugees
UNICEF	United Nations Childrens Fund
UNPDDESA	United Nations Population Division Department of Economic and Social Affairs

UVR	ultra-violet irradiation
VAPP	vaccine-associated paralytic poliomyelitis
WCECD	Word Commission on Environment and Development
WFP	World Food Program
WHA	World Health Assembly
WHO	World Health Organization
WRI	World Resource Institute
WWC	World Water Commission

Section 1

The global public goods for health concept

Chapter 1

Global public goods and health: Concepts and issues

David Woodward and Richard D Smith

1.1 Introduction

Public goods have, for centuries, been part of the economic analysis of government policy at the national level (Connolly and Munro 1999). However, as globalization progresses, it is becoming clear in many areas that matters which were once confined to national policy are now issues of global impact and concern. This has been evidenced, for example, in dealing with environmental problems, such as chlorofluorocarbon (CFC) emissions and ozone depletion, and carbon emissions and global warming. These affect the nation involved in their production, but also impact significantly on other nations; yet no one nation necessarily has the ability, or the incentive, to address the problem. Recognition of this led to the development of the concept of *Global Public Goods* (GPGs) (Sandler 1997), which has recently been advocated and supported by the United Nations Development Programme (UNDP) (Kaul *et al.* 1999).

At the same time, in this increasingly globalized world, health is an ever more international phenomenon, as each country's health affects, and is affected by, events and processes outside its own borders (Folland *et al.* 1997). The most obvious example of this is communicable disease, which is often a problem against which no single country can orchestrate a response sufficient to protect the health of its population. Similarly, international movements of goods which promote or damage health, and of health professionals, are increasing, as is cross-border marketing which promotes unhealthy behaviors, such as tobacco and alcohol consumption and unhealthy diets. With health moving up the global agenda, it is an opportune time to consider the application of the GPG concept to health and health care.

The aim of this chapter is to outline briefly the foundation of the GPG concept, and provide an overview of the main economic and political dimensions of this concept, as background to the series of case studies which follow. Following this introduction, Section 1.2 provides an overview of the concept of GPGs, and Section 1.3 illustrates how this concept may apply to health and health care.

Section 1.4 discusses the economic and political dimensions important in securing the provision of GPGs for Health (GPGH). The chapter concludes, in Section 1.5, with a summary of the main points, and foreshadows the following case-study chapters.

1.2 Public goods, access goods, and global public goods

What is a "Global Public Good," and how does it relate to health? This section outlines definitions and our understanding of what is meant by public goods and global public goods, and the policy relevance of the GPG concept.

1.2.1 What is a *public* good?

Most goods[1] are private in nature: their consumption can be withheld until a payment is made in exchange, and once consumed they cannot be consumed again. For example, the consumption of a cake can be withheld from the consumer until the consumer pays the baker a price, and once the consumer has eaten that cake it cannot be eaten again. A private good is therefore considered *excludable* and *rival in consumption*.

If purely private goods are seen as lying at one end of the spectrum of goods, at the other lie pure public goods, which are defined as having the opposite characteristics. That is, the benefits, once the good is provided, cannot be restricted and are therefore available to all (i.e. *non-excludable*), and consumption by one individual does not limit consumption of that *same good* by others (i.e. *non-rival in consumption*).

A classic example is the service provided by a lighthouse: the warning it provides is available to all who would benefit from it, and one ship's use of it does not limit the ability of other ships to use it. Virtually all public goods are such services or other intangibles, with few, if any, "commodities" (in the narrow sense of physical objects) meeting these criteria (the exception to this being physical infrastructure, such as sewage systems, which once completed are largely non-rival in consumption, and difficult to exclude people from using) (Kaul *et al.* 1999).

However, both excludability and rivalry are relative, not absolute, concepts. In terms of *excludability*, access to public goods in particular may be:

(1) *geographically specific* (e.g. conventional television broadcasts, while they broadly satisfy the criteria for a public good, reach only an area defined by the location of transmitters, the strength of signals and topographical constraints);

(2) subject to *indirect access costs* (e.g. following the above example, the cost of a television set), which may result in a "club good" (see below);

---

[1] Note that "goods" are here defined in their economic sense as anything that produces a benefit, be it a physical commodity or service.

(3) subject to *administrative control* (e.g. television licences creating a "club good" out of the public good); and/or

(4) subject to *change over time* as a result of technological changes (e.g. satellite and cable television technologies enable restriction, again creating a "club good").

Thus, some people *could* be (and often are) excluded from the benefits of most theoretically defined public goods through geographic, monetary, or administrative prohibition.

Similarly, *rivalry in consumption* may be relative to capacity, particularly in the case of physical infrastructure. For example, if a sewage system has spare capacity, its use is non-rival, but as the capacity constraint is approached use becomes rivalrous, whereby the person whose use of it causes capacity to be reached has effectively prevented the next person wishing to use it from doing so. Perhaps more usual is that the consumption of a particular good may not prevent others from using it, but simply reduce the benefits to them of using it. For example, one person's use of a road does not usually prevent use by others, but the use of roads becomes less beneficial as more people use them and they become more congested.

Between the extremes of pure private and public goods lie a range of private goods with externality effects[2] and public goods with private benefits. There are two particularly important categories of such goods. First, "common pool goods" are *non-excludable but rivalrous in consumption,* such as forests: the environmental benefits of forests are not excludable, but if they are used for logging these benefits are forgone. Second, "club goods," which are, conversely, *excludable but non-rivalrous,* with the benefits spread among a subgroup of the population, whose membership may be controlled by the providers of the good or others. Examples include cable and satellite television broadcasts, which have the characteristic of non-rivalry for those who subscribe to them, with non-subscribers being excluded.

Thus, the classification of a good as public or private may be somewhat misleading. Rather, it is more appropriate to discuss the degree to which goods may be subject to excludability and/or the degree to which their consumption is rival. It is the understanding of these characteristics of the good in question that may then allow remedial action to be taken to correct market imperfections in their supply, as indicated below. However, for the purposes of this chapter, and this book, the broad categorization of goods as *largely* private or public, and within public as *largely* common-pool or club goods, is made to facilitate ease of comparison and analysis.

1.2.2 The importance of "access goods"

Many public goods are only non-excludable to those who have the requisite private goods to access them. For example, a television is required to access

---

[2] Where "externality" refers to some positive or negative effects of production and/or consumption on a third party who does not control or play an active part in that action.

broadcasts, a computer to access the Internet and infrastructure to access clean water. Such private goods are here termed "access goods."

The requirement of access goods restricts the scope of the benefits of public goods. This not only reduces the overall benefits (making the balance between costs and benefits less favorable), but may also lead to perverse targeting: those who have access goods are likely to be the better off, so that the benefits of providing public goods will tend to be skewed away from the poor, who are likely to be in greatest need.

The non-rival nature of public goods means that it is desirable to increase coverage. If access goods are required, then this is achieved either by supplying access goods or by increasing demand for them. Demand may be increased through the provision of information and education where the private benefits of the public good are not immediate or not fully appreciated (e.g. in the case of vaccinations). However, while increasing demand is a "market friendly" approach, and will contribute to increasing coverage, it is likely to leave the problem of perverse targeting. This applies particularly where education and information themselves require access goods (e.g. literacy, access to media, and school attendance).

The direct supply of access goods is likely to be more expensive than increasing demand, even where effective targeting is possible, but it may be more effective than a demand-based approach in increasing coverage and countering perverse targeting. Decisions on the supply of access goods need to take account of alternative delivery mechanisms (e.g. the provision of access to computers through public libraries to facilitate access to the Internet) in terms of their cost and effectiveness in allowing access to public goods. It should also be noted that, even if access goods are supplied, there may still be a need to increase demand if there are indirect or non-financial costs (e.g. if vaccination requires traveling to a health center).

Overall, it may therefore be that the provision of some private goods is considered as a part of the "package" of securing the wider consumption of the public good. In this case, these private goods may be considered *as if they were public goods* for analytical and policy purposed.

In some cases, of course, the cost-effective supply of access goods may itself be a public good (according to our modified definition, presented in Section 1.2.4), as the cost of providing the access goods to those who do not have them may be no greater than the externalities arising from the additional consumption of the public good. In the case of vaccination against infectious diseases, for example, the externalities of increased coverage may well be sufficient to justify the subsidization of the costs of individual vaccination, as well as the infrastructure for the overall vaccination program. Other examples may include treatment for infectious diseases, such as tuberculosis (see Chapter 3 in this volume). A particularly strong case can be made for subsidization of access goods where universal or near-universal coverage is necessary to the benefits of the public good (e.g. eradication of polio, as detailed in Chapter 2). If some people do not have access to health services, for example, this may represent a major obstacle to disease elimination.

Access goods are also an important area of synergy, as essentially the same access goods may be required for a range of public goods. For example, public health infrastructure constitutes an access good for a range of public goods (see Chapter 8 in this volume). This represents a strong case for the provision of free health services as a public good at the national level.

1.2.3 What is a *global* public good?

What then is a "global" public good? The UNDP defines a *global* public good as:

> a public good with benefits that are strongly universal in terms of *countries* (covering more than one group of countries), *people* (accruing to several, preferably all, population groups) and *generations* (extending to both current and future generations, or at least meeting the needs of current generations without foreclosing development options for future generations). (Kaul *et al.* 1999, pp. 509–10; emphasis added)

However, we suggest that this definition is problematic for three reasons. First, it does not make explicit the distinction between *cross-border* and *within-country* externalities. In principle, this definition would include a public good whose benefits are limited to the country in which it is provided, so long as any country which provides it benefits from it. This allows, for example, broadcast television to qualify, although there is no obvious case for *international* provision or financial support.

Second, the implications of "strong universality" in terms of population groups could mean, for example, that women's health programs are excluded because they benefit only women, programs dealing with diseases affecting only the genetically predisposed (e.g. sickle-cell disease) or affecting racial or ethnic groups are excluded by virtue of this fact, or urban environmental programs are excluded as benefiting only urban populations. The irony is that this also suggests that programes benefiting only the poor would, in principle, fail to qualify.

Third, the requirement that neither present nor future generations should be harmed arguably creates a "temporal stalemate" whereby programs which only benefit current *and* future generations equally are acceptable. One implication of this is that disease eradication programs would be excluded, as they may require a reallocation of resources from uses that are of greater importance to the health of the present generation in order to benefit the next generation (even though disease eradication comes closer to satisfying the strict definition of a public good at the global level than possibly any other).[3] For example, while the reduction in the incidence of polio during the process of eradication benefits those who would otherwise suffer from it, the much greater benefits (to health and financially) of polio eradication *per se* accrue *after* it has been eradicated—that is, to future generations. Since the very considerable resources required to ensure that the last small pockets of infection are eliminated could be used instead for more

---

[3] There are also further conceptual problems with this definition when considering discounting, which we do not detail here.

cost-effective interventions,[4] the effect is to worsen the health of the present generation in order to benefit future generations.

In the light of the above problems, in this volume GPGs are considered to be goods exhibiting a significant degree of publicness (i.e. non-excludability and non-rivalry) *across national boundaries* (and thus not necessarily population or generational boundaries). To make the distinction between global rather than merely "international" GPGs, we also suggest that this cross-national characteristic must involve more than two nations, with at least one outside the traditional regional groupings (e.g. Europe, Sub-Saharan Africa, or South East Asia) of the other(s). There may be public goods across two or three close neighbors, but these would then be considered localized or regional public goods. Although many of the issues outlined in this chapter would nonetheless apply in these cases, the problems of collective action would be far smaller than that assumed below.

1.2.4 **What is the policy relevance of GPGs?**

Free markets under-supply public goods because: (i) non-excludability means that a price cannot be enforced, leading to "free-riding" (benefit from the actions of others without reciprocation); and (ii) non-rivalry means that efficient consumption is where individual marginal cost is just greater than zero—this will be below market price, leading to less than optimal supply.

While *both* non-excludability and non-rivalry in consumption are required by the strict definition of a public good, their relevance from a policy perspective is very different. Non-rivalry means that one person's consumption of a good does not reduce anyone else's consumption of it, so that, in the absence of negative externalities, it does not reduce anyone else's welfare. This suggests that broadening the provision of goods which are non-rivalrous in consumption (provided they do not have negative externalities) to make them available to all who would gain some positive benefit (irrespective of the size of that benefit) will increase overall welfare and is therefore an appropriate objective of policy.[5] This is irrespective of whether or not they are excludable (Connolly and Munro 1999).

Where a good is non-rivalrous in consumption, the extent to which it is excludable, and the means by which it may be made excludable, are relevant primarily because they affect how consumption can be broadened, and how provision can be financed. For example, where a non-rivalrous good is excludable the promotion of "clubs," as described above, is one means to broaden provision and secure partial financing.

---

[4] There were a total of 3,500 cases of polio worldwide during 2000; but the projected cost of the polio eradication program in April 2001 was US$ 1 billion (WHO Press Release No. WHO/17, April 3, 2001: "Polio Eradication: Final 1% Poses Greatest Challenge").

[5] In the case where the good does yield a negative externality then universal provision would be warranted up to the point where the marginal benefit from the *n*th consumer was at last as great as the marginal cost of the externality from that unit of consumption.

The fundamental problem arises, however, when beneficial non-rival goods are *not* excludable. Here, society will benefit from provision of the good, but non-excludability means that individuals or nations may free-ride (i.e. benefit from the actions of others without reciprocation), leading to under, or non, supply of the good and thus a societal loss of welfare[6] (Hargreaves-Heap *et al.* 1992).

> We argue, therefore, that the core policy issue is one of ensuring collective action at the global level to facilitate the production of, and access to, goods which are largely non-excludable and non-rival in consumption, and yield significant external benefits, across multiple nations.

Note that, importantly, *a good need not be a pure public good to suffer from a collective action problem*. Collective action problems also apply to private goods which have substantial positive externalities, as these too will be under-supplied (since externalities are not taken into account by private suppliers and consumers) (Hargreaves-Heap *et al.* 1992). For example, an individual secures only part of the benefit from his/her treatment for tuberculosis, as others benefit from the reduced risk of infection. However, it is only this private benefit that the individual will take into account when considering whether to seek treatment. Where the private benefit is less than the cost to the individual, they will not seek treatment, even though the population as a whole (including the individual sufferer) would be better off if the individual received treatment.

Thus, from a policy perspective it makes little sense to draw too categorical a distinction between private goods with large positive externalities and the pure public good case. In a sense, an intervention that would counter a nonpublic good-related collective action problem, so as to correct the under- or over-supply of positive or negative externalities widely spread among the population, can itself be considered a public good. For example, providing infrastructure capable of delivering timely and effective treatment for tuberculosis, and the policies to provide an incentive for individuals to seek and complete treatment, may have the characteristics of public goods even though the treatment of an individual is essentially a private good with positive externalities.

We therefore propose a definition, modified from that proposed by Kaul *et al.* (1999), to be used in this book which classifies as a GPG (or, for purists, a good which should be treated as a GPG for policy purposes):

> a good which it is rational, from the perspective of a group of nations collectively, to produce for universal consumption, and for which it is irrational to exclude an individual nation from its consumption, irrespective of whether that nation contributes to its financing.

---

[6] Although theoretically this may be resolved by philanthropy, this does not provide a dependable means of ensuring an adequate supply of all public goods, or of an appropriate prioritization of the public goods available.

Thus, we include some goods which are clearly not public goods in terms of the conventional definition, but which it is appropriate to treat *as if* they were public goods from a policy perspective. For example, vaccination against communicable disease is clearly both excludable and rivalrous in consumption, and its primary benefit is to the individual recipients and their respective nations. Nonetheless, if the effect on the risk of person-to-person or cross-border transmission of communicable disease is sufficient, it is not rational either to exclude an individual or nation from consumption, or to limit production to a level at which consumption is rivalrous.

1.3 Global public goods and health

In seeking to define the GPG concept with respect to health and health care, there are two dimensions to explore: (i) is health *per se* a GPG; and (ii) are there strategies to "produce" health which may themselves be GPGs? These questions are considered here.

1.3.1 Is *health* a GPG?

Health *per se* is not a public good, either individually or nationally. One person's (or one country's) health status is a private good in the sense that he/she (or it) is the primary beneficiary of it. To illustrate this, consider the parallel of a garden: if someone cultivates an attractive garden in front of his/her house, passers-by will benefit from seeing it; but it remains a private good, the main beneficiary of which is the owner, who sees more of it, and is able to spend time in it. An individual's health remains *primarily* of benefit to that individual, although there may be some (positive or negative) externalities resulting from it, such as exposure to communicable disease.

Further, in terms of the goods and services which are necessary to provide and sustain health, such as food, shelter and use of curative health services, "health" is often *rival* and *excludable* between individuals and nations. Nonetheless, there are two important externality aspects of health, both at the local level and across national borders, which may be amenable to conceptualizing as having GPG properties.

First, the *prevention or containment of communicable disease.* Preventing one person from getting a communicable disease (or treating it successfully) clearly benefits the individual concerned, but it also provides a significant positive externality to others by reducing their risk of infection (the primary motivation behind public health reforms in countries experiencing the "industrial revolution" of the eighteenth and nineteenth centuries). Similarly, the reduction of communicable disease within one country reduces the probability of cross-border transmission to other countries. However, while communicable disease control is non-rival in its *effect* (one person's lower risk of contracting a disease does not limit the benefits of that lower risk to others), its *production* requires excludable inputs, such as vaccination, clean water or condoms, as well as non-excludable inputs, such as knowledge of preventive interventions and best practice in treatment. In this sense, it may generally be considered a "club good" (non-rival but excludable), although its non-rival effect does imply that even if it is feasible to exclude people it may not be desirable, as the marginal effects on the health of others may outweigh the marginal savings from exclusion.

Globally, communicable disease accounted for 26 percent of deaths (14.5 million) in the year 2000, and approximately 30 percent of the global burden of disease (as measured by Disability Adjusted Life Years (DALYs) lost), with a disproportionate burden upon low- and middle-income countries, which account for more than 97 percent of communicable disease associated deaths and nearly 99 percent of the burden of disease (Murray *et al.* 2001, WHO 2001*b*). Within these low- and middle-income countries the three largest single causes of the burden of disease are all communicable (lower respiratory infections, HIV/AIDS and diarrheal diseases).

However, since not all communicable diseases are *global*, clearly only the prevention or containment of *some* communicable diseases may be considered as GPGs. For example, malaria control benefits only endemic areas, so can only be a "regional public good." Equally, some (richer) populations can avoid some infections, through vaccination or better living conditions, or avoid significant adverse health effects of diseases such as measles through better nutritional status. Thus, only for a sub-set of communicable diseases can the prevention/containment of such diseases be considered a GPG. These are outlined in Appendix 1.1. Within this volume, the series of case-studies of GPG in section two are therefore predominantly concerned (with the exception of the case-study on broader environmental effects on health) with this sub-set of communicable diseases and not a more comprehensive coverage of all communicable disease.

Furthermore, for this sub-set of diseases whose control can be considered a GPG, it is important to distinguish between control within a country or region, to limit the global "stock" of disease which may be disseminated (e.g. the polio eradication program of Chapter 2), and control of cross-border transmission (e.g. through the International Health Regulations, detailed in Chapter 10). These two approaches have very different implications, particularly for the distribution of benefits. Since transmission is predominantly from countries with a high incidence of disease to those with a low incidence, the benefit of limiting cross-border transmission is greatest where incidence is lowest. By contrast, programs based on in-country control focus on countries with high incidence, which therefore benefit most. Since the incidence of communicable diseases is generally lower in richer than in poorer countries, the approach chosen thus has important implications for equity.

A special case of communicable disease control is that of disease eradication. This is exceptional in two respects. First, once a disease has been eradicated globally, the benefits are neither excludable nor rivalrous, so that it clearly meets the criteria for a GPG. Moreover, unlike many health-related GPGs, access to effective health services is not necessary for populations to benefit from disease eradication (although their absence may impede its achievement). Secondly, it has time-limited costs while the benefits are permanent, strengthening the incentives for its provision. This is indicated in the case study in Chapter 2 with respect to polio eradication.

The second important externality aspect of health amenable to conceptualizing as having GPG properties is that of *wider economic externality effects*. The economic effects of ill-health on households may be considerable. While these effects appear essentially private, the *cumulative effect on the national/regional economy* of the resulting loss of production and income, and thus the potential gains from health improvements, may be substantial. For example, the difference in life expectancy between the developed countries and Sub-Saharan Africa, which increased from 26 years in 1980 to 31 years in 1999 (World Bank 2001, table 2.19), implies a reduction in Sub-Saharan Africa's relative income in the order of 20–50 percent in the last two decades.

On a more general level, the recent Commission on Macroeconomics and Health (CMH) reported that each 10 percent improvement in life expectancy at birth is associated with an increase in economic growth of at least 0.3 percentage points per year, holding other growth factors constant. The difference in annual growth accounted for by life expectancy at birth between a typical developed and developing nation is around 1.6 percent (CMH 2001, p. 24). Similarly, Bloom and Williamson (1998) estimate that health improvements may have accounted for as much as one-third of the East Asian economic "miracle," following the historical observation of the importance of breakthroughs in public health, disease control, and nutritional intake in supporting the economic "takeoff" of the UK in the eighteenth and nineteenth centuries, and the United States of America and Japan in the early twentieth century (CMH 2001, p. 22). This may then impact on other nations in terms of export markets, the provision of goods, or the profitability of, or opportunities for, foreign investment.

This effect is clear in the case of HIV/AIDS, which threatens economic development by decimating the young adult workforce, reducing productivity and discouraging savings and investment. Its effect is most conspicuous in Southern Africa (Bonnel 2000), where the incidence of HIV/AIDS is between 19 and 36 percent in most countries (World Bank 2001). Early estimates suggested that the epidemic might reduce growth by 0.6–1.1 percent p.a. in an average Sub-Saharan country, and by 0.7–1.5 percent p.a. in the ten worst affected countries in the region (Over 1992). A number of subsequent country-specific studies, for example, in Botswana, South Africa, Jamaica and Trinidad, and Tobago, have found effects broadly within this range, varying in line with HIV incidence (MacFarlan and Sgherri 2001, Arndt and Lewis 2000). In Botswana—which has the highest incidence of HIV globally, but greater capacity to withstand its economic impact than most Sub-Saharan countries—it has been estimated that national income will be 33–40 percent lower than it would otherwise have been by 2010 as a result of the epidemic (MacFarlan and Sgherri 2001). A previous study, considering a shorter period and predicting a substantially smaller impact on total income (8–10 percent between 2000 and 2010), nonetheless estimated that the proportion of households in poverty would be increased by 6–8 percent, and the average income of the poorest quarter of households would fall by 10–15 percent over the same period (BIPDA 2000).

Other communicable diseases also have a major impact on economic performance. For instance, Gallup and Sachs (2000) found that between 1965 and 1990 malaria slowed economic growth in Africa by up to 1.3 percent each year; with malaria-free countries averaging three times higher GDP per person than those with malaria, even after controlling for government policy, geography, and other factors affecting economic growth. This implies a cumulative effect on incomes in the order of 28 percent over this period, and the problem will be compounded by the growth of multi-drug-resistant (MDR) strains.

Furthermore, the close, mutual, relationship between poverty and disease—particularly communicable disease—has been recognized for generations (Strauss and Thomas 1998). Not only does disease reduce the productivity and incomes of people and nations, as indicated, but the resultant poverty also impacts on health through its effects on nutrition, education, housing, and health care, creating a cycle of ill-health and poverty which is hard to break (Lister 2000).

Thus, while a lower incidence of communicable disease may be considered as a public good, good health more generally is better viewed as a private good, although one which may provide substantial positive (health and economic) externalities. It is competitively produced, in the sense that its production requires mostly private goods as inputs, and, while there are substantial benefits to others, the primary benefits of one person's good health are to that person.[7] In both these respects, from a policy perspective, it makes sense therefore to consider *interventions to improve health internationally* as candidate GPGs, and the health improvements which they generate as the *mechanism* through which they produce externalities.

1.3.2 What may be GPG *for* health?

This leads us to explore the second dimension: what interventions may be classified as GPGs *for* health, yielding improvements in health and thus contributing to the externality effects specified above?

The scope of *potential* GPGs is wide, and their nature varied, and it is not possible to provide a comprehensive listing here. However, problems conducive to such solutions can be broadly divided between those which address in-country health problems with cross-country externalities (primarily communicable disease control, but perhaps also noncommunicable disease control to the extent that it

---

[7] Clearly, this is not to say that the improvement of health is not a worthy objective of private agents (e.g. NGOs), governments, and official agencies, and even where there are no positive externalities, social justice and equity are a sufficient justification for this (see Chapters 12 and 13 for more discussion of these aspects).

has economic effects), and those which address the cross-border transmission of factors influencing health risks (e.g. food safety, tobacco marketing, and international trade in narcotics). Within each of these categories, GPGs may then be classified in to three broad areas, each of which is covered in more detail in other chapters within this volume.

First, *knowledge and technologies* (broadly defined, to include, for example, understanding of health risks, preventive, diagnostic, curative and palliative interventions, and delivery systems). Information *per se*, such as on health risks and treatment régimes, is *in principle* both non-excludable and non-rival in consumption, at all levels from local to global. However, *in practice*, it may not be. For example, the surveillance and control of communicable disease relies on the generation and transmission of knowledge about the incidence of disease, which is non-rival and not easily excludable; but to work effectively it requires all countries both to produce and to act on the information, which requires an effective health infrastructure, and appropriate technical expertise, at the country level, thus excluding some countries.

Similarly, much of the technology for curative and preventive interventions is necessarily embodied in private goods such as pharmaceuticals and vaccines, turning what is otherwise a GPG into a club good (see Chapter 6). The nature of this transformation is determined largely by the international policy régime for intellectual property (issues explored further in Chapter 7, as well as outlined in more detail in Appendix 1.2). Again, knowledge of best practice in the treatment of diseases such as tuberculosis and malaria is a key element in strategies to limit the development of antimicrobial resistance (see Chapter 4); but the effectiveness of such knowledge is dependent on the existence of effective health professionals and services with which to apply it to the treatment of patients.

Second, *policy and regulatory régimes*. The collective nature of policies, whether in health or other sectors, makes them public goods (or bads!). However, it should be noted that policy can also be used to restrict access to public goods, either by enforcing its restriction to a limited sub-group of the population to make it a club good (e.g. television licensing), or by allowing its appropriation or retention by a particular agent (e.g. patent régimes). Regulatory régimes (e.g. for food and product safety or pharmaceuticals) essentially form a particular sub-set of policy, falling mainly in to the category of "club goods" (non-rival in consumption but may be excludable), as groups can be included or excluded by a regulation, but once a regulation exists it can apply to one or many (unless the cost of monitoring is very high, in which case regulation could possibly be considered rival in consumption). Chapter 9, on the case study of international law, discusses the role of international legal régimes in the production of GPGH more generally, and Chapters 10 and 11 provide more focused case-studies on International Health Regulations and the WHO Framework Convention on Tobacco Control as specific examples.

A less direct case is that of the international régime for intellectual property rights as it applies to technologies for preventive and curative interventions.

This balances the incentives for the overall production of such technologies, the prioritization of key health issues, and the affordability of the technologies produced; and how it does so will determine how many "clubs" are created, how many of them are relevant to different countries, and how many members can join each club. This is covered in more detail in Chapters 6 and 7.

Third, *health systems*. The role of health systems in relation to GPGs is analogous to that of *access goods*—private goods which are required to enable one to benefit from a public good (see Section 1.2.2). For example, just as a television is required to receive broadcasts, or a household's connection is required for it to benefit from a water or sanitation system, some GPGH require a functioning health system for a country to benefit from, or for the country to make the contribution necessary to the provision of, a GPG. Thus, the ease and cost of eliminating polio in a country will depend to a great extent on the existence of a functioning health system to deliver vaccines and to identify and treat cases, and controlling the incidence of MDR-TB will depend critically on the appropriate use of the right medication, which is dependent upon a functioning and adequate health system.

Effective interventions exist to reduce the mortality associated with all major communicable diseases (including those classified as GPGH), but hundreds of millions of people do not have reliable access to them because of inadequate health systems and lack of affordability. There are 1.4 million deaths per year in developing countries from childhood diseases readily combated by immunization, compared with fewer than 1,000 in developed countries. The lives of the estimated 33 million people living with HIV/AIDS in developing countries could be greatly extended by current treatment protocols—and extended further if improved technologies are successfully developed—but cost is a major barrier to access to these interventions.

This suggests that support for the health system in countries where it is currently ineffective or inaccessible may, in principle, be treated *as if they were GPGs* according to the modified definition presented earlier. Financial support of *national* health systems, including general equipment, professional training, and information systems, may therefore be justified in some countries on GPG grounds, as well as (and in some cases potentially as a precondition for) support for specific interventions. This is illustrated in Chapter 8, which considers the value of public health infrastructure as a foundational access good required to enable consumption of, and thus derive benefit from, other GPGH.

1.3.3 "Vertical" and "horizontal" approaches

This distinction made between Sections 1.3.1 and 1.3.2 may also perhaps be seen to represent a distinction between what may be considered to be "vertical" and "horizontal" GPGH. "Vertical" GPGH may be considered to be disease-specific programs, such as those represented in Chapters 2–4. These are the "traditional" means by which governments, NGO's, international bodies, and donors work in many countries, partly as a means of limiting the problems of working through under-resourced health systems. However, while such programs have saved many lives, they have also been seen as inefficient; giving rise, for example, to problems of coordination, skewing priorities from national toward donor concerns, diverting scarce human and other resources away from general health services, and generating costly duplication between parallel programs (LaFond 1995, Koivusalo and Ollila 1997).

These limitations of vertical programs arise primarily from the asymmetry in financing between these, relatively well-financed, vertical programs and grossly under-resourced "horizontal" health systems. For example, the World Bank's HIV/AIDS Rapid Response project in Gambia, approved in January 2001,[8] is equivalent to around 40 percent of total public expenditure on health in 1997[9] every year from 2001 to 2005, while its HIV/AIDS Project under preparation for Burundi[10] is equivalent to three years' public sector health spending at the 1997 rate. In Ethiopia, a World Bank HIV/AIDS Multisectoral Project approved in December 2000[11] is equivalent to 18 percent of 1997 public spending on health per year for $3\frac{1}{2}$ years. Together with projected funding for the Global DOTS Expansion Plan for tuberculosis (23 percent) and Roll Back Malaria (provisionally 15 percent) (Roll Back Malaria 2001, WHO 2001a), these three vertical programs alone are around 56 percent of the total public sector resources that were available for health in 1997.

However, there are significant categories of potential GPG *for* health, detailed in Section 3.2, that cut across diseases. Adequate health systems (Chapter 8), for example, would benefit many areas of communicable disease control, while modifications to international rules on pharmaceutical patents would apply to products across the spectrum of communicable, and indeed noncommunicable, diseases (see Chapters 6 and 7 for example).

Typically, these "vertical" and "horizontal" approaches may be seen to be competitors for funding: primary health-care systems in general competing with, for example, targeted immunization. However, an advantage of the GPG approach may be that in this case the horizontal and vertical approaches will be *complementary*, with a set of common horizontal GPGH creating the conditions in which disease-specific GPGs can then be provided more effectively, while a vertical program coordinates the provision of inputs needed for each disease, or group of related diseases. In developing such an approach, it is therefore important that relations between national level health programs are well managed and supported inter-nationally in such a way that these vertical programs facilitate and promote

---

[8] http://www4.worldbank.org/sprojects/Project.asp?pid=P060329.

[9] Figures for public expenditure on health in 1997 used in this paragraph are estimated from WHO 2000: annex tables 2 and 8.

[10] http://www4.worldbank.org/sprojects/Project.asp?pid=P071371.

[11] http://www4.worldbank.org/sprojects/Project.asp?pid=P069886.

the effectiveness of overall health systems and do not create inefficiencies in GPG production or health service provision more generally. Important synergies and tensions between programs (e.g. TB control and AMR containment) also require close collaboration *between* vertical programs at the national and international levels. It is therefore vital that vertical programs are placed within an overall institutional framework capable of ensuring effective coordination and collaboration between them, for example at the WHO. At the country level, Ministries of Health must be strengthened where necessary to play a similar role.

In raising these issues of the coordination of GPGH production and finance, it is therefore appropriate to consider the main economic and political dimensions of in ensuring the production of these GPGH, to which the chapter now turns.

1.4 **The economics and politics of providing GPGH: who pays the piper calls the tune?**

Public goods are characterized by the existence of a collective action problem: the community as a whole is better off if they are provided, but this requires collective action to avoid free-riding (individuals benefiting from the actions of others without reciprocating) and the "prisoner's dilemma" (lack of communication and information about each participant's actions, and lack of enforcement mechanisms, impeding cooperation[12]) (Hargreaves-Heap *et al.* 1992). Fundamental to securing the provision of *global* public goods is therefore the political process of ensuring collective action at the international level.

However, the political dimension is inextricably linked to the economic, as any global public good requires, to a greater or lesser extent, resources for its production: knowledge and information first need to be produced (e.g. through research); policies require implementation and enforcement; and regulatory mechanisms require policing. (Finger 2000, for example, estimates the average cost of implementing the WTO agreements on Trade-Related Aspects of Intellectual Property Rights (TRIPS), Sanitary and Phytosanitary Measures (SPS) and Technical Barriers to Trade (TBT) in a developing country at around $150 million). Some GPGH may also impose costs on third parties other than the costs of their production, and in some cases these may also have health effects. For example, imposing stricter safety standards on internationally traded foods may result in a major loss of export revenues for low-income countries and of incomes for producers (Otsuki *et al.* 2000).

The opportunity and incentive for each individual country to free-ride must therefore be overcome, as must the opposition of potential losers where they have the strength to block decisions to provide GPGs, or their involvement or cooperation

---

[12] It has to be acknowledged that communication of information is a "necessary but not sufficient" condition to prevent the "prisoners dilemma" problem arising, since the communication of information itself does not ensure the mechanisms to enable it to be acted upon.

is needed for provision. These points are considered in more detail with respect to specific contexts in the remaining chapters, but here we consider some common issues.

1.4.1 **Who pays for GPGH?**

Nationally, public goods, or private goods with significant externalities, are generally dealt with by government intervention, principally through direct provision, taxes, subsidies, or regulation (Connolly and Munro 1999). However, in the case of *global* public goods the absence of a "global government" means that the collective action problem becomes many times more complex, with the increased number of players involved and the absence of effective, collectively—enforced sanctions against non-compliance. The main potential contributors to the financing of GPGs are: international agencies, as fora for consensus-building and collective decision-making, co-ordinators, promoters and channels of government support, and supporters of control mechanisms and regulatory frameworks; national governments, as potential beneficiaries, sources of funding (internally and externally) and providers of many of the mechanisms for control; and transnational corporations (TNCs), as developers and suppliers of relevant medical technologies. However:

(1) While international agencies may provide a politically convenient means of *channelling* government support, they are financed and controlled (in varying ways) by their member governments, limiting their relevance as an independent *source* of financing.

(2) Most developing country governments, though the major potential beneficiaries of most prospective GPGs, have very limited resources to contribute to their financing, whether directly or through international agencies. Their resources, in general, are also inversely proportional to their likely benefits, as richer countries generally have fewer health problems than poorer ones.

(3) Transnational corporations are primarily motivated by profit, and will generally make contributions only to the extent that they expect to benefit (although this would include perceived improvements in their public image, as well as the more direct financial benefits), unless they can be effectively coerced. However, their political strength, the absence of effective legal mechanisms at the international level, and the problem of coordinating coercive measures between countries makes coercion difficult.

All of this suggests that developed country governments are the major prospective source of financing for GPGs, either directly or through international institutions.[13] However, if financing is skewed toward developed countries, this is likely

---

[13] The income disparity between rich and poor countries also represents a very strong case for financing the provision of GPGs as far as possible from resources provided by the developed countries, where the opportunity cost of the funds in welfare terms is much lower than in developing countries (provided the funds are not diverted from development assistance).

to mean that, in practice, developed countries will need to be substantial beneficiaries of the provision of a GPG (or of supporting and financing its provision) if
it is to be produced.[14] This is particularly important if the funding for GPGs
comes from existing aid budgets rather than from genuinely additional aid funds.

1.4.2 How could GPGH be financed?

Funding for the production of GPGH may be achieved in four main ways. First,
voluntary contributions are the most straightforward option, but are particularly
prone to the free rider problem—as demonstrated by the meager contributions
thus far to the Global Fund Against AIDS, Tuberculosis and Malaria[15]—since each
country has an incentive to minimize its contribution. If each party whose support
and co-operation is required gains more than it loses, each still has an incentive to
minimize its own contribution.

A system of *coordinated contributions* divided between parties according to an
agreed formula is therefore likely to be more effective. However, there are difficulties in adjusting the formula for contributions to reflect the ability of different parties to pay (particularly as benefits will often be non-financial and/or arise only in
the long term). Further, agreement of contributions, or the subsequent threat of
withholding them, may be used to distort GPG provision to the benefit of major
contributors and the detriment of the collective good; or a formal *quid pro quo*
may be demanded through voting mechanisms linked to the level of contributions
(cf. the International Monetary Fund and World Bank).

Second, *ear-marked national taxes coordinated between countries* might, in principle, be an appropriate approach where the achievement of health improvements
rests on the *discouragement* of particular activities, such as tobacco consumption
or pollution (the "polluter pays" principle). However, the political feasibility of
this approach is unclear, as there may be resistance to the concept of taxation policies being decided outside the country of enaction, and intractable disagreements
over their design (e.g. activities on which taxes should be levied, whether they
should be set in absolute or percentage terms and the rates at which they should be
set). The inclusion of low-income countries would seem particularly problematic,
as most have very low government revenues (giving rise to political pressure to
retain the revenues raised) and/or weak collection and enforcement mechanisms

---

[14] This does not mean that they need necessarily derive benefits directly from the GPG
itself sufficient to off-set the costs to them, as geopolitical and diplomatic objectives,
international reputation, domestic political constituencies (notably development and
environmental NGOs) and commercial interests may also contribute, as well as philanthropic or humanitarian concerns.

[15] The Global AIDS and Health Fund is an international fund, financed by donations from
governments, private foundations, and corporations, to support programs for health, principally HIV/AIDS, tuberculosis and malaria. It is to be run by governments independently
of, but with advice and support from, the UN system.

(giving rise to resentment in other countries that they were not making their full contribution, despite possibly being the greatest and most direct beneficiaries of the GPG provided). However, the latter perception might also arise if low-income countries were explicitly excluded.

Third, *taxes imposed and collected at the global level*, such as the "Tobin tax"[16] for example, has the potential to raise substantial sums, is increasingly seen as practicable, and is gathering substantial international support (Schmidt 1999). However, there are wide variations in estimates of the amount of, and many competing uses for, the proceeds, and it is likely to be resisted strongly by some major developed countries either as a matter of political principle, because of commercial interests, or because it threatens their dominance in international decision-making. It is therefore inadvisable to predicate the provision of GPGs on the implementation of such a proposal.

Fourth, *market-based mechanisms*, such as used in the Kyoto agreement to allow trading of emission rights (permits), have also been proposed as a possible solution to the growth of antimicrobial resistance (Smith and Coast 1998). However, they can only be used where there is something to trade, and they do not generate additional resources unless transactions are taxed (which reduces the efficiency of the market). There is also a risk that trading in rights to damage human health may be seen as less politically acceptable than trading in rights to damage the global environment.

It is clear, therefore, that whatever system, or combination of systems, of financing is considered, significant attention will have to be paid to the potential losers and gainers, and the means by which incentives can be created for collaboration and collective action to finance and/or produce the GPG in question.

1.4.3 What incentives should be used: coercion or compensation?

As described, those who may lose from the provision of GPGs, financially or otherwise, have an incentive for political and economic action against the decision to provide the public good, and no incentive to play any part in its provision. There are broadly two ways to negate these incentive problems: coercion (through formal legal instruments and/or through the exertion of influence and extra-legal pressures) and/or compensation.

The scope for *formal coercion* is determined legally and politically. At present, the limitations of international law (as compared with national law) impose serious constraints on the scope for formal coercion at the global level, even where political agreement exists (Fidler 1996, 1997). This means that there are no mechanisms available for formal coercion of national governments, and that formal

---

[16] The Tobin tax refers to a proposal by Nobel Economics Laureate James Tobin (Tobin 1978) to levy a tax at a very low rate on all currency conversion transactions conducted through the international clearing system.

coercion of non-state actors must rely on governments introducing laws voluntarily (or at least without formal coercion) within their respective jurisdictions. As a result, in the absence of a radical change in the system of global governance, the collective action problem will remain (Fidler 1996, 1997). Moreover, this problem is not limited to the initial decision to provide a GPG; each government (including new governments coming to office) will have the opportunity to reverse the laws which give effect to formal coercion at the national level.

This problem is compounded by the disproportionate influence conferred on companies, organizations and even influential individuals by most national political systems. Since companies and powerful individuals will often be the subject of GPG legislation (e.g. on marketing of unhealthy products, pharmaceuticals or food safety), this makes national legislation a still more unreliable mechanism in many contexts. The potential for TNCs to relocate their operations further discourages legislation which has substantial adverse effects on them, and provides a means of escaping its provisions if necessary.

Informal coercion and inducement is often used with respect to developing country governments. Mechanisms include, for example, offers of (or threats to withdraw or withhold) economic or military aid, favorable market access, and support for membership of, or loans from, international institutions. Informal coercion and inducement have the potential to at least reduce the collective action problem to one among the major developed countries, who have the resources and international influence to apply it effectively. However, as experience with structural adjustment programs has amply demonstrated, informal coercion has limitations even where solidarity is strong: while international agencies can be harnessed to apply pressure, and considerable economic rewards and sanctions are available, it is often easier to secure formal *agreement* than actual *compliance*, particularly where insufficient account is taken of the political dynamics of the country concerned (Fidler 1996, 1997). This problem may be compounded by a lack of "ownership," where there is a perception that changes are being imposed from outside, which may be exploited by vested interests resisting change. Similarly, the use of informal coercion to secure support for an initial decision to produce a GPG may seriously weaken the legitimacy of the decision-making process, as well as generate an agenda skewed in favor of the developed countries.

A similar compliance problem is also likely to arise in the case of TNCs. Moreover, the extra-legal nature of informal coercion means that TNCs may increasingly be as well placed as developed country governments to use it to exert pressure on developing countries (albeit through different mechanisms), both to limit their compliance or enforcement and to discourage their support for the initial proposal to provide a GPG. The main constraints on this type of activity by TNCs are the threat of developed country sanctions against them, and the potential impact on a company's image of using its economic power to pursue evidently self-serving objectives to the detriment of public health. The former constraint is weakened by the political strength of TNCs in most developed countries, the latter by carefully managed public relations.

However, even with informal coercion, *compensation* for any substantial costs incurred by low-income country governments is likely to be essential for the provision of GPGs. If such costs are not externally financed, they will be a major obstacle to their support for GPG provision (cf. TRIPS, SPS, and TBT as above). Even if support is nonetheless secured (e.g. by failing to make the costs explicit and/or through informal coercion) resource constraints are likely to prevent effective implementation of the measures necessary at the national level. If internally financed, there is also a serious risk that the cost of implementation would divert resources away from other health-related expenditure, to the detriment of public health.

There are also costs which go beyond those of establishing and operating institutions charged with GPG provision. For example, disease surveillance and reporting mechanisms may trigger travel restrictions or discourage tourism, while food safety regulations on international trade may lead to major losses of export earnings for the countries concerned, and of incomes for producers. In such cases, compensation for the negative economic effects of each instance of compliance are likely to be needed, to ensure compliance; and this needs to be certain, rapid, comprehensive, and at least as great as the costs involved.

Where NGOs are involved in the provision of GPGs, such as in the case of polio eradication, they are also likely to need compensation for their services, both to ensure that they participate (the rather vague definition of NGOs undermines the potential for formal or informal coercion to achieve this), and to ensure that their activities are adequately resourced.

In the case of TNCs, it would in principle make sense to use coercion to restrict activities which have negative health effects (e.g. the promotion of tobacco and alcohol consumption and unhealthy diets and behaviors), and compensation or reward to encourage them to provide health-favoring externalities (e.g. research into new drugs and vaccines). In practice, however, the limitations of formal and informal coercion at the national and international levels may require compensation to be used in the former case.

1.5 Conclusion

Increasing globalization has exposed a range of goods for which production is seen to be suboptimal, a number of which concern, to varying degrees, health. However, without an adequate consideration of *why* suboptimality occurs, there is a good chance that attempts to improve provision will, at best, be ineffective or, at worst, lead to greater sub-optimality.

In this chapter we have therefore explored how the concept of "global public goods" may be defined and applied to address this problem, and outlined the economic and political measures derived from such an analysis that may be used to improve the provision and finance of such goods. The essential characteristics of both pure and impure public goods were described, as was the meaning of "global" used in this volume. A definition of what we consider to be a GPG was then provided, and is used as the foundation to the consideration of the GPG characteristics for the chapters that follow.

It is worth highlighting three key aspects which result from the analysis provided here, as they foreshadow the reasons for, and discussions within, the following chapters. First, the importance of "access goods": private goods required to enable the public good to be fully accessed and/or utilized. The consumption of many goods classified as "public" goods will infact be determined by the ability of consumers to obtain the private good required to access them. In this respect, policies to improve the provision of public goods will be limited, or fail, and as such some goods, which are patently not public according to the strict definition, must nevertheless be classified *as if they were* public goods to ensure that the public good itself is consumed. This issue is emphasized throughout the chapters, but best exemplified in the discussion of public health infrastructure in Chapter 8, which underpins many of the other case-studies presented as a "archetypical" access good.

Second, health *per se* is not a GPG, but a private good, although one which may provide substantial positive (health and economic) externalities. Thus health is taken as an *objective* to be achieved, rather than as a *means* to achieve something else. The two caveats to this involve the role of communicable disease control as a GPG *per se*, and the significant positive economic externalities from improved which make health sufficiently important to qualify as being treated as a GPG.

Third, the "horizontal" nature of GPGs. The primary "horizontal" GPGH identified are knowledge and policy and regulatory regimes, with health systems being deemed a fundamental access goods to be included as if they were a GPG. These are "horizontal" goods. An important contribution of the GPG concept may be that it places such horizontal issues back in the centre of policy discussions, as a compliment to the historical focus upon more "vertical" streams.

These issues, amongst many others, are discussed in the following chapters, by a range of experts in economics, law, and public health. Once these have been explored, we summarize in Chapter 13 the lessons that have been learnt in assessing the utility of the GPG concept as applied in health.

Appendix 1.1 **GPG status of the control of major communicable diseases**

Malaria

Malaria is not a global disease. It may, with global warming, spread geographically, but otherwise cross-border movement of vectors is localized. Although it has a substantial effect in endemic areas, this is primarily among low-income households with limited integration in the global economy, limiting potential cross-border impacts. While a small proportion of the population of non-endemic countries may be at risk through travel, this is minimal with the availability of prophylaxis (notwithstanding the potential impact of MDR-malaria).

Malaria control and the inputs it requires are therefore regional rather than global public goods.

HIV/AIDS

HIV/AIDS is global in scope and cross-border transmission is both global and likely to be substantial, with the likelihood of onward transmission. Infection is not curable, and management is expensive, so that cross-border transmission has a potentially significant effect both on health and on health-care costs in low-incidence countries. HIV/AIDS has a major economic impact in some developing countries, with some potential effects on foreign investment through loss of human capital, although this is a secondary concern.

Control of HIV/AIDS may therefore be seen as a GPG, and the inputs it requires as GPGs or access goods.

Tuberculosis

Tuberculosis is global in scope, and has the potential for cross-border and onward transmission. While vaccination is routine in most developed countries, it is of limited effectiveness; but effective treatment is readily available and (except for MDR-TB) relatively inexpensive, limiting the effects of importation. MDR-TB is much more problematic: while its impact in developed countries is primarily on health-care costs, the high potential for onward transmission makes this cost potentially substantial.

Control of tuberculosis may therefore be seen as a GPG, although primarily as a means of controlling MDR-TB, and the inputs it requires as GPGs or access goods.

Acute respiratory infection

Acute respiratory infection (ARI) is global in scope, with the potential for onward transmission. However, it is primarily a disease of poverty, limiting the potential for non-local cross-border transmission. It is relatively easy and cheap to treat, and any cross-border transmission which does occur is therefore unlikely to have a significant effect either on health or health-care costs. Since it mainly affects children, its economic impact is very long-term in nature.

Control of ARI therefore cannot be considered as a GPG; but the inputs it requires may be.

Diarrheal disease

Diarrhea is analogous to ARI: cross-border transmission is limited to the local level by its concentration among low-income populations; the health impact of importation is limited by the ease and low cost of treatment; and the economic impact limited by its concentration among children. Infection is primarily through food and water, limiting the scope for onward transmission once imported.

Control of diarrheal disease cannot therefore be considered as a GPG; but the inputs it requires may be.

Maternal and neonatal health

Health problems related to child-birth are not communicable, and therefore not subject to cross-border transmission. Cross-border economic effects are also likely to be limited.

Control of maternal and neonatal health problems cannot therefore be considered as a GPG; but the inputs it requires may be.

Non-eradicable vaccine-preventable diseases

Vaccine preventable diseases (e.g. mumps and yellow fever) have limited potential for non-local cross-border transmission, dependent upon the prevalence of vaccination, which also limits onward transmission, particularly in developed countries. Treatment costs are often minimal, and health effects limited in countries with adequate nutrition, living conditions and health systems. Because they mainly affect children, cross-border economic effects are also minimal.

Control of non-eradicable vaccine-preventable diseases cannot therefore be considered as a GPG; but the technology embodied in a vaccine against a disease of global scope is a GPG.

Eradicable diseases

Communicable diseases, such as polio and measles, for which effective low-cost preventive interventions (e.g. vaccination) are available, and for which there is no non-human reservoir, have the potential for eradication. Reducing the incidence of these diseases is not a GPG, for the same reason as vaccine-preventable diseases; but global eradication allows those countries which would otherwise have continued to operate prevention programs to save resources by terminating these programs.

Where it is feasible, disease eradication (for diseases of global scope) can therefore be seen as a GPG, and the inputs it requires as GPGs or access goods.

Antimicrobial resistance

Antimicrobial resistance (AMR) generally arises within countries, due to inappropriate use of antimicrobial treatments. Once it exists, however, it has the potential for cross-border and onward transmission. Although AMR infection can often be treated in developed countries, and the risk of infection may be limited by vaccination, treatment cost is often considerable, and many diseases are becoming incurable. Lowering the risk of cross-border transmission may therefore have a significant effect on health-care costs in countries with strong health systems, as well as a major impact on health in those with weak health systems.

Control of AMR in diseases of global scope can therefore be seen as a GPG, and the inputs it requires as GPGs or access goods.

Appendix 1.2 **Knowledge and technology: public or private goods?**

Medical knowledge, as embodied in technologies such as vaccines and pharmaceuticals, is non-rival in consumption. Once the technology is known, one person's use of it does not prevent others from using it, or limit its benefits to them. In principle, it is also only partly excludable: without policy intervention (see below), access to knowledge is limited only by the secrecy of those who have access to it and the technical skills required for its application. This creates a potential incentive problem: as a public good, there is no commercial incentive for the development of new technologies.

This problem has been resolved by exploiting the need for the knowledge to be embodied in products, such as vaccines and pharmaceuticals, for delivery to users. Since these products are private goods—rival and excludable in consumption—they can be used to limit access to the technology they embody to those who pay, allowing commercial companies to sell the goods concerned at a profit. This turns the technology itself into a club good, limited to those who can afford to pay for the products which embody it.

However, this embodiment of medical knowledge within products is not sufficient by itself to provide a commercial incentive to invest in research and development (R&D). Producing the goods which embody the technology makes the knowledge available to other companies, allowing them to produce the same goods. The more companies produce a particular drug, the more competition will reduce prices and thus profits. Thus, while medical technology is a GPG as far as *users* are concerned, it is rival in consumption between *producers*.

Historically, this problem has been resolved (for pharmaceuticals, at least) by patent legislation. This amounts to using administrative mechanisms to turn the public goods of medical (and other) technologies into private goods, owned and controlled by the companies which pay for their development. This has the effect of endowing patent holders with monopoly rights, and therefore monopoly profits, for a fixed period. In response to the globalization of markets, this approach was extended internationally by the WTO Agreement on TRIPS in 1995, which also extends the period of patent protection to 20 years.

The result of patent legislation is that product development becomes essentially self-financing. The research is initially financed by commercial companies, but ultimately paid for by purchases of the resulting products by donors, governments, and individual users (together with a sufficient profit to provide a commercial rate of return and to compensate companies for the commercial risks). Thus incentives are created for the development of new medical technologies, where these provide a sufficient profit on the necessary investment in research and testing.

However, the resulting "market" for this essentially public good has important side-effects. In particular:

(1) The use of prices and profits as an incentive mechanism creates a major trade-off between the development of technologies and access to them once they have been developed, due to problems of affordability among low-income households.

(2) The pattern of R&D is determined by ability to pay, not health needs. This skews product development away from major health problems mainly affecting poorer populations, such as malaria and tuberculosis, and toward less important concerns of rich populations, such as impotence and hair loss.

(3) Since consumer willingness to pay is typically greater for the treatment of a current disease than for the prevention of contracting a disease, product development may be skewed away from cost-effective preventive interventions, such as vaccinations, and toward generally less cost-effective drugs for treatment, especially of chronic disease.

(4) Stimulating product development in areas of low public health priority may mean that research on prevention and on major poverty-related health diseases is reduced, if financial and human resources are diverted away from them, or the prices of scarce inputs necessary for research—notably specialized professionals—are inflated.

In short, the current approach of reliance on *commercial* development and production under patent protection reduces access to existing technologies among poorer households and does not increase—and may even reduce—the development of new technologies for most of their major health problems.

Various options are available to address these issues, including modifications to the international patent régime (e.g. Lanjouw 2001), increased public sector funding of R&D, public–private partnerships in R&D funding and production (Buse and Walt 2000), tax credits or advance purchase commitments (PIU 2001), promotion of differential pricing by pharmaceutical companies (charging countries according to their ability to pay) (Barton 2001, Scherer and Watal 2001), compulsory licensing and parallel imports (Corea 2000) and promotion of low-cost generic production.

Although none of these options is unproblematic, they may well be less problematic than the status quo. A system which would provide *an optimal combination of incentives for the development of technologies of public health priority, and access to them for populations in greatest need*, would provide very considerable health benefits. The international patent régime, modified as necessary, is central, but would need to be supplemented by other mechanisms to deal with specific areas of medical technology, according to their nature (e.g. vaccines compared with pharmaceuticals) and disease characteristics (e.g. geographical and socio-economic incidence).

Since the sharing of costs and benefits between the public and private sectors varies considerably between different options, it is also important to take account of the opportunity costs of public expenditure and tax concessions, as well as the large commercial (and associated political) interests in this area.

Vaccines have been treated differently. While processes developed for producing a particular vaccine are patentable, the vaccine itself is not generally patented.[17] This means that the initial developer has a relatively short period of monopoly profits, until competitors develop their own processes for its production. The result is to limit the incentives for vaccine development, but to make vaccines more affordable once they have been developed. The limited research incentives have been off-set by public sector intervention, particularly research in publicly funded institutions and "public private partnerships," such as Medicines for Malaria and the International AIDS Vaccine Initiative.

However, this situation rests on the absence of product patents on vaccines, which cannot necessarily be assumed. If the proteins in vaccines were subject to product patents, the same issues of incentives and affordability would arise as for pharmaceuticals, suggesting a need to exploit the flexibility in the TRIPS Agreement to define natural products as discoveries rather than inventions in the drafting of national patent legislation.

References

Arndt C, Lewis JD. *The Macro-implications of HIV/AIDS in South Africa: A Preliminary Assessment.* Africa Region Working Paper No. ARWPS-9, Washington DC; World Bank, 2000.

Barton J. *Differentiated Pricing of Patented Products.* CMH Working Paper No. WG4-1, Commission on Macroeconomics and Health.
http://www.cmhealth.org/docs/wg4_paper2.pdf, 2001.

---

[17] Whether biological materials such as proteins are patentable depends on whether they are considered as inventions or discoveries, which varies between patent laws in different countries (Corea 2000, chapter II).

BIPDA. *Impacts of HIV/AIDS on Poverty and Income Inequality in Botswana.* Botswana Institute for Development Policy Analysis. Paper presented at the International AIDS Economics Network (IAEN) Workshop, Durban South Africa, June 2000.

Bloom J, Williamson M. Demographic transitions and economic miracles in emerging Asia. *World Bank Econom Rev* 1998; **12**(3): 419–55.

Bonnel R. *Economic Analysis of HIV/AIDS.* Background Paper for the Africa Development Forum 2000, World Bank/UNAIDS, 2000.

Buse K, Walt G. Global public-private partnerships: Part II. *Bull WHO* 2000; **78**: 569–714.

Commission on Macroeconomics and Health (CMH). *Macroeconomics and Health: Investing in Health for Economic Development.* Geneva: World Health Organization, 2001.

Connolly S, Munro A. *Economics of the Public Sector.* Europe: Prentice Hall, 1999; chapter 4.

Corea C. *Integrating Public Health Concerns into Patent Legislation in Developing Countries.* Geneva: South Center, 2000.

Fidler D. Globalisation, international law, and emerging infectious diseases. *Emerg Infect Dis* 1996; **2**: 77–84.

Fidler D. Return of the fourth horseman: emerging infectious diseases and international law. *Minn Law Rev* 1997; **81**: 771–868.

Finger JM. *Statement by J. Michael Finger.* Developing Countries and the New Round of Multilateral Trade Negotiations Workshop, Harvard University, 5–6 November, 2000.

Folland S, Goodman A, Stano M. *The Economics of Health and Health Care.* New Jersey: Prentice Hall, 1997; chapter 22.

Gallup H, Sachs J. *The Economic Burden of Malaria.* Center for International Development, Harvard University, Working Paper No. 52, 2000.

Hargreaves-Heap S, Hollis M, Lyons B, Sugden R, Weale A. *The Theory of Choice. A critical Guide.* Oxford: Blackwell Publishers Ltd, 1992; chapter 7.

Kaul I, Grunberg I, Stern MA. *Global Public Goods: International Cooperation in the 21st Century.* New York: Oxford University Press, 1999.

Koivusalo M, Ollila E. *Making a Health World: Agencies, Actors and Policies in International Health.* London: Zed Books, 1997.

LaFond A. *Sustaining Primary Health Care.* London: Earthscan, 1995.

Lanjouw J. *A Patent Policy Proposal for Global Diseases.* Mimeo: World Bank. http://econ.worldbank.org/view.php?type=5&id=1733, 2001.

Lister G. *Global Health and Development: the Impact of Globalisation on the Health of Poor People.* In: *Eliminating World Poverty: Making Globalisation Work for the Poor,* DFID White Paper, London, 2000.

MacFarlan M, Sgherri S. *The Macroeconomic Impact of HIV/AIDS in Botswana.* Working Paper No. WP/01/80, Washington DC: International Monetary Fund, 2001.

Murray CJL, Lopez AD, Mathers CD, Stein C. *The Global Burden of Disease 2000 project: aims, methods and data sources.* GPE Discussion Paper No. 36, Geneva: World Health Organization, 2001.

Otsuki T, Wilson J, Sewadeh M. *Saving Two in a Billion: A Case Study to Quantify the Effects of European Safety Standards on African Exports.* Mimeo: World Bank, 2000.

Over M. *The Macroeconomic Impact of AIDS in Sub-Saharan Africa.* Mimeo: Population and Human Resources Department, Washington DC: World Bank, 1992.

Performance and Innovation Unit (PIU). *Tackling the Diseases of Poverty—Meeting the Okinawa/Millennium Targets for HIV/AIDS, Tuberculosis and Malaria.* London: Cabinet Office, 2001.

Roll Back Malaria. *Country strategies and resource requirements.* Draft for consultation, Geneva: World Health Organization, 2001.

Sandler T. *Global Challenges: An Approach to Environmental, Political and Economic problems.* Cambridge, New York and Melbourne: Cambridge University Press, 1997; chapter 5.

Schmidt R. *A Feasible Foreign Exchange Transactions Tax.* Mimeo: North South Institute, 1999.

Scherer JM, Watal J. *Post-TRIPS Options for Access to Patented Medicines in Developing Countries.* CMH Working Paper No. WG4-1, Commission on Macroeconomics and Health. http://www.cmhealth.org/docs/wg4_paper1.pdf, 2001.

Smith RD, Coast J. Controlling antimicrobial resistance: a proposed transferable permit market. *Health Policy* 1998; **43**(3): 219–32.

Strauss A, Thomas J. Health, nutrition and economic development. *J Econom Lit* 1998; **36**: 776–817.

Tobin J. A proposal for monetary reform. *Eastern Economic Journal* 1978; **4**(3–4):153–9. Reprinted in Patomäki H (2001) *Democratising Globalisation: The Leverage of the Tobin Tax.* London: Zed Books.

WHO. *World Health Report 2000, Health Systems: Improving Performance* 2000; National account Indicators, annex table 8.

WHO. *Global DOTS Expansion Plan: Progress in TB Control in High-burden Countries, 2001.* CDS/STB/2001.11, 2001*a*.

WHO. *World Health Report 2001.* Geneva: World Health Organization, 2001*b*.

World Bank. *World Development Indicators 2001.* New York: Oxford University Press, 2001.

Section 2

Global public goods for health: Case studies

Chapter 2

Polio eradication

R Bruce Aylward, Arnab Acharya,
Sarah England, Mary Agocs, and
Jennifer Linkins

2.1 Introduction

The control of an infectious disease is a classic example of a public good for health
(Zacher 1999). The *global* eradication of an infectious disease is a classic example of
a global public good for health (GPGH). Once a disease is eradicated no one person's receipt of this protection will diminish the protection everyone else enjoys,
and every newborn entering the global community is also protected.

After 15 years of program implementation the Global Polio Eradication
Initiative (GPEI) is unique in offering the most well-developed instance of a
GPGH in practice. As such it provides substantial experience from which lessons
may be drawn to facilitate the production of other possible GPGH outlined in this
volume. This chapter therefore considers the politics, practicalities, and economics
of producing the GPEI, summarizing lessons learnt.

Following this introduction, Section 2.2 provides background to polio disease
and control. Section 2.3 considers the GPGH aspects of polio eradication, with
Section 2.4 outlining the politics and practicalities encountered in conducting the
GPEI. Section 2.5 presents the economics of polio eradication, before Section 2.6
concludes with a discussion of the utility of the GPGH concept, and lessons from
the experience of the GPEI relevant to other potential GPGH.

The authors are extremely grateful to Ms Joan Hawe of the World Health Organization
(WHO) for her assistance with the references for this article, as well as Dr Robert
Beaglehole and Ms Anne-Lise Loomer of the WHO, for their detailed comments on
specific sections of the manuscript.

2.2 **Polio: The disease and its control**

Caused by three closely related viruses, paralytic poliomyelitis frustrated health officials and terrified the general population until the development of effective vaccines. As recently as the 1950s, polio outbreaks left tens of thousands of people permanently paralyzed, even in industrialized countries (Paul 1971, CDC 1994). Spreading primarily through the fecal–oral route, the three strains of the poliovirus eventually enter the spinal column and destroy nerve cells resulting in paralysis of the muscles (Sutter *et al.* 1999). Paralysis is usually permanent. Even among those who recover, one-third may experience a recurrence of muscle pain, exacerbation of existing weakness, or new weakness and paralysis, 15–40 years later as the "post-polio syndrome" (Ramlow *et al.* 1992). Because the majority of its victims survive the acute illness, as many as 20 million people are today living with the consequences of polio (Aylward *et al.* 2000*a*).

By 1963 an extraordinary scientific research program culminated in the licensing of two effective vaccines against the disease. The inactivated poliovirus vaccine (IPV), developed by Dr Jonas Salk, rapidly led to the virtual elimination of the disease from many industrialized countries (Sutter *et al.* 1999). With the licensing and widespread use of the oral polio vaccine (OPV), developed by Dr Albert Sabin, most of the final chains of poliovirus transmission were extinguished in "the West" (Sutter *et al.* 1999). This OPV, developed from a weakened (attenuated) strain of the virus, had the advantages of lower cost, simpler administration and heightened gut immunity, facilitating its use and impact in developing countries (Hull *et al.* 1994). By 1974, substantial progress toward smallpox eradication had

1988
>125 countries

2001
10 countries

Fig. 2.1 Distribution of endemic poliomyelitis in 1988, the year the World Health Assembly voted to eradicate the disease, and at end-2001

stimulated efforts to scale up national immunization services in developing countries, such that by 1990 routine childhood immunization coverage against polio had risen from 5 to over 70 percent worldwide (Lee *et al.* 1997).

Despite this global progress there remained significant disparities in levels of immunization coverage, particularly in Sub-Saharan Africa where more than 50 percent of children were still not being immunized by the late 1980s (WHO 2002*a*). As a result, in 1988, the year the global polio eradication goal was adopted, more than 350,000 cases of paralytic poliomyelitis occurred, the vast majority in developing countries (Hull *et al.* 1994, Aylward *et al.* 2000*b*). In war-torn countries such as Afghanistan and Cambodia, surveys in the mid-1990s were still finding polio to be a leading cause of permanent disability among children (Francois *et al.* 1998).

When the World Health Assembly (WHA) voted to eradicate polio in 1988, the causative virus was either proven or believed to be circulating in more than 125 countries on 5 continents (the number of "countries" defined using year 2000 geographic borders), with just over 90 percent of reported cases from low or lower-middle income countries (Fig. 2.1; by 2001 this was down to just 10 countries).

2.3 Polio eradication as a GPGH

The GPEI, launched by the WHA in 1988 to eliminate paralysis due to poliovirus (WHA 1988) is a classic GPGH: all people everywhere will share equally in the benefits of a polio-free world, possibly in perpetuity. Everyone in the world will be protected from polio and no one person's protection will decrease another's protection (i.e. it is non-rival). There will be no limit to the safety from polio that eradication will offer in terms of geographic reach or the number of people protected (i.e. it is non-excludable). As the goal of polio eradication is provided and pursued through the collective action of over 10 million people working or volunteering worldwide, polio eradication meets or approximates all of the GPG criteria set by various authors (see, e.g. Sandler 1997, Kaul *et al.* 1999).

The pursuit of polio eradication also illustrates the basic issues that arise in the pursuit of any GPGH, ranging from the "prisoner's dilemma" (i.e. making a decision in the absence of information as to how others will behave) to "free-riders" (i.e. those who will benefit from the GPGH without contributing to its production). As importantly, the experience gained through 15 years of the GPEI provides clues as to how such issues actually evolve in practice and thus lessons on the politics and economics of global public goods.

2.4 Politics and practicalities of polio eradication

2.4.1 The decision to pursue eradication

Although the success of smallpox eradication in 1977 created momentum for new eradication efforts, this enthusiasm was countered with concern that pursuing such targeted objectives could compromise efforts to develop strong primary health care systems (Dowdle and Cochi 2002). Further, within the scientific community there were doubts concerning the technical feasibility of eradicating any organism after smallpox (Anonymous 1982). Polio was considered particularly problematic due to the large number of asymptomatic infections and limitations of the vaccine and diagnostic tools, particularly in the tropical developing country setting (Horstman *et al.* 1984).

However, the ultimate proof that an organism can be eradicated is the interruption of its transmission in a large geographic area; a condition met for polio by the mid-1980s (de Quadros *et al.* 1992). Perhaps, the most important factor leading to the adoption of the GPEI was the decision by Brazil in 1980 to pursue polio control through nationwide rounds of OPV immunization (Risi 1984). By 1983, the disease had been virtually eliminated from this largest country in South America and other countries, notably Mexico and Costa Rica, had adopted the strategy with similar success. In 1985, the 37 Member States of the Pan-American Health Organization (PAHO) launched a regional polio elimination effort (PAHO 1985). Using a four-pronged strategy of routine immunization, national immunization days (NIDs), surveillance and laboratory investigation of all cases of acute flaccid paralysis (AFP), and house-to-house "mop-up" campaigns, the region was rapidly approaching zero polio by the end of 1987 (de Quadros *et al.* 1992). However, despite this progress, there was little support for extending this effort to a global eradication goal due to both scientific scepticism and concerns that such a goal was incompatible with the strengthening of primary health care systems (WHO 1978, Horstman *et al.* 1984, Dowdle and Cochi 2002).

The event considered to have been pivotal in transforming the regional PAHO elimination goal into a global effort was a March 1988 meeting convened by the Task Force for Child Survival and Development (Task Force for Child Survival and Development 1988). By the time of the meeting, the compelling data from the Americas had captured the imagination of the charismatic and persuasive leader of the United Nations Children's Fund (UNICEF), who became an ardent advocate for a GPEI. During this meeting, the Director-General of the WHO was also convinced of the merit of a global eradication effort and resolved to put the matter to the WHA only 2 months later.

In May 1988, the WHA, consisting of the Ministers of Health of all WHO Member States, unanimously endorsed the polio eradication resolution, after rewording to emphasize that eradication " . . . be pursued in ways that strengthen the development of the Expanded Programme on Immunization as a whole, fostering its contribution, in turn, to the development of the health infrastructure and primary health care" (WHA 1988). More importantly, and in part out of deference to advoc-ates of health systems development, significant lessons from the Americas were not reflected in the Resolution, particularly the need for the massive immunization campaigns that had been critical in the Western Hemisphere.

The eradication goal was subsequently reviewed and endorsed by the World Summit for Children in 1990, the largest ever gathering of Heads of State (World Summit for Children 1990). By 1989, each of the six WHO Regional Committees had also reviewed and adopted a Regional eradication goal. Health and political leaders from low-, middle-, and high-income countries have continued to reaffirm their commitment to polio eradication through resolutions adopted in forums such as the Organization of African Unity (OAU), the South Asian Association for Regional Cooperation (SAARC) and a G8 summit (Assembly of Heads of States and Government 1996, Andrus *et al.* 2001). These leaders have repeatedly reinforced and publicly demonstrated their leadership role by participating in highly visible events such as the launching of NIDs.

2.4.2 The "production" of polio eradication

In general, the effort required to eradicate polio has correlated inversely with a country's income. In the few high-income countries that were endemic in 1988, the elimination of polio was relatively straightforward because of the temperate climate, high levels of sanitation, and strong health systems (i.e. the presence of sufficient "access goods"). In such countries, the strengthening of routine immunization and surveillance services was generally sufficient to eliminate any remaining chains of polio transmission. In contrast, eliminating polio from the remaining endemic low-income countries has been an extraordinary challenge, requiring massive and sustained efforts over a 5–10 year period. Implementation of NIDs has been a particularly daunting challenge, reflected in the achievements of countries like China and India where approximately 80 and 150 million children, respectively were immunized during a 1–3-day period, and repeated 1 month later, over multiple years (EPI 1996*a*, 2000*a*). In a number of low-income countries, it was also necessary to double the number of NIDs conducted each year to compensate for low routine immunization coverage (EPI 2001*a*).

Because of the huge numbers of people and vehicles required, the management and implementation of high quality NIDs was beyond the capacity of the health sector in many low- and middle-income countries. Consequently, many countries have drawn heavily on their information, transport, defence, and other ministries to help solve the logistical challenges inherent in trying to reach all children, in all corners of a country, over a 1–3-day period. Even then, it was only by engaging the private sector, often on an extraordinary scale, that high immunization coverage could be ensured during NIDs. In the Philippines, for example, more than 140 private companies regularly donated personnel, vehicles, facilities, and financial support (Tangermann *et al.* 1997).

Even with high-quality NIDs in individual countries, people crossing borders could transmit polio in the interval between the NIDs in one country and its neighbor, thus reducing the efficacy of these activities. Recognizing this, many countries decided to synchronize their NIDs. In "Operation MECACAR" for example, 18 countries of the Mediterranean, Caucasus, Central Asian Republics, and Russia immunized 56 million children in April and again in May 1995 (EPI 1996*b*). Similar activities followed in South Asia and West Africa (Andrus *et al.* 2001, EPI 2001*b*). Perhaps, the most extraordinary of these activities began when the conflict-affected countries of the Democratic Republic of the Congo, Angola, Congo and Gabon decided to synchronize three rounds of NIDs in July, August and September 2001, reaching 15 million children (EPI 2001*b*, 2002).

Through the training of tens of thousands of health workers, deployment of thousands of vehicles, and development of an electronic communications network around the world, by the year 2000 all polio-infected countries were reporting standard data to WHO on acutely paralyzed children on either a weekly or monthly basis (EPI 2000*b*). In addition, standard performance data was allowing the comparison of information across all countries. Central to this surveillance capacity has been the development of a global laboratory network for enterovirus diagnosis that now comprises 147 facilities, covering every country in the world (EPI 2002). All of these facilities use the same methods, materials and quality control measures. Even in areas affected by conflict, such as Afghanistan, Congo, and Somalia, surveillance was nearing international (i.e. certification) standard by 2001.

By the end of 2001, every country in the world had introduced either the WHO-recommended polio eradication strategies or a variant thereof (Fig. 2.2) such that only 10 countries remained endemic for the disease, with just 480 confirmed polio cases in the world that year (Fig. 2.1). Worldwide, more than 10 million people are estimated to have volunteered their time to immunize 575 million children during NIDs in the year 2001 alone (EPI 2002).

2.4.3 **Coordination of the GPEI**

Though specific polio eradication activities have been led, co-ordinated, and implemented by the governments of polio-infected countries themselves, the support of an extraordinary partnership has been essential. This public–private partnership, spearheaded by the WHO, Rotary International, the US Centers for

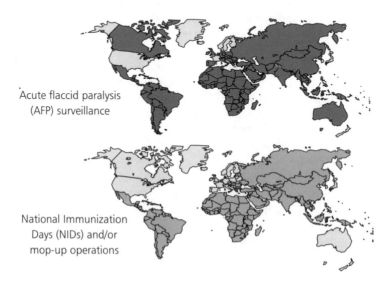

Fig. 2.2 Distribution of countries implementing the polio eradication strategies between 1985 and end-2001

Disease Control and Prevention (CDC), and UNICEF has facilitated the inputs of donor governments, other international organizations (e.g. UN funds, agencies, and programs), foundations, corporations, nongovernmental organizations (NGOs), and humanitarian organizations.

The most remarkable of the core polio eradication partners is Rotary International, the private sector service organization, which has played a central role in this global initiative through its "PolioPlus" Program and 1.2 million volunteers worldwide. Rotary has not only been central to the mobilization of financial resources from donor governments, but will also have contributed nearly US$ 600 million of its own resources by the end of 2005. In endemic countries, thousands of Rotary volunteers have assisted with social mobilization, NIDs, and other polio eradication activities. In both endemic and donor countries, it has been Rotary's high level advocacy that has often secured the necessary government support, whether financial or in-kind.

The non-governmental and humanitarian organizations that facilitate strategy implementation in the field have included the International Red Cross and Red Crescent Movement, The International Federation of the Red Cross, Médecins San Frontières, Save the Children Fund, World Vision, Cooperative for American Relief to Everywhere (CARE), and the US-based NGO umbrella-organization Congress of Racial Equality (CORE). These groups collaborate in micro-planning, training, transport, surveillance, and the administration of supplementary immunization, particularly in conflict-affected areas. UN agencies such as the United Nations Development Programme (UNDP), the World Food Programme (WFP), and the Office of the United Nations High Commissioner for Refugees (UNHCR) have facilitated activities at the country level through the provision of transport, human resources, security, and communications.

Civil society advocates, special ambassadors, business leaders, and celebrities from the arts, sciences, entertainment, and sports fields have supported the work of the polio eradication partnership, particularly in the areas of advocacy and communications. People such as UN Secretary General and Nobel Laureate Mr Kofi Annan, Microsoft Chairman Bill Gates and CNN founder Ted Turner have advocated on behalf of the eradication initiative.

To co-ordinate the inputs of such a diverse partnership, a variety of mechanisms were established at the global, regional, and country levels. Strategic planning, policy development, resolution of technical concerns, and priority setting are discussed and agreed through oversight bodies at the global and regional levels, usually known as Technical Consultative Groups (TCGs) convened by the WHO every 6–12 months. Resource mobilization efforts and coordination of financial inputs are managed through regular meetings of Interagency Coordinating Committees (ICCs), at the regional and country level. Polio endemic Member States play a central role in the TCG process and at the country level the Ministry of Health chairs the ICC. Similar mechanisms have been established to manage the core partnership, the global laboratory network, and the process for eventually certifying the world as polio-free.

2.5 **The economics of polio eradication**

Implementation of the GPEI has required substantial in-kind and financial contributions from both endemic and polio-free countries. In any given country, the proportion of costs estimated to have been incurred by national (internal) and international (external) sources for these activities correlates most closely with factors such as income level and health system capacity. China, for example, has estimated that over 95 percent of the costs of polio eradication strategy implementation were borne by the country itself. Even in the poorest countries with virtually nonexistent health systems, such as Somalia or Afghanistan, the community probably absorbs between 25 and 50 percent of the real costs of implementing the eradication strategies, particularly NIDs.

2.5.1 **National (internal) costs and expenditures**

Implementation of supplementary immunization days for polio requires significant national resources, particularly in terms of time spent by health workers and volunteers from all sectors of society. In most countries, this human resource input constitutes the largest component of polio-specific contributions from national resources (Mogedal and Stenson 1999). Because of the diversity of the communities, government administrative levels, and partners, that have contributed to the implementation of the GPEI, it is possible to estimate only the value of the financial and in-kind expenditures within a country.

Given the importance of understanding the scale and potential opportunity costs of this contribution, a conservative estimate was generated using the amount and value of the time that is contributed by volunteers, health workers, and others in the implementation of NIDs, the most expensive and labor-intensive of the polio eradication strategies. After quantifying the number of NIDs volunteer hours per country, wage rates from the year 2000 World Development Indicators statistical database were applied to establish a monetary value for this "volunteer" effort. Based upon these calculations, polio endemic countries will have contributed at least US$ 1.8 billion in volunteer time alone for polio eradication activities between 1988 and 2005.

Although external financing is used to help defray volunteer transport and food expenses in some low-income countries, this US$ 1.8 billion is nonetheless a very conservative estimate. For example, these calculations do not account for the fact that volunteer time is taken away from other regular duties, nor do they reflect the substantial government resources used at the national, state, province, district, and local community levels to pay for petrol, social mobilization, training, and other costs. Furthermore, some countries, such as India, have used World Bank IDA credit to cover part of the eradication-related costs. Many other countries, such as Nepal, incurred substantial additional opportunity costs by designating NIDs as national public holidays to facilitate the use of government personnel and other resources.

2.5.2 **International (external) contributions and financing mechanisms**

Between the launch of the GPEI in 1988 and its target date of 2005 for global certification, external sources will have provided at least US$ 2.75 billion to polio endemic countries to help cover the costs of implementing the necessary strategies. Approximately 40 percent of external financing has been used for OPV and 35 percent for NIDs operational costs (e.g. cold chain refurbishment, training, social mobilization). The strengthening of surveillance has absorbed 20 percent of external resources for equipment (e.g. vehicles, computers), supplies, training, personnel and related costs. The remaining 5 percent of external resources have been needed for enabling factors, such as the certification and containment processes, advocacy and resource mobilization, documentation, meetings, and administration.

The US$ 1.870 billion in external financing that was donated for activities between 1985 and 2001 came from a broad range of public and private sector sources (Fig. 2.3). Of the 175 external polio eradication donors to date, 26 will have contributed more than US$ 1 million over the lifespan of the initiative and 16 at least US$ 10 million. A number of these polio partners, such as Rotary International, are considered "non-traditional" overseas development aid (ODA) donors (Table 2.1).

A number of mechanisms have been used to channel these external resources to polio-endemic countries, the primary ones being multilateral funding through the WHO or UNICEF, and direct bilateral funding to recipient countries. This combination of mechanisms has allowed the initiative to accommodate the needs of

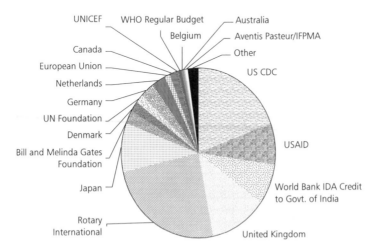

Fig. 2.3 Donors to the Global Polio Eradication Initiative, 1985–2001 (total contributions = US$ 1870 million)

Table 2.1 Major public and private sector donors to the GPEI (as of June 2002, including pledges through 2005)

Contribution (million US$)	Public sector partners	Development banks	Private sector partners
>500 m	United States of America	–	Rotary International
250–500 m	United Kingdom	–	–
100–249 m	Japan, Netherlands	–	–
50–99 m	Germany, Canada	World Bank ("grant" element)	Bill and Melinda Gates Foundation
25–49 m	Denmark, European Commission	–	United Nations Foundation
5–24 m	Belgium, Australia, Norway, WHO, UNICEF	American Development Bank (ADB)	Aventis-Pasteur, International Federation of Pharmaceutical Manufacturers Association
1–4 m	Italy, Switzerland, Ireland, Luxembourg	–	Anonymous, DeBeers, Wyeth Pharmaceuticals

both donors and recipient countries, while maximizing the efficient use of funds. To help achieve these efficiencies the WHO established a transparent process for tracking all external contributions, by funding source, and generating multiyear external resource requirement estimates, based on country-specific strategic plans (WHO 2001).

While the donor coalition that has been established to support the pursuit of this GPGH is impressive in terms of the size and breadth of the public and private sector partnership, there are a number of important "free riders." These free riders include traditional ODA donors from high-income countries, as well as middle-income "non-traditional" donor countries that have decided not to assist the work of polio-endemic countries despite a concerted effort by the Polio Advocacy Group to engage them. Of particular note is the non- or under-participation of some G7 countries and international financing institutions.

The reasons for this non-participation are many, but often stem from a philosophical disagreement with the pursuit of a "targeted" health objective, concerned that such pursuits could compromise or delay broader development efforts, particularly through the diversion of scarce human or financial resources. While these are valid concerns to which the Initiative must be extremely attentive and respond, there is little data to support them (Levin *et al.* 1999, Mogedal *et al.* 1999,

Loevinsohn *et al.* 2002). The only large-scale study to have looked at the impact of polio eradication on human resources concluded that there was sufficient "slack" in the public sector to absorb polio activities without major disruptions to other programs, particularly at the peripheral level (Mogedal *et al.* 1999). The sole detailed financing study found that there was a net increase in both national and international expenditure on routine immunization services during the period in which polio activities were implemented in the three countries studied (Levin *et al.* 1999).

2.5.3 Direct benefits: DALYs saved and cost-effectiveness

A number of studies have analyzed the benefits and costs of polio eradication. For example, Musgrove (1988) conducted a cost–benefit analysis of the PAHO Regional program, prior to the 1988 WHA resolution to pursue global eradication. Based on costs of treating polio derived from a 1982 study conducted in Brazil, and a 12 percent discount rate, the net present value of discounted savings resulting from polio eradication over the 15 years from the start of the campaign was estimated at US\$ 62.1 million, assuming a successful 5-year campaign and 10-year maintenance period, and that all polio victims were treated. The net present value of discounted savings was US\$ 0.6 million for the same period assuming that only a fraction of all polio victims were treated. Musgrove concluded "that polio eradication appeared economically justified solely in terms of reduced treatment costs, irrespective of reduced pain, suffering, and incapacitation. Moreover, the analysis found that eradication would still be economically justified if treatment costs were substantially lower, if substantially fewer cases occurred, or if somewhat fewer victims were treated."

Bart *et al.* (1996) conducted a similar cost–benefit analysis almost 10 years later, examining the more extended period of 1986–2040. Although only the benefits due to reductions in direct costs for treatment and rehabilitation were considered, the authors took into account the difference in vaccine costs in industrialized and developing countries. Their model "showed the 'break-even' point at which benefits exceeded costs was the year 2007, with a saving of US\$ 13,600 million by the year 2040. Sensitivity analyses revealed only small differences in the break-even point and in the dollars saved, when compared with the base case, even with large variations in the target age group for vaccination, the proportion of case-patients seeking medical attention, and the cost of vaccine delivery."

Because of developments within the GPEI and the global public health environment since the mid-1990s, the cost-effectiveness of this initiative was re-examined for the period 2001–40, using many of the assumptions of the original studies and standard discount rates of 3 percent (Acharya *et al.* 2001). Of note, calculation of the 2006–2040 costs was more complicated because there is now less international consensus on the appropriate polio immunization policy for the "post-certification" period (Global TCG 2002). In this analysis, the most realistic "best case" scenario would be simply the cessation of OPV immunization as soon as possible after the interruption of wild poliovirus transmission (set at 2010 for the purpose of this analysis). Conversely, the "worst case" scenario would be to replace routine OPV immunization with the more expensive IPV vaccine in all countries to avoid the risk of vaccine-associated paralytic poliomyelitis (VAPP) or of an outbreak due to a circulating vaccine-derived poliovirus (Global TCG 2001, EPI 2001*c*, Kew *et al.* 2002).

This analysis found that, even with improvements in routine immunization coverage, the burden of disease due to polio would still be significant were eradication not to take place. Between 2001 and 2040 there would be 10.6 million new cases of polio worldwide, representing the loss of 60 million Disability-adjusted Life Years (DALYs) (discounted at 3 percent), nearly all of which would occur in low-income developing countries (Table 2.2). Eradication would result in a cost savings in all countries if polio vaccination were to stop in 2010 wherever OPV is currently being used. Even in the "worst case" scenario, in which OPV would be replaced with a universal IPV strategy, and consequently a net cost of US$ 4.2 billion incurred by low-income countries, the cost per DALY saved would be low, at approximately US$ 50 per discounted DALY saved in developing countries (Table 2.2).

As noted, the cost-effectiveness of eradication is highly sensitive to international decisions on the most appropriate and feasible polio immunization policy in the post-certification era, particularly whether to stop routine use of OPV and whether to adopt universal IPV immunization in its place. Cost-effectiveness is also highly sensitive to the public sector price of IPV for low-income countries (set at US$ 0.50 per dose administered in this analysis). Finally, it is important to note that the benefits of eradication could rise considerably (perhaps by as much

Table 2.2 Discounted DALYs saved and estimated range of the cost-effectiveness of polio eradication, by World Bank income bracket, 2001–40

Income bracket	Discounted DALYs saved	Cost-effectiveness	
		Best-case scenario*	Worst-case scenario*
High	0	No change	No change
Upper middle	1,641,327	US$ 900 million savings	US$ 500 million savings
Lower middle	8,508,889	US$ 290 million savings	US$ 100 million savings
Low	46,480,358	US$ 1.4 billion savings	US$ 4.2 billion net cost**

* see text for description of the scenarios

** this option yields a cost-effectiveness ratio of US$ 52.50 per DALY saved as US$ 10 billion) should some or all industrialized countries decide to stop immunizing against polio in the post-eradication era.

2.5.4 Indirect benefits and costs

WHA Resolution 41.28, which launched the GPEI, explicitly states that eradication be pursued in ways that strengthen the delivery of primary health care services in general and immunization in particular (WHA 1988). Although there is widespread consensus that progress has been made in eradicating polioviruses (EPI 2002), there is substantial controversy as to whether this has strengthened the development of health systems or the delivery of other health services (Hall *et al.* 1998, WHO 2000). Some observers have felt that polio eradication has been detrimental to a sound, integrated approach to health systems development, while others have argued that any untoward effects of the initiative have been relatively minor and outweighed by the benefits (Aylward *et al.* 1998, Taylor and Waldman 1998).

A number of studies have attempted to reconcile these positions by examining the impact of the eradication initiative on the delivery of specific health services, or the development of health systems in general. From these analyses, three irrefutable benefits in the delivery of other health services have been found: (i) expanded Vitamin A distribution; (ii) enhanced global surveillance capacity; and (iii) improved cooperation among enterovirus laboratories worldwide (MacAuley and Verma 1999, Loevinsohn *et al.* 2002). Including the distribution of Vitamin A supplements during polio NIDs averted an estimated 400,000 childhood deaths during 1998–1999 alone, and strengthened the links between immunization contacts and micronutrient supplementation (Ching *et al.* 2000, Goodman *et al.* 2000). The surveillance capacity developed for polio eradication has been used to detect and respond to numerous outbreaks of important diseases, such as measles, meningitis, cholera, and yellow fever (Nsubuga *et al.* 2000). The international consensus on the value of this "indirect benefit" is reflected in widespread support for plans to expand and sustain this surveillance and laboratory capacity *after* polio eradication to enhance the control of other important public health problems.

More controversial has been the impact of eradication activities on the delivery of routine immunization services (Taylor Commission 1995, Aylward *et al.* 1997, Taylor *et al.* 1997). That the polio initiative has made a huge investment in the physical and human resources for routine immunization is incontrovertible; the cold chain, communications, and transport capacity has been largely replaced or refurbished in many low-income countries, particularly in Sub-Saharan Africa, and tens of thousands of vaccinators have been trained or retrained worldwide. The question remains as to whether the disruptions caused by polio NIDs will have only short-term effects or result in long-term impacts to routine services.

Despite studies on the broader impact of polio eradication on health systems, it has been difficult to generate more than anecdotal information. Most of these studies were hampered by a lack of credible baseline data, the absence of "control groups" and the concurrent implementation of major health system reforms, such as decentralization and sector-wide approaches (Mogedal and Stenson 1999, WHO 2000). However, most commentators agree that positive synergies exist between polio eradication and health systems development, but that these opportunities have seldom been fully exploited (Arora *et al.* 1999, Loevinsohn *et al.* 2002).

2.6 Conclusion

Reviewing the GPEI through the GPGH framework has proved valuable for a number of reasons, two of which may be particularly useful to other large public health endeavors. First, there are a number of lessons that could assist the planning of future GPGH, particularly in the areas of decision-making, production, financing, and benefits. Second, the GPGH concept provides a useful framework to advocate for, and sustain the societal and political commitment necessary for, large public health initiatives. The following sections outline four major lessons from the GPEI that may be applicable to other GPGH, and summarizes the utility of the GPGH concept for other public health initiatives, particularly eradication efforts.

2.6.1 Lessons for other GPGH

The first lesson derives from the decision-making process that eventually launched the GPEI. Of particular importance in this process has been the role played by "champions" who promoted and sustained the vision of polio eradication, beginning in individual countries in the 1960s, through the America's regional elimination effort of the 1980s, and today in the global initiative. While the humanitarian and economic benefits of eradication may appear self-evident, the international health environment was quite hostile to the idea of a "targeted program" in the years immediately following smallpox eradication, when the concept of primary health care was rising in the late 1970s. Overcoming such reticence required the unflagging promotion of polio eradication at the highest political levels by such credible luminaries as Dr Albert Sabin, the developer of the OPV, Dr Carlyle Guerra de Macedo, the former Regional Director of PAHO, and Mr James Grant, the visionary former leader of UNICEF. It was largely the single-minded support for global eradication by such people that brought the issue to a vote at the WHA in 1988 (Dowdle and Cochi 2002).

Though the WHA was the appropriate forum for discussing and debating the merits of an eradication initiative against polio, it has been argued that the delegates may not have had sufficient information to make a truly informed decision. No data were presented on the estimated human and financial resources that would be required, nor was there a clear statement on the strategies that would need to be pursued and in what timeframe (WHO 2002*b*). This lack of information had consequences for both endemic and polio-free countries, as well as the cost and efficiency of the eradication effort itself. For polio-endemic countries, the majority of which were low- or middle- income, it prevented a close evaluation of the opportunity costs of implementing the eradication strategies. For polio-free, predominantly high-income, countries it did not allow a calculation of the financial burden they might be expected to bear.

Perhaps as a result of this, it was not until 1992 that any country outside of the America's introduced the necessary supplementary immunization activities, and only in 1999, one year before the original target date for global eradication, that the last countries started. As important, the lack of a true consensus among important donor nations resulted in the eradication initiative being chronically short of funds. Until 1995 the number of major donors was very limited, with non-traditional development donors such as Rotary International and the US CDC providing most of the external financing. Many major overseas development agencies and traditional private sector health donors have yet to contribute on the scale that might be expected.

The late introduction of polio eradication strategies in endemic countries and slow engagement of donors from polio-free countries has been costly, not only in financial terms but also in opportunity costs and international goodwill, a critical element of any program requiring collective action on a global scale over a prolonged period. Although it is not possible to know whether better consensus building efforts and decision-making processes would have accelerated external financing and country level strategy introduction, they certainly would have helped in assessing and managing these risks to the eradication goal.

A second lesson from polio eradication relates to the actual production of a GPGH and the scale of the costs that may be incurred through collective action on a global scale. Though polio eradication requires that all countries implement the necessary strategies, the effort required to produce a GPGH can differ by orders of magnitude across geographic areas, populations and, perhaps most importantly, income brackets. Polio had largely been eliminated from high-income countries when the decision was taken to pursue global eradication. In fact, 99 percent of the disease burden was located in low- and lower-middle income countries. This resulted in the poorest countries of the world, with the weakest health systems, bearing the majority of the costs. An often heated debate has flared between and within ODAs, academics, NGOs, and the United Nations itself as to whether the massive opportunity costs of eradication, particularly to conduct National Immunization Days, were simply too high to merit the production of this GPGH. While the cost-effectiveness analysis presented here suggests that all countries stand to benefit from this investment, regardless as to the income bracket, this is not universally accepted.

Consequently, the importance of a sound understanding of the geographic areas and populations that will need to implement the necessary strategies to produce a GPGH cannot be overstated. Such an understanding is essential to evaluating the distribution of costs and burden of effort that will be required to produce a GPG.

A third lesson relates to financing. As with any GPGH, all countries stand to benefit economically from global polio eradication, whether in the form of eliminated treatment costs, reduced vaccination costs, enhanced productivity, or a combination of all three. Recognizing this, Rotary International, as part of its advocacy strategy on behalf of the GPEI, calculated "fair shares" of the total polio eradication budget to be financed by each major donor country. Using the rationale that WHO's regular budget of assessed contributions from Member States represented a "Global Public Good" for health, the polio eradication "shares" were based loosely on that formula. However, of the 22 WHO Member States who are members of the OECD's Development Assistance Committee that makes up the community of "traditional" ODA donors, only 16 have contributed to the eradication initiative. Of these, only 7 contributed the equivalent or more than their estimated "share," 6 are "free-riders" in that they made no financial contribution to eradication, while the remaining 9 contributed substantially less than their estimated "share" of the total budget of US$ 2,750 million dollars between 1985 and 2005.

The "fair share" concept has been most useful in negotiations with those donors who were institutionally committed to the concept of polio eradication and the global nature of the benefits that would result. Such donors readily engaged in discussion as to the "appropriate" level of contribution. The fair share concept had limited utility, however, when seeking donor government resources from those who were opposed, for whatever reason, to the concept from the outset. Recognizing this limitation of the fair share concept, the polio partnership devised alternate strategies for mobilizing resources in this setting, usually by raising the issue to a high political level and seeking a "one-off" contribution of substantial size. Overall, the fair share concept has been of great value for setting resource mobilization targets and in negotiating an appropriate level of contribution with interested donors, but its limitations must be recognized early, with alternate strategies for mobilizing funds in those settings where the fair share concept does not prove sufficient argument.

The final major lesson from polio eradication is in the measurement and valuing of the benefits and costs of producing a GPGH. Proponents of polio eradication have always argued that, in addition to the direct benefit of eliminating the target organism, this initiative would also strengthen health systems and the delivery of other health services. While this assertion was important in establishing a consensus on launching the eradication initiative in 1988, it has since presented significant difficulties for the program. The primary problem lies not in whether or not such indirect benefits can be achieved, but in whether and how they are measured. Without objective criteria and indicators for measuring the broader impact of polio eradication on health systems, proponents and detractors have both used anecdotal information to convincingly argue their cases.

Proponents of future GPGH should probably be very modest in arguing the indirect benefits of the proposed initiative, and ensure that there are agreed indicators for monitoring and pursuing such benefits. It might even be argued that the decision to pursue a GPGH should be made only on the basis of the direct benefits and costs of its production. The experience of the GPEI suggests that if the direct benefits alone are not sufficient for pursuing a GPGH, the launching of such an initiative should be questioned.

2.6.2 **The utility of the GPGH concept**

The concept of disease eradication is now much better understood than it was when the first eradication initiative was launched against a human pathogen nearly 100 years ago (Aylward *et al.* 2000*b*). Various criteria have been promoted for judging the "eradicability" of an organism, such that by 1999, most experts agreed that an organism could only be considered a candidate for eradication if three basic criteria were met (Dowdle 1998, Goodman *et al.* 1998). First, eradication must be biologically feasible. Second, the benefits of pursuing eradication must outweigh the costs of ongoing or heightened control measures. Third, there should be sufficient societal and political recognition of the value of eradication.

Of course, the GPGH framework does not provide additional insights into whether or not it is biologically possible to eradicate a particular organism. However, reviewing polio eradication in the context of GPGH has reaffirmed the soundness of the cost: benefit and societal/political commitment criteria for evaluating future eradication initiatives and it has helped to refine each. Indeed, this is not only useful for disease eradication, but suggests the importance of these criteria as constant elements in the decision-making process to pursue any large scale health initiative, regardless as to whether or not it is a global *public* good.

Considering polio eradication as a GPGH has helped formalize the understanding and presentation of the costs, financing, and benefits of eradication. The emphasis on concepts of "fair shares," identification of the bearer of burden, and opportunity cost, could prove particularly useful to future initiatives. For example, the efficiency of such initiatives would be markedly enhanced were it possible to establish an agreement on "fair shares" for external financing at the outset. Similarly, a more systematic evaluation of the opportunity costs of pursuing eradication, by income bracket, might allow safeguards to be developed while offsetting potential criticisms. Considering polio eradication as a GPGH has proven particularly useful in re-evaluating the need for, and relative merits of, promoting an eradication initiative on the basis of its potential indirect benefits.

Another useful outcome of this analysis has been the further development of the framework for evaluating, establishing, and sustaining societal and political support for future eradication initiatives. This criterion is undoubtedly the least understood aspect of disease eradication and thus the area where the risk of failure is greatest (Aylward *et al.* 2000*b*). With its focus on effective collective action, the GPGH concept emphasizes the importance of the consensus building and decision-making processes, not only for launching an eradication initiative, but also for ensuring the ongoing engagement of all stakeholders. The GPG concept thus reaffirms the need for appropriate forums to negotiate and sustain societal and political engagement at all appropriate levels. In the case of polio eradication, such forums have been necessary from the community through international levels.

The greatest benefit of the GPGH concept to polio eradication has been its utility as a powerful advocacy tool of the polio eradication partnership. From the 1970s, the concepts, if not the specific language, of GPGH were central to the arguments used by the proponents polio eradication. In fact it was the non-exclusive and non-rival nature of the benefits of global polio eradication that were largely responsible for the adoption of this goal by the WHA in 1988. From the mid-1990s, the concept of "fair shares" has been central to the successful expansion of the polio eradication partnership and its resource mobilization efforts.

By late 1999, the language of GPGH was an extremely effective mechanism for engaging decision-makers from beyond the area of health in the debate on the relative merits of the global eradication initiative. The idea of a global public good *for health* has provided a common, easily grasped framework that has been especially interesting for politicians, global bankers, business people, economists, and other non-health experts. However, loose application of the term "global public good" has threatened to undermine its value for initiatives that truly fit this definition. There is an increasing risk that this loose use of "GPGH" could begin to evoke scepticism and, even worse, cynicism when this argument is appropriately used to promote a truly global public good for health.

Although there are many health issues for which global action might be appropriate, particularly those such as malaria which primarily affect developing countries, most do not constitute true GPGHs. It will be important to preserve this distinction if the GPGH concept is to remain an effective argument, when appropriate, for mobilizing international cooperation. In the case of polio eradication, the GPGH framework has been central to freeing the discussion and debate of its value from the domain of health experts alone, thus ensuring a broader, more balanced perspective.

References

Acharya A, England S, Agocs M, Linkins J, Aylward B. *Production of a Global Public Good in Health: Technical Analysis of Polio Eradication.* Working Paper for the Macroeconomic Commission on Health. Geneva: World Health Organization, 2001.

Andrus JK, Thapa AB, Withana N, Fitzsimmons JW, Abeykoon P, Aylward B. A new paradigm for international disease control: lessons learned from polio eradication in Southeast Asia. *Am J Public Health* 2001; **91**: 146–50.

Anonymous. Report on the International Conference on the Eradication of Infectious Diseases. Can infectious diseases be eradicated? *Rev Infect Dis* 1982; **4**: 912–84.

Arora NK, Patwari AK, Lakshman M, Rewal S, Mathur P, Ganguly KK. *Pulse Polio Immunization Program Evaluation 1997–98.* New Delhi: All India Institute of Medical Sciences, 1999.

Assembly of Heads of States and Government. *Yaounde Declaration on Polio Eradication in Africa.* Yaounde, Cameroon: Organization of African Unity, 1996, Resolution AHG/Decl.1 (XXXII) 1996.

Aylward RB, Olivé JM, Hull HF, de Quadros CA, Melgaard B. Disease eradication initiatives and general health services: ensuring common principles lead to mutual benefits. In: WR Dowdle, DR Hopkins (eds) *The Eradication of Infectious Diseases: Dahlem Workshop Reports*. Chichester: John Wiley & Sons, 1998, pp. 61–74.

Aylward RB, Bilous J, Tangermann RH, Sanders R, Maher C, Sato Y, Omi S. Strengthening routine immunization services in the Western Pacific through eradication of poliomyelitis. *J Infect Dis*, 1997; 175(Suppl. 1): S268–71.

Aylward RB, Hull HF, Cochi SL, Sutter RW, Olivé JM, Melgaard B. Disease eradication as a public health strategy: a case study of poliomyelitis eradication. *Bull World Health Organ* 2000a; 78(3): 285–97.

Aylward B, Hennessey KA, Zagaria N, Olivé JM, Cochi S. When is a disease eradicable? 100 years of lessons learned. *Am J Public Health* 2000b; 90: 1515–20.

Bart KJ, Foulds J, Patriarca P. Global eradication of Poliomyelitis benefit-cost analysis. *Bull World Health Organ* 1996; 74(1): 35–45.

Center for Disease Control and Prevention (CDC). Summary of notifiable diseases— United States (1993). *MMWR* 1994; 42(53): 1–91.

Ching P, Birmingham M, Sutter R, Goodman T, Loevinsohn B. The impact of vitamin A supplements delivered with immunization campaigns. *Am J Public Health* 2000; 90: 1526–9.

de Quadros CA. (2000). "Polio" In: *Encyclopedia of Microbiology*, Vol. 3. New York: Academic Press pp. 762–72.

de Quadros CA, Andrus JK, Olivé JM, Guerra de Macedo C. Polio eradication from the western hemisphere. *Annu Rev Public Health* 1992; 13: 239–52.

Dowdle WR. The principles of disease elimination and eradication. In: *Global Disease Elimination and Eradication as Public Health Strategies*. Proceedings of a conference held in Atlanta, Georgia, USA, February 23–25, 1998. *Bull World Health Organ* 1998; 76 (Suppl. 2): 22–5.

Dowdle WR, Cochi SL. Global Eradication of Poliovirus: History and Rationale. In: BL Semler, E Wimmer (eds) *The Picornaviruses*. Washington DC: ASM Press, 2002, pp. 473–80.

EPI. Progress towards poliomyelitis eradication, 1990–1996: China. *Wkly Epidemiol Rec* 1996a; 71: 377–9.

EPI. Update: mass vaccination with oral poliovirus vaccine—Asia and Europe, 1996. *Wkly Epidemiol Rec* 1996b; 71: 329–32.

EPI. Progress towards poliomyelitis eradication, Southeast Asia, 1998–1999. *Wkly Epidemiol Rec* 2000a; 75: 213–16.

EPI. Performance of AFP surveillance and incidence of poliomyelitis, 1999–2000. *Wkly Epidemiol Rec* 2000b; 76: 299–301.

EPI. Progress towards global poliomyelitis eradication, 2000. *Wkly Epidemiol Rec* 2001a; 76: 126–31.

EPI. Progress towards poliomyelitis eradication, West and Central Africa, 1999–2000. *Wkly Epidemiol Rec* 2001b; 76: 158–62.

EPI. Acute flaccid paralysis associated with circulating vaccine-derived poliovirus, Philippines 2001. *Wkly Epidemiol Rec* 2001c; 76: 319–20.

EPI. Progress towards global poliomyelitis eradication, 2001. *Wkly Epidemiol Rec* 2002; 77: 98–107.

Francois I, Lambert ML, Salort C, Slypen V, Bertrand F, Tonglet R. Causes of locomotor disability and need for orthopaedic devices in a heavily mined

Taliban-controlled province of Afghanistan: Issues and challenges for public health managers. *Trop Med Int Health* 1998; **3**: 391–6.

Global Technical Consultative Group to the World Health Organization on the Global Eradication of Poliomyelitis. "Endgame" issues for the Global Polio Eradication Initiative. *Clin Infect Dis* 2002; **34**: 72–77.

Goodman RA, Foster KL, Trowbridge FL, Figueroa JP. Global disease elimination and eradication as public health strategies. Proceeding of a conference held in Atlanta, Georgia, USA: February 23–25 1998. *Bull World Health Organ* 1998; **76** (Suppl. 2): 1–162.

Goodman T, Dalmiya N, de Benoist B, Schultink, W. Polio as a platform: using national immunization days to deliver vitamin A supplements. *Bull World Health Organ* 2000; **78**(3): 305–14.

Hall RG, Acharya AK, Aylward RB, Gyldmark M, Hall AJ, Hinman AR, Kim A, Schwartlander B, Waldman RJ. Group report: what are the criteria for estimating the costs and benefits of disease eradication. In: WR Dowdle, DR Hopkins (eds) *The Eradication of Infectious Diseases: Dahlem Workshop Reports.* Chichester: John Wiley & Sons. 1998; pp. 107–15.

Horstmann DM, Quinn TC, Robbins FC (eds) International symposium on poliomyelitis control. *Rev Infect Dis* 1984; **6** (Suppl. 2): S301–601.

Hull HF, Ward NA, Hull BP, Milstien JB, de Quadros CA. Paralytic poliomyelitis: Seasoned strategies, disappearing disease. *Lancet* 1994; **343**: 1331–7.

Kaul I, Grunberg I, Stern MA. *Global Public Goods: International Co-operation in the 21st Century.* New York: Oxford University Press, 1999.

Kew O, Morris-Glasgow V, Landaverde M, Burns C, Shaw J, Garib Z *et al.* Outbreak of poliomyelitis in Hispaniola associated with circulating type 1 vaccine-derived poliovirus. *Science,* 2002; **296**: 356–9.

Lee JW, Aylward BR, Hull HF, Batson A, Birmingham ME, Lloyd J. Reaping the benefits: Getting vaccines to those who need them. In: GC Woodrow, MM Levine (eds) *New Generation Vaccines.* New York: Marcel Dekker 1997; pp. 79–88.

Levin A, Ram S. *The Impact the Polio Eradication Campaign on the Financing of Routine EPI: Findings of Three Case Studies.* Bethesda: Partnership for Health Reform, University Research Co, 1999.

Loevinsohn B, Aylward B, Steinglass R, Ogden E, Goodman T, Melgaard B. Commentary: Impact of Targeted Programmes on Health Systems—A Case Study of the Polio Eradication Initiative. *Am J Public Health* 2002; **92**(1): 19–23.

MacAulay C, Verma, M. *Global Polio Laboratory Network: A Model for Good Laboratory Practice—A Study of the Quality Principles within the Global Polio Laboratory Network.* Bethesda: Quality Assurance Project, University Research Co, 1999.

Mogedal S, Stenson B. *Disease Eradication: Friend or Foe to the Health System? Synthesis Report from Field Studies in Tanzania, Nepal, and Lao PDR.* Paper Presented at the Meeting on the Impact of Targeted Programmes on Health Systems: A Case-study of the Polio Eradication Initiative (PEI), World Health Organization, Geneva, Switzerland, December 16–17, 1999.

Musgrove P. Is polio eradication in the Americas economically justified? *Bull Pan Am Health Organ,* (1998); **22**(1): 1–16.

Nsubuga P, McDonnell S, Otten M, Perkins B, Sutter R, Quick L, Cochi S. *Impact of Acute Flaccid Paralysis Surveillance on the Surveillance of Other Infectious Diseases in Africa.*

Paper presented at the 49th Annual Epidemic Intelligence Service (EIS) Conference, Centers for Disease Control and Prevention, Atlanta, USA, April 10–14, 2000.

PAHO. Director announces campaign to eradicate poliomyelitis from the Americas by 1990. *Bull Pan Am Health Organ* 1985; **19**: 213–15.

Paul JR. *History of Poliomyelitis*. New Haven: Yale University Press, 1971.

Ramlow J, Alexander M, LaPorte R, Kaufmann C, Kuller L. Epidemiology of post-polio syndrome. *Am J Epidemiol* 1992; **136**: 769–86.

Risi JB. The control of poliomyelitis in Brazil. *Rev Infect Dis* 1984; **6** (Suppl. 2): S391–6.

Sandler T. *Global Challenges: An Approach to Environmental, Political, and Economic Problems*. Cambridge, New York and Melbourne; Cambridge University Press, 1997.

Sutter RW, Cochi SL, Melnick JL. Live Attenuated Poliovirus Vaccine. In: SA Plotkin, WA Orenstein (eds), *Vaccines*, 3rd edn. Philadelphia, PA: WB. Saunders Company, 1999; pp. 16: 364–408.

Tangermann R, Costales M, Flavier J. Poliomyelitis eradication and its impact on Primary Health Care in the Philippines. *J Infect Dis* 1997; **175** (Suppl. 1): S272–6.

Task Force for Child Survival and Development. *Protecting the World's Children: An Agenda for the 1990s*. Talloires, France: Tufts University European Center 1998.

Taylor Commission. *The Impact of the Expanded Program on Immunization and the Polio Eradication Initiative on Health Systems in the Americas*. Report number 1995-000003. Washington, DC: Pan Am Health Organ.

Taylor C, Cutts F, Taylor ME. Ethical dilemmas in current planning for polio eradication. *Am J Public Health*, 1997, **87**: 922–5.

Taylor CE, Waldman RJ. Designing eradication programs to strengthen primary health care. In: WR Dowdle, DR Hopkins (eds) *The Eradication of Infectious Diseases: Dahlem Workshop Reports*. Chichester: John Wiley & Sons, 1998 pp. 145–55.

WHA. *Global Eradication of Poliomyelitis by the Year 2000*. Geneva: World Health Organization, 1988; Resolution 41.28.

WHO. *Report of the International Conference on Primary Health Care, Alma-Ata, USSR, September, 1978*. Geneva: World Health Organization, 1978.

WHO. *Meeting on the Impact of Targeted Programmes on Health Systems: A Case Study of the Polio Eradication Initiative*. Geneva: World Health Organization, 2000, WHO Document No. WHO/V&B/00.29.

WHO. *Global Polio Eradication Initiative: Estimated External Financial Resource Requirements for 2002–2005*. Geneva: World Health Organization, 2001, WHO Document No. WHO/Polio /01.05.

WHO. (2002*a*). *WHO Vaccine-preventable Diseases: Monitoring System. 2001 Global Summary*. Geneva: World Health Organization, 2002*a* WHO Document No. WHO/V&B/01.34.

WHO. *Thematic Evaluations in 2001—Eradication of Poliomyelitis, Report by the Director-General*. Geneva: World Health Organization, 2002*b*, WHO Document No. EBPDC8/3.

World Summit for Children. *World Declaration on the Survival, Protection and Development of Children*. New York: United Nations, 1990.

Zacher MW. Global epidemiological surveillance: International cooperation to monitor infectious diseases. In: I Kaul, I Grunberg, MA Stern (eds) *Global Public Goods: International Cooperation in the 21st Century*. New York: Oxford University Press, 1999.

Chapter 3

Tuberculosis control

Jim Yong Kim, Aaron Shakow,
Arachu Castro, Chris Vanderwarker,
and Paul Farmer

3.1 Introduction

Tuberculosis (TB) is an airborne infectious disease caused by an organism, *Mycobacterium tuberculosis*, and is thought to infect almost one-third of the world's population. It commonly manifests as an infection of the lungs, usually with symptoms of coughing, weight loss and other constitutional symptoms (Iseman 2000). Known as the "white death" or "consumption" during the nineteenth century in western countries, TB was a major determinant of population health throughout the early twentieth century. The discovery of antibiotics and improvements in basic sanitation and living conditions, dramatically decreased the impact of TB in developed countries, but together with HIV/AIDS, it remains one of the two most important infectious causes of adult mortality in the world (WHO 2000a).

Because TB is airborne, the effectiveness of a particular TB control program can have individual, local, regional, and global impact. Treating the sick patient with antibiotics (usually for a minimum of 6 months) renders that patient non-infectious, thus halting spread to other close contacts in the home or in the community (Crofton 1962, Iseman 2000). Additionally, screening close contacts of a known case, such as family members or co-workers, and providing prophylactic treatment for the latently infected can further reduce the development of cases of active TB in a population (Nolan *et al.* 1999, Iseman 2000).

In 1993, the WHO declared TB a global emergency, and promoted the DOTS (Directly Observed Treatment with Short-course chemotherapy) strategy with great success in many nations (Anonymous 1993). Yet, after almost a decade of efforts to promote this effective and cost-effective strategy more broadly, less than a quarter of the active cases of TB in the world receive this treatment. This is especially disappointing as DOTS is much more effective than the therapies usually available in most developing countries (WHO 1998a).

As globalization has dramatically increased the movement of people across national boundaries, the transnational spread of TB has also grown. The percentage of cases that occur among the "foreign born"—people who were infected with TB in one country but developed the disease in another—has increased notably in the United States and other developed countries (Harvard Medical School 1999, Centers for Disease Control 2002, Geng *et al.* 2002). In addition, some especially virulent strains of TB, including multidrug-resistant variants, have spread quickly and broadly throughout the world (Bifani *et al.* 2002, Toungoussova *et al.* 2002). Thus, the powerful potential for cross-border effects from TB is a serious concern for everyone, including those who live in developed countries.

In a recent report from the Institute of Medicine (IOM) of the US National Academy of Sciences, TB experts charged with drafting a plan for the elimination of TB as a public health problem in the United States pointed out that it would be impossible for the United States to move toward elimination without addressing the problem of TB globally (Geiter 2000). The authors of this report clearly understood that effective global TB control would be non-rivalrous, in that all would enjoy its benefits, and that it would be non-exclusive, in that it would be impossible to exclude anyone from breathing air that was less contaminated with *M. tuberculosis*. Further, the report made it clear that the market had been failing and would continue to fail in responding adequately to tuberculosis globally. They concluded, therefore, that the United States should invest more in efforts to control TB in developing countries. TB control, we argue, is therefore clearly a "global public good for health" (GPGH), and publications like the IOM report and the recently published *Global Plan to Stop TB* have begun to give shape to that argument in a way that could be useful to both public health policy-makers and funders (Geiter 2000, Stop 2002).

Following this introduction, Section 3.2 introduces TB as an infectious disease, describes the most common signs and symptoms affecting sick patients, and outlines the social and economic consequences of widespread infection, especially among the poor. Section 3.3, details the global response to the epidemic, highlighting the notable success of the WHO recommended strategy for TB control: DOTS. Section 3.4 presents the argument for TB control as a global public good (GPG), and Section 3.5 describes the political and economic barriers to effective global TB control. Section 3.6 concludes with a discussion of strategies for achieving the elimination of TB as a public health problem.

3.2 **The burden of TB**

3.2.1 **Individual health burden**

TB is an airborne infectious disease caused by the bacillus *M. tuberculosis*. Once a patient is infected with the TB bacillus, most never develop active disease. Some patients, particularly the immunosuppressed, can progress quickly to active disease. Others do not develop active disease immediately—reservoirs of viable TB bacteria are held in check by the cell-mediated immune system. This state is referred to as "TB infection." Patients at this stage are not infectious and can be treated prophylactically with antibiotic drug regimens that are less intense than those required for active disease (Iseman 2000).

"Active TB" disease occurs either with direct airborne infection of the lungs leading to illness or when patients with TB infection progress to being actively sick with the disease. Though capable of infecting virtually every organ system of the human body, TB most commonly manifests itself as pulmonary disease, where symptoms include coughing, chest pain, hemoptysis, shortness of breath, and constitutional symptoms such as malaise, weakness, and fever. Once a patient develops active disease, without treatment up to two-thirds will die (Dye *et al.* 1999, Iseman 2000).

Transmission occurs by inhalation of droplet nuclei—small clusters of TB bacteria aerosolized by the coughing of a sick patient. TB is susceptible to ultraviolet light, including sunlight, but transmission is facilitated by overcrowding and poor ventilation. Additionally, the transition from infection to disease is highly dependent on the integrity of the host's immune system. Malnutrition and diseases compromising immune response, especially HIV/AIDS, greatly increase an individual's risk of progression from infection to active TB disease.

3.2.2 Population health burden

Fifty years after the introduction of effective chemotherapy, tuberculosis remains, with AIDS, the leading infectious cause of adult mortality in the world, causing between 1.5 and 2 million deaths per year (Bloom and Murray 1992, Dolin *et al.* 1994, Raviglione *et al.* 1995, Murray and Lopez 1997*a*, WHO 1997*b*, Dye *et al.* 1999). Fully one-third of the world's population, almost 2 billion people, is already infected with *M. tuberculosis* (Sudre *et al.* 1992), and the number of new TB cases each year climbed 6 percent between 1990 and 1997, from 7.5–8 million cases (Raviglione *et al.* 1995, Dye *et al.* 1999). It currently stands at 8.4 million (WHO 2001*b*).

Projections of the future toll of the global TB pandemic are even more sobering. Some estimate that less than half of all TB cases worldwide are ever diagnosed, and fewer than 60 percent of those diagnosed are cured (Raviglione *et al.* 1997, WHO 2000*c*). Without unprecedented efforts to improve TB control in regions hardest hit by the disease, incidence is expected to climb steadily. TB is projected to remain one of the world's top 10 causes of adult mortality by the year 2020; HIV is the only other infectious pathogen slated to remain on this list (Murray and Lopez 1997*a*,*b*). One estimate suggests 171 million new cases and 60 million deaths over this period in the "best-case scenario," and 249 million new cases and 90 million deaths in the "worse-case scenario" (Murray and Salomon 1998*b*).

Together TB and HIV display a noxious synergy that has led to the explosion of TB cases in regions of high HIV prevalence. While non-HIV-infected persons with TB have a 5–10 percent *lifetime* risk of developing TB disease, HIV-infected persons with TB have a 5–10 percent *annual* risk of progressing to active disease.

TB already accounts for approximately one-third of all AIDS deaths around the world, and in regions of Sub-Saharan Africa up to 70 percent of people living with AIDS are infected with *M. tuberculosis*. The consequences of this dual burden are not just increased deaths due to TB, but a larger pool of patients with active disease capable of spreading infection throughout the community, undermining basic control efforts in the area (Raviglione *et al.* 1995, Stop 2002).

TB is also much more difficult to diagnose in patients co-infected with TB and HIV. In Zambia, where TB case rates have trebled in the past decade, the proportion of smear-negative cases has risen even more dramatically (Bosman 2000). Drug-resistant strains of TB, the deterioration of public-health infrastructure, and novel demographic pressures likewise amplify the TB problem (Bloom and Murray 1992, Raviglione *et al.* 1994, Nolan 1996, Fatkenheuer *et al.* 1999, see also Chapter 4 concerning antimicrobial resistance, AMR).

3.2.3 Social burden

A century ago TB ravaged affluent and poor countries alike; today, rates of TB have become telling indicators of a society's wealth or poverty. At present, 95 percent of the 8 million new cases of TB, and 98 percent of deaths from TB, worldwide are in developing countries (Dye *et al.* 1999). In these regions, disease and death from TB occurs most often in the most economically active segment of the population; among the 1.5–2 million people dying annually from TB every year, 75 percent are between the ages of 15 and 54, with TB accounting for almost one-fifth of all deaths in this age group (Murray *et al.* 1993, Murray 1996). TB kills more women annually than all the causes of maternal mortality combined (World Bank 1993, Murray and Lopez 1996). Worldwide, some 900 million women of reproductive age are infected with TB, and at least 2.5 million every year develop active TB. Among women aged 15–44 years, TB accounts for the annual loss of an estimated 8.7 million years of life (WHO 1998*b*). Gender inequality also plays an obvious role. While men are more likely to have latent infection with *M. tuberculosis*, women are more likely to progress from infection to active disease (Murray 1991, Hudelson 1996, Holmes *et al.* 1998), and poor women are less likely to receive diagnostic and treatment services.

3.2.4 Economic burden

The demographics of TB suggest that the disease halts work in the formal and informal economies, as well as within households. Country studies document between three and four months work time lost annually to the disease, and lost earnings of 20–30 percent of household income (Ramachandran *et al.* 1997, Croft and Croft 1998). Families of persons who die from the disease lose about 15 years of income because of the premature death of the TB sufferer (WHO 2000*b*). As economic difficulties put pressure on state health budgets, the social cost of this lost productivity is compounded. In Thailand, out-of-pocket expenditure for the diagnosis and treatment of TB is over 15 percent of annual income for households already below the poverty line (Kamolratanaku *et al.* 1999). In Uganda, an estimated 70 percent of the cost of treatment was borne by patients or their families (Saunderson 1995). The whole economy suffers as the workforce is reduced, productivity falls, revenues drop and markets shrivel (WHO 2000*b*). Economic development itself is thus stunted by TB, as it is by malaria and HIV.

Like TB and development, TB and poverty are closely linked. Malnutrition, overcrowding, poor air circulation and sanitation—factors associated with poverty—increase both the probability of becoming infected and the probability of developing clinical disease (Farmer 1999). Together, poverty and the tubercle bacillus form a vicious cycle: poor people go hungry and live in close, unhygienic quarters where TB flourishes; TB decreases people's capacity to work, and adds treatment expenses, exacerbating their poverty. The direct and indirect cost of TB to individual patients causes, on average, a decline of 20–30 percent of household income. Meanwhile, the poor receive inadequate health care, preventing even the diagnosis of their tuberculosis. Treatment, if received at all, is often erratic or simply incorrect. The poor are also less likely to seek and receive care from medical practitioners when ill, and are two to three times more likely than other income groups to self-medicate (Pathania *et al.* 1997). Self-medication encourages the emergence of drug-resistant TB strains, further increasing the impacts on the poor and the risks to others in society.

The global burden of TB may be summed up in economic terms through a few brief computations. Given 8.4 million sick, according to the most recent WHO estimates, the bulk of them potential wage-earners, and assuming a 30 percent decline in average productivity, the toll amounts to approximately $1 billion yearly. Two million annual deaths, with an average loss of 15 years' income, adds an additional deficit of $11 billion. Every 12 months, TB causes somewhere near $12 billion to disappear from the global economy (Bloom 2001).

3.2.5 **TB and globalization**

The differential spread of diseases like TB underlines a stark moral dilemma: if these millions of human deaths are preventable, then inaction seems a blot on the modern conscience. But for wealthy countries, the fight against TB is also a matter of self-interest. In many of the regions where TB is already rife, inadequate therapy has led to selection for multidrug-resistant tuberculosis (MDR-TB), mutant organisms that do not respond to the medications of first resort (see also Chapter 4, concerning AMR). The legacy of these poor therapeutic practices is a reservoir of bacilli that cannot be treated with the standard TB treatment strategy, based on short-course chemotherapy regimens. Where MDR-TB is already widespread, the treatment efficacy of short-course chemotherapy—even when properly administered—is inadequate and can even worsen the problem (Becerra *et al.* 2000, Espinal *et al.* 2000, Furin *et al.* 2000), facilitating the development of new strains that are resistant to three or more antibiotics.

In an increasingly integrated world, these lethal TB strains do not stay at home in their "hot spots," but travel readily along with their human hosts via air, land, and sea. While 95 percent of all cases of TB occur in developing regions, people latently infected with TB travel and are making up an increasingly large number of the TB cases in industrialized countries. The case rate for foreign-born persons remains seven times that of US-born individuals, and 46 percent of all cases of TB in the United States in 2000 were among the "foreign born"; in 1992 these cases comprised just 27 percent of the national total (Centers for Disease Control 2002). When these patients are found to be sick with drug-sensitive TB, their care in the United States will cost many thousands of dollars and, in some settings, costs to treat fully susceptible TB can average as high as $60,000 per case (Wurtz and White 1999). When patients have MDR-TB, costs can go as high as $200,000 for a single case (Iseman 1993). Further, we now know that even highly virulent strains of tuberculosis have caused epidemics in many parts of the world and some of these epidemics have occurred with the multidrug-resistant form of the strain (Bifani *et al.* 1996, Glynn *et al.* 2002). For example, the Beijing strain of tuberculosis, the dominant form of tuberculosis in East Asia since 1950, has been implicated in a number of outbreaks in the United States, South Africa, Iran, Columbia, and Russia and some of these outbreaks have been caused by multidrug-resistant variants of this strain (Bifani 2002, Glynn *et al.* 2002).

3.3 **TB control**

Practically speaking, what *is* TB control? During the early 1990s, most public health professionals, if asked to describe it, would have produced a long list of interventions such as passive case finding, use of short-course chemotherapy, the importance of ensuring compliance with treatment, adequate drug supply, sound reporting and recording systems, and so on. The most crucial element was recognized to be the human one—having health workers or volunteers form a close bond with their patients to help them successfully complete treatment. This practice, known as directly observed therapy, or DOT, was first implemented in Madras, India, in 1958, when Wallace Fox led a study looking into patient compliance in an ambulatory setting versus a hospital setting (Fox 1958). Since then, Karel Styblo and others at the International Union Against TB and Lung Disease (IUATLD) have refined an approach to TB control in developing countries that promised to have an enormous impact on overall TB mortality and morbidity (Hopewell 2002).

In the face of these ironies—a completely treatable disease leading to millions of deaths—WHO declared TB a "global emergency" in 1993 (Anonymous 1993). That same year, the World Bank's *World Development Report* revealed that TB control using the WHO-recommended strategy, at an estimated cost of between $0.90 and $3.10 per year of life saved, was one of the most "cost-effective" of all health interventions (World Bank 1993, de Jonghe *et al.* 1994, Jha *et al.* 1998). The DOTS strategy has yielded cure rates as high as twice those of other treatment programs.

Indeed, DOTS may be one of the soundest interventions of any kind for countries struggling to pull themselves out of poverty (Kochi 1997). As promoted by WHO, "DOTS" has five elements, spanning the technical, the clinical, the programatic, and the political:

1. Government commitment to sustained TB control activities.

2. Case detection by sputum smear microscopy among symptomatic patients self-reporting to health services.

3. Standardized treatment regimens lasting at least 6–8 months for all confirmed sputum smear-positive cases, with directly observed treatment for the initial 2 months

4. A regular, uninterrupted supply of all essential anti-TB drugs.

5. A standardized recording and reporting system that allows assessment of treatment results for each patient and of the TB control program overall (WHO 1998a).

From the standpoint of TB treatment programs, particularly in developing countries, DOTS has a number of signal advantages. The standardized nature of its regimens has simplified drug-supply considerations, which allows for inexpensive and effective management even in areas where health-care infrastructure is scant or lacking. Because they are inexpensive, reproducible, and relatively easy to supervise on a local level, DOTS programs allow TB officials to direct their resources efficiently to areas with the highest caseloads. According to the World Bank, the cost of DOTS-based TB control is approximately $20–57 per death averted, and US$ 1–3 per disability-adjusted life year (DALY) gained. Indeed, these figures probably overestimate the costs of TB control, as drug prices have fallen as much as 75 percent since the estimate was made in the early 1990s (WHO 1999).

Whatever the cost estimate, DOTS has proved to be effective in curing people with TB. Without treatment, an estimated 70 percent of people with infectious TB will die of their disease (Dye *et al.* 1999, Iseman 2000). Even weak TB-control programs are able to decrease the mortality considerably, but have less impact on morbidity, as many people remain chronically ill and continue to transmit the disease—including drug-resistant strains—within their households and communities. Properly implemented, DOTS can rapidly reduce both mortality and morbidity from TB, often curing over 85 percent of patients. Meanwhile, since curing people with TB prevents them from infecting others, it serves an important preventive function as well, breaking the chain of transmission. Finally, the emergence of national TB control strategies based on DOTS has provided a crucial tool in slowing the generation of drug-resistant TB (Weis *et al.* 1994, WHO 1994, Anonymous 1996).

If DOTS has an Achilles' heel, it's that it is not being implemented quickly enough. Today, only 27 percent of people diagnosed with TB receive DOTS treatment (WHO 2001a). Intensified implementation and expansion of existing control strategies are needed, if TB trends are to be deflected from their present trajectory (Raviglione *et al.* 1997). While the number of countries implementing the DOTS strategy did increase slightly during 1999, less than half of the world's population had access to DOTS-based treatment—even in principle. In practice, the situation was even more grim: only 23 percent of estimated new TB cases were reported to DOTS programs in 1999, as compared with 22 percent in 1998. At this rate, WHO's goal of identifying 70 percent of TB cases worldwide through DOTS will not be realized until 2013; to achieve goals by 2005, programs would have to recruit at least 300,000 additional cases annually (WHO 2001*b*).

One obstacle for the DOTS strategy is that it was advanced tardily in many regions. In settings where drug-resistant disease is already prevalent, a significant fraction of patients will not respond to standardized short-course chemotherapy regimens, even if they are fully supervised to ensure compliance (Mitchison *et al.* 1986, Manalo *et al.* 1990, Espinal *et al.* 2000). This has been observed most recently and dramatically in the former Soviet Union (Centers for Disease Control 1999, Coninx *et al.* 1999, Kimerling *et al.* 1999). In such settings, where MDR-TB has become entrenched, supervised short-course chemotherapy cures significantly less than half of patients (Centers for Disease Control 1999, Farmer 1999, Harvard Medical School 1999, Kimerling *et al.* 1999). Simultaneously, decreasing death rates through improved treatment compliance and decreasing cure rates due to growing drug resistance leads to an increase in new infections, as the sick survive and continue to spread drug-resistant strains. Worse, when cure rates are high for drug-susceptible TB, but much lower for drug-resistant TB, strains of drug-resistant TB begin to constitute a growing proportion of new infections. Eventually, treatment efficacy will be compromized to the point that DOTS, once a cost-effective intervention, no longer remains one (Dye *et al.* 1999). And MDR-TB epidemics are of course only *briefly* local, since drug-resistant strains have rapidly traversed national borders (Harvard Medical School 1999).

To forestall such an occurrence, the global TB community had to embrace the notion that TB control must include effective therapy for patients already sick with drug-resistant TB (Farmer *et al.* 1998). As recently as 1999, no such consensus existed. Treatment of patients with MDR-TB takes longer than treatment of those with drug-susceptible TB and it is considerably more complicated than DOTS (Iseman 1993). The standard of care in MDR-TB therapy requires 18–24 months of treatment, as opposed to the six-month regimens used in DOTS; and MDR-TB therapy requires the use of "second-line" antituberculosis drugs, which are significantly more expensive than first-line drugs. Moreover, these medications are more toxic and often associated with difficult adverse effects, requiring close and attentive medical management, and attentive social support (Furin *et al.* 2001). For these reasons, WHO and other international bodies discouraged the use of second-line antituberculosis agents in developing countries (WHO 1996, 1997*a*). As the severity of the MDR-TB epidemic in countries like Russia became clear in the late 1990s, WHO was forced to change its position and began to spearhead a global effort to develop policy recommendations for poor countries facing the threat of drug-resistant tuberculosis.

HIV recently overtook the great influenza epidemic of 1918 as the most devastating infectious cause of adult death since the bubonic plague of the fourteenth century (Joint United Nations Programme on HIV/AIDS 2000). But TB is the leading cause of death among people with HIV infection, accounting, as noted, for a third of all AIDS-related deaths worldwide. In 1997, Sub-Saharan Africa had the highest observed TB-incidence rate of any region in the world. In several African countries, despite the existence of strong DOTS-based TB-control programs, TB incidence has risen significantly (Stop TB 2002). The global TB community has recognized the need to move beyond DOTS in high HIV-prevalence settings and the Global Stop TB Partnership has recommended that TB and HIV programs work together to offer, in addition to DOTS, isoniazid prophylactic therapy, treatment of other opportunistic infections and highly-active antiretroviral therapies. As in the case of MDR-TB treatment, many people in both the funding and global health communities have expressed concern that these additional interventions will move TB control as a whole from the "affordable and important" category into another category for which resource limitations will preclude appropriate action. It is precisely at this point where the GPGH concept might be most helpful.

3.4 **TB control as a GPGH**

In recent work on GPGH conducted by the Commission on Macroeconomics and Health, (CMH) and the United Nations Development Programme (UNDP), TB-control efforts are presented as a classic example of how a health program might be considered a global public good (Bradley 2001, Bumgarner 2001, Chen *et al.* 1999, Stansfield *et al.* 2001).

As stated, comprehensive TB control rests on the ability of national TB programs to successfully identify and treat patients. In other words, TB control is a product of TB treatment, epidemiological monitoring, case finding, and other essential elements. On an individual level, the treatment of TB has only limited value as a GPGH—the positive externalities to the community at large are balanced by the patient's consumption of specific commodities and s/he receives the private good of being cured of the disease. Many of the inputs necessary to sustain the distinct elements of TB control might also fit into the category of private goods; technical expertise, diagnostics, nutritional supplements, and health workers remain "rivalrous and excludable." However, the overall effect of these elements in the control of TB will have substantial global externalities. A patient cured of TB is one less person contributing to the continued spread of the epidemic: it is estimated that each infectious patient infects 25–50 percent of his household contacts (Adler and Rose 1996). In this instance we have a benefit that is both non-rivalrous (each person can benefit from the reduced risk of infection without impacting another's risk of infection) and non-excludable (reduced environmental exposure affects everyone in the community and none can be excluded). In this sense, it is the overall control of TB that has GPGH characteristics, and those private goods required to secure such control are necessary inputs.

Despite these benefits, and the deadly threat of TB, private markets will not achieve global TB control. The positive externalities of good TB control are magnified in the age of globalization and drug-resistance. Some may interpret the provision of TB treatment as a form of club good—that is, TB treatment is an attainable product for those nations and individuals willing and/or able to pay for TB control services. Such arguments have dominated international public health throughout the antibiotic era. However, as barriers to travel have come down the proportion of TB cases among the foreign-born in developed countries has increased and, in addition to treating all the cases that are appearing "downstream," TB controllers in the developed world are now being forced to look at more "upstream" solutions (Centers for Disease Control 2002). Meanwhile, drug resistance and HIV are now threatening the efficacy of our most effective interventions.

We therefore argue that TB control—the product of political commitment, surveillance, prevention, and treatment—is a GPGH because it is non-rivalrous and non-excludable, and is at risk of market failure. It also displays "weak link" characteristics—with globalization, the maximum attainable level of control in any particular country can be impacted by the level of control achieved in the worst national TB control program. TB control also suffers from "prisoner's dilemma" issues in that countries must make the decision to invest in TB control while not knowing if neighboring countries will do the same. In some instances, certain countries could become "free riders" by ignoring their own TB problems and leaving patients to seek care privately or in other countries that offer free, high-quality services.

3.5 The politics and economics of producing TB control

TB has been an extremely important determinant of morbidity and mortality worldwide for many centuries. In the last 50 years, TB control in developed countries has been mostly successful. Since it is a leading infectious killer, one might assume that TB control would become *de facto* top priority for global health for many decades. Yet, as recently as 1990 an integrated global approach to TB control did not exist. In that year, WHO had only one employee devoted solely to the control of TB, and despite the committed efforts of groups like the IUATLD and the Royal Dutch Netherlands TB Association, TB was very far down the list of priorities in global health, certainly in terms of funding (Holme 1998). Since 1990, the global TB community has made great strides, starting with the establishment of the Global TB Program at WHO in 1991 that led to the establishment of the Stop TB Global Partnership in 1998 in Bangkok, the signing of the ambitious Declaration of Amsterdam by all high-TB burden countries in 2000, and the publication of the consensus *Global Plan to Stop TB* in June of 2002 (Stop TB 2002).

All of these developments have helped to solidify a plan for greatly improved TB control. The *Global Plan*, though not specifically focused on the question of whether TB control is a GPGH, goes far toward making the case. George Soros, who funded the writing of the *Global Plan* through his Open Society Institute, has been a proponent of the GPGH framework as tool for guiding funding decisions (Soros 2002). In asking Partners In Health (an NGO funded by the authors) and the WHO to write a "business plan" for the TB world, he effectively requested a written argument making the case for TB control as a GPGH. The resulting document includes an analysis of the current state of TB control in the world, a budget that estimates the total cost of a comprehensive global TB control program, and detailed action plans for each of the six working groups that make up the Stop TB Partnership. These working groups include: the DOTS Expansion Working Group that works to establish and maintain basic DOTS programs in all countries facing TB epidemics; the TB–HIV Working Group that was recently formed to tackle the burgeoning co-epidemic of TB and HIV that has rapidly accelerated TB incidence rates in countries with high HIV burdens; the Working Group on DOTS-Plus for MDR-TB that coordinates programs to address drug resistance in developing countries; and three working groups focused on research and development (R&D) for new drugs, new diagnostics, and new vaccines respectively.

The first two sentences of the introduction to the *Global Plan* lay out the goal: "Eliminate tuberculosis as a public health problem. That and nothing less is the goal of the Global Partnership to Stop TB." With this ambitious plan, the global TB community completed a process in which it committed itself to a dramatically expanded program for TB control that it once considered impossible. The *Global Plan* sets out the framework for such a comprehensive effort and is the culmination of a rapid evolution of TB control strategy from 1990, when there was little commitment to the global coordination of TB control at WHO, to the mid 1990s, when TB control leaders argued that DOTS alone was sufficient to control the World's TB problem. There is now unprecedented commitment to the newly defined six-pronged strategy and total costs have been calculated. The cost of carrying out all the activities of the six working groups over the next 5 years was calculated at US$ 9.1 billion with a little more than half that amount coming from the poor countries in which TB is endemic. Approximately US$ 700 million per year is the amount that will be needed from external funding sources to reach the targets set out in the plan. Compared with the numbers that are now being discussed in relation to HIV prevention, care, and treatment in developing countries, a comprehensive approach to TB control now seems like quite a bargain.

As the *Global Plan* was being completed, prospects for expanded funding for TB control improved dramatically. The US government expanded its overseas donations for TB control from zero to $85 million for 2001. Bilateral aid from other countries, notably the United Kingdom, Canada, the Netherlands, Finland, and others, has also expanded. The World Bank continued to provide important loans for TB control and is now considering turning all loans into grants for the poorest countries. Large foundations such as the Bill & Melinda Gates Foundation, the OSI, the Rockefeller Foundation and others have also made very serious commitments to funding TB control efforts. Most importantly, the Global Fund to Fight AIDS, TB, and Malaria (GFATM) was formed in 2001 and in the first round of grants, the entire spectrum of TB activities was funded including funding for basic DOTS programs, treatment of MDR-TB and expanded programs for HIV treatment that could have a dramatic impact on TB incidence in countries with a high HIV burden. If the GFATM reaches its funding goals and if current levels of funding from foundations and bilateral and multilateral donors continue to increase, the resource mobilization goals outlined in the *Global Plan to Stop TB* should be easily achieved.

Yet, the obstacles to achieving global TB elimination are enormous. First, the political, financial, managerial, infrastructural, and (at times) clinical challenges of TB control are significant. TB treatment requires a minimum of 6 months of contact with health services, the first two of which should be directly observed. In regions where drug resistance is already a problem, short-course chemotherapy regimens are not effective and thus longer regimens involving more expensive and difficult to manage second-line drugs are required (Espinal *et al.* 2000). In high HIV-prevalence regions, the rapid rise in TB incidence rates despite the presence of good TB control programs is sobering. In these regions, prophylactic therapy for latent TB infection, enhanced diagnostic capabilities, and coordination with HIV programs which include the administration of antiretroviral therapy and other interventions will be required to bring TB under control. More fundamentally, both funders and TB controllers will have to embrace the difficult reality of comprehensive TB control. The current situation with both drug resistance and TB–HIV have illustrated that ignoring problems now will make them more expensive and difficult to resolve later. Happily, it seems that both funders and TB controllers are embracing the challenge of comprehensive global TB control. The GPGH concept should be helpful in keeping the focus on the importance of TB control as a whole and discourage approaches that would eliminate certain aspects of a comprehensive program using cost-effectiveness or other arguments. Rather than basing decisions about program design on the assumption that current resource levels for TB control are fixed, a GPGH model could be used to encourage both funders and TB controllers to design plans that will actually solve current problems in all their complexity. The *Global Plan* has done just this. At $9.1 billion over 5 years, comprehensive TB control is eminently affordable.

Secondly, while the TB community was able to reach consensus around the publication of the *Global Plan*, proponents of specific strategies have different opinions on priorities and timing within the overall plan. Prioritizing is important, but as the funding base for TB control shifts, the TB-control community has had to adjust some of its assumptions about what will and will not be possible in developing countries. For example, over the last decade, the predominant assumption was that sputum smear microscopy was the only diagnostic technology feasible in poor countries. Currently, the gold standard for TB diagnosis is culture, but because of the difficulty of establishing high-quality laboratories, culture and drug sensitivity testing were deemed unattainable for the vast majority of developing countries. With increasing awareness of the devastation of HIV in Sub-Saharan Africa and elsewhere, aspirations for infectious disease laboratory capacity in developing countries have been elevated dramatically and the TB community is beginning to alter its aspirations as well. As of the writing of this chapter, there was no clear consensus on how priorities would be redefined in the context of new funding opportunities like the GFATM but the TB community has come to understand that problems like drug resistance and TB–HIV are worse than anyone had predicted. Many developing countries are faced with difficult decisions in terms of prioritizing but with new funding sources and heightened public awareness in developed countries of the global threat of infectious diseases like TB and MDR-TB, the aspirations of TB controllers will likely have to rise within this changing environment. The GPGH concept for TB, if adopted by funders as suggested above, should help TB policymakers to take a broader view of their task and not be as restricted as in the past by lack of funding.

A third major obstacle to achieving global TB elimination is inadequate global coordination. Despite enormous efforts by TB-focused NGOs and the WHO, woefully inadequate funding has led to equally inadequate systems for both information gathering and dissemination. Lessons from the Global Polio Eradication Initiative (GPEI) could be very helpful for TB control. The political history of GPEI, as described in Chapter 2, is especially informative. TB control has not had "champions" at the level and scale of the GPEI. Heads of organizations like WHO and UNICEF have not made TB control a top priority, as they did with polio eradication, (WHO and UNICEF 2001) and while small agencies like IUATLD and the Royal Dutch Netherlands TB Association have played critical roles in pushing forward TB control efforts at a time when funding and attention to the problem were extremely limited, TB has never had the financial, administrative and political support of a large group like Rotary International. In other, more technical areas, the GPEI also offers important lessons. For example, the importance of the global surveillance system for the detection of cases of acute flaccid paralysis is an important lesson for the TB community. Further systematization and even computerization of, for example, global drug resistance surveillance data and/or the spread of best practices in treatment of MDR-TB or TB–HIV, for example, should be a high priority. Happily, the Stop TB Partnership has evolved rapidly to become a model for effective global coordination and with appropriate funding and support, it could become an extremely effective organizational core for coordinating all necessary activities for global TB elimination.

3.6 Conclusion

Given the history of concepts like cost-effectiveness, DALYs, and "appropriate technology" in global health, we began writing this chapter by asking ourselves if the GPGH concept might be another way of justifying inaction or lower aspirations in formulating a global response to tuberculosis. We think not. On the contrary, the GPGH concept could serve, if utilized practically, to both increase external funding for TB programs and push those involved in TB control to embrace an ambitious, comprehensive global plan that would move the world toward TB elimination.

The first advantage of a GPGH analysis for TB control is to move beyond nation-state based cost-effectiveness analyses. The DOTS approach is one of the most cost-effective interventions in all of global public health, but we now know that in many regions of the world it will not be enough to control the epidemic. Decisions for TB control in places such as South Africa, which has one of the worst co-epidemics of MDR-TB and HIV yet described, should not be made based on simple cost-effectiveness analyses and on the national government's willingness and/or ability to pay. MDR-TB and HIV in South Africa are a problem for the entire world and the GPGH concept gives us a way to begin the discussion about appropriate responses. Ultimately, first-world funders must embrace comprehensive TB control as of importance for them as well as others, and the GPGH concept, while new, could become increasingly important in guiding funding decisions (Stansfield *et al.* 2000, Soros 2002).

The GPGH concept could be helpful in moving TB control past "free rider" and "prisoner's dilemma" problems as well. If funders embrace the concept of global TB control as a GPGH, poorer countries may be able to move beyond national budget constraints in deciding whether or not to invest in TB control. Mandatory TB control for all countries in the world is a step that will require much thought and negotiation but if we become serious about TB elimination and eradication, it is an option that must be explored. As for the problem of imperfect information across national boundaries leading to a "prisoner's dilemma," bolstering the role of the Stop TB partnership as a central information management and dissemination mechanism, could be extremely helpful. The WHO is the only body that has direct contact with most countries in the world so Stop TB, through its close relationship with WHO, could both collect and disseminate information on the status of TB control activities in practically every country in the world. The GPGH concept is helpful once again in emphasizing the importance of comprehensive control in all countries as the desired endpoint of all TB control efforts.

The GPGH concept also brings attention to the problem of market failure in responding to problems like TB. Efforts to address market failures in TB control must be expanded and supported by global coordinating bodies like the Stop TB Partnership. One notable effort to address a market failure and reduce the price of second-line TB drugs began in August of 1999 when the Program in Infectious Disease and Social Change of Harvard Medical School and the Communicable Diseases Cluster of the WHO submitted an application to include seven second-line anti-TB drugs on the WHO's Model List of Essential Drugs. These drugs, the application read, would only be used, "in settings with established DOTS programs and in WHO-approved DOTS-Plus treatment regimens." Including these drugs on WHO's essential drugs list was intended to help ensure tighter control of second-line drugs as it would give national TB programs the power to regulate the distribution of these drugs. Irrational prescription of second-line drugs was an acknowledged reality and prohibitive pricing is one reason why this practice was not more widespread. The drugs were eventually included in the "reserve anti-microbial" section of WHO's Model List of Essential Drugs and by February of 2000, MSF (Doctors Without Borders) had agreed to procure all the drugs and provide them to approved programs at cost. Eli Lilly and Company, WHO and MSF began negotiations for agreement on supply of two key agents (capreomycin and cycloserine), and this combination of events led to dramatically lower prices.

Overall, the price reductions for the most expensive drugs have hovered in the 95 percent range in comparison with the prices Partners In Health was paying in 1996. In addition, a "Green Light Committee" was formed to ensure that only programs capable of utilizing second-line TB drugs appropriately would be given access to them at the reduced price. If programs do not have the technical expertise to qualify for Green Light Committee approval, the committee seeks to provide technical assistance so that countries and programs can eventually qualify (Gupta *et al.* 2001). Examples such as these illustrate both that the market will fail in TB control efforts and that coordinated efforts can overcome market failures.

The challenge to all concerned with the TB epidemic—patients and their families, TB-burdened nations and communities, health organizations and donors—is to articulate and embrace the characteristics of commitment that will be required to successfully control TB. To mobilize a worldwide campaign against TB means we must seek new partners, develop a communications strategy to expand awareness and motivation beyond the traditional TB constituency, and advocate for innovative strategies to increase the availability of resources.

What are the prospects for addressing the problem of tuberculosis through the assertion of a global public goods argument? Clearly, the collective action problems that led to the conception of global public goods in the first place will not disappear even if they are successfully enshrined in law. Public goods, whether local, national, or global, are chronically defeated by the differential incidence of power; simple declarations, even legislative initiatives, are unlikely to combat these differentials effectively. Far better to see the notion of GPGHs as a tool of analysis and advocacy, a way of expressing the relationship between individuals and collectivities on a global scale, rather than as a policy measure *per se.*

References

Anonymous. Tuberculosis: a global emergency. *World Health Forum* 1993; **14**(4): 438.

Anonymous. Results of directly observed short-course chemotherapy in 112,842 Chinese patients with smear-positive tuberculosis. China Tuberculosis Control Collaboration. *Lancet* 1996; **347**: 358–62.

Becerra MC, Freeman J, Bayona J *et al.* Using treatment failure under effective directly observed short-course chemotherapy programs to identify patients with multidrug-resistant tuberculosis. *Int J Tuber Lung Dis* 2000; **4**(2): 108–14.

Bifani PJ, Mathema B, Kurepina NE, Kreiswirth BN. Global dissemination of the *Mycobacterium tuberculosis* W-Beijing family strains. *Trends Microbiol* 2002; **10**(1): 45–52.

Bifani PJ, Plikaytis BB, Kapur V *et al.* Origin and interstate spread of a New York City multidrug-resistant *Mycobacterium tuberculosis* clone family. *J Am Med Assoc* 1996; **275**(6): 452–7.

Bloom BR, Murray CJ. Tuberculosis: commentary on a reemergent killer. *Science* 1992; **257**(5073): 1055–64.

Bosman MCJ. Health sector reform and tuberculosis control: the case of Zambia. *Int J Tuber Lung Dis* 2000; **4**(7): 606–14.

Bradley D. The biological and epidemiological basis of global public goods for health. *CMH Working Paper Series* 2001; Paper No. WG2: 15.

Bumgarner R. The evolving role of the international agencies in supplying and financing global public goods for health. *CMH Working Paper Series* 2001; Paper No. WG2: 20.

Centers for Disease Control. Primary multidrug-resistant tuberculosis—Ivanovo Oblast, Russia, 1999. *Morb Mortal Wkly Rep* 1999; **48**: 661–4.

Centers for Disease Control. Tuberculosis morbidity among US-born and foreign-born populations—United States, 2000. *Morb Mortal Wkly Rep* 2002; **51**(05): 101–4.

Chen L, Evans T, Cash R. Health as a global public good. In: I Kaul, I Grunberg, M Stern (eds) *Global Public Goods: International Co-operation in the 21st Century*. New York: Oxford University Press, 1999.

Coninx R, Mathieu C, Debacker M *et al.* First-line tuberculosis therapy and drug-resistant Mycobacterium tuberculosis in prisons. *Lancet* 1999; **353**(9157): 969–73.

Croft RA, Croft RP. Expenditure and loss of income incurred by tuberculosis patients before reaching effective treatment in Bangladesh. *Int J Tuber Lung Dis* 1998; **2**: 252–4.

Crofton J. The contribution of treatment to the prevention of tuberculosis. *Bull Int Union Tuber* 1962; **32**: 643–53.

de Jonghe E, Murray CJ, Chum HJ *et al.* Cost-effectiveness of chemotherapy for sputum smear-positive pulmonary tuberculosis in Malawi, Mozambique and Tanzania. *Int J Health Plann Manag* 1994; **9**: 151–81

Dolin PJ, Raviglione MC, Kochi A. Global tuberculosis incidence and mortality during 1990–2000. *Bull World Health Organ*, 1994; **72**: 213–20.

Dye C, Garnett GP, Sleeman K, Williams BG. Prospects for worldwide tuberculosis control under the WHO DOTS strategy. *Lancet* 1998; **352**(9144): 1886–91.

Dye C, Scheele S, Dolin P *et al.* Consensus statement. Global burden of tuberculosis: estimated incidence, prevalence, and mortality by country. *J Am Med Assoc* 1999; **282**(7): 677–86.

Espinal MA, Kim SJ, Suarez PG *et al.* Standard short-course chemotherapy for drug-resistant tuberculosis: treatment outcomes in 6 countries. *J Am Med Assoc* 2000; **283**(19): 2537–45.

Farmer P. Managerial successes, clinical failures. *Int J Tuber Lung Dis* 1999; **3**(5): 365–67.

Farmer P, Kim JY. Community based approaches to the control of multidrug resistant tuberculosis: introducing "DOTS-plus." *BMJ* 1998; **317**(7159): 671–4.

Farmer PE, Kim JY, Mitnick C, Timperi R. Responding to outbreaks of multidrug-resistant tuberculosis: Introducing DOTS-Plus. In: LB Reichman, ES Hershfield (eds) *Tuberculosis:*

A Comprehensive International Approach. 2nd edn. New York: Marcel Dekker Inc., 1999, pp. 447–69.

Farmer P, Bayona J, Becerra M *et al*. The dilemma of MDR-TB in the global era. *Int J Tuber Lung Dis* 1998; 2(11): 869–76.

Fatkenheuer G, Taelman H, Lepage P *et al*. The return of tuberculosis. *Diagn Microbiol Infect Dis* 1999; **34**(2): 139–46.

Fox W. The problem of self-administration of drugs; with particular reference to pulmonary tuberculosis. *Tubercle* 1958; **39**: 269–74.

Furin JJ, Becerra MC, Shin SS *et al*. Effect of administering short-course, standardized regimens in individuals infected with drug-resistant *Mycobacterium tuberculosis strains*. *Eur J Clin Microbiol Infect Dis* 2000; **19**(2): 132–6.

Furin JJ, Mitnick CD, Shin SS *et al*. Occurrence of serious adverse effects in patients receiving community- based therapy for multidrug-resistant tuberculosis. *Int J Tuber Lung Dis* 2001; **5**: 648–55.

Geiter L. *Ending Neglect: The Elimination of Tuberculosis in the United States*. Institute of Medicine Press, 2000.

Geng E, Kreiswirth B, Driver C *et al*. Changes in the transmission of tuberculosis in New York City from 1990 to 1999. *N Engl J Med* 2002; **346**(19): 1453–8.

Glynn J, Whitely J, Bifani P *et al*. Worldwide occurrence of Beijing/W strains of *Mycobacterium tuberculosis*: a systematic review. *Emerg Infect Dis* 8(8): 843–49.

Gupta R, Kim JY, Espinal MA *et al*. Responding to market failures in tuberculosis control. *Science* 2001; **293**(5532): 1049–51.

Harvard Medical School. *The Global Impact of Drug-resistant TB*. Boston; Program in Infectious Disease and Social Change, 1999.

Holme C. Tuberculosis: story of medical failure. *BMJ* 1998; **317**: 1260.

Holmes CB, Hausler A, Nunn P. A review of sex differences in the epidemiology of tuberculosis. *Int J Tuber Lung Dis* 1998; 2: 96–104.

Hopewell PC. Tuberculosis control: how the world has changed since 1990. *Bull World Health Organ* 2002; **80**(6): 427.

Hudelson P. Gender differentials in tuberculosis: the role of socioeconomic and cultural factors. *Tuber Lung Dis* 1996; **77**: 391–400.

Iseman MD. Treatment of multidrug-resistant tuberculosis. *N Engl J Med* 1993; **329**(11): 784–91.

Iseman MD. *A Clinicians Guide to Tuberculosis*. Philadelphia: Lippincott Williams & Wilkins, 2000.

Iseman MD, Cohn DL, Sbarbaro JA. Directly observed treatment of tuberculosis. We can't afford not to try it. *N Engl J Med* 1993; **328**(8): 576–8.

Jha P, Bangoura O, Ranson K. The cost-effectiveness of forty health interventions in Guinea. *Health Policy Plan* 1998; **13**: 249–62.

Joint United Nations Programme on HIV/AIDS. *AIDS Epidemic Update: December 2000*. Geneva: Joint United Nations Programme on HIV/AIDS, 2000.

Karnolratanakul P, Sawert H, Kongsin S *et al*. Economic impact of tuberculosis at the household level. *Int J Tuber Lung Dis* 1999; **3**: 1–7.

Kimerling ME, Kluge H, Vezhnina N *et al*. Inadequacy of the current WHO re-treatment regimen in a central Siberian prison: treatment failure and MDR-TB. *Int J Tuber Lung Dis* 1999; **3**(5): 451–3.

Kochi A. Tuberculosis control—is DOTS the health breakthrough of the 1990s? *World Health Forum* 1997; **18**: 225–32; discussion 233–47.

Manalo F, Tan F, Sbarbaro JA, Iseman MD. Community-based short-course treatment of pulmonary tuberculosis in a developing nation. *Am Rev Respir Dis* 1990; **142**: 1301–5.

McCarthy T. Kantian constructivism and reconstructivism: Rawls and Habermas in dialogue. *Ethics* 1994; **105**.

Mitchison DA, Nunn AJ. Influence of initial drug resistance on the response to short-course chemotherapy of pulmonary tuberculosis. *Am Rev Respir Dis* 1986; **133**(3): 423–30.

Murray CJ. Social, economic and operational research on tuberculosis: recent studies and some priority questions. *Bull Int Union Tuber Lung Dis* 1991; **66**: 149–56.

Murray CJ. Epidemiology and demography of tuberculosis. In: IM Timaeus, J Chackiel, and L Ruzieka (eds) *Adult Mortality in Latin America*. Oxford: Clarendon Press, 1996, 199–216.

Murray CJ, Lopez AD. *The Global Burden of Disease*. Cambridge, MA: Harvard School of Public Health, 1996.

Murray CJ, Lopez AD. Mortality by cause for eight regions of the world: global burden of disease study. *Lancet* 1997*a*; **349**(9061): 1269–76.

Murray CJ, Lopez AD. Alternative projections of mortality and disability by cause 1990–2020: global burden of disease study. *Lancet* 1997*b*; **349**(9064): 1498–504.

Murray CJ, Salomon JA. Modeling the impact of global tuberculosis control strategies. *Proc Natl Acad Sci USA* 1998; **95**(23): 13881–6.

Nolan CM. Nosocomial multidrug-resistant tuberculosis—global spread of the third epidemic. *J Infect Dis* 1997; **176**(3): 748–51.

Nolan CM, Goldberg SV, Buskin SE. Hepatotoxicity associated with isoniazid preventive therapy: a 7-year survey from a public health tuberculosis clinic. *J Am Med Assoc* 1999; **281**(11): 1014–18.

Pan American Health Organization. *Health of the Americas*. Country Report: Peru, 1999, pp. 413–27.

Pathania V, Almeida J, Kochi A. TB patients and private for-profit health care providers in India. TB Research No. 1 (WHO/TB/97.223). Geneva: WHO, 1997.

Ramachandran R, Balasubramanian R, Muniyandi M *et al. Economic Impacts of Tuberculosis on Patients and Family*. Tuberculosis Research Centre, Chennai, South India: Indian Council of Medical Research, 1997.

Raviglione MC, Rieder HL, Styblo K *et al.* Tuberculosis trends in eastern Europe and the former USSR. *Tuber Lung Dis* 1994; 75(6): 400–16.

Raviglione MC, Snider DE Jr, Kochi A. Global epidemiology of tuberculosis. Morbidity and mortality of a worldwide epidemic. *J Am Med Assoc* 1995; **273**(3): 220–6.

Raviglione MC, Dye C, Schmidt S, Kochi A. Assessment of worldwide tuberculosis control. WHO Global Surveillance and Monitoring Project. *Lancet* 1997; **350**(9078): 624–9.

Saunderson PR. An economic evaluation of alternative programme designs for tuberculosis control in rural Uganda. *Soc Sc Med* 1995; **40**: 1203–12.

Shimao T. Drug resistance in tuberculosis control. *Tubercle* 1987; **68**(2 Suppl.): 5–18.

Soros G. *George Soros on Globalization*. Oxford: Public Affairs, 2002.

Stansfield SK, Harper M, Lamb G, Lob-Levyt J. *Innovative Financing of International Public Goods for Health.* CMH Working Paper Series, Paper No. WG2: 22, 2001.

Stop TB. *The Global Plan to Stop TB.* WHO.CDS.STB.2001.16. Geneva: WHO, 2002.

Sudre P, ten Dam G, Kochi A. Tuberculosis: a global overview of the situation today. *Bull World Health Organ* 1992; **73**: 52–8.

Toungoussova OS, Sandven P, Mariandyshev AO *et al.* Spread of drug-resistant *Mycobacterium tuberculosis* strains of the Beijing genotype in the Archangel Oblast, Russia. *J Clin Microbiol* 2002; **40**(6): 1930–7.

Weis SE, Slocum PC, Blais FX *et al.* The effect of directly observed therapy on the rates of drug resistance and relapse in tuberculosis. *N Engl J Med* 1994; **330**(17): 1179–84.

World Bank. *Investing in Health: World Development Report.* New York: Oxford University Press, 1993.

WHO. *Tuberculosis Programme: Framework for Effective Tuberculosis Control.* WHO/TB.94.179. Geneva: WHO, 1994.

WHO. *TB/HIV: A Clinical Manual.* Geneva: WHO, 1996.

WHO. *TB Treatment Observer,* 1997*a*; p. 2.

WHO. *Tuberculosis control: the DOTS strategy: an annotated bibliography compiled by the Global Tuberculosis Programme and the Regional Office for South-East Asia.* Geneva: WHO, 1997*b*.

WHO. *Global Tuberculosis Control: WHO Report 1998.* Geneva: WHO, 1998*a*.

WHO. TB is single biggest killer of young women. WHO Press Release WHO/40 May 26. Geneva: WHO 1998*b*.

WHO. *Global Tuberculosis Programme. WHO Report 1999.* Geneva: WHO, 1999.

WHO. *World Health Report 2001.* Geneva: WHO 2000*a*, annex 1 and 2.

WHO. *The Economic Impacts of Tuberculosis.* Ministerial Conference, Amsterdam, March 22–24, WHO/CDS/STB/2000.5. Geneva: WHO, 2000*b*.

WHO. *Tuberculosis and Sustainable Development: Report from the Ministerial Conference in Amsterdam.* WHO/CDS//STB/2000.6. Geneva: WHO, 2000*c*.

WHO. *Global Tuberculosis Control: Surveillance, Planning and Financing. WHO Report 2002.* WHO/CDS/TB/2002.295. Geneva: WHO, 2001*a*.

WHO. *Global Tuberculosis Control: WHO Report 2001.* WHO/CDS/TB/2001.287. Geneva: WHO, 2001*b*.

WHO. *A Human Rights Approach to Tuberculosis.* Geneva: WHO, 2001*c*.

WHO. United Nations Educational, Scientific and Cultural Organization, Joint United Nations Programme on HIV/AIDS, United Nations Population Fund, World Bank. Health. *A Key to Prosperity: Success Stories in Developing Countries.* Geneva: WHO, 2001.

Wurtz R, White W. The cost of tuberculosis: utilization and estimated charges for the diagnosis and treatment of tuberculosis in a public health system. *Int J Tuber Lung Dis* 1999; **3**(5): 382–7.

Chapter 4

Antimicrobial drug resistance

Richard D Smith and Joanna Coast

4.1 Introduction

> We may look back at the antibiotic era as just a passing phase in the history of
> medicine, an era when a great natural resource was squandered, and the bugs proved
> smarter than the scientists. (Cannon 1995, p. 189)

Over the last 50 years humankind has had a new weapon in the war against
infectious disease: the antimicrobial "magic bullet". However, it is becoming clear
that although we have been winning many of the important battles, the war is far
from over, and we may soon be forced into retreat.

Antimicrobial Resistance (AMR) is one of the major challenges facing public
health in the twenty-first century, with the emergence of a "post-antibiotic" era
threatening current and future medical advances (Liss and Batchelor 1987, Neu
1992, Murray 1994, Tomasz 1994, Cannon 1995, ACSP 1996, Fox 1996). The
potential impact of increasing resistance on health care expenditure and population morbidity and mortality, is causing professional and public concern (US
Congress 1995, House of Lords Select Committee on Science and Technology
1998, Standing Medical Advisory Committee Sub-Group on Antimicrobial
Resistance 1998, WHO 2001). Indeed, the United States of America considers the
potentially destabilizing economic and social effects of AMR, as well as its potential in biological warfare, sufficient to classify AMR as a national security risk
(Kaldec *et al.* 1997, CIA 1999, World Bank 2001).

Although the effects of AMR are documented in developed and developing
nations alike, there is greater potential for harm in the developing world, where
many of the second and third line therapies for drug-resistant infections are
unavailable, and many of the narrow spectrum antimicrobials available in the
developed world are not affordable (Fasehun 1999, Smith 1999).

However, AMR is not easily isolated to any one country. It is a global problem,
resulting from a combination of the (mis)use of antimicrobials leading to the
emergence of resistance, and the worldwide transmission of these resistant micro-
organisms once they have developed. In an increasingly interconnected world,
AMR is a problem against which no single country can orchestrate a response

sufficient to protect the health of its population. An international response to AMR is therefore essential, and the maintenance of antimicrobial susceptibility, through measures to contain the emergence and transmission of AMR, is of global relevance.

This chapter explores the usefulness of applying the concept of "Global Public Goods for Health" (GPGH) to the problem of AMR, and to strategies to contain AMR. Following this introduction, Section 4.2 describes AMR and its conceptualization within economics. Section 4.3 considers whether containment of AMR *per se* is a GPGH, and/or whether strategies to contain AMR are themselves GPGH. Section 4.4 outlines the role international bodies may play in ensuring the provision and finance of AMR containment measures. Section 4.5 concludes by considering the usefulness of the GPGH concept when considering AMR and suggests future research priorities.

4.2 What is AMR?

4.2.1 AMR and its economic conceptualization

Micro-organisms are said to be resistant to a specific antimicrobial drug when they are able to multiply in the presence of drug concentrations higher than those achievable in humans receiving therapeutic doses.[1] The ability of micro-organisms to develop resistance to the effects of antimicrobials has been identified since such therapies were first introduced (Ashley and Brindle 1960). AMR is therefore a natural biological phenomenon, caused by the selection of resistant micro-organisms as a direct consequence of the use of antimicrobial treatments.

Development of resistance means that antimicrobials become ineffective in treating infections (Coast *et al.* 1996). However, the development and spread of resistance is a complex process that depends on many factors around which there is imperfect knowledge. There is considerable uncertainty resulting from poor knowledge about basic scientific, clinical, and epidemiological factors relating the development of resistance to health outcomes, with further uncertainties about the costs and benefits associated with treatment (Coast *et al.* 1996).

Resistance may be acquired by previously sensitive isolates from the environment, from other organisms, from bacteriophages or through random mutation (Standing Medical Advisory Committee Sub-Group on Antimicrobial Resistance

---

[1] Of importance is also the emergence and transmission of AMR within animals, from agricultural and veterinary use. Much of the resistance which occurs in animals is to antimicrobials which are used in human medicine. Although therefore of relevance, strategies for containing antimicrobial use and resistance in animals is outside the scope of this current paper, and interested readers are referred to the "WHO Global Principles for the Containment of Antimicrobial Resistance in Animals Intended for Food" (see: www.who.int/emc/diseases/zoo/who_global_principles.html), and chapter 4 of the WHO Global Strategy for the Containment of AMR (WHO 2001).

1998). The use of antimicrobials exerts a selection pressure favoring the emergence of resistance, but for any specific antimicrobial the correlation between consumption and resistance is complicated by factors such as the relative fitness of resistant and sensitive strains and linked multiple resistances (Magee *et al.* 1999). The direct development of resistance within an individual can happen when individuals take antimicrobials to treat one particular pathogen, but selection pressure is exerted on other organisms within the body at the same time. Alternatively individuals may acquire resistant organisms from food, animals, inanimate objects, or contact with others (Standing Medical Advisory Committee Sub-Group on Antimicrobial Resistance 1998). Once resistance has developed, its spread is exacerbated by a number of aspects of modern society, including increasing international travel, ecosystem disturbances, war, the rapid growth of large cities, and increasing numbers of people with compromised immune systems (Coast *et al.* 1996).

The development of resistance over time appears to follow a sigmoid distribution, illustrated in Fig. 4.1, with a lag phase before resistance appears (time *x*), then a relatively rapid increase in the proportion of resistant organisms, followed by a third phase (time *x* + *n*) in which this proportion reaches an equilibrium (Austin and Anderson 1999). This equilibrium level is determined by the relative fitness of resistant and sensitive strains, the genetic basis and stability of resistance, and the magnitude of the selection pressure. At this level, the proportion of resistant organisms may range from 10–90 percent (Anderson 1999).

Importantly, although a few studies have suggested that organisms may lose their resistance levels over time once drug exposure has been removed, in general, resistance is slow to reverse or often appears to be irreversible (Seppala *et al.* 1997).

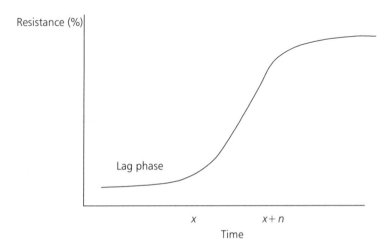

Fig. 4.1 Development of AMR over time expressed in terms of a particular bug that is resistant to an antimicrobial

This suggests that in the containment of resistance it is vital to act early to prevent emergence of resistance (e.g. in the "lag phase") rather than wait until resistance has begun to emerge.

Economists have tended to conceptualize antimicrobial resistance as a *negative externality* associated with the consumption of antimicrobials (Phelps 1989), but the economic analysis of AMR remains limited. The complexity associated with such analysis can be illustrated by the "net benefit equation" developed by Coast *et al.* (1998). This suggested that the net benefit resulting from antimicrobial usage in a particular time period would be a function of the direct benefit to the patient of taking the antimicrobial, the cost of the drug plus administration costs, the costs associated with side effects, problems caused by difficulties in diagnosis, the negative externality associated with the development of resistance, the positive externality associated with limiting the current spread of infection, the quantity of antimicrobials consumed, and a vector of other factors determining resistance within the community.

4.2.2 The health and economic costs and consequences of AMR

Patients infected with antimicrobial-resistant micro-organisms are less likely than those infected with a sensitive micro-organism to recover from infection with the first antimicrobial used in their treatment. They may require additional investigations and additional treatments (often with more toxic and more expensive antimicrobials). For some patients a cascade of antimicrobial drugs may be used before one is found to be successful in eradicating the infection. Patients may require longer hospital stays and longer periods of time away from work. Most serious is the increased likelihood of premature death (Smith *et al.* 1996).

Such findings have been noted in a number of epidemiological studies. In their review, Holmberg *et al.* (1987) found that, in almost every study, patients with resistant organisms had poorer health and economic outcomes that those patients with sensitive organisms. For example, in outbreaks of resistant Salmonella the mortality rate was 3.4 percent compared with a mortality of 0.2 percent for those with sensitive Salmonella strains during outbreaks investigated in the United States of America between 1971 and 1980 (Holmberg *et al.* 1987).

Assessments of the cost of AMR are crude. In 1995, the American Society for Microbiology estimated the annual health care costs associated with the treatment of resistant infections in the United States of America at over $4 billion (American Society for Microbiology 1995). More recent estimates have put this figure at more that $7 billion, with up to $4 billion incurred for the treatment of nosocomial infections due to AMR bacteria (John and Fishman 1997). In France, it has been suggested that there would be large cost savings if those costs associated with the 500,000 patients who acquire nosocomial infections each year could be avoided (Astagneau *et al.* 1999). In 1995, the cost of containing an MRSA (methicillin resistant staphylococcus aureus) outbreak in a district general hospital in the United Kingdom was estimated to be greater than £400,000 (Cox *et al.* 1995). As well as being relatively crude, the cost estimates that have been produced almost certainly underestimate the total current costs of resistance, as they are limited to medical care costs, with the majority of these being incurred by the health care system. Further, none of these estimates include any estimate of costs incurred by future generations—costs that will almost certainly be larger than those being currently experienced (Coast *et al.* 2002).

The economic and health costs of AMR, serious enough in the developed world, are often made more severe in many parts of the developing world (Okeke *et al.* 1999). The economic, health and infrastructure systems of these countries (e.g. irregular drug supply and availability of drugs from unofficial sources (Munishi 1991, Salako 1991, Hogerzeil *et al.* 1993)), lead to the inappropriate use of anti-microbials (Bojalil and Calva 1994, Nizami *et al.* 1996, Paredes *et al.* 1996, Hui *et al.* 1997, Reyes *et al.* 1997, Rodolfo *et al.* 1997), resulting in nosocomial infections from strains that are far more drug-resistant than those currently encountered in developed countries (Wolff 1993).

4.3 Is containment of AMR a GPGH?

It has already been stated that AMR is a negative externality resulting from private (i.e. excludable and rival) consumption decisions to take antimicrobials in the treatment of disease. Once AMR has developed, people cannot be *excluded* from catching the resistant bugs anymore than they can be excluded from catching sensitive infectious disease. Further, resistance is also *non-rival* in its effect: because one person has developed a resistant infection it does not stop another from catching it also. AMR is therefore non-excludable and non-rival in consumption and, because it generates ill-effects, fulfills the requirements of the economic terminology of a "public *bad* for health."

But is it global? Does it accrue to more than one group of countries, to several population groups and to both current and future generations? The answer is undoubtedly yes.[2] Resistance, like most infectious diseases, can be, and is, transmitted across international, cultural, and ethnic boundaries. Further, actions taken now will impact on the transmission and emergence of resistance in future generations. It may have particularly severe consequences for economies which already suffer greatly from infectious disease—countries where living conditions are poor and where there are high proportions of individuals with immunocompromise—but it will also have significant economic and health consequences at a global level, suggesting that resistance is a global public bad.

---

[2] Except, theoretically, where countries or localities (e.g. remote tribes) can be regarded as perfectly closed systems, with no movement of goods, people, animals etc. in or out of that country. However, this is a purely theoretical possibility and unlikely to occur (at least to any significant extent) in practice. Further, even this situation would leave the possibility of effects upon future generations within these localities.

The containment of AMR is, conversely, a public *good*: the reduced risk of infection by a resistant disease is both non-excludable and non-rival in consumption. As with AMR itself, the global nature of resistance, and particularly the intergenerational effects, make the containment of resistance *per se* a "GPGH."

It is perhaps most helpful to think about AMR as a *dynamic* model, with a number of interactions. There are people consuming antimicrobials, leading to the development of resistance, and there are "strategies" either to stop this consumption of antimicrobials, to ameliorate the resistance-inducing effects of taking antimicrobials or to ameliorate the transmission of resistance at any one time. A "contained" pool of resistance is merely one for which the strategies have reduced the effects of the further development of resistance (which itself arises through additional consumption of antimicrobials). Of particular relevance here are the strategies by which the global public good (GPG) of contained AMR is achieved, and the extent to which these are themselves seen as "intermediate" GPGH.

Before considering the nature of individual strategies and the possibility that they may comprise "intermediate" GPGH, however, it is important to note that the "eradication" of resistance is neither a realistic nor a desirable goal. To eradicate resistance entirely—or even to maintain resistance at current levels—would require significant, if not total, reduction in the use of antimicrobial agents, as the use of *any* agent will lead to the development of *some* resistance. Such a goal would imply allowing significant mortality and morbidity to be incurred. The aim must therefore be to use the available strategies to *optimize* the balance between the use of effective antimicrobials to treat infection, and thus reduce current morbidity and mortality, and the emergence and spread of resistance to these antimicrobials which in turn leads to increased future morbidity and mortality (Coast *et al.* 1998). This balance depends upon the relative costs and benefits of these positive and negative effects. It is determining this balance that is critical. Given the diverse contexts of developed and developing nations, it is likely that optimal strategies will vary considerably across them, but all strategies should share the same goals of achieving an optimal balance in the use of antimicrobial agents (WHO 2001).

4.3.1 Strategies for the containment of AMR as "intermediate" GPGH

If the containment of AMR itself is a "GPGH," then the next important step in the analysis of how this good may be provided is to consider the "intermediate GPG" aspects of strategies which may be used to contain resistance.

There are many strategies for containing AMR, some of which may be best pursued at the international level, and others of which will be pursued at more micro-levels (regional, national, or local), whilst still conferring benefits on other countries and to future generations. Some of these strategies will have public good characteristics, while others will clearly be private goods. However, even if these strategies do not themselves fulfill the qualities required to be considered intermediate GPGs, the fact that containing resistance is itself a GPGH means that they *may be treated as if they were public goods* according to the modified definition provided in Chapter 1.

One particularly important distinction between strategies is whether they aim to avoid the *emergence* of new resistance or the *transmission* of existing resistance. Of course, the second interacts with the first, but avoiding the *emergence* of new resistance could be seen as a primary goal in relation to the development of strategies to contain AMR. This is because, in terms of the health impact on future generations, the benefit of reducing the pressure toward greater selection of resistance is likely, in absolute terms, to be much greater (Coast *et al.* 1996, 2002). Policies to reduce transmission will never avoid all the ill health associated with a resistant organism, whereas policies that avoid resistance ever appearing could, potentially, avoid all such ill health. There is a further, third, strategy that relates neither to the emergence nor transmission of antibiotic resistance, nor indeed to the containment of resistance. Nevertheless it is an alternative solution to the problem of resistance as it comprises the development and production of wholly new antimicrobial treatments.

There are a wealth of strategies that may be pursued in containing the emergence and transmission of AMR. Table 4.1 summarizes the major strategies, and illustrates the variety of interventions that have been proposed to achieve them (complete descriptions of which can be found in Smith *et al.* (2001), and further discussion of the relative importance of such strategies in national contexts in the WHO Global Strategy for the Containment of AMR (WHO 2001)).

It is impossible to deal here with all the strategies that have been proposed as means of containing resistance. The focus is therefore limited to considering the extent to which strategies for avoiding the *emergence* of AMR are GPGH. Table 4.1(b), considering the transmission of resistance, is not considered further as, although resistance adds an extra element to the analysis of infectious disease transmission (in particular by altering the balance of costs and benefits of strategies to control transmission), such strategies are common in addressing infectious disease transmission in general. The analyses contained in Chapters 2 and 3 relating to the transmission of specific diseases (polio and tuberculosis, respectively) are therefore relevant to the containment of resistance by reducing its transmission. Table 4.1(c) is concerned with the development of new antimicrobial agents, which offers (in the short-term at least) an *alternative* to containing existing resistance, by producing agents that can treat these resistant infections. However, new agents are effectively public goods that are privatized by administrative arrangements concerning intellectual property rights and patent laws, which is an area considered in more detail in Chapter 6.

In Table 4.2, each of the strategies designed to contain the emergence of resistance (Table 4.1(a)) are thus considered in more detail with respect to whether they are intermediate "GPGs." For each, the authors' view about whether the strategy is excludable and rival in consumption is given, as is the likely level of intervention (classified as local, national, regional, and global). This is the basis for determining whether each of these strategies comprises an intermediate GPGH.

Table 4.1 Strategies for containing antimicrobial resistance

Objective	Strategy	Intervention
(a) Preventing emergence		
↓ Selection Pressure*	↓ Antimicrobial use in humans and agriculture	• Education of professionals • Education of patients • Rapid diagnosis of bacterials • Control of sensitivity data released to prescribers • Antibiotic policies • Restriction of availability • Financial incentives/ disincentives • Antimicrobial cycling • Regulation on the use of antibiotics in agriculture
↓ Opportunity for Resistance Emerging*	Optimal use of existing agents	• Ensuring optimal agent, dose and dose frequency for each infection • Removal of potential septic foci • Emphasizing/ensuring compliance • Use of antibiotic combinations
↑ Range of Agents Available	Consider use of alternative treatment options	• Antiseptics • Cranberry juice for UTI • Probiotics
↓ Requirement for Antimicrobials	↑ Immune competence	• Vaccination • Nutrition • Minimize time patient is immunocompromised
(b) Control transmission		
↓ Transmission	Early recognition of resistant organisms	• More rapid techniques • Surveillance • Screening patients/staff
	↓ Infectivity ↓ Opportunities for transmission	• Use of antimicrobials • Isolation • Handwashing • General hygiene • Patient/staff ratios • Bed spacing
	↓ Susceptibility to infection	↑ Immunity ↑ Nutrition
(c) Develop new antimicrobials		
↑ Range of Agents Available	Discover/develop new agents	• Modification of existing agents/ discovery of new antimicrobials

Table 4.1 Strategies for containing antimicrobial resistance

Objective	Strategy	Intervention
		• Discovery of new drug targets through microbial gene analysis
		• Genetic manipulation
		• Computer modeling

* Although it may appear that these two aspects are the same, here "reducing selection pressure" refers to reducing antimicrobial usage, whereas "reducing opportunity for resistance emerging" refers to ensuring that, where used, antimicrobials are used in a way that minimizes the likelihood of resistance emerging, which may involve *increasing* the use of antimicrobial therapies rather than necessarily reducing them

The rationale for completion of Table 4.2 is as follows. All strategies that involve the provision of antimicrobials (strategies 8, 10, 13) or the provision of alternative treatments (strategies 3, 11, 14, 15, 16, 17, 19) are *private goods* (in the economic sense, although they may be provided through publicly funded health care systems, insurance systems, or by direct purchase by individuals). They are excludable and rival in consumption and they are provided at the individual level, although policies may be local or national. The argument for nutrition (strategy 18) being a private good is similar.

All forms of regulation (strategies 4, 5, 6, 9) are excludable, but are non-rival in consumption. Groups can be included or excluded by a regulation, but once a regulation exists it can apply to one person or many (the exception to this is if the cost of monitoring is very high, in which case regulation could possibly be considered rival in consumption). These strategies therefore fall into the category of *club goods*. Regulation may operate at local, national, regional, or global levels (with the latter two particularly in relation to the use of antimicrobials in farming and food safety).

The only area where interventions could be considered *full public goods* is in relation to the provision of information and/or education (strategies 1, 2, 12). Information is non-excludable and non-rival in consumption, and this is particularly so with some modern technologies such as the use of the Internet (although in practice such access is restricted to those with access to computing facilities). Specific educational strategies may, however, be excludable, particularly in relation to health professionals. Information provision may operate at all levels from local to global.

Financial incentives/disincentives (strategy 7), for example, to prescribe or not, utilizing taxation, subsidy, or permits (Coast *et al.* 1998), are excludable, as they can be (differentially) applied to specific groups (e.g. prescribers, patients, companies). However, although *incentive* payments may be classed as rival in consumption (such that, for example, payment to one prescriber cannot be paid to another), *disincentives* are usually non-rival in consumption (the penalty applied to one prescriber can equally be applied to another for example). Again, these strategies may be applied at levels ranging from the local to the global, although the spill-over effects in other areas (e.g. if applied to one antimicrobial, the impact on prescription of others) need to be carefully assessed.

Table 4.2 Characteristics of strategies for containing the emergence of resistance

Strategy	Excludable?	Rival in consumption?	Level of intervention
1. Education of professionals on appropriate clinical indications	Either	Non-rival	Local/national/regional/global
2. Patient education	Non-excludable	Non-rival	Local/national/regional/global
3. Rapid diagnosis of bacterials	Excludable	Rival	Local
4. Control of sensitivity data related to prescribers	Excludable	Non-rival	Local
5. Antimicrobial policies	Excludable	Non-rival	Local/national
6. Restriction of drug availability	Excludable	Non-rival	Local/national
7. Financial (dis)incentives	Excludable	Rival (incentives) Non-rival (disincentives)	Local/national/regional/global
8. Antimicrobial cycling	Excludable	Rival	Local
9. Regulation on the use of antimicrobials in agriculture	Excludable	Non-rival	Local/national/regional/global
10. Choosing the optimal agent, dose and dose frequency	Excludable	Rival	Local
11. Removal of potential septic foci	Excludable	Rival	Local
12. Emphasizing/ensuring compliance	Non-excludable	Non-rival	Local/national/regional/global
13. Use of drug combinations	Excludable	Rival	Local
14. Antiseptics	Excludable	Rival	Local
15. Cranberry juice for UTI	Excludable	Rival	Local
16. Probiotics	Excludable	Rival	Local
17. Vaccination	Excludable	Rival	Local/national
18. Nutrition	Excludable	Rival	Local/national
19. Minimize time patient is immunocompromised	Excludable	Rival	Local

There is one further area in relation to AMR, not incorporated in Table 4.2, where there is almost certainly a GPGH: the production of research that would eliminate many of the uncertainties associated with the development and containment of resistance. This includes basic scientific and epidemiological research, as well as clinical and economic studies of the costs and effectiveness of alternative strategies. Such research, as with all information, has the characteristics of being non-excludable and non-rival in consumption.[3] Steps should be taken to ensure that such research—particularly in relation to clinical and economic studies—is of global relevance, by being undertaken in both developing and developed countries, where different contexts may result in quite different costs and effectiveness being associated with interventions (see also Section 4.4.5).

It is clear that, whilst the containment of AMR is itself a GPGH, the strategies leading to this containment are, in general, not strictly intermediate GPGH. Whilst some information and regulatory strategies may be pursued at the international level, the majority will be pursued at micro-levels, although they may still confer benefits on other countries and to future generations. As mentioned, since the containment of resistance is a GPGH, it may be that strategies to achieve this GPGH may be treated *as if they were GPG* (see Chapter 1). However, research to reduce the uncertainty associated with development and containment of AMR may be the closest to an actual intermediate GPGH in this area.

4.4 Finance and provision: the role of international agencies with respect to GPGH and AMR

Although many of these strategies are not intermediate GPGH themselves, they may be treated as such to the extent that international coordination of their finance and provision would lead to a more optimal outcome in the GPGH of containment of AMR than if each nation acts independently (Sandler 1997). Although in large part this would be through overcoming the "prisoners dilemma" danger inherent in this area, there are also other constraints faced by countries in implementing these strategies. For example, many countries lack the necessary financial, health, and/or technical infrastructure to provide many of the strategies outlined, and for some poorer nations the national cost–benefit equation for these activities may be far lower than for alternative health-producing activities. In this case, establishing the impact of non-concordance with the rest of the "community of nations" is vital to persuade these other nations of the rationality of ensuring that the country in question is assisted in finance and/or provision of the strategy in question. To this extent, international support to strengthen national health provider systems may be an important input to the containment of AMR.

Nationally, public goods, or those imposing significant externalities, are dealt with by government intervention; either in the establishment of property rights, and hence excludability, coercive payment, such as through taxation, financial incentives,

---

[3] Although again, in practice, it is possible to impose excludability, such as through patent rights or database access, to generate a "club good" approach to information dissemination.

or compensation (e.g. the purchase and sale of "rights," such as permits, to perform activities with negative health consequences (Smith and Coast 1998)) or actual provision. However, in the case of *global* public goods the absence of a "global government" means that the central issue is how *national provision may be fostered and co-ordinated.* International agencies, such as the World Health Organization (WHO), World Bank, and United Nations, have a key part to play in the organization and facilitation of such a global response. WHO has already begun this process with their recent "Global Strategy for the Containment of AMR" (WHO 2001), and we envisage such agencies having key roles in five fundamental areas, detailed below.

4.4.1 Raising awareness of the importance of AMR and the interdependency of nations in containing AMR

Although international collective action is essential to deal with the global problem of AMR, responsibility for health is still predominantly national: controlled by national government and legislation (Fidler 1998). It will be national legislation, regulation, and health systems that will determine the production and delivery of strategies to contain AMR. National recognition of the problem that AMR represents, the interdependency of all nations, and thus the impact and responsibility each nation has on global health, is a prerequisite to effective action.

A fundamental role for international organizations involves raising awareness and lobbying governments about the importance of AMR (APUA 2000). Key to this will be the establishment of the economic, health, and political costs and benefits to each nation of pursuing containment strategies on a uni- or multilateral basis (Sandler 1997). Each nation will incur costs in implementing any of the strategies mentioned, but at present the corresponding benefits are unclear. The working hypothesis is that each country will benefit from another's actions, but this needs quantifying to assess the potential for free-riding, and the loss of benefit which might result from non-concordance, in order to appeal to the self-interested, as well as altruistic, nature of governments.

Further, the impact that the interaction of strategies pursued by different (neighboring) nations may have upon the effectiveness of these strategies is also unclear. For example, the European Union (EU) has banned the use of four antimicrobial products which are important for human treatment but were used in animal feed (EU 1997, 1998)—although the effects of this action may be diminished if their use is still adopted, or even increased, in other countries through drug company marketing pressure. There may therefore also be a role for international bodies to review the possible implications from, and co-ordinate implementation of, strategies to maximize beneficial synergies and reduce negative ones.

4.4.2 Support for the creation, monitoring, and enforcement of national legislation, and regulation mechanisms to ensure production of strategies to contain AMR

The optimal provision of strategies will require national support for the introduction and enforcement of appropriate legislation and regulation, as well as funding for adequate provision and delivery. The large number of actors involved in the process of developing and implementing these strategies include: national governments; national and transnational corporations; non-governmental organizations (NGOs); health organizations; and citizens. This creates significant potential for political, policy and collective-action problems (e.g. free-riding, prisoner's dilemma[4]) in ensuring adequate production and delivery of strategies.

In particular, each actor will have different vested interests in the provision, or non-provision, of AMR containment as a GPGH, and in strategies aimed at achieving containment. For example, government attitudes are likely to be broadly split between those who stand to gain from an increase in foreign aid if AMR is treated as a GPGH, or who are able to "free-ride," and those from whom the aid will be sought. Private (pharmaceutical) industry attitudes will most likely be against restrictions on antimicrobial use, which may be seen as a threat to profitability.[5] The attitudes of populations will also differ across nations, as some may experience a reduction in "health" from restricted availability of antimicrobials, yet others may be more positive as appropriate use will mean an increase in access to antimicrobials therapies and an increase in "health." These vested interests will reflect the economic and political costs and benefits that result from AMR containment being treated as a GPGH, and proposed strategies to contain AMR. In order to develop and implement mechanisms to ensure containment of AMR it is vital that these costs and benefits are quantified, as discussed in Section 4.4.1.

An important role for international bodies is therefore in identifying, and quantifying, the input required from agencies that might be involved in the production/supply of these strategies (which will vary according to the type of strategy). This information will enable the strengthening of agencies or networks as required, and the prevention of potential losers (politically or economically) blocking provision of the good or limiting effectiveness through non-concordance.[6] In some cases, new

----

4 Where free-riding refers to nations benefiting from the actions of others without reciprocation, and prisoners dilemma refers to a lack of communication, and/or lack of mechanisms to ensure collaboration, resulting in a sub-optimal decision for all parties compared to the decision which could have occurred with improved communication and/or mechanisms to ensure collaboration (Hargreaves-Heap *et al.* 1992).

5 Restrictions on the use of new antimicrobials (reserved as "last-line" drugs) will provide a disincentive for companies to invest in developing new drugs. Given the lag time in development and marketing of new drugs, this is not an optimal long-term outcome if all currently available drugs develop high levels of resistance. This suggests that some system, similar to the "orphan-drug" system, should be established to encourage new drug development, but not at the "cost" of increased antimicrobial use, and therefore increased resistance.

6 Although unlikely, it may be that there will be some gainers as a side-effect of strategies who may be able to "compensate" the losers.

"institutions" and/or legislative frameworks will be required to achieve this. Here, international bodies can provide advice and assist in the co-ordination of multi-national support for nations in pursuing reform (Sandler 1997).

International agencies can also provide a framework for collaboration between different agents. While this role can be undertaken in part by national governments, lack of capacity and limited influence with some key actors (notably transnational companies) may require, in addition to collaboration between national governments, international organizations to play a part.

4.4.3 Facilitate production and dissemination of information within and across nations

Surveillance is commonly identified as the fundamental stage in a global strategy for the containment of resistance, as it provides the information required to establish, for example, the location of an AMR problem, its growth, transmission and direction of travel, and the impact of interventions to contain it (WHO 2001). Co-ordination of surveillance systems and alert mechanisms for notifying nations about the emergence and spread of resistant strains, although technically a "club good," would thus have considerable external benefit to all nations who have access to that information. The establishment and maintenance of a global database of AMR surveillance data to which nations contribute, and from which they have access to the information and alert mechanisms, could therefore be extremely valuable to each nation in planning to deal with AMR (e.g. MDR-TB surveillance (WHO 2000b)). A major challenge in achieving this, however, is the multiplicity of laboratory susceptibility testing techniques across the world. An important step in this area may therefore be in the specification and co-ordination of international standards in laboratory susceptibility testing techniques.

Similarly, educational material (e.g. medical education, information to pharmacists and citizens), although often costly to develop, may be repeatedly used at a low marginal cost. Thus, the provision and/or co-ordination of the collection of, and access to, such material, and its translation, could be undertaken by international bodies (e.g. WHO 2000a).

Research and development of new drugs and vaccines, and evaluation of strategies to contain AMR, is often expensive and time-consuming to conduct, yet the results are relatively cheap to disseminate. Thus, international agencies can encourage and co-ordinate international research networks, utilizing a core set of standard methods, to undertake epidemiologically-sound clinical trials in different patient groups and geographical regions, and to report the outcome of strategies where implemented. They could also act as a repository for information from nations about current research projects, and implementation and evaluation of strategies to tackle AMR.

Information has to be communicated to be of any use. International agencies, through activities such as those mentioned, could therefore also assist in maintaining communication channels to reduce the potential for the "prisoners dilemma" problem arising in cross-national communication.[7]

4.4.4 Advocate for international funding structures to assist in the implementation of strategies

The co-ordination of national surveillance and research information has economic and political implications. As discussed, collection of surveillance data will, for example, be difficult for countries that lack the necessary financial and/or technical infrastructure, and support to strengthen these structures may be necessary. This both undermines the political will to cooperate and limits effective participation in international communicable disease control, impeding effective global action. Even the creation of a legal *duty* does not ensure *compliance*, as this depends on having adequate resources to fulfil such obligations (Fidler 1996, 1997).

Similarly, for the dissemination of information the "community of nations" should recognize that it is irrational to exclude a country from consumption because the marginal benefit from that country's consumption of it outweighs the marginal cost of enabling it to be freely available.

Advocating the rationale for "pooling" of resources to be used internationally is an important area in ensuring provision and distribution of many of the strategies mentioned, and leading to strategies to contain AMR being pursued in each individual nation. The lack of strong mechanisms for the formal coercion of national governments, and the lack of effective sanctions against transnational corporations (who, for example, may threaten to relocate if economic and/or political changes are unfavorable), makes financial support the obvious means to secure concordance with international decisions. In addition, to avoid counterproductive incentives, compensation for the negative health or economic effects of such concordance may be required in some instances (this may also apply to households as well as governments if low-income households bear significant costs as a result of GPGH provision).

In the case of transnational companies, it would in principle make sense to use either formal coercion or "voluntary codes of practice" (and associated informal coercion related to "public image") to restrict activities which have negative health effects (e.g. the promotion of antimicrobials), and compensation or reward systems to encourage provision of health favoring externalities (e.g. research into new antimicrobials). In practice, however, the limitations of formal and informal coercion at the national and international levels may require compensation to be used in both cases. The importance of avoiding unintentional and perverse effects should also be noted.

---

[7] It has to be acknowledged that communication of information is, in this respect, a "necessary but not sufficient" condition to prevent the "prisoners dilemma" problem arising, since communication of information itself does not ensure the mechanisms to enable it to be acted upon (see also Section 4.4.2).

4.4.5 Provide an agenda, funding and coordination for research in the area of AMR to address knowledge gaps and improve areas of uncertainty

There is a substantial lack of information surrounding AMR, including the natural history of resistance, its emergence and transmission, the relationship between resistance and use of antimicrobials, the health and economic impact of resistance, and the cost and effectiveness of strategies to contain it (Smith *et al.* 2001). Given the wealth of information that could be collected, and limited research time and funding, it is important that a clear research agenda is developed and pursued which maximizes these resources.

At present there is no one global body that defines, co-ordinates, and supports priorities for research. This is an area where international bodies could play a significant role. WHO has begun in the Global Strategy to define key aspects for future research in a number of areas (WHO 2001). For example, assessing the effects of different methods of prescriber payment, different forms of patient charges, and manner of health insurance on levels of AMR, factors influencing the prescription of antimicrobials, and links and interactions between AMR in hospitals, nursing homes, and the community.

However, identification of a research agenda is of limited value unless it is prioritized, implemented, and co-ordinated. Clearly there will be a disparity between countries in this regard, although the information obtained from each nation will be of use to others. International agencies could therefore provide a central role in the coordination of a "global" agenda for research, reflecting the needs of developed and developing nations, and the funding and conduct of that agenda. Cross-subsidization of research funding and expertise will be required, and for this some element of "pooling" of a proportion of research funds, or GDP, could be one way in which a central "global" fund for research is established and distributed. There is some precedent for such international R&D support for diseases that pose significant international concern, such as the "Medicines for Malaria Venture,"[8] a multiagency program supported by WHO and the World Bank to co-ordinate research on antimalarial products (Butler 1997, Gallagher 1997, Mons *et al.* 1998).[9] Another means of achieving this could be to simply co-ordinate collaboration between *national* research agencies and bodies in the funding and conduct of research in different nations. Linked with this will be the requirement to hold and disseminate the research findings, as detailed in Section 4.4.3 above.

---

[8] http://www.malariamedicines.org. See also: http://www.malariavaccine.org

[9] There are other examples, such as the Sexually Transmitted Infections Diagnostic Group, International AIDS Vaccine Initiative and the Medicines for Malaria Venture, all of which involve multiagency partners from academia, international organizations (e.g. WHO, UNAIDS), NGOs, a variety of charitable organizations (e.g. Bill and Melinda Gates Foundation) and private industry, as explored by Buse and Walt (2000).

4.5 **Conclusion**

Antimicrobial resistance is a global problem. No single nation, however effective it is at containing resistance within its national borders, can protect itself from the importation of resistance through travel and trade. The health of future generations is in the hands of the current generation, and will depend heavily upon how well the current generation manages its consumption and development of new antimicrobial agents. This global nature of resistance calls for a global response.

As outlined in Section 4.3, AMR is non-excludable and non-rival in consumption, across countries, peoples, and time. In this sense, AMR may be classified as a global public *bad* for health, and thus its containment a global public *good* for health. This is useful in emphasizing the interdependency of nations, peoples, and generations in containing AMR, and that containment in any one country is dependent upon the overall level of global containment. The GPGH concept is therefore relevant, and is useful in highlighting not just the transnational, but also cross-population and intergenerational aspects of AMR, and emphasizes the importance of international bodies and international action in the creation of mechanisms and institutions required to ensure the production of strategies to contain AMR. Although, as outlined in Section 4.3.1, most of the strategies to contain AMR (except information and education) are private or club goods, provided on a national or regional basis, their role in achieving the GPG of AMR containment means that, under the related concept of "access goods" outlined in Chapter 1, they may be considered *as if they were* GPG.

The real value of the GPGH concept is in highlighting the global nature of the problem of AMR. Much of the discussion concerning the role of international bodies, detailed in Section 4.4, follows from this. Five key roles of such bodies were outlined which focus upon ensuring the provision of strategies at a predominantly national level. The usefulness of the GPGH concept is in illustrating the externality effect of AMR on a global scale, and the requirement for countries to consider strategies for containing AMR in not just their own, but also in other, countries. This may be particularly important in encouraging a cross-subsidization between rich and poor countries to maximize global containment of AMR, as it makes an appeal to the self-interest of developed countries which should reinforce existing humanitarian-based aid.

In terms of the GPGs identified of information and education, these are areas that are common across a number of contexts in which the GPGH concept is being considered, both in this volume and beyond (Kaul *et al.* 1999). There will therefore be common issues in ensuring the finance and provision of information and education for these areas and AMR. There will also be interaction in the containment of AMR with other possible GPGH. The most obvious example for this is the containment of infectious disease, where AMR may alter the balance of the costs and benefits of such disease and strategies for its containment.

4.5.1 **Future research priorities**

In addition to general research in the area of AMR, there are three fundamental areas of research (within which a more detailed specification of research questions will obviously be required) that form priorities arising *specifically* from the discussion in this paper:

1. Establishment of the economic, health, and political costs of AMR to each nation.

2. Establishment of the mechanism and size of the economic and health externality created by AMR from nation to nation.

3. Establishment of the economic, health, and political costs and benefits to each nation (and industry and NGOs) of pursuing containment strategies on a uni- or multilateral basis.

Given the paucity of data concerning AMR, its variability across countries, and the time required to generate the data required, the danger is that uncertainty will lead to inaction. Our *primary recommendation* is therefore that effort be placed first in the development of a conceptually and methodologically sound economic model of the costs and effects of AMR (Smith *et al.* 2001). Although the cost and time to develop such a model should not be underestimated, it will provide a cost-effective means by which to structure the main variables of relevance to the problems being addressed, and provide preliminary indications of the three areas highlighted here. Such a model could also enable prioritization of empirical data collection, and identify the key research questions within these areas.

To conclude, the GPGH concept provides useful pointers for health policy and intervention. Its value is in ensuring rigorous thought around challenging issues, prior to the commissioning of policies. However, ultimately, it is not the GPGH status, or otherwise, of these issues that is of importance. Rather, it is the rigor of the analysis that is used in the development and evaluation of those policies whose implementation will actually make a difference to the global community of people that is vital.

References

ASCP Susceptibility Testing Group. United States geographic bacteria susceptibility patterns 1995, *Am J Clin Pathol* 1996; **106**: 275–81.

Alliance for the Prudent Use of Antibiotics (APUA). *Action Needed to Curb Antimicrobial Resistance: A Synthesis of Recommendations by Expert Policy Groups (1987–2000).* WHO/CDS/CSR/DRS/2000.9, 2000.

American Society for Microbiology. Report of the ASM task force on antibiotic resistance. *Antimicrob Agents Chemother* 1995; Supplement: 1–23.

Ashley DJB, Brindle MJ. Penicillin resistance in staphylococci isolated in a casualty department. *J Clin Pathol* 1960; **13**: 336–8.

Astagneau P, Fleury L, Leroy S et al. Cost of antimicrobial treatment for nosocomial infections based on a French prevalence survey. *J Hosp Infect* 1999; **42**: 303–12.

Austin DJ, Anderson RM. Studies of antibiotic resistance within the patient, hospitals and the community using simple mathematical models. *Philos Trans R Soc Lond* 1999; **354**: 721–38.

Bojalil R, Calva JJ. Antibiotic misuse in diarrhea: a household survey in a Mexican community. *J Clin Epidemiol* 1994; **47**: 147–56.

Buse K, Walt G. Global public-private partnerships: Part II. *Bull World Health Organ* 2000; **78**: 569–714.

Butler D. Time to put malaria control on the global agenda. *Nature* 1997; **386**: 535–6.

Cannon G. *Superbug. Nature's Revenge.* London: Virgin Publishing, 1995.

Central Intelligence Agency (CIA). The global infectious disease threat and its implications for the United States. www.odci.gov/cia/publications/nie/report/nie99–17d.html, 1999.

Coast J, Smith R, Miller MR. Superbugs: should antimicrobial resistance be included as a cost in economic evaluation? *Health Econ* 1996; **5**: 217–26.

Coast J, Smith RD, Millar MR. An economic perspective on policy antimicrobial resistance. *Soc Sci Med* 1998; **46**: 29–38.

Coast J, Smith RD, Karcher AM, Wilton P, Millar M. Superbugs II: How should economic evaluation be conducted for interventions which aim to reduce antimicrobial resistance? *Health Econ* 2002; **11**: 637–47.

Cox RA, Conquest C, Malaghan C *et al.* A major outbreak of methicillin-resistant Staphylococcus aureus caused by new phage-type (EMRSA-16). *J Hosp Infect* 1995; **29**: 87–106.

European Union (EU). *Decision 97/87/EC.* Official Journal L356, 1997.

European Union (EU). *Decision 98/84/EC.* Official Journal L15, 1998.

Fasehun F. The antibacterial paradox: essential drugs, effectiveness and cost. *Bull World Health Organ* 1999; **77**: 211–16.

Fidler D. Globalisation, international law, and emerging infectious diseases. *Emerg Infect Dis* 1996; **2**: 77–84.

Fidler D. The globalisation of public health: emerging infectious diseases and international relations. *Indiana J Global Leg Stud* 1997; **5**: 11–51.

Fidler D. Legal issues associated with antimicrobial drug resistance. *Emerg Infect Dis* 1998; **4**: 169–77.

Fox R. The post-antibiotic era beckons. *J R Soc Med* 1996; **89**: 602–3.

Gallagher R. Global initiative takes shape slowly. *Science* 1997; **277**: 309.

Hargreaves-Heap S, Hollis M, Lyons B, Sugden R, Weale A. *The Theory of Choice. A Critical Guide.* Oxford: Blackwell Publishers Ltd, chapter 7, 1992.

Hogerzeil HW, Bimo Ross-Degnan D, Laing RO. Field tests for rational drug use in twelve developing countries. *Lancet* 1993; **342**: 1408–10.

Holmberg SD, Solomon SL, Blake PA. Health and economic impacts of antimicrobial resistance. *Rev Infect Dis* 1987; **9**: 1065–78.

House of Lords Select Committee on Science and Technology. 7th Report. London: HMSO, 1998.

Hui L, Li X-S, Zeng XJ, Dai YH, Foy HM. Patterns and determinants of use of antibiotics for acute respiratory tract infection in children in China. *Pediatr Infect Dis J* 1997; **16**: 560–4.

John J, Fishman NO. Pragmmatic role of the infectious diseases physician in controlling antimicrobial costs in the hospital. *Clin Infect Dis* 1997; **24**: 471–85.

Kaldec R, Zelicoff A, Vrtis A. Biological weapons control: prospects and implications for the future. *J Am Med Assoc* 1997; **278**: 351–6.

Kaul I, Grunberg I, Stern MA. *Global Public Goods: International Cooperation in the 21st Century.* New York: Oxford University Press, 1999.

Liss RH, Batchelor FR. Economic evaluations of antibiotic use and resistance— a perspective: Report of Task Force 6. *Rev Infect Dis* 1987; **9**: S297–313.

Magee JT, Pritchard EL, Fitzgerald KA *et al*. Antibiotic prescribing and antibiotic resistance in community practice: retrospective study, 1996–8. *BMJ* 1999; **319**: 1239–40.

Mons B, Klasen E, van Kessel R, Nchinda T. Partnership between south and north crystalises around malaria. *Science* 1998; **279**: 498–9.

Munishi GK. The development of the Essential Drugs Program and implications for self-reliance in Tanzania. *J Clin Epidemiol* 1991; **44** (Suppl. 2): 7S–14S.

Murray BE. Can antibiotic resistance be controlled? *N Engl J Med* 1994; **330**: 1229–30.

Neu HC. The crisis in antibiotic resistance. *Science* 1992; **257**: 1064–73.

Nizami SQ, Khan IA, Bhutta ZA. Drug prescribing practices of General Practitioners and Pediatricians for childhood diarrhoea in Karachi, Pakistan. *Soc Sci Med* 1996; **42**: 1133–9.

Okeke I, Lamikanra A, Edelman R. Socio-economic and behavioural factors leading to acquired bacterial resistance to antibiotics in developing countries. *Emerg Infect Dis* 1999; 5(1). Serial online, available from: http://www.cdc.gov/ncidod/eid/vol5no1/okeke.htm

Paredes P, de la Pena M, Flores-Guerra E, Diaz J, Trostle J. Factors influencing physicians' prescribing behavior in the treatment of childhood diarrhoea: knowledge may not be the clue. *Soc Sci Med* 1996; **42**: 1141–53.

Phelps CE. Bug/drug resistance. Sometimes less is more. *Medical Care* 1989; **27**: 194–203.

Reyes H, Guiscafre H, Munoz O. Antibiotic noncompliance and waste in upper respiratory infections and acute diarrhea. *J Clin Epidemiol* 1997; **50**: 1297–304.

Rodolfo J, Lozano J, Ruiz J, Londono D, Rodriguez M, Ruiz A. Drug prescription patterns of recently graduated physicians in Colombia [abstract]. *J Clin Epidemiol* 1997; **50** (Suppl. 1): 26S.

Salako LA. Drug supply in Nigeria. *J Clin Epidemiol* 1991; **44** (Suppl. 2): 15–9S.

Sandler T. *Global Challenges: An Approach to Environmental, Political, and Economic Problems.* Cambridge, New York and Melbourne: Cambridge University Press, chapter 5, 1997.

Seppala H, Klaukka T, Vuopio-Varkila J *et al*. The effect of changes in the consumption of macrolide antibiotics on erythromycin resistance in group A streptococci in Finland. Finnish Study Group for Antimicrobial Resistance. *N Engl J Med* 1997; **337**: 441–6.

Smith RD, Coast J, Millar MR. Over-the-counter antimicrobials: the hidden costs of resistance. *J Antimicrob Chemother* 1996; **37**: 1031–2.

Smith RD, Coast J. Controlling antimicrobial resistance: a proposed transferable permit market. *Health Policy* 1998; **43**(3): 219–32.

Smith RD. Antimicrobial resistance: the importance of developing long-term policy. *Bull World Health Organ* 1999; **77**: 862.

Smith RD, Coast J, Millar MR, Wilton P, Karcher A-M. Interventions against anti-microbial resistance: a review of the literature and exploration of modelling cost-effectiveness. Geneva: Global Forum for Health Research, http://www.globalforumhealth.org/pages/index.asp, 2001.

Standing Medical Advisory Committee Sub-Group on Antimicrobial Resistance. *The Path of Least Resistance*. Department of Health, London. The Publications Unit, PHLS Headquarters Office, 61 Colindale Avenue. London NW9 5DF. Also available at http://www.doh.gov.uk/smac/htm, 1998.

Tomasz A. Multiple-antibiotic resistant pathogenic bacteria. A report on the Rockefeller University Workshop. *N Engl J Med* 1994; **330**: 1247–51.

US Congress, Office of Technology Assessment. *Impacts of antibiotic-resistant bacteria*. OTA-H-629 US Government Printing Office, Washington DC, 1995.

WHO. *World Health Organisation Report on Infectious Diseases 2000. Overcoming Antimicrobial Resistance*. Geneva: WHO, 2000*a*, WHO/CDS/2000.2.

WHO. *Global Tuberculosis Control: WHO Report 2000*. Geneva: WHO, 2000*b*, WHO/CDS/TB/2000.275.

WHO. *Global Strategy for the Containment of Antimicrobial Resistance*. Geneva: WHO, 2001, WHO/CDS/CSR/DRS/2001.2.

Wolff MJ. Use and misuse of antibiotics in Latin America. *Clin Infect Dis* 1993; **17**: S346–51.

World Bank. *World Development Report 2000/01*. New York: Oxford University Press, 2001.

Chapter 5

Global environment

Anthony J McMichael, Colin D Butler, and Michael J Ahern

5.1 Introduction

Earth's biophysical environment constitutes the basic "goods and services" upon which our existence depends (Costanza *et al.* 1997, Daily 1997). Although societies within a given environment have, through the millennia, learnt how to conserve natural resources, these environmental assets have often been taken for granted; the tendency being to exploit natural resources to increase the carrying capacity of the environment. This scale of exploitation has increased exponentially over the past two centuries, as human numbers have expanded and as the material- and energy-intensity of economic activity has increased (Diamond 1997, Redman 1999, UNPDDESA 2001). Some of the longer-term consequences for human health are expected to be commensurately more serious.

Several assessments have concluded that humanity is now incurring a significant and increasing "ecological deficit," evidenced by an increasing decline in global environmental and ecological resource stocks (Wackernagel and Rees 1996, Loh *et al.* 1998, Butler 2000*a*). These include, for example, depletion of ocean fisheries, fresh water, and fertile soil. Perhaps more fundamentally, there is disruption to the recycling of nutrients and the gaseous composition of the lower and middle atmospheres. These processes exacerbate the unprecedented rate of loss of species, and threaten many local indigenous populations.

From the local to the global, the biophysical environment is our basic life-support system, fundamental to human health. Unlike most "goods and services," the basic environment is an endowment to humanity, one which all can use and from which none are excluded; making it a clear "global public good" (GPG) (Sandler 1997, Kaul *et al.* 1999). The purpose of this chapter is, however, to consider the environment as a global public good *for health*, and assess how the conceptual framework of "Global Public Goods for Health" (GPGH) might be useful in mitigating the adverse consequences of environmental degradation.

Following this introduction, Section 5.2 considers the GPG properties of a number of key environmental "goods." Section 5.3 describes adverse human health consequences of climate change, with Section 5.4 outlining the economic impact. Section 5.5 explores the political aspects of ensuring environment management, with Section 5.6 concluding with an assessment of the usefulness of the GPGH concept and recommendations for policy.

5.2 **The environment as a GPGH**

The linkages between the environment and the conceptual framework of GPGs are complex. For example, the degree to which aspects of the environment, such as clean air or water, can be described as a GPG is influenced by both spatial and temporal factors, determining the position of each environmental "good" along a spectrum from "pure" to "impure" GPGs. In an attempt to simplify these complex linkages for subsequent analysis, Tables 5.1 and 5.2 provide cross-sectional representations of both the "heritage" and "current" GPG status of some key environmental goods.

Table 5.1 shows the "original" endowment of environmental goods, all of which are classified as being non-rival on a global scale (and, therefore, regional and local scale), although some being excludable (and thus "club goods"). However, especially over the last few decades, this classification has changed considerably, with population growth ensuring that virtually all environmental goods are now rival in nature, and some becoming excludable, together with a more complex division in rivalry and excludability spatially. These are indicated in Table 5.2, and a brief discussion of the current state of these key goods provided below.

Table 5.1 The "heritage" status of major environmental "goods"

"Good"	Excludable?	Rival in consumption?	Level of application
Clean riparian waters	Yes	Non-rival	National/regional/global
Clean aquifer waters	Yes	Non-rival	National/regional/global
Unpolluted oceanic waters	No	Non-rival	Regional/Global
Fertile soil	Yes	Non-rival	National/regional/global
Biodiversity	Yes	Non-rival	National/regional/global
Unpolluted air	No	Non-rival	Global
Stratospheric ozone "shield"	No	Non-rival	Global

Table 5.2 The "current" status of major environmental "goods"

"Good"	Excludable?	Rival in consumption?	Level of application
Clean riparian waters	Yes	Rival	National
Clean aquifer waters	Yes	Rival	National
Unpolluted oceanic waters	No	Rival	Regional
Fertile soil	Yes	Rival	National/regional
Biodiversity	Yes	Rival	National/ regional/global
Unpolluted air	Yes	Rival	National
Stratospheric ozone "shield"	No	Rival	Regional/global

5.2.1 Air

At all spatial levels (local, regional, and global) "air" is quantitatively non-excludable and non-rival, and thus a "pure" GPG. However, over time, human activities have degraded the quality of air, so that the location of this good along the spectrum is determined by geographical location and socio-economic status. Thus "clean air" has become both rival and/or excludable (and hence a private, club, or common-pool good) according to geographical location, and cannot now be considered as a pure GPG in practice, although conceptually it remains thus.

5.2.2 Water

Equally, the public good status of water has become increasingly influenced by spatial factors. Most of the world's accessible water is contained within three[1] systems (oceanic, riparian,[2] and aquifer), and for most of human history all three systems were quantitatively and qualitatively "pure public goods." However, with time, this degree of "purity" has diminished. For instance, until recently, the contribution of the oceans to stabilization of the global climate has been a pure GPG. However, oceanic warming, at least in part because of human activities, suggest that even this GPG can be damaged (Levitus *et al.* 2000).

Furthermore, the overharvesting of oceanic species is reducing the trophic level of the marine harvest (Pauly *et al.* 1998) and many fisheries face collapse (Hutchings 2000). The GPG status of the oceans as a source of human food has become rival as its resources are depleted. These resources are increasingly excludable, through limitations of both physical access and pricing mechanisms.

---

[1] A considerable fraction of fresh water also exists as polar ice caps. Even with present technology, this source remains largely inaccessible, because of cost.

[2] In lakes, dams, and rivers, including from the seasonal melting of alpine glaciers.

The role of riparian and aquifer waters in the climate system is comparatively non-exclusive and non-rival, and thus both are "pure" public goods. However, the immediate benefit of these goods is on a national or regional scale: as such they are best described as regional public goods. But the role of riparian and aquifer water as providers of water for drinking, irrigation, and industry, as well as fishing and hydroelectric power is potentially excludable and rival (WWC 2000, Gleick 2000, 2001). These characteristics operate at a local and regional scale, and can potentially lead to conflict with devastating human health consequences (Homer-Dixon *et al.* 1993, Homer-Dixon 1994, 1999, Snooks 1996, El Betagy 2000).

5.2.3 Soil

The role of soil in the climate system is, again, historically non-exclusive and non-rival on a global scale. However, the role of soil in the food chain is excludable because its main product—food—is a private good. Most agricultural land, with the most fertile soil, is also privately owned, and thus excludable and rival. But much soil is also found on commonly owned land, for example in forests. These two characteristics will be exacerbated by the continuing spread of land degradation (Pimentel 2000).

5.2.4 Stratospheric ozone layer

An intact stratospheric ozone layer (SOL) is clearly a GPG. Until the early 1970s its public good status was relatively "pure" (although there was a natural variation in the thickness of the SOL, depending on latitude, season, and volcanic eruptions etc.). In recent years, because of certain industrial and agricultural gaseous emissions, the SOL has deteriorated in quality at a global scale, and has thus become rival. This can be partly compensated for by behavioral changes, such as applying sunscreen and wearing hats and sunglasses. But the SOL remains non-excludable; though of lesser quality, the residual UVR screen remains open to all.

5.2.5 Biodiversity

As human demand for space, materials, and food increases, so populations and species of plants and animals are being increasingly extinguished (Pimm *et al.* 1995). An important consequence for humans is the disruption of ecosystems that provide "nature's goods and services," and therefore underpin life and health (Daily 1997). These include, for example, recycling of nutrients, cleansing of water, stabilizing of surface water runoff, climatic stability, and pollination. Biodiversity loss also means that we are losing, before discovery, many of nature's chemicals and genes, of the kind that have already conferred enormous health benefits (Myers 1997).

5.3 Health impact of climate change

The large diversity of possible environmental goods, and their varying status as "pure" GPGs, creates complexity in the quantification of their health and economic impact, as well as measures to ameliorate their decline. Thus, for the remainder of this chapter, analysis is focused on the most fundamental environmental good: that of climate. Here, the health impact of climate change is outlined, focusing upon global climate change and stratospheric ozone depletion.

5.3.1 Global climate change

There is now clear recognition that anthropogenic activities are having a profound impact on national, regional, and global climatic conditions (Chapin *et al.* 2000). For example, evidence suggests that human-induced alteration of atmospheric composition, mainly from burning fossil fuels, has contributed to the rise in global temperatures over the last century (IPCC 1996). Current predictions are for a further rise of around 2–3 °C (5.5 °C according to Cox *et al.* 2000) within a plausible range of 1.4–5.8 °C (IPCC 2001) over the next century, representing a greater rate of change than at any time in the last 100,000 years.

Global climate change, occurring because of human augmentation of the "greenhouse effect" (accumulation of heat trapping gas in the lower atmosphere), is a potent manifestation of an unprecedented, human-caused, large-scale environmental change. Average world temperatures increased over the last quarter of the twentieth century, and weather patterns in many regions have displayed increased instability (Easterling *et al.* 2000). Scientists, the public and policymakers have become increasingly aware of these human-induced climatic changes, and questions about future health consequences of climate change are now firmly on the environmental health agenda.

The health effects of climate change have been classified as direct and indirect (McMichael and Haines 1997). While some health outcomes in some populations would be beneficial—some tropical regions may become too hot for mosquitoes, for example, and winter cold-snaps would become milder in temperate-zone countries where death rates typically peak in winter time—most of the anticipated health effects would be adverse (IPCC 1996).

Direct health effects include changes in mortality and morbidity from an altered pattern of exposure to thermal extremes, respiratory health consequences of increased exposures to photochemical pollutants and aeroallergens, and the physical hazards of the increased occurrence of storms, floods, or droughts (Bouma *et al.* 1997). Intensified rainfall, with flooding, can overwhelm urban wastewater and sewer systems, leading to contamination of drinking water supplies, especially in large crowded cities where infrastructure is old or inadequate.

Indirect health effects are, as might be expected, more diffuse, with arguably the three most important impacts being the spatial dispersion of disease vectors, effects of sea-level changes, and crop yields. These are considered below.

Spatial dispersion of disease vectors

Climate change leads to alterations in the geographical range (latitude and altitude) and seasonality of certain vector-borne infectious diseases. These include malaria, dengue fever, schistosomiasis, leishmaniasis, Lyme disease, and tick-borne viral encephalitis (Fenwick *et al.* 1981, Patz *et al.* 1996, Martens *et al.* 1999,

McMichael *et al.* 1999*a*, Lindgren and Gustafson 2001), as well as seasonal peaks of food-borne infections, such as salmonellosis.

Climate change is also expected to influence various directly transmitted infections, especially those due to contamination of drinking water and food. Many bacteria and protozoa are sensitive to temperature. Changes in the pattern of rainfall can disrupt surface water configuration and drinking water supplies. Hence, the occurrence of infectious diseases such as cryptosporidiosis and giardiasis, spread via contaminated drinking water, may be influenced by a changed climate. The consequences will vary from region to region, but the burdens are likely to fall disproportionately on the poorer populations in low-income countries, and on those made vulnerable by age or pre-existing illness.

Sea-level change

Sea-level rise is another environmental consequence of climate change. Oceans are thermally expanding, while most glaciers are already shrinking (Thompson *et al.* 2000). In consequence, the sea level is forecast to rise by approximately 40 cm by 2100 (IPCC 1996). This rate of rise would be several times faster than has occurred over the past century. This is important, since over half of the world's population now lives within 60 km of the sea, with vulnerable countries including Bangladesh and Egypt, with huge river delta farming populations, and Pakistan, Indonesia, and Thailand, all of which have large and relatively poor coastal populations.

Such a rise is likely to have widespread adverse public health impacts for these vulnerable populations. For example, a half-meter rise (at today's population) would approximately double, to around 100 million, the number who experience flooding annually. Further, sea-level rise will damage coastal structures and arable land, salinate coastal freshwater aquifers, particularly those beneath small islands, and affect sewage and wastewater disposal. There would be inevitable adverse physical and psychological health consequences resulting from consequent population displacement and economic disruption. However, because sea-level rise is a relatively slowly occurring physical process, protective action should be possible in many coastal regions, particularly in wealthy nations. The disproportionately large ratio of coastline to total area, allied with poverty, imperils the survival of many island states, including the Maldives and many small Pacific Ocean nations (Gillespie and Burns 2000).

Crop yields

Climate change effects food production in a number of ways, including temperature effects on plant physiology, soil moisture effects on plant physiology, carbon dioxide fertilization effects (gains in plant water-use efficiency), plant disease occurrence, crop losses via pest species, damage due to extreme weather events (e.g. floods and droughts), and, as mentioned, sea-level rise causing increased salination and inundation of coastal land.

Scientists have used dynamic crop growth models to simulate the effects of climate change, in conjunction with increased atmospheric carbon dioxide on cereal crop yields (which represent almost two-thirds of world food energy). One pioneering modeling study estimated the additional number of hungry people attributable to standard projections of climate change by the year 2060, within a range of plausible future trajectories of demographic, economic and trade-liberalization processes at between 40 and 300 million (Parry *et al.* 1999).

Regionally, most of this nutritional adversity would occur in Sub-Saharan Africa. The resultant additional hunger and malnutrition would increase the risk of infant and child mortality and cause physical and intellectual stunting. In adults, energy levels, work capacity, and health status would be compromised. The uncertainties inherent in this sort of attempt to model future climate change impacts on world food production are well illustrated by the spread of estimates obtained in other global studies (Winters *et al.* 1999, Rosenzweig *et al.* 2000).

It is important to note also the potential impacts of climate change upon food yields from the marine and freshwater aquatic environment (approximately one-sixth of all protein consumed by the world population is of aquatic origin, and in many developing countries it accounts for the majority of animal protein) (O'Brien *et al.* 2000). The Intergovernmental Panel on Climate Change (IPCC), in its Third Assessment Report, noted that, while weather impacts and seasonal rhythms have long been recognized by the global fishing industry, decadal-scale shifts in climate have only recently been acknowledged as a factor in fish and marine ecosystem dynamics (IPCC 2001). In fact, various life-stages of fish populations are sensitive to temperature: spawning, growth rates (in part because of temperature influences on food availability), migratory patterns, and breeding routes.

The important question of how global climate change is likely to affect food production remains complex and uncertain. There are finite, and increasingly evident, limits to agroecosystems and wild fisheries. Our capacity to maintain food supplies for an increasingly large and increasingly expectant world population will depend on maximizing the efficiency and sustainability of production methods, incorporating socially beneficial genetic biotechnologies, and taking pre-emptive action to minimize the future course of detrimental, ecologically damaging, global environmental changes.

5.3.2 Stratospheric ozone layer depletion

The depletion of stratospheric ozone, first observed in the 1970s over Antarctica, is primarily caused by the build-up of human-made ozone-destroying gases in the stratosphere (e.g. CFCs), which cause artificially high ultraviolet irradiation (UVR) at the Earth's surface (Farman *et al.* 1985, McKenzie *et al.* 1999).

This increase in UVR can be expected, in the first half of the twenty-first century, to cause an increase in the severity of sunburn, the incidence of skin cancers in fair-skinned populations, and the incidence of various disorders of the eye (especially cataracts) (Longstreth *et al.* 1988). Since cataract accounts for a majority of the tens of millions of cases of blindness in the world, even a marginal impact of increased UVR exposure on their occurrence would be significant. Some UVR-induced

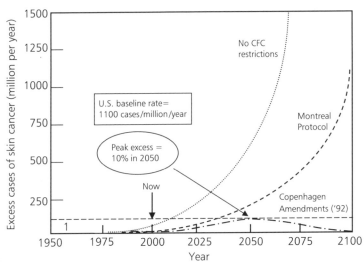

Fig. 5.1 Estimates of ozone depletion and excess skin cancer incidence to examine the Montreal Protocol achievements
Source: Based on H Slaper *et al.* (1996)

suppression of immune functioning may also result, thus increasing susceptibility to infectious diseases and perhaps reducing vaccination efficacy (WHO 1994, UNEP 1998). The health impacts of SOL depletion are difficult to quantify, but Longstreth *et al.* (1988) and Slaper *et al.* (1996) have provided broad projections of the burdens of skin cancer and other UV-related disease under various scenarios of emission containment, as illustrated in Fig. 5.1.

A potentially more important, although more indirect, health detriment could arise from ultraviolet-induced impairment of photosynthesis on land (terrestrial plants) and at sea (phytoplankton; Neale *et al.* 1998). Such an effect could reduce both the world's food production, and also harm the oceanic carbon sink (Field *et al.* 1998). However, few quantitative data are yet available.

5.4 **Economic impact of climate change**

The IPCC (1996) recognized that estimates of the economic impact of climate change are uncertain, and that such uncertainty is not only applicable to the science of climate change but is also associated with:

♦ limited knowledge of regional and local impacts

♦ difficulties in measuring the economic value of impacts even where impacts are known (particularly for non-market impacts and the impacts in developing countries)

- difficulties in predicting future technological and socio-economic developments
- the possibility of catastrophic events and surprises.

However, recognizing such imprecision, the IPCC (1996) reviewed the literature on CO_2 emissions and, based on best-guess central estimations (that include both market and non-market impacts, and adaptation costs), concluded that the economic impact from a doubling of CO_2 would be in the order of 1.5–2.0 percent of world GDP, split in to a developed country impact of 1–1.5 percent of GDP and developing country impact of 2–9 percent of GDP.

Although these figures were based on a large number of simplifying and often controversial assumptions, and are subject to regional variations, there is a marked difference in the impact on developing countries compared with developed countries. This is particularly important as developing countries have less capacity to adapt and are more vulnerable to climate change damages, just as they are more vulnerable to other stresses (IPCC 2001).

In addition to the impact on GDP of a doubling in CO_2 emissions, the IPCC (1996) estimated the monetary value of the marginal damage of carbon emitted to be in the order of US\$ 5–125 per additional tonne. However, Costanza (1997) discusses how sensitive the marginal cost per tonne of carbon is to the assumptions used, and argues that it can plausibly vary by a factor of about 100. He reports that though Nordhaus found the marginal cost per tonne of carbon to be US\$ 5 per tonne regardless of time, Azar and Sterner found it to be US\$ 590 per tonne for a 1,000-year period of impacts. As with other estimations of climate change impacts, the assumptions upon which such values are based are subject to debate (especially concerning time frame and discount rate).

More recently the IPCC (2001) reported that any attempt to enumerate the health costs of climate change will be complex because of the great heterogeneity of such impacts. It will also be controversial because of the difficulties in assigning monetary values to a diverse range of health deficits across varied cultures and economies, and using an appropriate time-discounting factor. Recognizing the current dearth of such data, the IPCC (2001) has catalogued some of the recent approximations that have been published of the impact on national economies of major infectious disease outbreaks that might occur more often under conditions of climate change. For example:

- An outbreak of plague-like disease in Surat, north-west India in 1994 cost an estimated US\$ 3 billion in lost revenues to India alone (John 1996, WHO 1997).
- The cost of the 1994 dengue hemorrhagic fever (DHF) epidemic in Thailand was estimated to be between US\$ 19–51 million (Sornmani *et al.* 1995).
- The cost of the 1994 epidemic of dengue/DHF in Puerto Rico was estimated to be US\$ 12 million for direct hospitalization costs alone (Rodriguez 1997, Meltzer *et al.* 1998).

5.4.1 **The cost (and benefit) of reducing "greenhouse gas" emissions**

There will be costs associated with reducing degradation in climate. For example, reducing "greenhouse gas" (GHG) emissions is fundamental to arresting predicted increases in average global temperature, and one of the main commitments made by parties to the Kyoto Protocol. However, there are difficulties in estimating the costs and/or benefits to society from cutbacks in GHG emissions. Controversy also envelops the impact that GHG emission cutbacks may have on individual economies. The latter is one particular line of argument taken by the current US administration, who argue that the costs of Kyoto would be prohibitively high, and would represent "the difference between robust [economic growth] and a recession" (The Royal Institute of International Affairs 2001).

The IPCC (2001) has recently summarized results from many sectoral studies, largely at the project, national, and regional level, with some at the global level, providing cost estimates of potential GHG emission reductions in 2010 and 2020. While these emission reductions take account of potential overlaps between and within sectors and technologies, it is important to recognize that the range of emissions reductions reported "reflect the uncertainties of the underlying studies on which they are based" (IPCC, WGIII, Summary for Policymakers, p. 4). Half of the potential emissions reductions in Table 5.3 may be achieved by 2020 with direct benefits (energy saved) exceeding direct costs (net capital, operating, and maintenance costs), and the other half at a net direct cost of up to US$ 100/tC$_{eq}$ (at 1998 prices).

Whilst there are costs associated with the reduction of GHG emissions, these reductions are also likely to generate health benefits. For example, Davis *et al.* (2000) produced an analysis of the ancillary benefits of GHG mitigation. They calculate that controlling air pollution from fossil fuel combustion in the United States of America might result in an annual reduction in the number of air pollution-related deaths equivalent to the number of deaths that currently occur as a result of traffic accidents or HIV. On a global scale such reductions in air pollution, tied with mitigating GHG, could reduce 4–12 million excess deaths by 2020. Davis *et al.* (2000) provide evidence on monetary values (which considers the benefits and costs), and cite the most recent analysis of the benefits and costs of air quality legislation in the United States of America ("The Benefits and Cost of the Clean Air Act Amendments of 1990"). This analysis indicated that the reductions in premature mortality (due to air pollution) are valued at US$ 100 billion annually out of US$ 120 billion in total benefits, compared to costs of about US$ 20 billion (Davis *et al.* 2000, p.153). Such analysis would suggest that the more developed richer nations, like the United States of America, should reduce their GHG emissions if not for the benefit of other less wealthy and less able nations, then at least as a matter of self-interest.

Table 5.3 Estimates of potential global GHG emission reductions in 2010 and in 2020

Sector	Potential emission reductions in 2010 (MtC_{eq}/year)	Potential emission reductions in 2020 (MtC_{eq}/year)	Net direct costs per tonne of carbon avoided
Buildings CO_2 only	700–750	1000–1100	Most reductions are available at negative net direct costs
Transport CO_2 only	100–300	300–700	Most studies indicate net direct costs less than $25/tC but two suggest net direct costs will exceed $50/tC
Industry CO_2 only -energy efficiency: -material efficiency:	300–500 ~200	700–900 ~600	More than half available at net negative direct costs Costs are uncertain
Industry, Non-CO_2 only	~100	~100	N_2O emissions reduction costs are $0–10/$tC_{eq}$
Agriculture Non-CO_2 only	150–300	350–750	Most reductions will cost between $0–10/$tC_{eq}$ with limited opportunities for negative net direct cost options
Waste CH_4 only	~200	~200	About 75% of the savings as methane recovery from landfills at negative direct cost; 25% at a cost of $20/$tC_{eq}$
Montreal Protocol replacement applications Non-CO_2 only	~200	Not available	About half of reductions due to difference in study baseline and Special Report on Emissions Scenarios baseline values. Remaining half of the reductions available at net direct costs below $200/$tC_{eq}$
Energy supply and conversion CO_2 only	50–150	350–700	Limited net negative direct cost options exist; many options are available for less than $100/$tC_{eq}$
Total	1,900–2,600	3,600–5,050	

Source: Adapted from IPCC WGIII Summary for Policymakers (2001, p.14)

5.5 Politics and economics of environmental "husbandry"

At a global level, where there is no government, the key question to be addressed is how the biophysical environment as a GPG is to be managed to support population health for present and future generations. Many challenges face policymakers trying to preserve GPGs, including their provisioning, financing, and political dimensions. This section considers major political and economic factors of importance.

5.5.1 Politics of environmental "husbandry"

The development of global efforts to monitor, protect and restore the global environment mirrors (though with a lag) the emergence of attempts at global governance, evidenced by the League of Nations and the United Nations. It has been greatly assisted by science, including the growing understanding of the interrelatedness of Earth's biological, chemical, and physical processes, and by satellite technology, which has transformed both the global monitoring database and public perceptions of the planet (Lovelock 1988, Schellnhuber 1999).

Concern for what we now recognize as environmental GPGs accelerated in the 1960s (Carson 1962, Ehrlich 1968, Mooney and Ehrlich 1997) and led to the first United Nations Global Environment Conference, held in Stockholm in 1972. The subsequent Limits to Growth debate (Meadows *et al.* 1974) and various reports to the Club of Rome (Mesarovic and Pestel 1974) attracted intense public interest. The oil shock of the early 1970s strengthened interest in renewable energy sources, to reduce Western dependence on imported oil. In the 1980s, formal concerns over global environment changes emerged, impelled principally by confirmation of stratospheric ozone depletion—continuously monitored by satellite since 1978— and renewed concern over global warming (WCED 1987). In 1992 the "Earth Summit" in Rio de Janeiro drew numerous heads of state and thousands of activists in an effort to save the planet. The 1990s were forecast by optimists as the "environmental decade."

Lack of space precludes more than a sketch of subsequent events. The last decade has seen an encouraging increase in global public awareness of the importance and fragility of many aspects of the global environment, but incommensurate ability to translate this into effective action. The inability of Al Gore, author of "Earth in the Balance" (Gore 1992), to bring about genuine environmental reform during his 8 years as US Vice President encapsulates this paradox, as does the collapse of the recent round of climate change negotiations, in the Hague (Dickson 2000). The causes are clearly complex (McMichael *et al.* 1999*b*, Butler 2000*a*).

However, despite the recent rejection of the Kyoto Protocol by the new US government, hope remains. This rejection enhanced public awareness of climate change in many countries, in both the First and Third Worlds, and the Bush administration may be forced to reconsider its position if allies can bring sufficient pressure to bear. There are hopes that public concern outside the United States will accelerate the process of signature and ratification of the Kyoto Protocol, even without immediate US participation.

The Kyoto Protocol targets are widely recognized as inadequate for stabilizing GHG concentrations (Bolin 1998). A key reason for US rejection of the Kyoto Protocol is its perception that low-income countries, allowed under the Protocol to increase their GHG emissions, are "free-riders"—an argument not supported by evidence. The United States, with only 4 percent of the global population, emits as much as 25 percent of the annual total GHG burden; on a cumulative basis, the United States has emitted far more than even this high proportion over the last century. The United States has used these emissions not only to ensure a high living standard for many of its current citizens, but to develop its industrial and military capacity. A clever marketing campaign, allied with rapid adoption of the Kyoto Protocol by the other high-income Annex 1 countries, may embarrass, cajole, and ultimately help to galvanize a US public, which still remains largely uneducated and uncertain about the reality and risks of climate change.

This is not necessarily utopian. This pressure could be magnified by forces even more potent than national pride, which may be about to emerge within US policy, and lead to a similar outcome. These are the twin issues of US security and US living standards. Paul O'Neill, erstwhile treasury secretary in the Bush administration, is on record as warning, concerning climate change, that "a real danger to civilisation is that . . . we don't do anything for 10 years" (Haimson 2001).

Recently, echoing some of the arguments expressed herein, an editorial in the New York Times warned that environmental change, water shortages, and third world poverty pose a risk to US security (January 29, 2001). The 11th September attacks in the US give additional credence to these warnings. Voices are increasingly emerging in the United States (Friedman 2001, Lewis 2001) arguing that a fairer world is also a safer world. The British Prime Minister has also recently argued this (Blair 2001).

5.5.2 Economics of environmental "husbandry"

Analysts of the current climate change impasse point to the excessive influence within US policymakers, of "cornucopian" economists, such as the late Julian Simon (Simon 1981, Simon and Kahn 1984), and conservative think tanks (Beder 1998). These policies were particularly effective in reducing US concern and action regarding development and population growth in low-income countries. Simon and his supporters argued that human beings—even those who are functionally and intellectually impaired by desperate poverty, illiteracy, micronutrient-deficiency, and contamination by environmental pollutants such as lead—are an "ultimate resource" who can, and will, generate successful solutions to their plight. Simon and his supporters also argued that global environmental risks were grossly exaggerated. Absurd as Simon's arguments appear to ecologists, environmentalists, and human rights activists, we suggest that they helped to enable the recent, largely *laissez faire* US foreign policy approach to population growth in the Third World.

Simon's arguments represent a form of intellectual permission, justifying the comparative abandonment of the world's poor with the retention of a clear conscience.

The emerging field of ecological economics, which bridges the divide between economics and the physical sciences (Dasgupta 1996, Wilson 1998), must become more mainstream. Economic forecasts and analysis, including the risks from climate change (Nordhaus 1991), are only as good as their assumptions (Costanza 1997). Once policymakers grasp the scale of the risk being taken we are confident that economic projections will become favorable. The principles of ecological economics already demonstrate that "full cost" accounting will help to make many environmentally sustainable technologies competitive (Daly 1991, 1996). Economies of scale will further help to lower the costs of sustainable technologies. For example, cars powered by fuel cells manufactured using GHG-neutral energy, such as geothermal (Pearce 1999), solar, or hydro-electric, will be far cheaper to run than those fueled by oil, once harm to the GPG status of the climate is properly factored in.

Low-income countries, not yet encumbered with expensive, fixed, and long-lived carbon-intensive power stations can cost-effectively "leapfrog" (Reddy and Goldemberg 1990) from animal to solar power. It is vital, however, that aid to the Third World does not end with technology, though, by its ability to facilitate communication, this will also improve education, information, and accelerate the demographic transition. Despite an aversion by many sectors, including environmentalists, to consider this issue, there is no doubt that the maximum size of the forecast human populations in low-income countries is a vital strategic issue, including for the powerful countries of the North. This is not principally because impoverished populations in the South continue to drive large numbers of refugees to the North, but mainly because of the cumulative damage to GPG that large populations cause, even if their per capita impact is small.

Even an effort on the scale of a global Marshal Plan (Gore 1992) will not guarantee success. Regional food insecurity, ongoing ecosystem system decline—even at a slower rate—and inertial effects in both the atmospheric concentration of GHG and the broader climatic system ensure that risks of civilization failure, due to the erosion of GPGH, will remain for at least another century (Butler 2000b). However, the strategies described here, because of their emphasis on cooperation, are likely to make an environmentally imperilled world far safer and more tolerable than the current global economic and political direction can.

Economic historians identify an oscillation between poles of capitalism, characterized by different degrees of co-operation and competition (Hirschman 1982, Gray 1999, Szreter 1999). There is increasing evidence, from both game theory and evolutionary biology (Dugatkin 1999, de Waal and Berger 2000, Field et al. 2000, Wedekind and Milinsky 2000), that a form of diluted marketism, with a mixture of competition and co-operation, is more consistent with evolutionary principles than undiluted competition. This rediscovery of the value of cooperation undermines the conceit of "homo economicus," used by supporters of marketism to privilege the pursuit of individual selfishness (Nowak and Sigmund 2000).

The simplistic view that humans are primarily selfish—and that this inevitably leads to the maximization of total economic gain—may have arisen from a misunderstanding of evolutionary theory, as well as of Adam Smith's "invisible hand" (Schlefer 1998). In fact, "survival of the fittest" might more properly be considered "survival of the fittest population," among populations distinguished by greater or lesser degrees of cooperation, while Smith warned of the dangers of monopolization and the risk of social degradation from the pursuit of profit for its own sake.

Both the Ultimatum Game and the Prisoner's Dilemma (Nowak *et al.* 2000) illustrate how self-interest is improved by cooperation, a principle understood intuitively by every pack and herd animal. While it is clear that human progress has also been facilitated by the ability of individuals and groups to take risks, to deceive,[3] and to occasionally "free ride", such behavior is unlikely to be rewarded for long unless any gains are shared (Bowles and Gintis 2002).

Not only general economic benefits, but crucial environmental GPGH have been harmed by the behavior of a comparatively small population of wealthy free riders. This has occurred because: (i) the damaged GPG remain largely hidden; (ii) the corollary of a world view of isolated nation states is that environmental threats remain primarily local; and (iii) of a continued belief in the alleged advantages of an economic system based upon "homo economicus" disguises the social harm that has occurred. As discussed, developing countries have been labeled as free riding by some Annex 1 countries, particularly the United States. The success of this perverse strategy depends on a very narrow view of environmental GPG. The loosening of national identity that globalization promises may help a better understanding of humanity's common dependence upon environmental GPG and to uncover strategies to escape the current zero sum game. In other words, both wealthy and poor populations may come to realize that both are prisoners, and that greater cooperation will be of mutual benefit.

We also anticipate a swing toward cooperation, based not on "altruism" as generally defined, but self-interest. Humans are well adapted to endorse such a strategy. Extreme adherence to unrestrained market principles has contributed to the epidemic of BSE ("mad cow" disease), the manipulation of Californian electricity prices by the failed energy company Enron, and the corruption of advisers such as accountancy firms and stock-market analysts. It has also intensified global inequality (Butler *et al.* 2001). Clearly, faith in the unrestrained market is not justified by its results. In other words, a blend of cooperation and selfishness, with human behavior encouraged to preserve, rather than destroy, environmental GPGs, is far more likely to be successful than the current, largely *laissez faire* approach (Ridley and Low 1993). The recognition of environmental GPGs, once widely disseminated, will provide a powerful lever for their protection, by increasing self-interested public demand for their preservation.

---

[3] Such behavior is not confined to humans (Dugatkin 1999, Emery and Clayton 2001).

For the present, growth in this demand is not only hampered by ignorance of the risks, but by the tendency to prefer smaller, immediate, and tangible rewards over those that are deferred and more conceptual, even if larger (Fehr 2002). This characteristic can be overcome by the use of legal codes and penalties, enforced through international treaties, just as enforced rules have been used to prevent past "tragedies of the common" (Buck 1985). Economic incentives can be used to protect tropical forests in poor countries, using the clean development mechanism (CDM) proposed under the Kyoto Protocol. This would lead to the transfer of funds from wealthy to poor countries, in exchange for a carbon credit, allowing the wealthy population to continue to produce excess GHG emissions. Provided the funds transferred are sufficient, this would compensate the poor country for its foregone logging opportunity, and maintain the local and global environmental public goods embedded in the forest (Kremen *et al.* 2000). Such a win–win scenario is only plausible if wealthy countries can be convinced that the transfer of funds is economically sensible.

Private-sector signals have important roles to play in the transition to sustainability. The progressive withdrawal of most of the world's leading car and energy companies from the Global Climate Coalition—a once influential conservative business consortium that denied the science of climate change—has been followed by many of these same companies jostling for environmental leadership and future market share by developing hybrid and hydrogen cars, and going "beyond petroleum" (Gelbspan 2000). The Dow Jones sustainability index, launched in 1999, seeks to reward companies that develop environmentally benign technologies, as do ethical investments and consumer boycotts (Hay 2002). While still comparatively small, these forces may be approaching "tipping points" beyond which industry, market and consumer behavior will change radically (Raskin *et al.* 2002).

Given sufficient demand by an informed and concerned public, supported by a mature and influential ecological economics discipline, even an organization as resistant to environmental concerns as the World Trade Organization could be transformed to one that promotes the protection of environmental GPG, for example by framing and enforcing uniform carbon taxes on traded goods. Similarly, the United Nations, though marred since its inception by the self-interest of its various constituent blocks, is the logical forum to debate and develop institutions for global environmental protection (Hawken *et al.* 1999).

While some scholars argue that this depends on wealthy populations accepting a form of global environmental governance, we argue that GPGH, at least in this century, will more plausibly be protected by a concerted campaign led by wealthy nations. The adoption of the treaties governing the production of ozone depleting substances and the banning of atmospheric nuclear weapons tests shows that this is possible without formal global governance.

Finally, it is important to emphasize that the complexity of these large-scale environmental issues means that there is inevitably a hierarchy of uncertainties that bear on scientific assessments and policy decision-making. It is for this reason that there is an emerging accommodation with the ideas of the Precautionary

Principle as a means of decision-making in situations of uncertainty and potentially great future risk. The adoption of this principle in the international decision-making process is necessary if we are to solve the huge challenge of curbing global climate change in time to avert serious damage to the global environment and serious risk to human wellbeing and health.

5.6 **Conclusion and recommendations**

Recognition and discussion of environmental GPGH presents a paradox: they are much easier to recognize when they start to lose their pure public good status through declining quality and accessibility. Until their deterioration (or partial "privatization"), they are taken for granted. However, what illumination does the GPGH analysis offer? A recent presentation by the former chairman of the UN Framework Convention on Climate Change (UNFCC) might provide some guidance (Watson 2000).

First, the focus upon temporal (i.e. generational), as well as geographical, populations makes it clear that policymakers are obliged to respond to the long-term risks posed by anthropogenic GHG emissions and other long-acting environmental change agents (Ceballos and Ehrlich 2002). Although uncertainty complicates matters, it should not preclude preparations to cope with adverse climate change scenarios and to protect against potentially costly future outcomes. Decisions taken now limit future policy options; for example, high near-term GHG emissions will necessitate deeper future reductions to meet any given GHG concentration target. Delayed action might reduce the overall costs of mitigation because of future technological advances, but risks increasing the rate and eventual magnitude of climate change, and hence the adaptation and damage costs. Delay is likely to impair future capacity to deal with climate-change-related adversity and to increase the possibility of costly and even irreversible consequences. Actions which mitigate or help to adapt to climate change, and which can be justified for other reasons are particularly desirable.

Second, the GPGH concept recognizes the principle of differentiated responsibilities, as does the UNFCC. High-income countries, and countries with economies in transition, should take the lead in limiting their GHG gas emissions, taking account of their historical and current GHG emissions and their current financial, technical, and institutional capabilities. GHG emissions by developing countries are currently much lower, both in absolute and per capita terms, than industrialized countries. Even though, as well recognized, emissions from developing countries are increasing rapidly and are likely to surpass those from wealthier countries within a few decades (in absolute terms, not per-capita), the contribution of the South to global warming will not equal that of the North until nearly 2100—since the climate system responds to the cumulative, not annual, emissions of greenhouse gases.

Many crucial environmental GPGH are already damaged. Increasing scientific understanding indicates that most will decline further in coming decades

(Flannery 1994). As well, future surprises can be expected, some of which are likely to further damage GPG. Some will occur as interactions between existing elements of the Earth system; some may be totally novel (Lawton 2001). A deepening of global democracy, strengthened by a fairer distribution of information, including a less commercialized media, may impel another vital component of the earth system—humanity—to self-organize in ways to protect the GPG upon which civilization depends.

A key mechanism in this will be the widening global franchise resulting from increasing educational and economic opportunities to the population of the South. This population will be increasingly able to persuade reluctant politicians to exchange their perceived self-interest with a longer-term vision, in which the preservation of environmental GPG for health takes a high priority. A shift away from marketism (Gray 1999) and a wider appreciation of ecological economics (Daly 1996, Gardner 2001) will also accelerate the sustainability transition. WHO, in concert with other international bodies, environmental and development NGOs, and corporations developing the necessary transitional technologies, has a vital role in mobilizing global public opinion (McMichael *et al.* 2000). It needs to devote as much, or more, attention to this topic as to any other. It will find many allies.

References

Beder S. *Global Spin: The Corporate Assault on Environmentalism.* Melbourne: Scribe Publications, 1998.

Blair A. Speech to the Labour Party conference (4.10.01) http://www.smh.com.au/news/webdiary/2001/10/04/FFX7UQ9GDSC.html 6.10.01, 2001.

Bolin B. The Kyoto Negotiations on climate change: A science perspective. *Science* 1998; **279**: 330–1.

Bouma M, Kovats RS, Goubet SA, Cox JS, Haines A. Global assessment of El Niño's disaster burden. *Lancet* 1997; **350**: 1435–8.

Bowles S, Gintis H. Homo reciprocans. *Nature* 2002; **415**: 125–8.

Buck SJ. No tragedy on the commons. *Environ Ethics* 1985; **7**(Spring): 49–61.

Butler CD. Inequality, global change and the sustainability of civilisation. *Glob Change Hum Health* 2000*a*; **1**(2): 156–72.

Butler CD. Entrapment: global ecological and/or local demographic? Reflections upon reading the BMJ's "six billion day" special issue. *Ecosys Health* 2000*b*; **6**(3): 171–80.

Butler CD. Epidemiology, Australians and global environmental change. *Aust Epidemiol* 2001; **8**(1): 13–16.

Butler CD, Douglas RM, McMichael AJ. Globalisation and Environmental Change: implications for Health and Health Inequalities. In: R Eckersley, J Dixon, R Douglas (eds.) *The Social Origins of Health and Wellbeing,* Cambridge, Cambridge University Press, pp. 34–50.

Carson R. *Silent Spring.* Boston, Houghton Mifflin, 1962.

Ceballos G, Ehrlich PR. Mammal population losses and the extinction crisis. *Science* 2002; **296**: 904–7.

Chapin III FSI, Zavaleta ES, Eviner VT *et al.* Causes, consequences and ethics of biodiversity. *Nature* 2000; **405**: 234–42.

Costanza R. Review of: Climate Change 1995: economic and social dimensions of climate change. In: James P. Bruce, Hoesung Lee, Erik. F. Haites (eds). *Ecol Econom* 1997; **23**: 75–7.

Costanza R, d'Arge R, Groot R *et al.* The value of the world's ecosystem services and natural capital. *Nature* 1997; **387**: 253–60.

Daily GC. (ed.) *Nature's Services: Societal Dependence on Natural Ecosystems.* Washington DC: Island Press, 1997.

Daly HE. From Empty-World Economics To Full World Economics: Recognising An Historical Turning Point In Economic Development. In: R Goodland, H Daly, SE Serafy, R Costanza (eds). *Economically Viable Sustainable Development—Building upon Brundtland.* UNESCO/World Bank, 1991.

Daly HE. *Beyond Growth.* Boston: Beacon, 1996.

Dasgupta P. The economics of the environment. *Proc Br Acad* 1996; **90**: 165–221.

Davis D, Krupnick A, Thurston G. The Ancillary Health Benefits and Costs of GHG Mitigation: Scope, Scale, and Credibility. In: *Ancillary Benefits and Costs of Greenhouse Gas Mitigation, OECD, Proceedings of an IPCC Co-Sponsored Workshop*, March 27–29, 2000, Washington DC 2000.

de Waal FBM, Berger ML. Payment for labour in monkeys. *Nature* 2000; **404**: 563.

Diamond J. *Guns, Germs and Steel.* London: Jonathan Cape, 1997.

Dickson D. Deadlock in The Hague, but hopes remain for spring climate deal. *Nature* 2000; **408**: 503–4.

Dugatkin L. *Cheating Monkeys and Citizen Bees: The Nature of Co-operation in Animals and Humans.* Cambridge, Massachusetts, Harvard University Press, 1999.

Easterling DR, Meehl GA, Parmesan C, Changnon SA, Karl TR, Mearns LO. Climate extremes: observations, modelling, and impacts. *Science* 2000; **289**: 2068–74.

Ehrlich PR. *The Population Bomb.* New York: Ballantyne, 1968.

El Betagy A. Strategic options for alleviating conflicts over water in dry areas. In: *Food, Water and War. Security in a World of Conflict*, Canberra: Australian Centre for International Agricultural Research, 2000; pp. 67–82.

Emery NJ, Clayton N. Effects of experience and social context on prospective caching strategies by scrub jays. *Nature* 2001; **414**: 443–6.

Fenwick A, Cheesmond AK, Amin MA. The role of field irrigation canals in the transmission of Schistosoma mansoni in the Gezira Scheme, Sudan. *Bull World Health Organ* 1981; **59**: 777–86.

Farman JC, Gardiner BG, Shanklin JD. Large losses of total ozone in Antarctica reveal seasonal ClOx /NOx interaction. *Nature* 1985; **315**: 207–10.

Fehr R. The economics of impatience. *Nature* 2002; **415**: 269–72.

Field CB, Behrenfeld MJ, Randerson JT, Falkowski P. Primary production of the biosphere: integrating terrestrial and oceanic components. *Science* 1998; **281**: 237–40.

Field G, Shreeves G, Sumner S, Casiraghi M. Insurance-based advantage to helpers in a tropical hover wasp. *Nature* 2000; **404**: 869–20.

Flannery TF. *The Future Eaters*. Melbourne: Reed Books, 1994.

Friedman TL. A tweezer defense shield? New York Times 19.10.01 http://www.nytimes.com/2001/10/19/opinion/19FRIE.html?todaysheadlines 19.10.01, 2001.

Gardner G. Accelerating the shift to sustainability. In: L Starke (ed.) *State of the World 2001*, New York, WW Norton, 2001; pp. 189–206.

Gelbspan R. Help Me, I'm Melting! Grist Magazine 2000. (Online environmental magazine). http://www.gristmagazine.com/grist/maindish/gelgspan 092900.

Gillespie A, Burns WC. (eds). *Climate Change in the South Pacific: Impacts and Responses in Australia, New Zealand, and Small Island States*. Dordrecht, Boston, and London: Kluwer Academic Publishers, 2000.

Gleick PH. *The World's Water, The Biennial Report on Freshwater Resources*. Washington DC: Island Press 2000.

Gleick PH. Safeguarding our water: making every drop count. *Sci Am* 2001; **284**(2): 28–33.

Gore A. *Earth in the Balance*. Boston, Houghton Mifflin, 1992.

Gray J. *False Dawn. The Delusions of Global Capital*. London, Granta, 1999.

Haimson L. The five biggest climate stories of 2000. Grist http://www.gristmagazine.com/grist/heatbeat/thisjustin011101.stm 12.1.01, 2001.

Hawken P, Lovins AB, Lovims LH. *Natural Capitalism: Creating the Next Industrial Revolution*. Boston: Little Brown & Company, 1999.

Hay A. Ethical activists buy stocks to force change http://www.planetark.org/dailynewsstory.cfm/newsid/14746/story.htm 27.2.02, 2002.

Hirschman AO. Rival interpretations of market society. *J Econ Lit* 1982; **20**: 1463–84.

Homer-Dixon TF. Environmental scarcities and violent conflict: Evidence from cases. *Int Security* 1994; **19**(1): 5–40.

Homer-Dixon TF. *Environment, Scarcity, and Violence*. Princeton, New Jersey: Princeton University Press, 1999.

Homer-Dixon TF, Boutwel JH, Rathjens GW. Environmental change and violent conflict. *Sci Am* 1993; **268**(2): 16–23.

Hutchings JA. Collapse and recovery of marine fishes. *Nature* 2000 **406**: 882–5.

Intergovernmental Panel on Climate Change (IPCC). *Second Assessment Report. Climate Change 1995 (Vols. I, II, III)*. Cambridge: Cambridge University Press, 1996.

Intergovernmental Panel on Climate Change (IPCC). *Third Assessment Report*. Cambridge: Cambridge University Press, 2001.

John TJ. Emerging and re-emerging bacterial pathogens in India. *Indian Journal of Medical Research* 1996; **103**: 4–18.

Kaul I, Grunberg I, Stern MA. *Global Public Goods: International Cooperation in the 21st Century*. Oxford University Press, New York, 1999.

Kremen C, Niles JO, Dalton MG *et al*. Economic incentives for rain forest conservation across scales. *Science* 2000; **288**: 1828–32.

Lawton J. Earth system science [editorial]. *Science* 2001; **292**: 1965.

Levitus S, Antonov JI, Boyer TP, Stephens C. Warming of the World Ocean. *Science* 2000; **287**: 2225–9.

Lewis A. The inescapable world New York Times 20.10.01, http://www.nytimes.com/2001/10/20/opinion/20LEWI.html?todaysheadlines 21.10.01, 2001.

Lindgren E, Gustafson R. Tick-borne encephalitis in Sweden and climate change. *Lancet* 2001; **358**: 16–18.

Loh J, Randers J, MacGillivray A *et al*. *Living Planet Report*. Gland, Switzerland: WWF International, New Economics Foundation, World Conservation Monitoring Centre, 1998.

Longstreth J, de Gruijl FR, Kripke ML *et al*. Health risks. *J Photochem Photobiol B: Biol* 1988; **46**: 20–39.

Lovelock J. *The Ages of Gaia. A Biography of our Living Earth*. Oxford: Oxford University Press, 1988.

Martens WJM, Kovats RS, Nijhof S *et al*. Climate change and future populations at risk of malaria. *Global Environ Change* 1999; **9** (Suppl.): S89–107.

McKenzie R, Connor B, Bodeker G. Increased summertime UV radiation in New Zealand in response to ozone loss. *Science* 1999; **285**: 1709–11.

McMichael AJ, Haines A. Global climate change: The potential effects on health. *BMJ* 1997; **315**: 805–9.

McMichael AJ, Kovats RS, Martens WJM, Nijhof S, de Vries P, Livermore M. Comparative scenarios of climate change and health: Modelling future patterns of malaria and thermal stress. In: G Jenkins (ed.) *Global Climate Change and Its Impacts*. London: Department of Environment and Bracknell: Hadley Centre for Meteorological Research, 1999*a*.

McMichael AJ, Guillebaud J, King M. Contrasting views on human population growth. One wisdom justifies complacency: the other demands action now [editorial]. *BMJ* 1999*b*; **319**: 931–932.

McMichael AJ, Smith KR, Corvalan CF. The sustainability transition: a new challenge [editorial]. *Bull World Health Organ* 2000; **78**(9): 1067.

McNeill JR. *Something New Under the Sun. An Environmental History of the Twentieth-Century World*, New York: Norton, 2000, pp.162–6.

Meadows D, Meadows D, Randers J, Behrens III W. *The Limits to Growth*. London: Pan, 1974.

Meltzer MI, Rigau-Perez, Clark GG, Reiter P, Gubler DJ. Using disability-adjusted life years to assess the economic impact of dengue in Puerto Rico. *American Journal of Tropical Medicine and Hygiene* 1998; **59**: 265–71.

Mesarovic M, Pestel E. *Mankind at the Turning Point*. New York: EP Dutton & Co, 1974.

Mooney HA, Ehrlich PR. Ecosystem Services: A Fragmented History. In: GC Daily (ed.) *Nature's Services: Societal Dependence on Natural Ecosystems*, Washington DC, Island Press, 1997; pp. 11–19.

Murray CJL, Lopez AD. (eds). *The Global Burden of Disease: Global Burden of Disease and Injury Series, Vol.1*. Boston: Harvard School of Public Health, Harvard University, 1996.

Myers N. Biodiversity's genetic library. In: GC Daily (ed.) *Nature's Services: Societal Dependence on Natural Ecosystems*. Washington DC, Island Press, 1997.

Neale PJ, Davis RF, Cullen JJ. Interactive effects of ozone depletion and vertical mixing on photosynthesis of Antarctic phytoplankton. *Nature* 1998; **392**: 585–9.

Nordhaus W. To slow or not to slow: the economics of the greenhouse effect. *Econ J* 1991; **101**: 920–37.

Nowak MA, Sigmund K. Shrewd investments. *Science* 2000; **288**: 819–20.

Nowak MA, Page KM, Sigmund K. Fairness versus reason in the ultimatum game. *Science* 2000; **288**: 1773–5.

O'Brien CM, Fox CJ, Planque B, Casey J. Climate variability and North Sea cod. *Nature* 2000; **404**: 142.

Parry M, Rosenzweig C, Iglesias A, Fischer G, Livermore M. Climate change and world food security: a new assessment. *Global Environ Change* 1999; **9**: S51–67.

Patz JA, Epstein PR, Burke TA, Balbus JM. Global climate change and emerging infectious diseases. *J Am Med Assoc* 1996; **275**: 217–23.

Pauly D, Christensen V, Dalsgaard J, Froese R, Torres F. Fishing Down Marine Food Webs. *Science* 1998; **279**: 860–3.

Pearce F. Iceland's power game. *New Scientist* 1999 (May 1): 20–21.

Pimentel D. Soil Erosion and the Threat to Food Security and the Environment. *Ecosyst Health* 2000; **6**: 221–6.

Pimm SL, Russell GJ, Gittleman JL, Brooks TM. The future of biodiversity. *Science* 1995; **269**: 347–54.

Raskin P, Gallopin G, Gutman P, Hammond A, Kates R, Swart R. *Great Transition: The Promise and Lure of the Times Ahead.* Boston: Stockholm Environment Institute, 2002.

Reddy AKN, Goldemberg J. Energy for the developing world. *Sci Am* 1990; **263**(3): 63–72.

Redman CL. *Human Impact on Ancient Environments.* Tucson, USA: University of Arizona Press, 1999.

Ridley M, Low BS. Can selfishness save the environment? *Atlantic Monthly* 1993; **272**(3): 76–86.

Rodriguez E. *Dengue outbreak in Puerto Rico (1994–95): Hospitalization Cost Analysis.* World Health Organization, Geneva, Switzerland 1997.

Rosenzweig C, Iglesias A, Yang XB, Epstein PR, Chivian E. Climate Change and US Agriculture: *The Impacts of Warming and Extreme Weather Events on Productivity, Plant Diseases and Pests.* Harvard Medical School, USA: Centre for Health and the Global Environment, 2000.

The Royal Institute of International Affairs. Energy and Environment Programme Meeting Report: President Bush might have done Kyoto a favour. http://www.riia.org/Research/eep/Kyotodeadreport.pdf 16.5.01, 2001.

Sandler T. *Global Challenges: An Approach to Environmental, Political and Economic Problems.* Cambridge, New York and Melbourne; Cambridge University Press, 1997; chapter 5.

Schellnhuber HJ. 'Earth system' analysis and the second Copernican revolution. *Nature* 1999; **402**: C19–C23.

Schleffer A. Today's most mischievous misquotation. *Atlantic Monthly* 1998; **281**: 16–19.

Simon JL. *The Ultimate Resource.* Oxford: Martin Robertson, 1981.

Simon JL, Kahn H. *The Resourceful Earth.* Oxford: Blackwell, 1984.

Slaper H, Velders G, Daniel JS, Gruijl FR. d, Leun JC. Estimates of ozone depletion and skin cancer incidence to examine the Vienna Convention achievements. *Nature* 1996; **384**: 256–258.

Snooks GD. *The Dynamic Society. Exploring the Sources of Global Change.* London: Routledge, 1996.

Sornmani S, Okanurak K, Indaratna, K. *Social and Economic Impact of Dengue Haemorrhagic Fever in Thailand.* Social and Economic Research Unit, Bangkok, Thailand 1995.

Szreter S. Economic growth, disruption, deprivation, disease and death: on the importance of the politics of public health. *Popul Dev Rev* 1999; **23**(4): 693–728.

Thompson LG, Yao T, Mosley-Thompson E, Davis ME, Henderson KA, Lin, P-N. A High-Resolution Millennial Record of the South Asian Monsoon form Himalayan Ice Cores. *Science* 2000; **289**: 1916–19.

United Nations Environment Programme (UNEP). *Environmental Effects of Ozone Depletion.* Lausanne, Switzerland: UN Environment Program, 1998.

United Nations Population Division Department of Economic and Social Affairs (UNPDDESA). *World Population Prospects: The 2000 Revision.* New York: United Nations, 2001.

Wackernagel M, Rees W. Our ecological footprint: Reducing Human Impact on the Earth. Gabriola Island, BC: New Society Publishers, 1996.

Watson R. Presentation to the United Nations Framework Convention on Climate Change Conference of the Parties, The Hague, 2000.

Wedekind C, Milinsky M. Co-operation through image scoring in humans. *Science* 2000; **288**: 250–252.

Wilson EO. *Consilience. The Unity of Knowledge.* New York: Alfred A Knopf, 1998.

Winters P, Murgai R, de Janvry A, Sadoulet E, Frisvold G. Climate change and agriculture: effects on developing countries. In: G., Frisvold, B. Kuhn (eds) *Global Environmental Change and Agriculture.* Cheltenham, Gloucester, Edward Elgar Publishers, 1999.

World Commission on Environment and Development (WCED). *Our Common Future.* Oxford: Oxford University Press, 1987.

World Health Organization (WHO). *Ultraviolet Radiation. Environmental Health Criteria No 160.* Geneva: WHO, 1994.

World Health Organization (WHO). *Plague-India 1994: Economic Loss.* World Health Organization, Geneva, Switzerland 1997.

World Health Organization (WHO). *Health and Environment in Sustainable Development.* Document WHO/EHG/97.8. Geneva: WHO, 1997.

World Water Commission (WWC). *A Water Secure World. Vision for Water, Life and the Environment.* The Hague, 2000.

Knowledge: The central global public good for health

Chapter 6

Medical knowledge

Jayati Ghosh

6.1 Introduction

Medical knowledge, central to the improvement of health, comprises a wide variety of elements, from the understanding of health risks, through the impact of preventive, diagnostic, curative, and palliative procedures, to the effect of different delivery systems for medical technologies. All these forms of knowledge are subject not only to public (government and non-profit organization) and commercial involvement, but often also to direct community interest in the form of "traditional" knowledge.

"Pure" knowledge, in the sense of information, wisdom or learning, has long been recognized as having characteristics which differentiate it from other "goods": once it exists, knowledge may be "consumed" by all without depletion of that knowledge "stock," and its dissemination is very hard to restrict (it is hard to stop people gaining this knowledge) (Arrow 1962). Knowledge is thus often portrayed as the "archetypal" public good (Stiglitz 1999).

However, most medical knowledge tends to be made "artificially" excludable, such as through patent laws, and/or physically excludable, through embodiment in specific products (e.g. pharmaceuticals). Further, the ability to benefit from medical knowledge often depends upon the systems designed to deliver that knowledge and the nature of the existing health and infrastructure services; issues covered further in Chapter 8 of this volume.

With advances in information technology, the increasingly rapid and widespread global dissemination of knowledge makes it important to consider whether medical knowledge comprises a "Global Public Good for Health" (GPGH), and the usefulness of this concept in improving global knowledge production, dissemination, and use. In considering these issues, this chapter focuses upon both "modern" and "traditional" medicines, as examples reflecting similar processes for other forms of medical knowledge.

Following this introduction, Section 6.2 considers the applicability of the global public good classification to (aspects of) medical knowledge. Section 6.3 discusses the production of medical knowledge, with Section 6.4 outlining issues in the dissemination and consumption of knowledge. Section 6.5 looks at strategies for promoting and financing the production, dissemination, and consumption of medical knowledge, with conclusions in Section 6.6.

6.2 **Medical knowledge as a GPGH**

As defined in Chapter 1, a "global public good" (GPG) is a good exhibiting a significant degree of "publicness" (non-rivalry and non-excludability) across a number of geographical borders. Knowledge *per se* is a public good because it is fundamentally non-rivalrous in nature, and difficult, if not impossible, to exclude from consumption. It is also one of the few public goods whose inherently global nature has never been questioned. Clearly, for example, mathematical theorems are non-rival, non-excludable, and universally applicable.

However, knowledge is usually *embodied* in forms that may be rival and/or excludable to some degree. Typically, some form of exclusion is generated through legislation or commercial product, generating a "club good": non-rival in consumption to those with access through either formal or informal (e.g. based on purchasing power) membership. Often such a "club good" approach is encouraged through legislation, to provide an incentive for commercial "production" of knowledge; resulting in "dynamic gains." However, it is also clear that there is a trade-off as "static losses" are incurred, given the characteristics of non-rivalry, through the under-utilization of knowledge (Stiglitz 1999). That is, private agents will not have the incentive to provide knowledge widely since they cannot ensure profits in this way. Public action to ensure the adequate provision of medical knowledge needs to balance these static and dynamic considerations.

In the application of the GPG concept to medical knowledge, the distinction between the production, dissemination and consumption (or end use) of medical knowledge is therefore important. As Table 6.1 illustrates with respect to several examples of medical knowledge, the GPG nature of knowledge differs according to whether one is considering the production of knowledge, its dissemination or access, and its final consumption or use.

Broadly, one can see that knowledge *production* (defined as the existence of "pure" knowledge) is non-excludable and non-rival in nature, at a global level (which, obviously, encompasses the local, national, and regional levels). However, the *dissemination* of, or access to, "pure" knowledge may be excludable or rival according to the form of that dissemination, and thus may be a club good or common pool good; often also limited to the local or national level. The *consumption*, or final use, of knowledge is predominantly excludable and rival, and thus a private good, because it is generally embodied in a physical product or service: a tablet, for example, cannot be consumed by more than one person, and can be withheld from that person until a price is paid (of course, the *effect* of that tablet may be less excludable and rival e.g. reduction in infectivity). This "private" nature of the newly embodied knowledge applies, of course, at all levels from local to global.

Table 6.1 The GPG characteristics of medical knowledge

Category of knowledge	Excludable?	Rival in consumption?	Geographical applicability
Production			
Diagnostic	No	No	Global
Preventive	No	No	Global
Curative/Palliative	No	No	Global
Delivery	No	No	Global
Dissemination			
Education/training for health professionals	Yes	Sometimes	Local/national
General access (e.g. internet)	Sometimes	No	Global
Consumption			
Access to products (e.g. drugs)	Yes	Yes	Local/national/ regional/global

Thus, the GPG characteristics of knowledge decrease as one moves from the existence of knowledge, through its dissemination, to its use. There will be specific factors important at all these levels, to encourage or discourage the production of information *per se*, as well as its dissemination and use. It is important to note that in general it is neither production nor dissemination that ensures that knowledge is valuable: it is only when the knowledge is used (consumed) that value from it is ensured, and so this is the key endpoint to be strived for. It is thus important to recognize that although the three elements are dealt with separately for analytical purposes below, in practice they are interdependent. Nevertheless, it is clear that the consumption of knowledge is largely a matter of access to private goods, and it is only in the production and dissemination of that knowledge that the GPG concept applies.

6.3 **Production of medical knowledge**

The production of medical knowledge requires investment. However, because of the non-excludability of such knowledge, there is a danger that levels of required investment (and thus levels of knowledge produced) would be socially sub-optimal, in both static and dynamic senses, if left solely to "the market."[1]

---

[1] With the possible exception, of course, of the charitable sector. However, financing of "basic" knowledge production by charitable organizations is small, as most prefer to (be seen to) invest in the application or dissemination of knowledge.

This is because third parties may "free-ride" in their use of the knowledge produced.

Given the structure of international production in this area, the major players are private industry (typically large multinational corporations), international organizations and, increasingly, civil society organizations with some amount of lobbying power. However, the key players are governments, who, singularly at the national level and occasionally jointly at the regional or global level, intervene to "solve" this failure of the market to ensure production of knowledge; typically in one or more of three ways:

1. Assignment of *property rights* over the use of knowledge, such as patent regimes and other systems of recognizing private intellectual property rights.

2. Ensuring sufficient *incentives for private investment*, through various non-property right means, such as public pre-purchase agreements.

3. Direct *public funding* and organization of medical research.

Each of these strategies is considered in more detail below.

6.3.1 **Property rights**

The incentive problem facing private investment in the production of knowledge is typically dealt with through the assignment of private rights (e.g. patent regimes) to generate (temporary) monopoly profits. However, in addition to the higher than socially optimal prices that result (which is a known and accepted trade-off to encourage the investment) this leads to the research agenda being set by private industry, which is influenced by interests of commercial profitability rather than social need.

Within the global arena, there have been particular concerns relating to the implementation of the World Trade Organization Agreement on Trade-Related Aspects of Intellectual Property Rights (TRIPS), with respect to drug patents in particular, and growing recognition that such a regime may not be quite the GPG its protagonists would suppose (see also Chapter 10 in this volume for more discussion of TRIPS and GPGH). Concerns about the enforcement of the TRIPS agreement emerge particularly with reference to health conditions in developing countries, since the agreement is seen as increasing the power of large corporations who may be in a position to capture patents, *vis-à-vis* state regulatory authorities. Some of the most frequently expressed concerns are that:

1. Increased patent protection leads to both higher drug prices and fewer drugs of importance from a public health perspective (e.g. emphasis on "lifestyle" drugs).

2. TRIPS will not reduce the access gap between developed and developing countries, and between rich and poor within countries, especially as producers in developing countries have to wait 20 years before they can have access to knowledge to produce a local affordable generic version.

3. The shift from process to product patents in certain developing countries will have adverse effects on local manufacturing capacity and remove a source of generic innovative quality drugs on which the poorer countries depend.

Growing public concern about these effects of TRIPS prompted the WTO Doha Declaration of December 2001 on TRIPS and Public Health. While this did not provide legally binding commitments, and is therefore a political rather than legal document, it still provides a framework for dealing with the use of the TRIPS agreement by large companies in the developed world, especially in matters relating to public health. Similarly, while it is still vague about the possibilities for export of cheaper drugs produced using compulsory licensing, it leaves open the possibility that this can be decided positively by the TRIPS Council. Thus, it emphasized that: each member country has the right to grant compulsory licences and the freedom to determine the grounds upon which such licences are granted; and each member country has the right to determine what constitutes a national emergency or other circumstance of extreme urgency.

However, there are still many changes that may make the TRIPS agreement more open to meeting global public health concerns, and avoid the exclusion that currently faces producers of medicines. For example, revision of Article 27.1 in order to exclude the patentability of "essential medicines" listed by the World Health Organization (WHO), revision of Article 30 to incorporate an explicit recognition of an "early working" exception for the approval of generic products before the expiration of a patent, and revision of Article 31 in order to clarify the right to grant compulsory licenses for public health reasons.

This form of intervention through property rights, while it provides incentives to private players, may reduce the ability of governments to meet public health goals and ensure wider public access to knowledge. This in turn may conflict with other economic objectives of governments where such private players are large employers and contribute substantially to national income. In addition, incentives to particular private players may become constraints on the knowledge-development ability of other private players, leading to dynamic losses. Or they may create social/political tensions, highlighted by civil society organizations.

6.3.2 Incentives for private investment

Rather than develop property-rights to "solve" the question of non-excludability causing market failure in the production of knowledge, other fiscal incentives (e.g. tax breaks or subsidies) may be used to promote medical research and development. This currently occurs at the national level. For example, the US Orphan Drug Act was designed to encourage the private development of drugs for which the market may otherwise be too small for profitable commercial exploitation. It provides tax credits and exclusive marketing for a specific period as recompense for developing products used to diagnose, treat or prevent rare diseases or conditions.

The right to patents and data exclusivity becomes especially significant in these cases, when the company cannot itself claims a patentable invention. The infamous case of the drug paclitaxel (Taxol), for which the company Bristol Myers Squibb received tax benefits and exclusive marketing rights even though it contributed little to drug development, has added to the controversy surrounding the Orphan Drug Act (Love 2000). It has also led to the company attempting to establish exclusive marketing control in other countries. Thus, such legislation can lead to global monopolistic practices with respect to essential or important drugs, and can even operate to inhibit further innovation in other countries. The Taxol case has shown that national level incentives can have cross-border effects, suggesting the need to consider even such a *national* intervention from a GPG perspective, and allow for international co-ordination and monitoring of such practices.

International organizations have a role to play, both in providing incentives to private players and in preventing the misuse of such incentives. The key issue, from a *global* public goods perspective, is that such intervention(s) may not be feasible and/or desirable at the international level for a number of reasons. First, many developing country governments simply do not have the fiscal means to provide the necessary incentives for desired medical investment. This would further reinforce the problem of inadequate investment in knowledge relating to diseases of the poor. Second, because of the cross-border effects of some research, even if they can afford to, individual country governments are unlikely to spend sufficient amounts, in the form of subsidies or other incentives for private investors, to enable investment to reach the socially optimal level from a global perspective. Third, many developing countries simply do not have the infrastructure or resources to enable adequate testing of drugs to ensure safety and public knowledge of effects and side-effects, and therefore can be at a disadvantage when confronted with the superior lobbying and advertising power of multinational drug companies.

There is clearly a case, therefore, for international action to be led by pan-national organizations, such as the United Nations, WHO, and/or World Bank. But what would such "action" include? There are a variety of options currently used or proposed which would be worth considering. For example, pre-purchase agreements would ensure markets, and therefore profitability, for investment into (and subsequent manufacture of) particular drugs or diagnostic and therapeutic techniques. Alternatively, international organization-led funding for medical research could be used to bring together research teams in universities and other private laboratories based in different countries. Similarly, international level surveillance and regulation, with internationally organized testing institutions, recognized criteria for drug acceptance, and wide publication/dissemination of knowledge relating to the drugs, could also be led by such organizations.

6.3.3 Direct public investment

Over the past two decades, there has been a growing reliance on private activity in the production of knowledge. However, this has been associated with a change in research patterns, with movement toward areas of high profitability (e.g. "lifestyle" drugs) and away from areas of arguably greater social importance (e.g. prevention of infectious disease in poor countries). For example, of 1,223 new drugs developed by private industry between 1975 and 1997 only 4 were relevant to tropical diseases (Pecoul *et al.* 1999, p. 361). Further, even within diseases or treatment of more general relevance, private investment tends to focus on products that may be attractive from a commercial point of view but which add little to therapeutic innovation. Often, for example, "new" formulations are "me-too" products that imitate existing drugs rather than providing significant therapeutic improvement (t'Hoen 2000).

One cross-border implication of this "commercialization" of knowledge production is the attempt by private companies to find least-cost methods of clinical testing, which is typically one of the more expensive aspects of drug development. There is growing evidence of companies moving to undertake such tests on poorer populations in developing countries, especially in Africa and India, where, for example, regulation and surveillance standards are lower and the test subjects do not have full knowledge of the risks involved. Not only is this ethically problematic, it can also reduce the quality of the results provided, and affect populations in other countries who then take the drug so tested (Pecoul *et al.* 1999).

Finally, there are concerns that when medical research is left to private agents, the costs, especially of drug development, can be greatly exaggerated. While information about the costs of developing new drugs vary widely, and tend to be shrouded in secrecy, these unreliable estimates form the basis of important public policy decisions. As Love (2000, 2001) highlights, there can be confusion surrounding the actual costs of drug research and development because of: the extent of allowance for risk and the opportunity cost of capital; varying definitions of what is a new drug and the description of "me-too" products as completely new innovations; private agents taking credit for research expenses not actually borne by them, such as when they purchase rights to, or otherwise appropriate, the fruits of publicly funded research or traditional knowledge; and skewed samples, and therefore misleading averages of costs and expenses incurred. Some estimates suggest that, even according to the drug companies' own data, the level of R&D expenditure is not enough to warrant high monopoly prices being charged.[2]

These concerns with private sector involvement in knowledge production suggest the need for strong *international* regulatory mechanisms to control and monitor private research (the GPG aspects of such international regulatory frameworks are considered further in Chapter 9). However, they also suggest that there is a strong case for direct public involvement in knowledge production.

---

[2] One study of the nine top pharmaceutical companies in the United States of America found that eight of them spent twice as much on marketing, advertising, and administration as on R&D, and all of them made more profits than their total R&D spending (Families USA Foundation 2001).

It is important to remember, for example, that until the mid-to-late 1980s, even in the United States of America, most research was funded and conducted by governmental and quasi-governmental agencies, other public bodies and universities, rather than by corporations. Even today, much of the final research on medicines done (and patented) by private companies remains based on the research carried out by public agencies or under public funding. Indeed, there are increasing concerns that public funds have been substantially used to develop drugs or therapeutic techniques, which have subsequently been patented privately.[3] The "free rider" possibilities inherent in such mechanisms emphasize that, with increased public activity in the funding and direction of medical research, the control over such technologies would also need to remain in the public domain, in many case a global domain.

At one level this can be seen as a disincentive for private players, but if knowledge development is essentially an add-on process of steps, then ultimately it operates as an incentive to further knowledge production. This is especially clear when the links between traditional and modern medical knowledge are considered, and the extent to which much modern, private company-generated, knowledge has drawn upon the freely available wisdom of communities is recognized.

A key problem with public funding of research is, of course, that it can simply replace "market failure" with "government failure," leading to misdirection of resources for other reasons, such as the inefficient functioning of government-run laboratories and research institutions. While these may be problems at the national level, the losses associated with some possibly wasted resources are likely to be far outweighed by the benefits, in terms of increased production and access to relevant medical knowledge. Further, when considered on a global scale these problems may be less apparent. Of more relevance on the global scale is the interaction between countries in setting a research agenda for knowledge production and whether this agenda is any more reflective of the needs of the poorer nations than an agenda set by commercial enterprises reflecting demand structures in wealthy countries.

6.3.4 Traditional knowledge

"Traditional" knowledge may be defined as "a tacit type of knowledge that has evolved within the local (grassroots) community and has been passed on from one generation to another, encompasses not only local or indigenous knowledge, but also scientific and other knowledge gained from outsiders" (Rahman 2000, p. 2). It should be remembered that a significant section of the population in many

---

[3] Thus, for example, most work in gene isolation has been undertaken by public institutions using funds provided by governments and charities. However, most gene patents are in the hands of private companies who use the fruits of public research to complete the final stages of work and are more rapid in applying for patents (Sexton 2001). See also Chapter 7 on genomics.

developing countries (which could be as many as several hundred million people) still relies mainly on traditional practitioners, including traditional birth attendants, herbalists, and bonesetters, as well as local medicinal plants, to satisfy their primary health-care needs. It is therefore very much a "living" tradition in many respects, and in some instances the boundaries between it and modern medicinal practice may be hard to draw precisely.

Traditional knowledge is typically tacit, non-codified, and not clearly articulated along modern scientific lines, even though it may be very "scientific" in reasoning. It tends to be embedded in the experiences of communities, handed down across generations, and often involves intangible factors including beliefs, perspectives, and value systems. Many traditional medicine systems, including those widely prevalent in Asia (such as the acupuncture and acupressure-based systems of China, and the ayurveda and siddha systems of India) are holistic in orientation, treating the entire patient rather than addressing a symptom or disease alone, as is common in modern allopathic medical practice.

Like other knowledge, traditional knowledge can also be considered as a GPG, because it shares the non-rivalry and non-excludability features of other medical knowledge. However, the issues involved in case of traditional knowledge are in some ways more complex, simply because commercial relations and the inevitable codification that typically accompanies commerce, are much less developed. Further, since much traditional knowledge is the result of historical evolution and community understanding, rather than individual scientific or other behavior, the creation of such knowledge is not really something that has to be subject to public intervention. This is why traditional knowledge, while potentially as important from the GPG perspective, poses rather different challenges, which relate more fundamentally not to its creation, but to its dissemination and consumption.

With respect to the "production" of such knowledge, traditional systems have always relied on some degree of "commercial viability." Thus, in some traditional medical systems in China or India, such as acupuncture/acupressure or ayurveda, there is a history of (attempts at) commercialization of some products of traditional medical knowledge, and attempts have even been made to codify them over time. This suggests a substantial interest in exploiting traditional knowledge to reap at least some commercial rewards. By contrast, in other cultures, such as for some Native American communities and Australian aboriginal groups, such traditional knowledge is actively sought to be kept secret within the community in order the maintain the community's identity, and any attempt at commercialization is therefore rejected. There can be further complexity even within communities.

The key concern is that, by definition, traditional knowledge is produced within communities and based on tradition and historical legacy to a significant extent. The danger is therefore not so much that investment in such knowledge does not take place, but that existing knowledge may be lost because of insufficient demand. Here again, cross-border issues are significant, as the loss of knowledge confined to a particular community implies a loss to humanity as a whole.

Incentives to promote the development of traditional knowledge need to be thought out carefully, since the standard incentives provided to private players, such as patent rights, may not be as useful in this context. However, direct public funding and providing fiscal incentives can still be important. International bodies can play a role as well in terms on cross-border standardization that promotes wider acceptability. However, since this issue is closely tied with problems of dissemination and consumption of traditional knowledge, the problems and possible interventions are considered in more detail below.

6.4 Dissemination and consumption of medical knowledge

In the case of medicines, it is hard to distinguish the *dissemination* of knowledge from its *consumption*. That is, although dissemination is more directly focused on how the produced knowledge is made available, which may be through the drug formulation made available through the Internet, print media, formal education or training, word of mouth etc., in the case of medicines dissemination is typically within an embodied product which has to be consumed, in this case "the medicine" itself. Nonetheless, the key issue concerning the dissemination and consumption of medical knowledge is *excludability*: both from the medical knowledge itself, as a result of patent regimes or inadequate dissemination (as in the case of traditional knowledge), *and* exclusion from the products embodying such knowledge, such as pharmaceuticals (typically the latter is, of course, a result of the former). The cost of this "artificial" excludability, which may be developed to ensure the "dynamic" gain of private sector involvement in the production of knowledge, is felt in the "static" loss of less than optimal consumption of it. From a GPG perspective, there are three important factors to consider in the dissemination and production of medical knowledge.

First, differential patenting legislation creates differential consumption. The Indian Patents Act, for example, recognizes only process patents in pharmaceuticals, allowing for reverse engineering for chemical products (working out a process to manufacture using the end-product only). This patent regime, which has been in operation since the 1970s, has contributed to the major price advantage that Indian companies are able to offer, both because of the ability to engage in reverse engineering and because of the consequently more competitive nature of the domestic industry. This allows for very substantial differences in drug prices between India and other developing countries.[4] Similarly, the prohibitive cost of

---

[4] Thus, for example, drug prices in Malaysia, where the patent laws did not allow for the emergence of a vibrant domestic drug industry, were between 12 and 200 times the prices of the same drugs in India in the 1990s. Even Pakistan, a country with similar per capita income, had drug prices which were several multiples of those prevailing in India.

anti-viral drugs for treatment of HIV/AIDS in countries most affected, as a result of the market power of patent holders of such drugs, have been widely discussed (Chandrasekhar and Ghosh 2001).

Second, regardless of its production, knowledge consumption becomes a "club" good, with membership dependent on purchasing power. That is why 15 percent of the world's population accounts for 86 percent of drug spending (Pecoul *et al.* 1997). The role of such a purchasing power differential in affecting not just the development of a drug but its continued production is dramatically illustrated in the case of eflornithine (or DFMO), a treatment for sleeping sickness. This disease, transmitted by the tsetse fly, kills around 150,000 people every year, mainly in Africa. The drug is currently not produced, because of "lack of commercial opportunities." Similarly, a drug for bacterial meningitis was not produced between 1995 and 1998 because of poor profitability (that is, low incomes of those affected) despite hundreds of thousands of sufferers each year, mainly in developing countries (Pecoul *et al.* 1997). Thus, whether knowledge translates into products that can be consumed depends upon international distribution of wealth. This is not only a problem for current populations, but has significant intergenerational effects.

Third, the difficulty of ensuring even a minimum degree of access to drugs is compounded by the high degree of concentration in the international drug industry which is associated with a range of monopolistic practices, including the use of brand names to generate market power and, hence, high prices on many drugs. The issue is especially complicated because of the asymmetric information that characterizes the drug market—since consumers do not know the actual composition of the drugs they are taking they often rely on brand names to ensure quality (Chowdhury 1995). This may be warranted where other manufacturers are providing spurious combinations or cheaper substitutes, but this cannot be predetermined or claimed to be true in all cases. As a result, established manufacturers often use the advantage of the brand name to charge higher prices even when other generic manufacturers are producing the same or equivalent drugs at lower prices. Together, brand names and patents insulate drug companies from price competition. Market segmentation allows for wide variation in the price of the same drug, not only by different companies but even by the same company in different markets.

Both national governments and international organizations have to stress the importance of "access goods," required to ensure that knowledge can be accessed and, therefore, used. There are pros and cons of the various methods adopted as solutions to this problem. Information failure that is characteristic of the drug market is expensive to rectify, and especially so in developing countries, with low levels of public education. This implies that governments with limited resources may be forced to choose between expenditures promoting the production of knowledge and expenditures designed to improve dissemination and consumption. On the other hand, for private players it is not incentive provision so much as regulation and disincentives which are required, but these too can be expensive for governments. There is a major opportunity for the other important players, international organizations, and civil society organizations, to be more active in providing more information and encouraging its wider spread across potential users.

6.4.1 Dissemination and consumption of traditional knowledge

Lack of dissemination is especially important in the case of traditional knowledge, because such knowledge, especially as exists in the oral tradition or vested in particular social groups, may die out because of lack of dissemination or insufficient training of practitioners (Lama 2000). This makes the problems rather different from those associated with standard medical knowledge, where the concerns often arise out of the "clubness" of the good, and the potential for secrecy and control. It may appear that this makes the issue simpler for traditional knowledge, but in fact encouraging wider dissemination and consumption of traditional knowledge is not so straightforward, partly due, ironically, to the *lack* of commercialization.

Traditional knowledge may be difficult to adapt to large-scale, homogenized production. For example, it tends to be expressed in very individualistic patient-oriented forms of treatment, often relying on natural products, such as fresh herbs. Further, the quantity and quality of safety and efficacy data are typically far from adequate to meet the demands placed by those used to more stringent modern testing techniques. This means that there are some important processes which will be crucial to the wider dissemination of traditional medicinal products and associated knowledge, including codifying the knowledge in accessible and standardized formats, providing resources and logistical support for testing of products, ensuring some degree of standardization of dosage and quality of products, standardizing qualifications of practitioners and increasing the shelf life of traditional medical products.

However, there is a significant tension between any process of commercialization, which is clearly necessary for dissemination, and the possibility of bio-piracy (theft of traditional knowledge). Bio-piracy is most evident in the intellectual property claims made on the various fruits of traditional knowledge, which may exist in non-codified form. It is obviously problematic in terms of rights and claims of the communities involved, since it involves (arguably false) claims to novelty and invention for traditionally evolved knowledge, divests scarce biological resources to monopoly control of corporations thus depriving local communities and indigenous practitioners, and creates market monopolies and excludes the original innovators from their rightful share to local, national, and global markets (Research Foundation for Science, Technology and Ecology 2000). Further, it may also result in high prices of medical products or therapeutic forms which effectively exclude or reduce the access of large numbers of lower-income groups, and may even exclude the very communities from which the knowledge originally came.

Currently, there is no international protocol governing traditional medical knowledge, despite the Convention on Biodiversity, although one of the most commonly suggested ways in which to deal with this relates to evolving mechanisms of "benefit sharing." These tend to operate within existing international intellectual property tights regimes, by accepting not only the patentability of such knowledge but also the *desirability* of such assignment of intellectual property rights, and focusing essentially on the distribution of the gains from such rights. For example, the Mataatua Declaration (1993) suggested that a body be established with appropriate mechanisms to: preserve and monitor the commercialism or otherwise of indigenous cultural properties in the public domain; generally advise and encourage indigenous peoples to take steps to protect their cultural heritage; and allow a mandatory consultative process with respect to any new legislation affecting indigenous peoples cultural and intellectual property rights. It also suggested that, in full cooperation with indigenous peoples, an additional cultural and intellectual property rights regime be developed, incorporating: collective (as well as individual) ownership and origin—retroactive coverage of historical as well as contemporary works; protection against debasement of culturally significant items; cooperative rather than competitive framework; first beneficiaries to be the direct descendants of the traditional guardians of that knowledge; and multigenerational coverage span.

Sahai (2000) describes the effective implementation of such a strategy in the context of the leaves of the "arogyapacha" plant, traditionally eaten by the Kani tribe of the Eastern Ghats in Northern Kerala, India, which was developed as a commercial strength-giving product "Jeevani" in 1995. While transferring the technology for production of the drug to a pharmaceutical firm, it was agreed to share the licence fee on a 50 : 50 basis. In addition to this, 2 percent of royalties from sales go to the tribal community. The proceeds from this are being managed by a Trust established for the purpose, with 60 percent of Kani households represented.

However, as well as illustrating success, this example also serves to highlight the difficulties of trying to implement strategies of community benefit-sharing that rely on commercial intellectual property rights. For example, what constitutes the community? Does it relate to all the population, to its representatives or to a segment of it? Does it refer only to those who are resident in the relevant locality? How are other generations (past and future) accounted for? Then there are questions of how to ensure that monetary or financial returns are used to the benefit of the "community," however defined. Which is the best agency for this? Who decides how the money is to be spent? And in stratified communities (whether stratified on the basis of class, gender, or other social category), how can it be ensured that the benefits will be equally or democratically spread rather than concentrated among a few? Finally, there are logistical questions of how such resources are to be garnered and managed. Overall, there are formidable difficulties in assigning essentially private intellectual property rights to a community; this being possible in the case of the Kani community largely because of their small number, limited geographical spread, and relatively homogenous society.

To a substantial extent, such difficulties therefore stem from the more basic problem of the notion of private intellectual property, which runs counter to the very concept of traditional or community knowledge. Of course, all knowledge in societies rests on a bed of tradition and history of intellectual development, and even the marginal increments to knowledge that are now patented as inventions are very dependent upon this previous knowledge base. But seeking to patent the base itself inevitably creates a philosophical, and indeed practical, problem. Who exactly is to be rewarded for such knowledge? The earlier generations who developed it, the current generation who has received it and maintained it, or the future generations who will be its repository? And what if it spreads to other areas and other peoples who are not part of the original community?

It can therefore be argued that to insist on forcing traditional or community knowledge into the straitjacket of the private appropriability of the fruits of knowledge is fundamentally misguided. Rather, it may be more useful to insist on the irrelevance of all patenting in such areas, to deny the possibility of product patents for all matters relating to natural products, whether in the pharmaceutical or food industries, and to allow only process patents for the products of nature or any extensions of them. This in turn means that other forms of public intervention have to be considered, primarily of increased funding for the recording, codification, and dissemination of such knowledge and for testing along accepted principles. These discussions need to be engaged in both at national and international levels, given the strong cross-border externalities in consumption of such knowledge.

6.5 **Strategies to harness medical knowledge for GPH**

Appropriate national policies remain fundamental to ensuring that knowledge is created and made available for public benefit. However, it is apparent that many of the issues discussed above cannot be dealt with adequately by national strategies alone, especially in developing countries. Further, national policies are themselves increasingly influenced by international regimes, such as TRIPS, and by the structure of the international market for medical knowledge and products. Since the protection of public health should have primacy over commercial interests, an initial starting point is the revision to those aspects of international trade agreements and other regimes that directly, or indirectly, have implications for public health at both national and global levels. For example, changes to the TRIPS regime might include:

1. Article 27.3 (b) of the TRIPS Agreement, relating to the patenting of life-forms, should be removed or dramatically diluted.

2. Article 29 of TRIPS, which requires disclosure in the case of patent applications, should also cover all patent applications that use the fruits of traditional knowledge.

3. For all inventions based on nature—that is, plant-based pharmaceutical or food innovations—only process, not product, patents should be allowed. This will control both bio-piracy and theft of traditional knowledge, and monopolies in these product categories.

4. The possibility of patenting genes needs to be seriously reconsidered.

5. Even apart from this, special status should be given to essential health-care products with respect to their patenting for private commercial purposes.

6. The scope for compulsory licensing needs to be made wider and the use of it to prevent monopolistic practices should be encouraged rather than discouraged through the TRIPS regime. Ideally, TRIPS should contain a positive list of industries and product categories for which compulsory licensing is recommended, determined on the basis of their importance from a GPG perspective.

In addition, there are other possible global interventions (several of which require the implicit or explicit involvement of WHO and related international bodies), as outlined briefly below, with respect to production, dissemination, and consumption.

6.5.1 Interventions related to the production of medical knowledge

1. There should be global strategies to ensure the development of essential medical technology. A Global Fund for essential medical research is one important suggestion, but linking it to new taxes (as proposed in some "Tobin Tax" type proposals) may not be so useful as that could delay, and perhaps prevent, the emergence of such a Fund. Instead, the demand for such a Fund should be treated as a matter of urgency, to which resources should be allocated on priority basis.

2. Incentives such as market exclusivity for certain drugs should be discouraged as these are liable to misuse and can create global monopolies.

3. The international community should evolve explicit protocols that prohibit or prevent some governments (influenced by powerful corporate lobbies) from exerting unilateral pressure on governments of other countries, especially developing countries, to adopt legislation on patents, health care, or services that is not in the interests of public health.

4. There is a strong case for centralized international purchase funds for existing drugs or treatments known to be useful in dealing with diseases common to poor populations. Such funds (which could combine public and private donor resources in various ways) would guarantee manufacturers large sales volumes and would therefore encourage private production of certain essential drugs.

6.5.2 **Interventions related to dissemination**

1. There is need for an international body to set standards for deciding upon and monitoring drug efficacy and quality, for both modern and traditional medicinal products.

2. International resources should be allocated toward organizing, codifying, testing, and disseminating various forms of medical knowledge emanating from traditional medical systems across the world.

3. Public health systems need to be geared to greater and more rapid transmission of medical knowledge. This dominantly involves training health-care practitioners at a national level, but such activities could be supported (especially financially) at a global level. New technologies such as the Internet provide cheap and easy ways of transmitting such knowledge and should be used more extensively.

4. The general public needs to be better informed about the nature of pharmaceutical and other medical technologies it is using. Once again, using media such as the Internet to inform patents and other consumers about aspects of drugs in use and their differences, as well as in costs, is something that could be organized with a global orientation, by WHO and others.

6.5.3 **Interventions related to consumption**

1. Many drugs are currently developed primarily with public funding. Governments—especially in rich countries—should evolve policies (which could be developed in consultation with WHO) to make such drugs available to poorer groups, and to populations in poor countries, at affordable rates.

2. Reliable data on the costs of developing new drugs should be made public and the specific contributions of different agents (public and private) toward developing particular drugs should also be made generally available to the public on a regular basis. Once again, WHO could take this up.

It could be asked why governments of rich countries should concern themselves with these matters—at least to the extent to committing more resources—other than for purely altruistic reasons. The answer lies in the global nature of the effects—in terms of both positive and negative outcomes. It is not just the far greater possibility in the current world of the cross-border transmission of a range of diseases. There are also the economic losses of output and productivity that result from higher levels of morbidity in the developing world and adversely affect aggregate output and demand growth in the world economy. The need to ensure wider and more equitable access within countries stems not only from basic equity concerns but also from consideration of the possible social tensions and conflicts that may otherwise emerge. And, of course, the possibility of civil society organizations improving their lobbying power to force governments, international organizations and private players to change their strategies, must also be recognized.

6.6 **Conclusion**

The GPG perspective is vital in the analysis of the production, dissemination, and consumption of medical knowledge. The public good characteristics of knowledge mean that it cannot be left to the market alone (because it would then be below socially desired levels). Further, since many of the positive and negative effects of investment in knowledge are cross-border in nature, even individual governments need not intervene to the extent that is socially desirable, and there is clearly a case for coordinated joint action or intervention by international bodies, such as WHO.

However, although some of the possible interventions were outlined above, there is a significant research agenda to be developed, concerning the existing problems and possible solutions in this area. For example, some key issues concern:

- The nature of medical innovation itself, and the degree to which it is actually influenced by the extent of private appropriability (do patents actually encourage more innovation?).

- The role played by international monopolies—both public and private—in limiting access to innovation and knowledge, and particularly access in developing countries.

- The experience of international regulation in other areas, and the lessons they can provide for international cooperation and joint regulation in this area.

- The extent to which varying national standards of medical regulation and control spill over in terms of cross-border effects on the efficacy of disease control.

- The scope for new international incentives for developing and disseminating the fruits of traditional knowledge.

Clearly, therefore, this is an important area with much scope for more relevant work and especially for a focus on more creative design of new forms of public intervention.

References

Arrow K. Economic welfare and the allocation of resources for innovation. In: Nelson D (ed.) *The Rate and Direction of Inventive Activity*. New York, 1962.

Chandrasekhar CP, Ghosh J. *New Approaches to Harnessing Technological Progress for Children*. UNICEF Project on "Harnessing globalisation for children," Florence: Innocenti Research Centre, 2001.

Chowdhury Z. *The Politics of Essential Drugs: The Makings of a Successful Health Strategy—Lessons from Bangladesh*. New Delhi: Vistaar Publications. 1995.

Families USA Foundation. *Off the Charts: Pay, Profits and Spending by Drug Companies*. Washington DC, 2001.

Lama A. *Peru: Traditional Knowledge Enhances Modern Medicine*. Third World Network, available at www.twnside.org, 2000.

Love J. *How Much does it Cost to Develop a New Drug?* Consumer Project on Technology, http://www.cptech.org, 2000.

Love J. *Paying for health care R&D: Carrots and Sticks.* Consumer Project on Technology, http://www.cptech.org, 2001.

Mataatua Declaration. *The Mataatua Declaration on Cultural and Intellectual Property Rights of Indigenous Peoples.* First International Conference on the Cultural and Intellectual Property Rights of Indigenous Peoples, Whakatane, New Zealand, June 12–18, 1993.

Pecoul B, Chirac P, Trouiller P, Pinel J. Access to essential drugs in poor Countries: a lost battle? *J Am Med Assoc* 1999; **281**: 361–7.

Rahman A. *Development of an Integrated Traditional and Scientific Knowledge Base: A Mechanism for Accessing, Benefit-sharing and Documenting Traditional Knowledge for Sustainable Socio-economic Development and Poverty Alleviation.* Paper presented to UNCTAD Expert Meeting on Systems and National Experiences for Protecting Traditional Knowledge, Innovations and Practices, Geneva, 30 October–1 November, 2000.

Research Foundation for Science, Technology and Ecology. *Biotechnology Factsheet, New Delhi*, available on www.vshiva.net, 2001.

Sahai S. *Commercialisation of Indigenous Knowledge and Benefit Sharing.* Paper presented to UNCTAD Expert Meeting on Systems and National Experiences for Protecting Traditional Knowledge, Innovations and Practices, Geneva 30 October–1 November, 2000.

Sexton S. No patent, no cure. *Health Matt* 2001: 31.

Stiglitz JE. Knowledge as a global public good. In: Inge Kaul, I Grunberg, MA Stern (eds) *Global Public Goods: International Cooperation in the 21st Century*, Oxford University Press, 1999, pp. 308–25.

t'Hoen E. *Globalisation and Equitable Access to Essential Drugs.* Third World Network, available at http:www.twnside.org, 2000.

Chapter 7

Genomics knowledge

Halla Thorsteinsdóttir, Abdallah S Daar,
Richard D Smith, and Peter A Singer

7.1 Introduction

[I]t is clear that the science of genomics holds tremendous potential for improving
health globally . . . The specific challenge is how we can harness this knowledge
and have it contribute to health equity, especially among developing nations.
(Brundtland 2002)

It is clear that the increased molecular understanding of diseases and their causa-
tion will have a tremendous impact on the way we identify, prevent, diagnose,
treat, and modulate diseases in the new millennium. At the same time, a balance
has to be struck between genomics and more conventional health-care methods,
and the complex economic, social, and ethical issues of genomics dealt with. This
calls for societies to develop new norms and frameworks to ensure that the use of
genetic technologies will be secure and palatable to peoples' tastes and needs.
This involves, for example, ensuring that peoples' privacy is not violated, that the
gains of genomics are accessible to rich and poor alike, and that they are accessible
globally (WHO 2002).

However, as revolutionary as genomics may be, it nonetheless represents a progression in the tradition of advancements in the quest for *knowledge*. In essence,
genomics concerns information gathering aimed at increasing our knowledge
about health, nutrition, agriculture, forestry, and the environment. This knowledge is then available to be used creatively in the development of new diagnostic

Grant support was provided by the Program in Applied Ethics and Biotechnology
(supported by the Ontario Research and Development Challenge Fund, GlaxoSmithKline,
Merck and Co., Sun Life Financial, The University of Toronto, The Hospital for Sick
Children, Mount Sinai Hospital, Sunnybrook and Women's College Health Sciences Centre,
and the University Health Network), and the Canadian Program on Genomics and Global
Health (supported by Genome Canada). PAS is supported by an Investigator award from the
Canadian Institutes of Health Research.

technologies, treatments, and preventive programs. Yet "knowledge" has long been viewed to have characteristics that lead it to be portrayed as the "archetypal" public good (Stiglitz 1999). The case of genomics is therefore timely as a specific, and very important, example of the challenges faced in ensuring the global generation, dissemination, and utilization of knowledge.

The objective of this paper is to consider the value of the "global public goods" (GPGs) concept to the analysis of the global generation, dissemination, and utilization of genomics knowledge. Following this introduction, Section 7.2 describes briefly what genomics is, and its applications. Section 7.3 outlines the potential costs and benefits of genomics, and Section 7.4 considers the GPGs elements of genomics. Section 7.5 outlines strategies for promoting and financing the production of genomics knowledge, with Section 7.6 concluding with a discussion of the value of the GPGs concept for the development of genomics.

7.2 **What is genomics?**

7.2.1 **Genes and genomes, genetics, and genomics: Concepts and distinctions**

Genes carry information about physical and functional inheritance vertically between generations. They are composed of deoxyribonucleic acid (DNA), arranged in the famous "double helix," which carries the genetic instructions for making living organisms, establishing how a particular organism with its own unique characteristics will be formed (Morange 1998, Bourgaize *et al.* 1999, The Human Genome Project 2002). Although genes play a paramount role in the formation of the individual, they interact with various environmental factors in a complex manner to produce the final outcome. *Genetics* is the study of these genes. Importantly, it is the study of single, or a small number of, genes to determine specific gene roles in diseases or physical characteristics of an individual.

The *genome* refers to an organism's *entire* genetic material, their complete *set* of DNA (Billings and Koliopoulos 2001, p. 19). The human genome is therefore the genetic material that "makes" a human, estimated at between 30,000 and 40,000 genes (International Human Genome Sequencing Consortium 2001, Venter 2001).[1] *Genomics* is the examination of an organism's entire set of genes and their interactions in a comprehensive analysis of the genetic components of organisms. This involves *structural genomics*, the "mapping" and "sequencing"[2] of the entire genome of an organism, and *functional genomics*, which seeks to discover the function and interaction of gene sequences (Lacadena 2001, p. 33).

....

[1] As traditionally defined and recognized, although there are others who believe the number could be as many as 120,000 (Cohen 2001).

[2] Sequencing refers to the "determination of the order of nucleotides (base sequences) in a DNA or RNA molecule or the order of amino acids in a protein" (The Human Genome Project 2002).

Genomics is thus primarily concerned with the generation, dissemination, and utilization of knowledge about the genetic attributes of organisms. This requires massive amounts of genetic information to be collected and analyzed. It has only evolved in the last few decades as a result of developments in analytical tools, such as DNA sequencers and genotyping techniques, which make it possible to easily characterize large numbers and types of genes in a single experiment. Advances in information technology have also contributed to the growth of genomics by providing the means to manage and process these large databases (Thomas 1999*a*, p. 134).

7.2.2 Application of genomics: The case of the Human Genome Project

Genomics can be applied to understanding the genes of simple bacteria, plants, animals, and humans. By February 2001, the genome had been sequenced on 599 viruses and viroids, 205 naturally occurring plasmids, 185 organelles, 31 eubacteria, 7 archae, 1 fungus, 1 plant, and 2 animals (International Human Genome Sequencing Consortium 2001, p. 860). However, the largest and best-known genomics project is the Human Genome Project.

This is a large-scale global project, involving research teams in 20 different countries, allocated over US$ 3 billion in public sector funding alone (Collins 1999). It arose from the belief that taking a *global* view of genomics was required to tackle this complex subject and to accelerate biomedical research. Begun in 1990, by February 2001 94 percent of the human genome had been sequenced. It is expected to be completed in 2003, two years earlier than in the original plan. The public nature of the exercise was confirmed by the "Bermuda Accord" between major players, including some pharmaceutical companies, which made data publicly available without restrictions within 24 hours of assembly. However, the speed of research efforts was undoubtedly accelerated by the announcement in 1998 by Celera, a private biotechnology company, that it would use a faster sequencing method and make the (patented) data accessible only through private subscription.

7.3 Potential costs, benefits, and risks of genomics

7.3.1 The potential benefits of genomics

Mapping the human genome is the basis for developing a variety of products to improve the identification, treatment, and prevention of ill health. These will not only have impacts on health, but also on economic growth.

The *identification* of disease genes can have applications in clinical diagnostics and predictive testing. For example, the polymerase chain reaction (PCR) technique, a highly sensitive and accurate genome-based diagnostic method that multiplies the DNA of a pathogen making it easier to detect. It can be used in various ways, including to detect the presence of pathogens, such as HIV, in samples.

Importantly, this method can be simplified and used in poor countries to diagnose infectious diseases, such as leishmaniasis and dengue fever, more rapidly, accurately, and less costly than by conventional techniques (Harris 1998). These and other initiatives raise hopes that genome-related biotechnologies may be used to improve the health of poor, as well as wealthy nations (Singer and Daar 2001).

Genomics can also be used to develop new *treatments* for disease, by identifying new drug targets[3] or tailoring drugs to specific genetic characteristics of individuals. Pharmaco-genomics in particular focuses on how minor genetic variations between people can affect the ways in which they respond to drugs for both infectious and noninfectious diseases, allowing medication to be adjusted to individual characteristics. For example, differential drug absorption can influence dosing levels and side effects. Similarly, genomics may predict how individuals or communities will respond to particular treatment. For example, it has been found that some West Africans may not respond to anti-retroviral therapy because of a genetic mutation (Schaeffeler *et al.* 2001).

Increased molecular understanding of diseases can also be applied to develop *preventive* measures, such as new and improved vaccines. For example, genomics can help identify multiple vaccine targets, useful in developing vaccines for organisms with a complex multihost life cycle, such as the malaria parasite (Carucci 2001). Genomics also has potential in the development of therapeutic vaccines for autoimmune diseases and allergies (Andre 2001).

Genomics has a strong role in the diagnosis, prevention, and treatment of both noncommunicable and communicable diseases. Noncommunicable diseases are not only a problem of the developed world, as they currently account for 60 percent of all deaths in developing countries (WHO 2001). Genomics is speeding the discovery of human drug targets for use in the treatment of various noncommunicable diseases. Further, although communicable diseases often affect developing countries more severally than the developed world, increasing globalization means that such diseases spread rapidly and widely over the globe, and many, such as tuberculosis, are resurgent, often in drug-resistant form (Chen *et al.* 1999). The use of genomics to avoid communicable diseases will therefore benefit developed as well as developing countries.

There may also be direct *economic* benefits. Genomics will be a significant contributor to the biotechnology sector, which, although still in its infancy, has major income generating potential (Ernst and Young 2001): the genomics-based pharmaceutical market is expected to grow from US$ 2.2 billion in 1999 to US$ 8.2 billion in 2004 (UNDP 2001, p. 34). However, genomics will not only benefit the major economic players in the world. Cuba, for example, has invested heavily

---

[3] The results of the Human Genome Project are estimated to increase the number of potential drug targets in humans from the current number of 500 to approximately 10,000 (Sanseau 2001).

since the 1980s in research infrastructure and manufacturing in biotechnology, producing several successful products, including the world's only meningitis B vaccine and holding at least 400 patents in the biotech field (Aitsiselmi 2001). As a result, biotechnology is destined to become a major export industry in Cuba (Carr 1999).

Genomics therefore has the *potential* to benefit both developing and developed countries, providing both high cost "designer drugs" as well as more lower cost health options. However, in order to reap direct economic benefit from genomics, countries will have to be active participants in the development and manufacture of genomics products. Those countries that will benefit the most from genomics are those that have appropriate health products to improve the health of their populations and who are active in developing and supplying those products.

7.3.2 The potential costs and risks of genomics

The potential benefits of genomics are significant. However, there are also costs and risks involved. Principal among these is the potential for a "genomic divide" between rich and poor nations.

There is a sizeable gap between spending on R&D in developed and developing countries. For example, average R&D expenditure as a proportion of GNP for 1987–97 was 2.4 percent for Organization for Economic Cooperation and Development (OECD) countries and just 0.6 percent for the countries of South Asia, with 3,141 and 152 scientists per 100,000 population respectively (UNDP 2001). In 1998, the 21 OECD countries with 14 percent of the world's people filed 86 percent of the world's patent applications and authored 85 percent of articles published in the world's scientific and technical journals (UNDP 2001). The capacity for researching local problems and/or transferring and absorbing scientific knowledge produced elsewhere is therefore extremely limited in many developing countries.

This limited human, institutional, infrastructure, and financial capacity is reflected in health-related research (Global Forum for Health Research 2000, Harris and Tanner 2000, Freeman and Miller 2001, Mills 2001, UNDP 2001). Further, much of the biotechnology R&D in industrialized countries is now the result of private finance, or public–private partnerships, whereas in developing countries there is typically almost no private sector involvement in biotechnology, which limits their potential to develop and commercialize genomics (Mugabe 2000, Lall 2001).

As a result of limited research capacity in developing countries, there is insufficient research on local health problems. It has been estimated that globally the private and public sector spend around US$ 70 billion a year on health research, yet only 10 percent of those funds are devoted to the health problems of 90 percent of the worlds population (Global Forum for Health Research 2002). Multinational pharmaceutical companies do not research and develop medical products for developing countries because the latter cannot afford them (Mills 2001). As a result, of the 1,223 new drugs introduced to the world market between

1975 and 1996, only 13 were aimed specifically at treating tropical diseases and only four resulted directly from pharmaceutical companies (UNDP 2001).[4]

These experiences suggest that developing counties may be severely disadvantaged through the "genomic revolution" in health, in a manner similar to the "agricultural genetic divide" that has been identified (Juma 2001). In health, a genomics divide such as this will result in the benefits of genomics being disproportionately directed to industrialized countries, with genome-related research not addressing the health problems of the developing world. Such a "genomic divide" will not only lead to widening health and economic inequalities between the industrialized countries and the developing world, but this in turn is likely to increase political and social unrest (Forbes 2000). This is unlikely to be localized to a few countries or regions; the impact is likely to be worldwide. A genomic divide could, therefore, have global consequences and it would be in the self-interest of industrialized countries to avoid its development.

These problems highlight the need to secure approaches and strategies to ensure that the benefits of the genomics revolution are available to be shared by all. The following sections consider the potential for the "GPG" concept to assist in achieving this end.

7.4 Genomics as a global public good for health (GPGH)

7.4.1 Public good aspects of genomics

Genomics is principally about knowledge; *typically* considered to be the archetypal public good (Stiglitz 1999). Knowledge, particularly that produced by basic research such as genomics, is often costly to produce, but once produced is virtually costless to reproduce and reuse (Arrow 1962). Once it is generated, it is difficult/costly to *exclude* people from access to knowledge. In terms of genomics, much of what is found will typically be published in international journals, or on the Internet,[5] open to all who wish to, and are able to, acquire it. For example, a completely new class of antimalarials was discovered through bioinformatics applied to the DNA sequence of the malaria parasite being freely available on the Internet (Jomaa *et al.* 1999).

Knowledge is also *non-rival* in consumption. Numerous people can, for example, utilize the information contained in the genome to generate new diagnostic

---

[4] Further, several developing countries are playing a central role in genomics without receiving due benefits. Typically, this is by populations from developing countries providing genetic material for important discoveries, but not sharing in the benefits of the discoveries (Andrews and Nelkin 2001). It is partly because of this kind of inequitable activity that the Ethics Committee of the Human Genome Organization has produced a statement on Genetic Benefit Sharing (HUGO 2000*a*).

[5] For example, through "GenBank," administered by the National Center for Biotechnology Information of the NIH in the United States (NCBI 2002).

tests or treatments. The knowledge itself is not depleted when used, and thus the marginal cost of sharing it is minimal. This makes it possible for additional individuals to use knowledge for various purposes.

However, although *theoretically* the knowledge produced by genomics research is a public good, this does not mean that the goods within which the knowledge is *embodied*, that the *utilization* of genomics, will not be excludable or rival. This is considered further in Section 7.4.4.

7.4.2 Global aspect of genomics

Humans share about 99.9 percent of their genome with one another (International Human Genome Sequencing Consortium 2001). In a *symbolic* sense, then, the genome is a common global heritage of humanity (UNESCO 1997, Article 1). Genomics may, then, be considered a *global* good because it is based on examining this globally shared resource of the human genome. Further, the global nature of genomics has been reinforced by the impressive free collaboration between scientists, laboratories, and countries in deciphering the human genome. This reflects the wish to make knowledge from the human genome available for the common good of humankind, with as few proprietary intrusions as possible.

However, there is perhaps a distinction to be made between the global *production* and *dissemination* of genomics knowledge, and its *utilization*. The paper now turns to consider this distinction.

7.4.3 Global public good aspects of the *utilization* of genomics knowledge

Although genomics *per se* may display public good characteristics, such knowledge has to be *produced, disseminated, and used* before it is of any value to society. Much will therefore depend on the degree to which its *applications* are non-rival and non-excludable. The GPG status of several illustrative applications of genomics knowledge is provided in Table 7.1.

The use of genomics for *individual* disease control, to diagnose, prevent, or treat diseases in individuals, represent private (rival and excludable) goods. For example, to diagnose dengue fever or use predictive technologies to identify individual predisposition to genetic diseases, such as breast cancer, represent private good applications of genomics (even though they may be provided by publicly funded health-care systems).

Applications of genomics for *population* disease control have a range of characteristics from pure public to pure private goods. For example, preventive technologies for the eradication of disease are non-rival and non-excludable, across a global population. In contrast, tests and vaccines are typically excludable and rival: they can be withheld from individuals and not reused on different individuals. However, vaccination will yield an *externality* effect, since after a certain proportion (say 90 percent) of the population is vaccinated, herd immunity is achieved, making the *results* of vaccination (although not the vaccine product itself)

Table 7.1 Global public good status of applications of genomics to health

Applications	Excludable or non-excludable	Rival or non-rival in consumption	Level of application	GPGH potential
(1) *Individual applications* Diagnosis of diseases (e.g. PCR for Dengue)				
Predictive tests (e.g BRAC for breast cancer)	Excludable	Rival	Local	No
Vaccines Pharmacogenomics adapted to the individual				
(2) *Population applications* Screening tests (e.g. for sickle cell disease)				
Mass immunization	Mixed	Mixed	Local/national/ regional/global	Yes
Pharmacogenomics adapted to the population				
(3) *Other applications* Accessing genomic databases on the Internet				
Genomics regulation				
Genomics governance	Mixed	Non-rival	Local/national/ regional/global	Yes
Education of professionals				
Education of general public				
Environmental improvement (e.g. bioremedation w/GMO)				
Genomics to avoid bioterrorism (e.g. biosensors)				

non-rival in nature. Similarly, future generations will benefit from effective current measures in disease eradication, again making the application of genomics, as it influences disease eradication, a GPG.

Accessing genomics databases on the Internet, genomics regulation, and education activities have more definite public goods characteristics. Regulations can be excludable or non-excludable depending on who they are aimed and the focus of regulation (e.g. exclusion from incentive, but not from disincentive structures), but they are non-rival in consumption and can as easily be applied to one or numerous individuals. The same applies to the application of genomics to avoid public "bads," such as bioterrorism. They are typically non-excludable and the benefits can extend widely across national borders. This could involve, for instance, using genomics to detect and develop vaccines against "bio-weapons" such as anthrax or smallpox (Enserink 2002). Transferring genomics knowledge to educate specific populations or the public at large also displays relatively strong public goods characteristics as it is typically non-excludable, depending on the target groups, and is generally non-rival in consumption. It is in the interest of humans to have these education activities totally non-excludable, at the global level, in order to encourage public engagement in formulating the application of genomics, which is most palatable to human beings. As stressed above, the human genome is the common global heritage of humanity and the application of genomics should therefore benefit and be acceptable to the majority of humankind.

7.4.4 Problems in the application of genomics knowledge at the global level

Although *in principle* genomics knowledge has considerable GPG characteristics, *in reality* knowledge does not always express the public goods characteristics that it is claimed to possess. Of importance are two major factors which compromise the public good characteristics, and therefore application, of genomics knowledge.

Intellectual property rights and patent legislation

First, knowledge, as a public good, will lack incentives for its production if those producing it are not able to secure a return on their investment through the property of exclusion. This may be addressed either through direct public finance and/or provision (e.g. academic research institutions) or through regulation or financial incentive structures for private companies. This latter approach is the essence of intellectual property regulations and the patent system. Patents, common in many scientific fields for decades, provide an incentive for inventors to develop inventions by granting them temporary monopoly, through artificial legislative exclusion, on commercialization of their discoveries to enable costs to be recouped (Gold 1999, Thomas 1999*b*).

Thus, by definition, patenting encourages genomics to be an excludable good. This presents a paradox. The knowledge itself remains non-rival, and thus with minimal marginal cost of consumption, implying that it should be consumed by all who derive a positive marginal benefit from it. However, to ensure its production its application is made artificially excludable, thus effectively creating a "club good" to ensure sufficient return on investment. Such excludability in the presence of non-rivalry generates socially suboptimal consumption of the good. This paradox is traditionally solved by the direct finance and/or provision by the state at minimal or no cost at point of use. What is unusual in the genomics situation is that medical technologies have been historically dealt with via the patent system, rather than direct government involvement.

However, traditional intellectual property and patent laws have not been adapted to reflect the new developments presented by genomics. It is puzzling to people, for example, how naturally occurring substance like DNA can fit under the realm of "novel invention" and thus be patented. In this case, prior instances of patenting natural chemical substances have been used to justify patenting the DNA. For example, patenting vitamin C in an isolated and purified form (Andrews and Nelkin 2001), or an oil-eating bacterium (Diamond v. Chakrabarty 1980).

Patenting in genomics began with genes associated with protein products, but has rapidly expanded to include expressed sequence tags (ESTs), single nucleotide polymorphisms (SNPs) and even the computer programs for the analysis of genomic information (Meyers *et al.* 2000). This has been in direct contradiction to the Human Genome Organization and the draft guiding principles of the World Health Organization (WHO) which recommend against patenting of DNA outside of the context of credible utility (Daar and Mattei 1999); a position supported by the Presidents of the (British) Royal Society, the Nuffield Council on Bioethics and the American Academy of Sciences (HUGO 2000*b*, Nuffield 2002). As a result, the utility requirement has recently been tightened in the United States of America and several other countries.

Patents are therefore an incentive for genomic research, but can also act as a barrier to further research using this basic knowledge, and the application of such knowledge in products (Heller and Eisenberg 1998). Patents on genomics that embody research tools can be especially detrimental to the development of the field of genomics. Researchers who do not have open access to the necessary tools for developing their fields will be limited in their ability to move their research forward (Eisenberg 1997). To date, patents have been sought on as broad a scope as possible, resulting in numerous, and often overlapping, patents being granted in relatively limited fields. This results in lower levels of research, as users need access to multiple patented input to create a single useful product (Heller and Eisenberg 1998).

It is especially unclear how patents will affect the diffusion of genomics knowledge in developing countries. Although much information is freely available in public databases to those who have access to the Internet, such access is still extremely limited. It is also unclear whether access to information itself is sufficient to enable research or product development and use in these countries where funds are even more restricted (see Section 7.4.2). Further, the inability of developing countries to pay high prices for the resultant patented product means that there is less incentive to invest specifically in diseases most relevant to those countries at the expense of diseases of more interest to the wealthier developed world.

A value of the GPGs concept is to highlight the need for a change in patent systems; to capitalize on private sector involvement, but ensure it is undertaken equitably (Gold 1999). This may be pursued through a variety of means. For example, development of "cross-licenses" to permit the patented technology to be used freely in specific countries or regions, such as that pioneered by the "SNP Consortium" of pharmaceutical and technology firms, which the Wellcome Trust was instrumental in forming (SNP 2002). This consortium funds identification of certain SNPs and places the information freely in the public domain. A second approach could be to change patent laws, especially with respect to research exemption doctrines (Gold 1999). This would shift the balance of patenting of certain forms of genomics knowledge to the research exemption category. Changes in patent law would need to be consistent with international agreements, such as the World Trade Organization Agreement on Trade-Related Aspects of Intellectual Property Rights (TRIPS), but amendments to such agreements could be called for. With any of these approaches, it is clear that policies for the patenting of genomics-related knowledge are (universally) required. This is an obvious area for leadership by international organizations, such as WHO (Bobrow and Thomas 2001, WHO 2002).

Furthermore, with TRIPS it is becoming increasingly difficult to follow the strategy of formalizing and enforcing intellectual rights gradually as countries build up their technological capacity. Several industrialized countries did not, for example, provide patent protection for pharmaceutical products until the late 1970s, and could in the meantime build up their local capacity to develop and manufacture pharmaceutical products (Chang 2001). The effects of TRIPS can therefore hamper the development of genomics and pharmaceutical development in developing countries as they do not provide the opportunity to shelter local endeavors. Most developed countries already have the capacity to develop and manufacture genomics products and will benefit from the global strengthening in intellectual property rights. Increased emphasis on patenting is likely to be a disincentive for developing countries with limited genomics capacity, but will provide incentives for increasing genomics development in richer countries.

Turning knowledge in to practice: The importance of "access goods"

Some research on science and technology development questions the notion that knowledge is actually an archetypal public good (Callon 1994, Cowan et al. 2000, Pavitt 2000). Although knowledge may, theoretically, be freely disseminated, practically there are constraints on being able to utilize this knowledge. For example, education and training, physical access to journals or the Internet, research infrastructure, and the ability to establish the necessary production processes to turn genomic knowledge in to a pharmaceutical, all constrain the ability to make practical use of genomics knowledge. These factors generate different degrees of excludability and rivalry. Important here are two main restrictions to the applications of knowledge.

First, the tacit dimension of knowledge: that knowledge is uncodified, embedded in people rather than in texts (Polanyi 1958, 1967). A necessary element of knowledge is that it is disseminated by hands-on experience, requiring more knowledge than just that presented in published articles. Due to the tacit dimension, knowledge is therefore deficient of public goods characteristics, as those embodied with the knowledge are rival (can only be in one place at once) and excludable (can refuse to cooperate). Further, the marginal cost of knowledge transmission has been argued to rise rapidly with "distance" from the context within which such knowledge was generated (Cowan *et al.* 2000). The tacit dimension of knowledge therefore restricts the dissemination of information presented both in patents and in publications.

Second, the absence of local R&D capacity. This is as valid for codified, as for tacit, knowledge. In order to absorb and make use of basic knowledge considerable investment is required in skills and training, equipment, institutions, and networks (Callon 1994). As a result there is a distinction between "free availability" (access unregulated) and "free use" (accessing and *using* information without cost) (Callon 1994). Different types of "access good" are therefore required to make use of the freely available scientific information: goods that are private in nature and are a necessary investment to reap benefits of public goods (see Chapter 1).

The fact that knowledge does not travel freely makes it difficult for countries to be "free riders" and use the basic research produced elsewhere to innovate. This explains why countries without a strong basic research capacity seem to have difficulties in engaging in technological development, and why countries which have been economically successful, such as the newly industrialized countries of East Asia, and the Nordic countries in Europe, have all placed emphasis on producing their own basic research (Pavitt 2000). Research has shown that firms place significantly less importance on foreign sources of knowledge than on national sources, and that this de-emphasis is larger for public than private knowledge (Arundel and Soete 1995). Hence, many of the benefits of nationally funded basic research stay national (Pavitt 2000).

Genomic knowledge is not likely to travel easily, despite the fact that massive amounts of genomic data are available free of charge on the Internet. Noncodified genomic-related knowledge is necessary in order to reproduce these results. Further, in order to absorb and develop applications of genomics, extensive investments are necessary in, for example, skills, research instrumentation, and networks. In that sense, genomics is not a public good to those (developing) countries that cannot afford to put sizeable resources into developing genomic research capacity. The publicness of the *utilization of genomics knowledge* is therefore not exhibited to a significant degree across national boundaries, which limits its globalness. Developing countries will require several "access goods" in order to develop appropriate applications from genomics for their needs, and become active participants in the genomics development.

7.4.5 **Summary**

Although knowledge is the archetypal public good, genomics as a form of knowledge can only be seen to display public goods characteristics in certain contexts. Although it is not depleted when used, and is therefore a public good in the sense of being *non-rival*, many factors, such as patenting and limited research capacity in genomics, have the potential to make genomic knowledge *excludable* in practice. Genomics is therefore in danger of becoming a "club good;" open for admittance only to the richer (industrialized) countries.

The value of the GPG approach in making this explicit is seen further when considering means to reduce the suboptimal global use of genomics for improving global health. The next section, describing strategies for promoting genomics (with particular emphasis on global health and developing countries), demonstrates how the GPGs framework can be a useful tool to define and establish a mechanism to direct the development of genomics and to foster the efficient sharing of its benefits.

7.5 Strategies for promoting and financing genomics for global health

If the "genomic divide" is to be averted, there is urgent need for strategies at the local, national, regional, and global levels to encourage the production, dissemination, and use of genomics knowledge more equally. These strategies will involve a mix of government, nongovernment, private, and international bodies, and collaboration will therefore be fundamental, as stressed by several international organizations. Both WHO in its Genomics and World Health Report and UNESCO in its Declaration on the Human Genome and Human Rights place emphasis on several measures to strengthen genomics in developing countries through international cooperation. These include building capacity for genetic research and seeking means to ensure that developing countries benefit from genomic research (UNESCO 1997, WHO 2002, Article 19). Several key strategies, concerning capacity strengthening, research, public engagement and consensus building, and financing of genomics, are therefore outlined below.

7.5.1 Capacity strengthening

The capacity to absorb, plan, and develop genomics knowledge is central to its development. As discussed in Section 7.4, although capacity strengthening involves private goods, it is an "access good" in that it is necessary in order to reap benefits from the public good of genomics. In developing countries especially, limited capacity in genomics is a serious constraint on its publicness. Strategies to increase capacity in the developing world will therefore result in greater, and more equitable, development, dissemination, and use of genomics knowledge. The strategies to increase capacity in genomics are typically specific to certain regions and thus have features of *regional* public goods. However, if genomics capacity is increased in many regions around the globe, it will start to take on the characteristics of promoting a GPG.

Capacity strengthening can be conduced and supported by several actors, including national governments, philanthropic organizations, and international organizations. A central part of capacity strengthening in genomics is building capacity to conduct genomics research and to develop and manufacture new health products based on genomics. To build the human resources capable of active participation in genomics is an essential step in capacity building. WHO has stressed the importance of strengthening genomics capacity in developing

countries and declared its intention to assist Member States in establishing training programs based on collaboration between developed and developing countries
(WHO 2002).

Capacity refers, however, to more than simply training people to be capable of
genomics research. Developing countries need also to strengthen their capacity in
ethical, legal, social, and policy aspects of genomics and biotechnology to craft an
operational system in genomics (Singer and Benatar 2001, WHO 2002). This
would, for example, involve educating judges and policymakers about genomics,
to provide them with expertise in addressing the ethical issues associated with
genomics and biotechnologies. For example, one could develop a series of regional
courses on genomics and public health policy for opinion leaders from different
sectors, including government, industry, academia, NGOs, and others. Such courses
can encourage collaborative efforts amongst and between developing and developed countries in addressing the ethical, legal, social, and policy aspects of
genomics.

Capacity strengthening methods developed in one country might also be useful
in other countries. However, due to differences in prevailing cultural and social
values it may not always be possible to transfer systems directly between countries.
Strong capacity in genomics would also strengthen the ability of developing countries to participate in international negotiations on genomics issues, which itself
could strengthen genomics as a GPG.

7.5.2 Facilitating research

For genomics to have a global presence and develop solutions to worldwide health
problems, more research has to be conducted in to the health problems of the
developing world. Here again, "access goods" are integral. Health research requires
research infrastructure that is often beyond the means of many developing countries. Initiatives to provide developing countries with private goods for R&D in
genomics will contribute toward strengthening genomics as a public good. The
Commission on Macroeconomics and Health, for example, called for a significant
increase in financing global R&D for diseases affecting developing countries
(WHO 2001), and the report of the Advisory Committee for Health Research
declared that WHO has a clear role in advocating an increase in the availability
of resources for genomics research targeted to the health needs of developing
countries (WHO 2002). It is important that these efforts in themselves are
research-based, and examine factors that stimulate and dampen the development
of genomics in developing countries (Singer and Daar 2001).

The UNDP has recommended that emphasis be placed on creating innovative
partnerships and new incentives for R&D as a strategy to make new technologies work for human development (UNDP 2001). In order to advance genomics
research in developing countries, it is important to create innovative partnerships. As
mentioned, this emphasis on collaboration and partnership is echoed by UNESCO
and WHO (UNESCO 1997, Daar and Mattei 1999). Increased collaboration in

research is an emblem for the changing nature of science and technological development (Ziman 1994, Gibbons *et al.* 1994). To develop innovative ideas and applications, different types of knowledge are required. Networks and partnerships are the keys to gaining access to this necessary knowledge and can be seen to be "access goods" for the development of science and technology. The collaborations need to be between very different types of actors, from the universities and public research system, to the private sector, and government. Close coordination of these actors is called for within regions and nations, but international collaboration is also of paramount importance for any new developments in genomics.

Private sector involvement is increasingly required for development of new technologies. As the private sector in most developing countries is underdeveloped, incentives are required to encourage its formation. This could, for example, involve tax incentives to firms for the development and manufacture of genomics products. Intellectual property legislation could also be modified to encourage pharmaceutical companies to find profits from products for high-volume, low-margin, markets in the developing world more comparable with the low-volume, high-margin markets of North America, Europe, and Japan.

7.5.3 Public engagement and consensus building

In order to promote genomics development that is acceptable and fulfils the needs of as many people as possible, worldwide public engagement is required. Education of the general public on genomics risks and benefits, and their involvement in planning and carrying out genomics, should be encouraged. Global public engagement, if successful, will ensure that the voices of inhabitants across the range of nations, cultures and races are heard. For example, it can be argued that in agricultural biotechnology the debate was focused on industrialized countries and risks. This pre-empted the ability of policy makers in developing countries to make their own choices about whether and how to use genomics and biotechnology to improve food security in their countries (Singer and Daar 2000).

Public engagement will also pave the way for the next step required in the development of genomics: consensus building by stakeholders, including government, industry, academics, NGOs, and the public. Although this is likely to be a difficult exercise, in light of the different interests of these multiple stakeholders it is essential for stakeholders to focus on the common interest of eliminating health inequity, providing strategic direction, and considering how genomics may best be regulated. One of the lessons of the experience with agricultural biotechnology is the need to create a platform for discussion and trust building among these different stakeholders (Singer and Daar 2000).

However, while public involvement it widely proclaimed as critical to the development of "palatable" genomics, there is no single accepted method for establishing this. For example, "research foresight" can be a part of consensus building. Here, different actors focus on what type of research they would like to see over a given period, and what action steps are required in order to realize their vision.

This involves communication about different needs and visions, consensus making and a commitment to a common plan (Martin 1995, 1996). Revising international DNA patenting is an example of a task that would benefit greatly from global consensus making. At present, this debate is highly polarized, and there is a call for developing a mutually acceptable balance between private incentives for innovators and the public interest of maximizing access to the fruits of innovation (Gold 2000, UNDP 2001).

An "international commission on genomics and global health" might also be a constructive platform for consensus building to ensure that the benefits of genomics are shared by everyone, including those in developing countries (Dowdeswell *et al.* 2003).

7.5.4 **Financing genomics production and dissemination**

National governments will still be expected to develop and/or enforce legislation or structures developed to finance GPGs. The challenge is how this may be fostered and coordinated. From the global perspective, it is therefore the role of international bodies in the organization, advocation, and regulation of mechanisms at the local, national, and regional level that is fundamental.

As discussed in Chapter 1, several mechanisms for financing GPGs are available, including voluntary contributions, coordinated contributions, global taxes, "market"-based systems, and "club" arrangements. It is argued there that voluntary and coordinated contributions are unlikely to be successful when addressing global health problems, such as communicable disease control, especially when a wide range of countries are involved. In these circumstances market-based systems and/or a global tax would be more fitting.

It seems likely that the same limitations of financing via voluntary and coordinated contributions apply to financing genomics. This is supported by empirical evidence from the Global Fund to Fight AIDS, Tuberculosis, and Malaria, established by the United Nations. Even though the fund is very promising, and it is expected to be a significant force in improving health in developing countries, it has been hard for it to reach its target funding. The target funding to address HIV, Tuberculosis, and Malaria at a global level was set at US$ 7–10 billion per year, and in less than one year of operation almost $2 billion has been donated (UNF 2002). There is hope that the impact of the Commission on Macroeconomics and Health will strengthen the Global Fund. The Commission recommended that $27 billion of total grants assistance for health needs in low-income countries should be reached by 2007 (WHO 2001). Perhaps, this is too ambitious, but the recommendation pushes the limited funds for health research for developing countries more firmly onto the international agenda.

There is increased awareness that the globalization of financial markets and the growth of transnational corporations has caused a misallocation of resources between private and public goods (Soros 2002). This has created an uneven playing field for developing countries. However, it has been proposed that the elements of the international financial markets themselves may be used to level this field

(Soros 2002). For example, resources could be increased and better distributed by using the International Monetary Fund's Special Drawing Rights (SDRs) to meet needs of developing countries. Soros (2002) stresses that although we cannot rely *solely* on the market mechanism to take care of our global collective needs and improve social justice, richer countries should not only help developing countries for altruistic reasons but also for their own sake.

There are also options for using market mechanisms in more innovative ways. For example, one possible market-based funding system has been developed by Globalegacy, a UK-based organization with the vision of building an alliance that will create long-term social and economic growth through the implementation of commercial ventures in developing, and developed urban, communities. In essence, to build a business model around a social purpose (Globalegacy 2002). This model could be used to establish an investment fund to channel funds toward developing applications of health genomics and biotechnology for developing countries.

One might also build upon the various "ethical investment funds" that currently flourish nationally to reduce, for example, investment in tobacco companies or weapons suppliers (Social Investment Forum 2002). Their potential in the global arena has not been fully tested. The objective would be to provide capital to initiate genomics research and utilization in developing countries to ensure that genomics is a global public good offering global health benefits. It would be based on private equity principles and need commitments of capital from investors for a fixed period. Investment would be expected to come from both public and private sources. For governments, it might be an appealing and focused use of official development assistance. For industry, especially multinational pharmaceutical companies, it might be a useful way to contribute constructively to the potential market failures for their genomics-based products in developing countries. The fund would support projects with clear health benefits to developing countries but, at the same time, the projects would be required to demonstrate future commercial benefits. The criteria for investment proposals would balance commercial imperatives with social and humanitarian values.

7.6 **Conclusion**

This chapter has argued that aspects of genomics span the range of private and public goods, and local to global levels of activity. Some elements have clear private good characteristics and are best left to the private sector or local or national government institutions (e.g. individual applications of genomics in developed countries), whilst others, such as population applications of genomics and genomics regulations, have more clear public good and global attributes. The message is that genomics has significant GPGs characteristics, but that they are suboptimally developed and utilized in developing countries. In order to strengthen genomics as a GPG, concerted, collective, and focused effort by international organizations and developing countries is needed.

Clearly, the GPGs concept is only a conceptual device to analyze the generation, dissemination, and application of genomics knowledge. However, we maintain that this concept can be helpful, both in gaining new insights and identifying ways to improve global health, in four ways.

First, we have demonstrated that genomics has significant GPGs characteristics and thereby provide a justification that the promotion of genomics needs to take its GPGs nature into account.

Second, our analysis points to a gap in the GPG characteristics of genomics: that although knowledge *per se* may be considered to have GPG aspects, this does not necessarily mean that the production, dissemination, and utilization of such knowledge are similarly global/public. The GPGs concept has therefore helped dissect the different elements of genomics and its different attributes, aiding identification of those elements to focus on when promoting genomics for global health.

Third, the GPGs concept has identified the importance of "access goods," and therefore helps identify the necessary mechanisms by which to promote genomics. It makes clear the importance and value of the provision of such "private goods" to ensure that the value of public goods, in this case, genomics knowledge is fully exploited.

Fourth, and most importantly, this analysis has shown that the greatest gap between the different elements of genomics and its suboptimal utilization is likely to be in developing countries. The GPGs concept makes clear the interconnected fate of nations—rich and poor. Given the divergent abilities of countries currently to invest in genomics, it is clear that the more wealthy will be required to support initiatives within poorer nations to enable the generation, dissemination, and use of genomics for their own health concerns. The GPGs concept makes this relationship explicit and points to strategies to address this gap and optimize genomics investment in developing countries.

The overall value of the GPGs analysis of genomics is therefore to advance our knowledge about genomics and pinpoint ways to advance it to improve global health. It highlights what requirements need to be in place for genomics knowledge to be fully exploited and its full potential value realized as widely as possible. It thereby lays the foundation for strategies on how to optimize not only the generation of genomics knowledge but also how to advance it and use it. It helps understand why collective actions are required in promoting genomics and which collective actions are most likely to result in realizing its potential. By helping analyze genomics and identify strategies to promote it, the GPGs concept strengthens the vitality of this powerful tool to improve global health and ameliorate one of the major ethical challenges of our time: inequities in global health.

References

Aitsiselmi A. *Medical Research in Cuba: Strengthening International Cooperation.* Paper presented at the Pugwash Meeting No. 259, Havana Cuba, 2001.

Andre FE. The future of vaccines, immunisation concepts and practice. *Vaccine* 2001; **19**: 2206–9.

Andrews L, Nelkin D. *Body Bazaar: The Market for Human Tissue in the Biotechnology Age.* New York: Crown Publishers, 2001.

Arrow KJ. The implications of learning by doing. *Rev Econom Stud* 1962; **29**: 155–73.

Arundel A, Soete L. *Innovation Strategies of Europe's Largest Industrial Firms.* Maastrict: MERIT, 1995.

Billings P, Koliopoulos S. What is the human genome? In: J-F Mattei (ed.) *The Human Genome.* Strasbourg: Council of Europe Publishing, 2001.

Bobrow M, Thomas SM. Patents in a genetic age: the present patent systems risks becoming a barrier to medical progress. *Nature* 2001; **409**: 763–4.

Bourgaize D, Jewell TR, Buiser RG. *Biotechnology: Demystifying the Concepts.* Addison, Longman: Wesley, 1999.

Brundtland GH. Foreword from the Director General. In: *Genomics and World Health, Report of the Advisory Committee on Health Research.* Geneva: World Health Organization, 2002.

Callon M. Is science a public good? Fifth Mullins Lecture, Virginia Polytechnic Institute. *Sci Technol Hum Values* 1994; **19**(4): 395–424.

Carr K. Cuban biotechnology treads a lonely path. *Nature* 1999; **398**(Suppl.): A22–3.

Carucci DJ. Genomic tools for gene and protein discovery in malaria: Toward new vaccines. *Vaccine* 2001; **21**(19(17–19)): 2315–18.

Chang H-J. *Intellectual Property Rights and Economic Development—Historical Lessons and Emerging Issues.* Human Development Report 2001 Background Paper, 2001.

Chen LC, Evans TG, Cash RA. Health as a global public good. In: I Kaul, I Grunberg, MA Stern (ed.) *Global Public Goods, International Cooperation in the 21st Century.* New York: Oxford University Press, 1999, pp. 284–304.

Cohen J. Consulting biotech's oracle. *Technol Rev* 2001; **104**(8): 70.

Collins FS. Shauttuck lecture—Medical and societal consequences of the human genome project. *N Engl J Med* 1999; **341**(1): 28–37.

Cowan R, David PA, Foray D. The explicit economics of knowledge codification and tacitness. *Indus Corp Change*, 2000; **9**(2): 211–53.

Daar AS, Mattei J-F. *Medical Genetics and Biotechnology: Implications for Public Health.* Geneva: WHO, 1999, WHO/EIP/GPE/00.1.

Diamond v. Chakrabarty. 447 US 303, 1980.

Dowdeswell E, Daar A, Singer P. Bridging the genomics divide. *Global Govern J* 2003 (in press).

Eisenberg R. Patenting research tools and the law. In: NR Council (ed.) *Intellectual Property Rights and Research Tools in Molecular Biology: Summary of a Workshop Held at the National Academy of Sciences, February 15–16, 1996.* Washington, DC: National Academy Press, 1997.

Enserink M. TIGR begins assault in the anthrax genome. *Science* 2002; **255**: 1442–3.

Ernst, Young. *Focus on Fundamentals: The Biotechnology Report. 15th Annual Review,* 2001.

Forbes I. *Health Inequalities: Poverty and Policy.* London: Academy of Learned Societies for the Social Sciences, 2000.

Freeman P, Miller M. *Scientific Capacity Building to Improve Population Health: Knowledge as a Global Public Good.* Commission on Macroeconomics and Health Working Paper Series, 2001. Paper No. WG2:3.

Gibbons M, Limoges C, Nowotny H, Schwartzman S, Scott P, Trow M. *The New Production of Knowledge*. London: Sage Publications, 1994.

Global Forum Health Research. *10/90 Report on Health Research*, 2000.

Globalegacy. Retrieved February 6, 2002, from the World Wide Web: www.globalegacy.com/model.html, 2002.

Gold ER. Making room: Reinventing basic research, health policy and ethics into patent law. In: TA Caulfield, B. Williams-Jones (ed.) *The Commercialization of Genetic Research, Ethical, Legal and Policy Issues*. New York: Kluwer Academic, 1999, pp. 63–78.

Gold ER. Moving the gene patent debate forward. *Nature* 2000; **18**: 1319–20.

Harris E. *A Low-cost Approach to PCR*. New York: Oxford University Press, 1998.

Harris E, Tanner M. Health technology transfer. *BMJ* 2000; **321**: 817–20.

Heller MA, Eisenberg RS. Can patents deter innovation? The anticommons in biomedical research. *Science* 1998; **288**: 698–701.

HUGO. *Statement on Benefit-sharing*. HUGO Ethics Committee. Retrieved April 9, 2000, from the World Wide Web: www.gene.ucl.ac.uk/hugo/benefit.html, 2000*a*.

HUGO. *HUGO Statement on Patenting of DNA Sequences*. HUGO Ethics Committee. Retrieved February 6, 2002, from the World Wide Web: www.gene.ucl.ac.uk/hugo/patent2000.html, 2000*b*.

International Human Genome Sequencing Consortium. Initial sequencing and analysis of the human genome. *Nature* 2001; **409**: 860–921.

Jomaa H, Wiesner J, Sanderbrand S *et al.* Inhibitors of the nonmevalonate pathway of isoprenoid biosynthesis as antimalarial drugs. *Science* 1999; **285**(3): 1573–6.

Juma C. *The New Genetic Divide: Biotechnology in a Globalizing World*. Paper presented at the ICTSD Workshop on Biotechnology, Biosafety and Trade: Issues for Developing Countries, Bellevue, Switzerland, July 18–20, 2001.

Lacadena J-R. An ethical code for human genetics. In J-F Mattei (ed.) *The Human Genome*. Strasbourg: Council of Europe Publishing, 2001.

Lall S. *Harnessing Technology for Human Development*. Human Development Report 2001 Background Paper, 2001.

Martin BR. Foresight in science and technology. *Technol Anal Strategies Manage* 1995; **7**(2): 139–67.

Martin BR. Technology foresight: Capturing the benefits from science-related technologies. *Res Eval* 1996; **6**(2): 158–68.

Meyers TC, Turano TA, Greenhalgh DA, Waller PRH. Patient protection for protein structures and databases. *Nat Struct Biol* 2000; **7**(Suppl.): 950–2.

Mills A. *Technology and Science as Global Public Goods: Tackling Priority Diseases of Poor Countries*. The World Bank Group background paper prepared for the Annual Bank Conference on Development Economics, Barcelona, June 25–26, 2001.

Morange M. *A History of Molecular Biology*. Cambridge, Mass: Harvard University Press, 1998.

Mugabe J. *Biotechnology in Developing Countries and Countries with Economies in Transition*. Background paper prepared for the United Nations Conference on Trade and Development (UNCTAD), Geneva, Switzerland, 2000.

NCBI. *GenBank*. National Center for Biotechnology Information. Retrieved February 6, 2002, from the World Wide Web: www.ncbi.nlm.nih.gov/, 2002.

Nuffield Council on Bioethics. *The Ethics of Patenting DNA*, A Discussion Paper, 2002.

Pavitt K. Public policies to support basic research: What can the rest of the world learn from US theory and practice? (And what they should not learn). *Indus Corp Change* 2000; **10**(3): 761–79.

Polanyi M. *Personal Knowledge: Towards a Post-critical Philosophy.* London: Routledge and Keegan Paul, 1958.

Polanyi M. *The Tacit Dimension.* New York: Doubleday, 1967.

Sanseau P. Impact of human genome sequencing for in silico target discovery. *Drug Discovery Today* 2001; **6**(6): 316–23.

Schaeffeler E, Eichelbaum U, Brinkmann U *et al.* Frequency of C3435T polymorphism of MDR1 gene in African people. *Lancet* 2001; **358**(9279): 383–4.

Singer PA, Benatar SR. Beyond Helsinki: a vision for global health ethics. *BMJ* 2001; **322**: 747–8.

Singer PA, Daar AS. Avoiding Frankendrugs. *Nat Biotechnol* 2000; **18**: 1225.

Singer PA, Daar AS. Harnessing genomics and biotechnology to improve global health equity. *Science* 2001; **294**: 87–9.

SNP. The SNP Consortium. Retrieved February 6, 2002, from the World Wide Web: http://snp.cshl.org/, 2002.

Social Investment Forum. Retrieved February 6, 2002, from the World Wide Web: www.socialinvest.org/, 2002.

Soros G. *George Soros on Globalization.* Oxford: Public Affairs, 2002.

Stiglitz JE. Knowledge as a global public good. In: I Kaul, I Grunberg, MA Stern (ed.) *Global Public goods: International Cooperation in the 21st Century.* New York: Oxford University Press, 1999, pp. 308–25.

The Human Genome Project. http://www.ornl.gov/hgmis/. Retrieved January 28, 2002, from the World Wide Web.

Thomas SM. Genomics and intellectual property rights. *Drug Discovery Today* 1999a; **4**(3): 134–38.

Thomas SM. Intellectual property rights and the human genome. In: TA Caulfield, B Williams-Jones (ed.) *The Commercialization of Genetic Research, Ethical, Legal and Policy Issues.* New York: Kluwer Academic, 1999b, pp. 55–62.

UNDP. *Human Development Report 2001: Making New Technologies Work for Human Development.* New York: United Nations Development Programme, 2001.

UNESCO. *Universal Declaration on the Human Genome and Human Rights.* Retrieved February 6, 2002, from the World Wide Web: www.unesco.org/human_rights/hrbc.htm, 1997.

UNF. *The Global Fund to Fight AIDS, Tuberculosis and Malaria.* United Nations Foundation. Retrieved February 6, 2002, from the World Wide Web: www.globalfundatm.org/contribute.html, 2002.

Venter JC. The sequence of the human genome. *Science* 2001; **291**: 1304–51.

WHO. *Investing in health research and development; Ad Hoc Committee on Health Research Priorities.* Geneva: WHO, 1996.

WHO. *Macroeconomics and Health: Investing in Health for Economic Development Report of the Commission on Macroeconomics and Health.* Geneva: WHO. who.int/

whosis/cmh/cmh_report/e/report.cfm?path=cmh,cmh_report&language= english, 2001.

WHO. *Genomics and World Health, Report of the Advisory Committee on Health Research.* Geneva: World Health Organization, 2002.

Ziman J. *Prometheus Bound, Science in a Dynamic Steady State.* Cambridge: Cambridge University Press, 1994.

Chapter 8

Public health infrastructure and knowledge

John Powles and Flavio Comim

8.1 **Introduction**

One of the most striking features of mortality decline during the twentieth century was its decreasing dependence on national income levels. As the century progressed, populations were able to attain ever-higher life expectancy at given levels of real income, gaining from "shifting the curve" relating income to life expectancy, rather than from "moving along the curve" (World Bank 1993, p. 34).

Fundamental to "shifting the curve" has been developments in the production, use, and dissemination of public health infrastructures and their associated knowledge, which have acted synergistically to improve health. The institutions and commodities that may be defined as "infrastructure," together with knowledge, can be seen as the three main interacting determinants of health levels in populations, each of them having medical and non-medical aspects,[1] as illustrated in Fig. 8.1.

The importance of these three factors operating together may be seen when, for example, considering the importance of commodities. Alone, command over commodities (real income) is an imperfect predictor of health status. As argued by Sen (1992, 1999), individuals' conversion of commodities into health is contingent on their capabilities and the institutions and knowledge available to facilitate that conversion. Two populations may, for example, have equivalent purchasing power for food, yet one may have access to a "Mediterranean" diet, and the other may not, or one may be aware of the health benefits of such a diet and the other may not. In either case, infrastructure—such as physical availability of food types or as publicly assimilated knowledge of the effects of specific diets on health—may

---

[1] Throughout this chapter we use "medical," usually in a broad sense, when referring to institutional responses to disease and reserve "health" to refer to the condition of being free of disease and disability. Considerable loss of meaning can result from confusing the two.

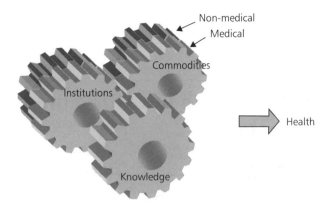

Fig. 8.1 A schema of the major determinants of health levels in populations

explain differences in rates of coronary heart disease, rather than the commodity of "food" *per se*. It is therefore important to emphasize the role of public health institutions and knowledge as determinants of health, as well as what may more traditionally be seen as commodities, and to note the complex links between them.

The purpose of this chapter is to examine the nature of such institutions, knowledge, and commodities to the extent that they constitute "public health infrastructures." More directly, the chapter will consider the extent to which these infrastructures may usefully be seen as either global public goods for health (GPGH) in themselves, or, more indirectly, as "access goods," which serve to support other GPGH.

The remainder of this chapter is divided into four parts. Section 8.2 examines the concept of public health infrastructures and notes, in particular, the extent to which such infrastructures tend to be embedded in other social structures. Section 8.3 examines public health infrastructures through the lens of economics, and considers the extent to which they may appropriately and usefully be viewed as (global) public goods, as intermediate goods or as access goods. Section 8.4 considers the action that might be taken to consolidate and build public health infrastructures, and notes the fundamental role played in such endeavors by the creation and transmission of knowledge. The fourth part concludes.

8.2 **What are public health "infrastructures"?**

Rutherford has defined infrastructures as "the basic services or social capital of a country, or part of it, which make economic and social activities possible . . ." (Rutherford 1992, p. 226). In terms of public health, they are the formal and enduring structures that support public health, having both tangible and intangible aspects and existing inside and outside the governmental sector. They may be directly protective of health—as in public sanitation systems—or they may support other activities that protect and enhance health.

The elements of public health infrastructure that tend to be easiest to recognize and to describe are those concerned with areas such as communicable disease control (including the safety of food), the protection of the health of mothers and children, and the control of environmental contamination. Less easy to identify are those infrastructures related to the control of noncommunicable disease and injury. However, in all these cases, effective improvements in public health require the three elements alluded to earlier, namely:

(1) *institutions* and capacity appropriate to respond to these problems and associated tasks (given the needs and circumstances of the country involved);

(2) *knowledge*, as assimilated and put to use both by the general population and by professional and administrative staff; and

(3) necessary *commodities* (resources or "tangible" infrastructure).

Each of these three elements is outlined in more detail below.

8.2.1 **Institutional capacities**[2]

Public health activities have two prerequisites. First, and arguably most important, is an appropriate legal and regulatory framework to enforce public health measures, in concert with the wider contribution of health-related civic organizations. CEA Winslow, the respected US public health leader, writing at the end of a period of very rapid mortality decline in the first quarter of the twentieth century thought that "the discovery of the possibilities of wide-spread social organization as a means of controlling disease was one which may almost be placed alongside the discovery of the germ theory of disease itself as a factor in the evolution of the modern public health campaign" (Winslow 1929, p. 200).

Such institutional capacities—encompassing both state and non-state actors—require a country's political and social institutions to accord due priority to collective measures to control disease. The political recognition of this priority will typically be supported by the perceived social and political legitimacy of public health endeavors. This legitimacy derives both from the intrinsic importance of health to wellbeing, and from the importance of health to economic and social development (WHO 2002). Politicians who have become used to thinking of spending on health services as a form of discretionary consumption need to be convinced that disease control also plays an important role in economic development (Arora 2001, Bhargava *et al.* 2001). Issues relating to regulatory structures are considered further Chapters 9 and 10.

---

[2] We use "institution" in its sociological sense, to be distinguished from "organizations," such that "organizations are the players—for example, individual providers, hospitals, clinics, pharmacies, and public health programs. Institutions are the rules (formal rules and informal customs)—the socially shared constraints that shape human interactions, along with the mechanisms by which these rules are enforced." (WHO 2000, p. 61).

Second, public health services need the capacity to monitor and respond to changing patterns and determinants of disease. Just as national public health agencies are oriented in their tasks by systematic surveillance of trends within the populations for which they are responsible, so too can they benefit from an appreciation of where their own country's health experience fits in relation to the experiences of countries in broadly similar circumstances. International public health surveillance performs this role but remains highly dependent on national surveillance capacities that have, in turn, their own institutional requirements. In middle- and high-income countries surveillance systems can typically be built on the foundations provided by comprehensive systems for the registration of vital events and of notifiable diseases. In low-income countries surveillance systems will, of necessity, be less comprehensive, but some effective system remains essential. Communicable disease surveillance in all countries requires laboratory facilities to identify pathogens and assess their antimicrobial sensitivities. Surveillance also requires mutually intelligible systems of disease classification, such as the WHO sponsored "International classification of diseases, injuries and causes of death"; now in its tenth revision.[3] Surveillance has also been highlighted as important in other chapters, such as that concerning antimicrobial resistance, AMR (see Chapter 4).

8.2.2 Staff education and training, and wider knowledge

Staff with appropriate competences do not emerge from nowhere, and nor can they function effectively in professional isolation. The quality of institutions for vocational and research training in public health disciplines is an important determinant of staff effectiveness. Their capacity to absorb the evolving international professional culture of public health and to acquire and assimilate the latest knowledge—increasingly with the aid of digital technologies—will also determine their effectiveness. The capacities of countries to absorb and make good use of the global stock of knowledge has been shown in the work of Jamison and colleagues to be a very powerful predictor of mortality decline: "some countries are better than others at absorbing ideas and technology from the world, harnessing technological and intellectual developments outside their country to boost those within it, and implementing new solutions as they become available" (Jamison *et al.* 2002).

As Powles (2001) has shown, increases in knowledge bring health benefits not only by enhancing the effectiveness of professional medicine and public health, but also by contributing to changes in public consciousness and behavior. If the assimilation of knowledge by the whole population is important, and if, in many

---

[3] Such conventions themselves provide fine examples of GPGH, but there is unfortunately not space to explore these in more detail here.

important instances, such assimilation depends on informal channels rather than formal public health programs, then it makes little sense to talk about health as some commodity-like entity that can typically be "delivered" by "interventions."

8.2.3 **Physical infrastructures**

Industrialization increased wealth but, initially at least, reduced health, with rapid urbanization associated with rising mortality levels (Szreter and Mooney 1997, Haines *et al.* 2000). Overcoming this "urban penalty" required a deliberate (i.e. politically, rather than market-mediated) reconfiguration of the physical infrastructures of cities (Szreter 1988). Sewers were laid, and safe water supplies secured. House construction was regulated with aim of making it more conducive to health. Later, industrializing countries were able to draw on this experience to foreshorten or abort their experience of the "urban penalty," and today mortality tends to be lower in urban, rather than rural, areas in low-income countries (Jin *et al.* 1998).

The means by which urban life has been made compatible with low transmission risks for serious food- and water-borne infection are an important component of public health infrastructures, but they are now so widely "taken for granted" as to be virtually invisible. Thus, during the period of intense debate about "sanitary reform" in British cities in the mid-to-late nineteenth century, the protection of public health was seen to entail, above all, the provision of safe public water supplies and systems for sewage disposal. Yet few, if any, countries today count spending on sewers and safe water supplies as part of their spending on health. Thus, although in the early twenty-first century safe water supplies and sewerage systems continue to be important parts of the public health infrastructure, they now have their own formalized systems of administration and their distinct visibility as part of the public health infrastructure has reduced. Successful measures to control the health risks associated with living in cities have thus been incorporated into the fabric of modernity itself and, paradoxically, have lost their salience as public health infrastructures. Analogous examples could be drawn from areas such as road safety, product safety, and pollution control. It may, therefore, be salutary to remember that what one "has" in the way of public health institutions may be rather more than what one "sees."

8.3 **Public health infrastructures: global public goods or "access goods"?**

As indicated in Chapter 1, "pure" public goods are those goods that are non-excludable and non-rivalrous in consumption. These characteristics lead to such goods being undersupplied. Although there are few goods that would be classified as "pure" public goods in this way, there are many which have varying degrees of "publicness," where we might find heuristic or practical value in treating them *as if they were* public goods. A further important category of goods with respect to public health are those which may be termed "access goods," defined in Chapter 1 as those "nonpublic" goods which are necessary for populations to access the public good of primary interest. The extent to which the elements of public health infrastructure outlined above are considered to be public goods, and the degree to which they may be treated as such under the guise of "access goods," is considered in more detail here.

First, to what extent are public health infrastructures GPG etc. Table 8.1 outlines the three main elements of public health infrastructure highlighted in Section 8.2 (institutions, knowledge, and physical infrastructure), and assesses them according to their degree of rivalry, excludability, and globality.

These broad elements of public health infrastructure may therefore, at best, be classed as "impure" public goods—goods that present strong externality effects, but are subject to some degree of excludability or rivalry—most notably goods that, while often non-rivalrous in consumption, are to some extent excludable and thus "club goods" (see Kaul *et al.* 1999, p. 2).[4]

Further, in terms of the geographical dimension, public health infrastructures are typically limited in the "sharing" of their benefits by their local context. In addition, the pharmaceutical, medical, institutional and practical knowledge, or capabilities involved in the constitution of public health infrastructures seems also to fit a description of "club" or "imperfect" public good: they present very high positive externalities but individuals can be excluded from their benefits. A complex picture thus emerges when we think of the connections between public health infrastructures and GPGs.

8.3.1 Public health infrastructure as "access" goods

The criteria for "public" and "club" goods ignore the more foundational properties of much of public health infrastructure in providing *access* to other (global public) goods for health. For example, the control of cross-national transmission of communicable disease has strong elements of non-excludability and non-rivalry. However, this control has to be achieved utilizing nonglobal, and nonpublic, goods, such as policy regimes, surveillance, and intervention to control relevant infection. These elements are not themselves GPGH, but the GPGH of control of the transnational spread of communicable disease is contingent upon their provision and implementation, and hence their importance as access goods to that final GPGH (see also Chapter 4). Similarly, stratospheric ozone depletion and global warming are now generally accepted as consequences of the disruption of natural processes by human productive activities. Over the longer term, increasing weather instability may cause major degradation of food producing resources (by shifts in agro-climatic zones) and the inundation of cropland, for example, the Ganges

---

[4] It must be noted that both excludability and rivalry are, of course, questions of degree. These three elements of public health infrastructure are influenced by a diversity of circumstances, and it is therefore important to analyze their determinants and how they might be influenced by different policies and funding arrangements.

Table 8.1 Characteristics of elements of public health infrastructures that extend to the global level, with illustrative examples

Element	Excludable?	Rival?	Level of intervention	Comment
(1) *Institutions—overall*	Either	Non-rival	Local/national/ regional/global	
Example: International public health organizations in support of global smallpox eradication	No: all benefit from eradication	Partly	Global	Enormously favorable benefit/cost ratios even for major funders for whom smallpox imposed mainly regulatory costs (eg US contribution repaid by regulatory savings each 26 days)
(2) *Staff education/ training (embodied knowledge)—overall*	Excludable	Rival	Local/national/ regional/global	
Example: Professional division of labor in public health and systems of training for professional roles	No	Partly	Mainly national	Strongly influences the capacity of countries to assimilate knowledge for the control of disease. Global externalities of national public health competencies may constitute GPG
(3) *Resources—overall*	Excludable	Rival	Local/national/ regional/global	
Example: IT infrastructure supporting knowledge transmission (including internet-accessible scientific journals and bibliographic databases)	Excludable	Partly	Local/national/ regional/global	Electronically published journals will soon be more accessible than paper journals for health professionals in low-income countries

delta in Bangladesh. Stocks of natural resources are in many cases, intrinsically global, and their preservation a GPG (see Chapter 5). Avoidance of the potential adverse health effects of ecological degradation depends on the development of international regimes to control, for example, greenhouse gas emissions, and these regimes may depend in turn on systems for monitoring carbon releases, meteorological conditions, and so on. So yet again, achievement of the preservation of this good of an undisrupted human habitat is contingent upon the mostly national goods that help provide access to it.

The spatial dimension of the three elements of public health infrastructure, may be envisaged as extending from the local through to global level. However, it is more likely that the national provision of these elements will contribute to global externality effects within the realm of public health. For example, the prevention of the international transmission of disease, of lifestyles both favorable and unfavorable to health and of environmental health risks, constitute important GPGH. The global transmission of medical knowledge (broadly considered to include both popular and professional public health knowledge) and of organizational solutions to health problems may thus help provide the tools to tackle those tasks, and itself exert an important externality effect in contributing to improved health in countries other than the one in which the relevant disease control methods were developed.

Public health infrastructures may therefore best be seen as "access goods," because they contribute to the provision of final GPGH. This may be directly, such as through the provision of sewers, but also indirectly, through externality effects. For example, in the case of medical and organizational knowledge, positive externalities may have an international domain, as in the case of the smallpox eradication program in Africa (1959–80), which "trained African assistants, developing dispensary skills in many communities and leaving a legacy of usable and transferable skills for other vaccination and control programs" (Malowany 2000, p. 344). For practical purposes then, the provision of access goods may be seen as part of the general provision of GPGH. The degree to which these goods are then excludable or not then becomes important to the extent of assessing different methods of finance, since, because these goods produce externalities, the impact of alternative financial regimes on their provision may be significant (see Chapter 1).

8.4 Building public health infrastructures: Aspects of provision and financing

Public health infrastructures tend to be national by nature. Thus, the national and local aspect of their provision and finance is critical to their global availability and benefit. Although this depends on the tangible dimension of infrastructure (e.g. public health laboratories, number of doctors, and sanitation), consideration should not be limited to it. This is primarily because local conditions will influence the absorption and adaptation of knowledge, the less tangible aspect of public health infrastructure referred to in this chapter.

The national public health institutions of rich countries, and the global public health institutions that are heavily dependent on their material support, provide some help for the development of public health infrastructures in poor countries. The externalities that arise from the strengthening of public health infrastructures in poor countries yield, in turn, GPGs for all, as already noted, in areas such as communicable disease transmission. This is a major justification—and for some, a sufficient one—for support for these endeavors from rich countries.

However, the benefits of global investment in public health infrastructures in poor countries may transcend the sphere of public health issues. It is well known that health is an important element of human capital formation, and that the improvement of health produces a positive effect on the generation of economic growth and productivity. Rich countries face other serious international problems, such as those of illegal immigration and lack of external demand for their goods, which could be partially helped by the provision of a better quality of life for people living in poor countries.

8.4.1 Knowledge and public health infrastructures

"Just as there are national public goods, so there are international ones, and many types of knowledge fall into this category. No single country will invest enough in the creation of such goods, because the benefits would accrue to all countries without the creating country receiving full compensation. But international institutions, acting on behalf of everyone, can fill this gap" (World Bank 1998, p. 6).

As indicated, knowledge is a vital, albeit less tangible, element in the characterization of public health infrastructures. Although knowledge is considered to be an archetypal public good (Stiglitz 1999), it is often made excludable through, for example, patents, copyrights, or fees for educational establishments. However, most importantly, once knowledge is produced it is non-rival, and under these circumstances it is not efficient to artificially exclude people from using it. In this case, the issue becomes one of how the production of such knowledge is to be achieved, as it is only through exclusion that the private sector will reap the profits needed to justify their investment in research. The paradox to be solved is thus how to ensure both the incentive to produce knowledge whilst ensuring that all may benefit from it (see Chapter 6).

One of the main (international) collective-action problems concerning public health infrastructure concerns balancing the incentives for the generation of new knowledge with the need for its optimum social provision. Attempts at universalizing the provision of pharmaceutical knowledge, for example, might undermine the incentives for the protection of property rights of investments made in this field. Conversely, the undersupply of trained staff, physical infrastructure, and medicines that are crucial for basic public health in poor countries should not be seen exclusively as a problem of the governments of those countries, but as part of an international division of labor that does not favor the production of these goods in all places where they are needed. *International* institutional solutions, rather than merely national ones, are needed to overcome this coordination problem, with private provision complemented by international arrangements that entitle countries to achieve optimum levels of social provision.

There are two forms of financing that warrant mention in this respect. First, subsidies and incentives could be given to the *production* of new knowledge. Second, the costs of *transmission*, absorption, and adaptation of this knowledge could be reduced. These are discussed in more detail below.

Production of knowledge

Reductions in the price of knowledge could be funded either by taxes or by changes in the mark-ups of big producers of knowledge (their products are usually price-inelastic). This will not be adequate alone; final production will be determined by participatory and social processes that will point out the extent of their undersupply. Financing mechanisms and incentives should also be given at a local level where these GPG will be adapted, modified and used.

However, in addition to direct finance and production, there are wider determinants of the provision and consumption of public health infrastructures. Key amongst these are: the very close link with poverty—programs aimed at poverty reduction may strengthen the sense of empowerment and opportunity, and reduce the feeling of vulnerability, of the poor, contributing to the efficiency in the building of public health infrastructures in their communities; and the close link with schooling (especially primary schooling)—it is well known that the higher the levels of literacy of a population, the lower the levels of under-5 mortality rates.

Of special concern in the context of public health infrastructures are those areas of research need which lack commercial or institutional incentive for investigation—for example "orphan diseases" affecting only the poor, who cannot be expected to pay prices (for e.g. for drugs) that would be sufficient to reimburse commercial R&D expenditures. International action is occurring to secure "public–private partnerships" to fund work in these areas (see e.g. the Global Alliance for TB Drug Development (http://www.tballiance.org). It is in this respect that international institutions have a pivotal role as intermediaries in the provision of knowledge for many countries.

Transmission of knowledge

Yet, it is not just the provision of knowledge that is of importance: perhaps even more so is its transmission. Although the production of knowledge can be costly, and may in some cases involve very low levels of publicness, when knowledge is produced its transmission might be subject to external economies or diseconomies. When the transmission of knowledge is subject to economies, externalities and the divergence between private and social returns may be high. External economies in the transmission of knowledge may result from a decrease in the marginal costs of transmission due to new technologies e.g. the Internet. There are two primary elements determining the degree to which transmission of knowledge is achieved.

First, knowledge must be *usable or embodied*. Knowledge can be *usable* when it consists of advice or general information to the population that is easily communicable (e.g. knowledge of how to treat common illnesses), or can be *embodied* when it consists of knowledge incorporated in routines, codified operations, and techniques that are needed for the implementation of public health infrastructures (e.g. knowledge of how to attain high coverage in a vaccination program). Knowledge embodied in public health infrastructure can be more or less adaptable to local conditions, can take more or less advantage of new information technology and reduced costs of communication, and can be more or less trusted. Trust is perhaps the most underrated element determining the success of knowledge use, with the World Bank suggesting that "access to knowledge is of little benefit if people do not trust the source. Health workers can suggest good contraception techniques, but poor women might not use them because they suspect that the workers do not understand their life circumstances" (World Bank 1998, p. 13). Two-way information flows is therefore crucial to ensure that full advantage of the knowledge embodied in public health infrastructures is taken.

Second, the dissemination of knowledge depends also on the levels of schooling of local populations. New knowledge may be blocked by traditional practices so that people do not become aware, for example, of the potential benefits of antibacterial drugs and vaccines. The observation that parental, especially maternal, schooling predicts child survival in many low-income populations points to the importance of the household as a locus of "medical practice": that is, a place where the application of modern knowledge about disease can save lives (Hobcraft 1993, p. 164). Caldwell (1986), for example, suggests that schooling is important to health improvement because it enhanced the authority of "outside" knowledge relative to local (traditional) knowledge. Fears that the communication dimension of globalization will damage health by the "transmission of unhealthy lifestyles," such as cigarette smoking, have some credibility. However, openness to cosmopolitan knowledge appears to have strongly favorable effects on child survival.

Medical professionals (of all kinds, not just physicians) and scientists tend to be universalists by professional culture. Insomuch as they value the advance of knowledge, they are also likely, therefore, to value its widespread application. This professional culture, plus the falling marginal costs of information transmission by digital means, has combined to make medical journal editors and others aware of new ways of facilitating information transfer to low- and middle-income countries. Not only are medical literature databases, such as Medline, available free of charge, there are strong moves to increase the range of full text literature available free on-line. Pub Med Central, supported by the US National Library of Medicine, is inviting "all journals to join those that have already committed to creating this resource for people all over the world."[5] Biomed Central, based in the United Kindgom, has started publishing more than 50 free-access on-line journals

---

[5] http://www.pubmedcentral.nih.gov/about/intro.html.

covering the whole of biology and medicine.[6] Given the fundamental importance of the dissemination of knowledge to health improvement, developments such as these represent significant new GPGH. Their accessibility in low-income countries will naturally depend on the development of infrastructures for digital communication but these are likely to develop quickly in the near future (Godlee *et al.* 2000).

Overall, the global nature of knowledge cannot be taken for granted. It depends not only on the externalities it can generate, but also on difficulties in propagating these externalities. These difficulties may be due to problems related either to its transmission or local adaptation. The effective use of knowledge can be facilitated by institutions and policies that simultaneously recognize the importance of its global nature and the array of difficulties in its transmission and use.

8.5 Conclusion: The role of public health infrastructures

Public health policies and programs can be classified as either "vertical" or "horizontal." Global programs to date have been largely dedicated to specified objectives, typically in relation to specific diseases. These "vertical" programs, with experts marshaled from around the globe, support from dedicated funding, hierarchical management structures, and quantitative objectives, are likely to appeal both to those with backgrounds in business and to those wary of the capacity of local institutions to make good use of international aid. They also undoubtedly have impressive achievements to their record. Smallpox was eradicated by such a "vertical" program, and polio may soon succumb to another (see Chapter 2). Currently, vertical programs are being developed for malaria ("roll back malaria"), HIV/AIDS and tuberculosis (see Chapter 3).

"Horizontal" programs are locally based and directed. Village-based programs in a low-income country aimed at increasing the capacity of mothers to prevent and manage diarrheal disease is an example. Vertical and horizontal approaches are best considered complementary, with some public health problems best addressed by one, some by the other and many by elements of both.

Whilst programs with a "vertical" emphasis have an important role to play, the current concentration of international public health assistance on programs of this type is unwise. Such an emphasis cannot compensate for the neglect of public investment in local public health infrastructures. And it is not "evidence-based" to the extent that it is incongruent with evidence on the relative importance of different factors to mortality declines over recent decades (Jamison *et al.* 2002). Care should therefore be taken to ensure that the mobilization of resources for vertical programs is not at the expense of the continuing development of broad-based— "horizontal"—programs, which, in most cases, remain the best candidates for achieving further major gains in health.

---

[6] http://www.biomedcentral.com/info/whatis.asp.

Consideration of public health infrastructures from the perspective of GPGs does not disallow justifications for widening the provision and finance of such goods on an international basis for other reasons, such as strategic or security grounds. For example, a world in which the least advantaged national populations fail to benefit from public health advances may be judged less safe—especially since the events of September 11, 2001—than a world in which there is coordinated action to strengthen public health institutions in all populations (the relevant expectation would be that a strengthening of such infrastructures would help improve health in the least advantaged populations and by this means to improve global security). Alternatively, global action to strengthen public health infrastructures could also be based on the expectation that it would help to legitimize concurrent processes such as financial globalization and trade liberalization that were desired for other reasons. Committing resources with the aim of giving globalization a "human face" (Koh 1999) or "making globalization work for all" could, plausibly, be seen as a defensible political objective by some parties, given the vocal force of recent opposition to "globalization."

Neither of these two types of justification—the strategic nor the legitimizing—requires that the case for global public action be coherent with economic theory. However, the economic perspective is equally important, as strategic or legitimizing justifications need to be proven feasible. The concept of GPGH (and the associated concept of "access goods") therefore need not compete with more extensive action motivated by a sense of human solidarity, or by the legitimation needs of the proponents of other policies or by the perceived strategic needs of states. The concept provides a useful analytic concept for identifying (minimum) global common interests and the international actions they indicate on the grounds of the rational self-interest of relevant actors, free of other considerations.

Considering public health infrastructures under the GPGH lens may thus have heuristic value, for example in helping to clarify why it may be in the interest of the citizens of rich countries to support the strengthening of public health infrastructures globally. We have however, reservations about viewing public health infrastructures through the lenses of "GPGs" or "access goods." There is the danger (even though it is not instrinsic to the concept) that the analytic device of regarding public health infrastructures as "goods"—or as the means of access to such goods—can encourage the false idea that decisions can readily be made to "produce" more of them or not, depending mainly on the availability of vertically commandable resources—that is, that the availability of money is the main constraint on the production of such goods. We argue instead that the connections of such infrastructures to an array of social institutions must first be understood.

We have argued that public health infrastructures could be understood in a wider framework than the one based exclusively on the criteria of non-rivalry and non-excludability. By overcoming a narrow dichotomy between public and private goods, we might be able to understand the mechanisms attached to the degree of publicness of different goods. More importantly, perhaps, we might be able to define a set of economic policies concerning regulations, externalities, exclusion, and transmission costs, etc that could guide governments and international institutions in the strengthening of global public health infrastructures as a means of protecting global public health.

Future work on the importance and effect of public health infrastructures in the provision of GPGH should therefore focus on the international transmission mechanisms that may allow the financing and support of these goods. Emphasis should be given to the international coordination problems that would need to be overcome in order to produce coherent, efficient, and equitable patterns of provision and distribution of infrastrcutures. A more comprehensive assessment of the effects of health improvements in poor countries would also deserve further scrutiny.

References

Arora S. Health, human productivity and long-term economic growth. *J Econom Hist* 2001; **61**: 699–749.

Bhargava A, Jamison DT, Lau LJ, Murray CJ. Modeling the effects of health on economic growth. *J Health Econom* 2001; **20**(3): 423–40.

Caldwell JC. Routes to low mortality in poor countries. *Popul Dev Rev* 1986; **12**: 171–220.

Godlee F, Horton R, Smith R. Global information flow: publishers should provide information free to resource poor countries. *BMJ* 2000; **321**: 776–7.

Haines MR, Craig LA, Weiss T. *Development, Health, Nutrition and Mortality: The Case of the "Antebellum puzzle" in the United States.* National Bureau of Economic Research, Cambridge, MA (NBER Working paper series on historical factors in long run growth No: h 0130), 2000.

Hobcraft J. Women's education, child welfare and child survival: A review of the evidence. *Health Transit Rev* 1993; **3**(2): 159–75.

Jamison DT, Sandbu M, Wang J. Why has infant mortality decreased at such different rates in different countries? Background Paper 4, Working Group 1, WHO Commission on Macroeconomics and Health, 2002.

Jin SG, Yang GH, Bos E *et al.* Child mortality patterns in rural areas of Anhui and Henan provinces in China, 1990. *Biomed Environ Sci* 1998; **11**: 264–76.

Kaul I, Grunberg I, Stern MA (eds) *Global Public Goods: International Cooperation in the 21st Century*, New York: Oxford University Press for The United Nations Development Programme, 1999.

Koh T. Prologue, In: I Kaul, I Grunberg, MA Stern (eds) *Global Public Goods: International Cooperation in the 21st Century*, New York: Oxford University Press for The United Nations Development Programme, 1999, pp. x–xi.

Malowany M. Unfinished agendas: Writing the history of medicine of sub-saharan Africa. *African Aff* 2001; **99**: 325–49.

Powles JW. Healthier progress: Historical perspectives on the social and economic determinants of health. In: R Eckersley *et al.* (eds) *The Social Origins of Health and Well-being: From the Planetary to the Molecular.* Cambridge: Cambridge University Press, 2001, pp. 3–24.

Rutherford D. *Routledge Dictionary of Economics.* London: Routledge, 1992.

Sen A. *Inequality Reexamined*. Oxford: Clarendon Press, 1992.

Sen A. *Development as Freedom*. Oxford: Oxford University Press, 1999.

Stiglitz J. Knowledge as a global public good. In: I Kaul, I Grunberg, MA Stern (eds) *Global Public Goods: International Cooperation in the 21st Century*. New York: Oxford University Press for The United Nations Development Programme, 1999, pp. 308–25.

Szreter S. The importance of social intervention in Britain's mortality decline c.1850–1914: A re-interpretation of the role of public health. *J. Soc Social Hist of Med* 1988; **1**: 1–37.

Szreter S. Mooney G. Urbanisation, mortality and the standard of living debate: New estimates of the expectation of life at birth in nineteenth-century British cities. *Econom Hist Rev* 1997; **51**: 84–112.

Winslow CEA. *The life of Hermann M. Biggs*. Philadelphia; Lea and Febiger, 1929.

World Bank. *Investing in Health: World Development Report*. Oxford: Oxford University Press for the World Bank, 1993.

World Bank. *World Development Report 1998—Knowledge for Development*. Oxford: Oxford University Press for the World Bank, 1993.

World Bank. *World Development Indicators, 2000*, Book and CD ROM edn. Washington: World Bank, 2000.

WHO. *World Health Report 2000: Health Systems: Improving Performance*. Geneva: World Health Organization, 2000.

WHO. *Macroeconomics and Health*. Geneva: World Health Organization, 2002.

Enabling global public goods for health: the importance of legislation

Chapter 9

International law

David P Fidler

9.1 Introduction

In the national context, governments have primary responsibility for the production and/or finance of public goods. In the international context, however, no central government exists to structure interstate relations, and as such states interact in a condition of "anarchy." International law, as "a body of rules governing the mutual interaction not only of states but of other agents in international politics," emerges from this anarchical structure of international relations (Bull 1977).

In international relations theory (IRT), schools of thought explain international cooperation (and the lack of it) differently (a brief description of the position of four leading schools of IRT *vis-à-vis* international cooperation, the concept of Global Public Goods (GPGs) and any role for international law in the production of GPGs is provided in Table 9.1). Although each school of IRT differs on the *nature* of international cooperation and the role of international law within it, all posit that the *function* of international law in international relations is to facilitate interstate cooperation. Indeed, arguments that international law is an "intermediate" GPG are based on the same basic conclusion—that international law is a tool that states frequently use to structure cooperation in the international system (Kaul *et al.* 1999, Taylor and Bettcher 2000).

This chapter focuses on international law as a tool in the production of Global Public Good for Health (GPGH). Section 9.2 describes the importance of international law and its practical and normative elements. Section 9.3 outlines the various actors that are the subjects of international law, and Section 9.4 examines the main sources of international law. Section 9.5 discusses the use of international law in the production of GPGH, and Section 9.6 reviews a number of limitations in the use of international law in this context. Section 9.7 concludes with a discussion of key issues in the application of international law to GPGH production.

Table 9.1 GPGs, international law, and international relations theories

International relations theory	Does the theory recognize the concept of GPG?	What is the role of international law in the production of GPG?
Realism	No, interstate cooperation in the condition of anarchy is weak, fragile, and vulnerable to defection because of state pursuit of power	International law reflects either (1) a temporary convergence of national interests based solely on expediency; or (2) the exercise of power by the strong against the weak
Institutionalism	Yes, states can learn to overcome the difficulties anarchy poses and build cooperation based on concerns of mutual interest	International law is critical to institutionalism's explanation of how states cooperate in the condition of anarchy to achieve common objectives
Liberalism	Yes, but the concept of GPGs is colored by liberalism's emphasis on individual liberty, democracy, and free trade	International law is central to liberalism's descriptive explanations and normative outlook on international relations
Constructivism	Yes, states can socially construct their interactions in anarchy in ways that accommodate the idea of GPGs	International law is often seen as a fundamental mechanism through which states socially construct anarchy in different ways to achieve common interests and values

9.2 International law: A practical and normative necessity

Since the development of the territorial state in the late European Renaissance, humanity has been divided into sovereign states, producing a particular political structure for human interaction—the international system (Watson 1984). An international system "is formed when two or more states have sufficient contact between them, and have sufficient impact on one another's decisions, to cause them to behave—at least in some measure—as part of a whole" (Bull 1977). The international system contains independent territorial units that are interdependent because they interact and affect each other's fate. Because no supreme power controls state behavior in an international system, the potential for cooperation and conflict exists. As interaction is unavoidable, states need mechanisms for regularizing their contacts. A chief mechanism devised for this purpose over the historical development of the international system has been international law.

International law differs from law within a state because it arises from a different political structure. The argument that international law is an illusion because it cannot be enforced flows from the wrong assumption that domestic law, which can be enforced, reflects the nature of law in every context. International law was developed, however, because no supreme political authority exists in the international system. To argue that international law is not enforceable like domestic law simply describes the factual context of international relations, rather than saying anything interesting about international law. International law arises and operates within a very particular political structure, and it is within this structure that we have to understand the function of international law in facilitating international cooperation.

The facilitation of international cooperation by international law comprises both a *practical* and a *normative* element. The development of international law embodies the realization of states that rules and procedures were needed to regulate their day-to-day interactions, such as rules governing the exchange of diplomats, the exercise of jurisdiction, and the formation of international agreements. All states share a common interest in regularizing their political and economic contacts to produce order and stability in the international system. International law fulfills this *practical* need by providing rules that stabilize and harmonize systemic interactions.

International law also fulfills the *normative* need created by the anarchical structure of international relations. In facilitating cooperation, international law helps states create the "anarchical society": states interacting in anarchy use international law as a means to construct an international society, which exists "when a group of states, conscious of certain common interests and common values, form a society in the sense that they conceive themselves to be bound by a common set of rules in their relations with one another, and share in the working of common institutions" (Bull 1977).

The rules of international law therefore form the sinews of international society for several reasons. First, as previously indicated, international law fulfills practical day-to-day needs of the international system. Second, fulfilling practical systemic needs over time creates, refines, and deepens a process that structures how states deal with new problems. New rules may be needed to facilitate cooperation in the face of novel problems or threats. International law provides a mechanism for the international system to change and evolve. As states adapt to new challenges, the practical and normative range of common state interests and values expands, as does the body of international law that contains the rules facilitating cooperation. Third, the deepening and broadening of international law allow states to raise deeper normative questions and issues that ask whether the prevailing international order is just, equitable, or moral. Figure 9.1 illustrates how the normative functions of international law build on the foundation laid by international law's practical organization of systemic interaction.

The development of public health as an issue in international relations illustrates the dynamic depicted in Fig. 9.1. The body of international law regulating the day-to-day interactions of states developed historically without reference to public health. International diplomacy on public health did not emerge until the

Fig. 9.1 Functions of international law

mid-ninteenth century, when infectious disease control became a matter of interstate concern. International control of infectious diseases in the nineteenth century posed a new normative and practical problem for which new procedures, represented by a series of international sanitary conferences, and new rules, embodied in international sanitary conventions, were created but which were built on the existing edifice of international law (Howard-Jones 1975). In the twentieth century, the normative and practical vision for public health expanded through: the creation of international health organizations, which began to look at global public health problems beyond infectious disease control (Goodman 1971); and the evolution of radically new legal and moral concepts such as health as a fundamental human right constitution of the World Health Organization 1946.

Global public goods are equivalent to the common interests and values that define the nature of the international society among states. International law represents the common set of substantive rules used by states in their interactions to achieve their common interests and values. States also use international law to create common institutions, such as international organizations (IGOs), that become focal points for cooperation on problems of mutual concern. Through IGOs, states use international law to create ongoing diplomatic processes that allow substantive approaches to new problems to develop as the regime evolves.

This description of the role of international law in the production of GPGs echoes both institutionalism and constructivism because it: recognizes that states use international law for practical, selfish reasons to address problems that cannot be handled except through international cooperation; and captures how international law can be adapted to receive new ideas and approaches that affect both the normative and practical aspects of state interaction.

9.3 Subjects of international law and GPG production

Thus far analysis has focused exclusively on states as the relevant actors in the use of international law in the production of GPGs. However, the environment in which international law operates is more complicated: while, historically, only states were subjects of international law, the list of subjects has expanded to include not only IGOs but also non-state actors, such as individuals, nongovernmental organizations (NGOs), and multinational corporations (MNCs). The expansion in the subjects of international law reflects the extent to which states have, in the development of international society, created new tools (e.g. IGOs) and crafted new public–private partnerships with NGOs and MNCs as part of international cooperation (Buse and Walt 2000*a*,*b*). The production of GPGs through international law is therefore not strictly *international* but *global* in that states and non-states actors are involved in the production and implementation processes.

The World Health Organization (WHO) Framework Convention on Tobacco Control (FCTC) is a prime example because it involves an effort to include non-state actors more formally into the treaty-making process (see Chapter 11). Prior to intergovernmental negotiations, WHO invited submissions from non-state actors about the proposed treaty and the global tobacco problem (WHO 2000). WHO received more than 500 submissions from non-state actors and held two days of public hearings on the proposed FCTC in which more than 170 non-state actors participated. WHO's effort to reach out to civil society groups widens the FCTC process from one that is strictly international into a global public health initiative.

Similarly, WHO seeks more involvement from non-state actors in the revision of the International Health Regulations (IHR) (see Chapter 10). WHO has proposed including in the revised IHR the authority for the Organization to receive disease information from WHO Member States *and* non-state actors (WHO 2001). Under this proposal, WHO may approach Member States confidentially about information received from, for example, NGOs (WHO 2001). The IHR process for ensuring maximum protection against the international spread of disease with minimum interference with world traffic will, if this proposal survives, be globalized through the involvement of global civil society.

Non-state actor involvement in the production of GPGs through international law does not, however, mean that non-state actors have equal status or authority with states. States remain the dominant subjects of international law for the purposes of GPG production. Rules of international law overwhelmingly address state rights and duties in the international system. This fact is important for understanding the production of GPGs. Whether at the national or international level, public goods require governmental intervention because private actors have insufficient incentives or resources to produce the goods. The growth of NGO and MNC involvement in international law does not, by itself, represent progress in the production of GPGs because whether states—the public actors—actually produce the public goods remains the central question.

9.4 **Sources of international law and GPG production**

International law is often associated with treaties, even though two other important sources of international law are customary international law (CIL) and "general principles of law recognized by civilized nations" (Brownlie 1995). The dynamic depicted in Fig. 9.1 helps explain why treaties have gained the lion's share of attention in GPG analysis. Historically, rules governing the day-to-day, practical interactions of states developed through the process of CIL. A rule of CIL forms when states exhibit general and consistent state practice with respect to an issue and display, in following the practice, a sense that they are legally obligated to do so (Brownlie 1998). CIL produced various GPGs, such as orderly diplomatic intercourse and the process for states to enter binding agreements.

When new problems confront states, existing rules of CIL are often not responsive. The start of international health cooperation in the mid-nineteenth century provides a good example. Because international cooperation on infectious disease control had not featured in international politics prior to the convening of the first international sanitary conference in 1851, no general and consistent state practice existed on which to base rules of CIL for infectious disease control. States turned to treaty law to create rules to deal with the new problem. As a general matter, every public health issue subsequently addressed through international law had to be approached through treaty law rather than CIL because state practice did not contain any generality, consistency, or sense of legal obligation with respect to any approach to the public health problem.

Even in situations where a rule of CIL arguably exists in a public health context, states need treaty law to advance the GPG in question. For example, some international environmental lawyers argue that states have a CIL duty to conserve natural resources, such as rain forest (Birnie and Boyle 1992, WHO 1997). Leaving aside whether state practice actually supports such a duty, CIL also recognizes that states have permanent sovereignty over their natural resources and can exploit them according to their own economic and environmental policies (Fidler 2001). The two customary duties conflict, and the only way to overcome this conflict is through the negotiation of a treaty on deforestation that balances the right to exploit with the duty to conserve.

Another problem with CIL in connection with the production of GPGs relates to the generality of customary rules. For example, international lawyers argue that states have a customary duty not to cause damage to the territory of other states through transboundary pollution (Birnie and Boyle 1992). Even though many international legal experts believe that CIL imposes this duty, treaty law on transboundary air pollution has been necessary to make the international legal obligation more precise and effective (Fidler 2001). The generality and ambiguity of many customary rules do not support specific action on global problems, necessitating the resort to treaty law to construct a more appropriate approach and substantive rules (Fidler 1996).

As for "general principles of law recognized by civilized nations," this source of international law is not used much in any context (Brownlie 1998), so it does not represent a robust source of international law for the production of GPGs. Under general principles of law, international lawyers attempt to find domestic rules of law that are present in many states that may be extracted from their domestic context and applied internationally. Typically, this exercise occurs when international courts or tribunals experience a gap in treaty or CIL while resolving a dispute (Brownlie 1998). For example, how should an international court treat circumstantial evidence in a dispute between two states? No treaty or customary rule provides guidance, so international courts have looked at how national court systems deal with circumstantial evidence and then molded those domestic principles into an approach suitable for the international dispute. This "gap-filling" function cannot support vigorous international action against perceived global problems.

The predominant importance of treaty law has positive and negative effects for the production of GPGs. Positively, states can use treaties to create institutions and specific rules that directly address global problems. The formation and interpretation of treaties is also a well-defined area of international law (e.g. Vienna Convention on the Law of Treaties 1969), which makes working with treaties easier than with CIL. On the negative side, treaties are the source of international law that is most sensitive to sovereignty. States are not bound by treaties unless they give their affirmative consent to be bound. By contrast, rules of CIL are universally binding on all states except those that persistently object to the rule, which has proved a difficult exception to meet (Charney 1985). Treaty law's strong recognition of sovereignty often means that states refuse to join treaties designed to produce GPGs, or states withhold their consent until treaty obligations are diluted such that joining the treaty imposes less onerous burdens. In either case, treaty law's sensitivity to sovereignty contains the potential for states to undermine international public action on global problems.

9.5 International law and GPGH

Global public health provides an excellent case study of the importance of international law to the production of GPGs. This section analyzes two important issues in the relationship between international law and the production of GPGH.

9.5.1 The neglect of international law by WHO

An interesting feature of the role of international law in the production of GPGH has been the historical neglect of international law by WHO (Taylor 1992, Fidler 1998). WHO's Constitution empowers WHO to adopt treaties on any matter within the competence of the Organization and to adopt binding regulations in specific areas of international public health concern, such as the international spread of infectious diseases (Constitution of the World Health Organization 1946). To date, WHO has not adopted a single treaty on any public health issue, and has only twice used its power to adopt binding regulations: once in connection with nomenclature issues (Fluss 1998) and once to adopt the IHR on infectious disease control (IHR 1969). WHO's indifference toward international law is also evident in the way the Member States of the Organization allowed the IHR to become irrelevant to the international spread of infectious diseases (Fidler 1999). Nor did WHO pay particular attention to many international legal regimes being developed and implemented by states and other IGOs that affected its public health mission.

WHO's historical lack of interest in international law in producing GPGH is a complex phenomenon, but three reasons for this neglect of international law can be identified. First, the neglect may reflect WHO's institutional culture, which is dominated by public health experts, physicians, and medical researchers (Taylor 1992). In such an environment, the use of national and international law received low or no priority. Second, WHO came into existence at the beginning of a revolutionary period for biomedical tools, such as antibiotics and vaccines. Its activities were therefore focused on delivering these and other new tools of public health and medicine directly within countries, and international legal initiatives were not necessarily needed to accomplish these tasks (Fidler 1998). Third, WHO's limited experience with trying to create regulatory regimes are fraught with controversy and conflict. The story of the development of the international code on the marketing of breast-milk substitutes provides one example of the acrimony WHO interest in the regulation of international trade for public health purposes generated among WHO Member States (Shubber 2000).

Despite WHO's attitude toward international law, the activities of the Organization depend on international law, primarily through the structure and processes created and supported by the WHO Constitution—a treaty between WHO Member States. International law thus formed the foundation for the international regime that WHO developed, so even WHO's experience substantiates the idea that international law is practically and normatively necessary for the production of GPGH.

During the 1990s, WHO launched two initiatives suggesting that international law may be seen as a more important instrument of global public health policy in the future. The first involved the revision of the IHR to make them more relevant to the global problems faced from emerging and re-emerging infectious diseases (see Chapter 10) (Fidler 1999). The second was the decision to develop the FCTC (see Chapter 11). This effort marks the first time in its history that WHO is exercising its treaty-making powers (Taylor and Bettcher 2000). Also in the 1990s, WHO began to show more awareness of other international legal regimes, such as international trade law and the World Trade Organization (WTO), that affect its public health mission.

Important as it may be, focusing only on WHO's neglect of international law nonetheless produces a distorted image of the role of international law in the area of public health. The protection of human health is an objective that states, IGOs, and NGOs have embedded in many areas of international law (Fidler 1999). A significant proportion of international environmental law exists, for example, to protect human health (Fidler 2001); yet none of this international law was developed within WHO. Other areas of international law that contain rules and institutions that protect human health include international trade law, international human rights law, international humanitarian law, international law on arms control, international law on narcotic drugs, and international labor law, as illustrated in Table 9.2.

The frequency with which international law addresses the protection of human health suggests that this objective represents a strongly held common interest and value among states in the international system (Guerrant and Blackwood 1999). In other words, the shared value of protecting human health is part of what characterizes contemporary international society. The widespread presence of international legal rules on the protection of human health also underscores the practical and normative importance that states, IGOs, and NGOs attribute to such protection in the operation of the international system. These observations reinforce this chapter's argument that international law is necessary to the production of GPGH.

9.5.2 The use of international law in the production of GPGH

The large body of international law relevant to the protection of human health makes summarizing the contribution of international law to the production of GPGH difficult, but four conceptual uses can be identified.

First, states use international law to construct formal institutions empowered to work on global public health problems. WHO provides the classical example of such an institution; but other organizations, such as the United Nations Environment Programme (UNEP) and the International Labour Organization (ILO), also engage in the production of GPGH. Such institutions engage in many activities that contribute to the production of GPGH, including scientific and policy research, information gathering and dissemination, promulgation of "best practices," policy coordination and leadership, and technical assistance to Member States.

Second, states use international law to establish procedures through which states and non-state actors come to grips with specific global public health problems. In the infectious disease control area, the IHR set up the process through which WHO Member States attempt to achieve maximum protection against international disease spread with minimum interference with world traffic (IHR 1969). Another example of the procedural approach is found in the framework convention strategy used in many areas of international environmental law. Framework conventions contain few, if any, substantive duties but focus on creating a diplomatic process that concentrates on a given problem, such as transboundary air pollution, ozone depletion, protection of biodiversity, and climate change. WHO adopts this procedural approach in its efforts to negotiate the FCTC.

Third, states use international law to craft substantive duties in connection with particular global public health challenges. The IHR obligate WHO Member States, for example, to notify the Organization of specific disease outbreaks and to restrict health-protecting trade measures to specified responses (IHR 1969).

Table 9.2 International law and the protection of human health

Area of international law	Recognition of the value of protecting human health	Specific examples
International environmental law	Rules seek to protect human health from exposure to health-damaging substances or processes	Treaties on transboundary movements of air pollution, water pollution, hazardous wastes, hazardous chemicals and pesticides, depletion of the ozone layer, and climate change
International trade law	Rules allow trade restrictions that are necessary to protect human health	Principles in multilateral (e.g. WTO) and regional (e.g. NAFTA, EU) that regulate the application of health measures that restrict trade
International human rights law	Rules that protect individuals from torture and that provide that health is a fundamental human right	Treaties protecting civil and political rights and treaties promoting economic, social, and cultural rights
International labour law	Rules that protect worker safety and health in the workplace	Treaties on occupational safety and health and on protecting workers from hazardous workplace conditions
International humanitarian law	Rules that protect individuals and populations from health threats in times of armed conflict	Treaties protecting prisoners of war, treatment of civilians under occupation, and prohibiting attacks on civilian populations
International law on arms control	Rules that ban the development and use of weapons especially harmful to human health	Treaties prohibiting chemical and biological weapons
International law on narcotic drugs	Rules that regulate the illicit use of narcotic drugs and prohibit their illicit use	Treaties harmonizing national policies on the manufacture, trade, and consumption of narcotic drugs
International law on genetic engineering	Rules that regulate the scope of genetic engineering and the subsequent products	Treaties banning cloning of humans and regulating the international trade in genetically modified organisms

In ILO occupational safety and health treaties, ILO Member States undertake to reduce worker exposure to specific harmful substances and workplace conditions (ILO 1981). In the international legal regime on ozone depletion, the protocol to the framework convention obligates states to reduce emissions of ozone-depleting substances by specific amounts (Montreal Protocol on Substances that Deplete the Ozone Layer 1987). International human rights treaties prohibit states from engaging in torture and other forms of inhuman or degrading treatment or punishment of prisoners and detainees (United Nations Convention against Torture and Other Cruel, Inhuman or Degrading Treatment or Punishment 1984).

Fourth, states can create, through international law, mechanisms to enforce substantive legal duties against states that accept them. Enforcement mechanisms come in many forms, from states' self-reporting of progress made in connection with certain goals articulated in a treaty, as found in United Nations human rights treaties (International Covenant on Civil and Political Rights 1966, International Covenant on Economic, Social, and Cultural Rights 1966), to formal adjudication of state-to-state disputes by an international tribunal, as seen in the WTO's dispute settlement mechanism (Understanding on Rules and Procedures Governing the Settlement of Disputes 1993).

The four uses of international law in the production of GPGH differ in the breadth and depth of their impact on global public health problems. The institutional approach offers breadth of coverage, as illustrated by the myriad public health problems dealt with by WHO, and breadth of membership, as evidenced by WHO's near universal membership. While making such breadth possible, the WHO Constitution lacks depth in terms of the legal obligations of Member States with respect to any given public health problem. The WHO Constitution imposes only two substantive duties on Member States, which are to: pay their share of the WHO budget; and submit periodic reports on various public health matters (Constitution of the World Health Organization 1946).

The construction of procedural approaches to specific public health problems provides more legal depth but less breadth because specific public health problems are singled out for greater attention (e.g. international infectious disease or tobacco control). Adoption of specific substantive rules regulating state behavior produces greater depth and less breadth because such rules seek to channel state behavior in ways that will reduce the public health problem in question. Enforcement mechanisms represent the deepest and narrowest layer because states have decided not to tolerate violations of specific substantive rules.

This four-level typology of international law suggests that the production of GPGH would benefit most when states have created international legal rules at all four levels. Historically, WHO's approach to the production of GPGH remains largely at the institutional level because it does not, outside the IHR, deepen its legal approach to any global public health problem. Outside WHO, states and IGOs have attempted to create deep international legal regimes in trade, human rights, labor, and environmental protection by crafting procedural mechanisms, substantive rules, and sometimes enforcement strategies.

WHO's move to revise the IHR and to negotiate the FCTC perhaps represents a sea change at the Organization concerning the role of international law in the production of GPGH. Other experts are also encouraging much more precise international legal regimes on global public health problems. For example, in 1999–2000 four proposals were aired concerning the need for special treaties on the rights of the mentally ill (WHO 1999), funding global vaccine supplies (Barton 2000), pandemic influenza vaccine supply, global alcohol control (Jernigan 2000), and improving global access to essential drugs and vaccines (Pecoul 2000).

9.6 The limitations of international law in the production of GPGH

The global public health community believes that GPGH are seriously undersupplied. Many commentators have noted how globalization may exacerbate public health problems nationally and internationally, from the global spread of infectious diseases to the worsening of occupational safety and health conditions worldwide. Clearly, at the very least, this perspective suggests that, although international law may be *necessary*, it is not *sufficient* for the production of GPGH. This section explores some (but by no means all) of the limitations that confront the use of international law in the world politics of public health.

9.6.1 The role of power in global public health

The emphasis of Realism (see Table 9.1) on power in international politics means that it has no robust concept of GPGs or international law. Realism posits that GPGs only come into being when powerful states want or need cooperation on a given issue. Power politics determines the agenda and the outcome of international cooperation. Those familiar with the world politics of public health know that power still matters in shaping the global public health agenda and the nature of international cooperation. If the great powers of public health, such as the United States of America and the European Union, are not engaged in the production of specific GPGH, then the chances for producing such goods are diminished. One need look no further than the HIV/AIDS debacle in Sub-Saharan Africa to see the consequences of great power indifference toward a global public health problem (Attaran and Sachs 2001). Further, great power opposition to certain international legal regimes can place the production of certain GPGH in jeopardy, as illustrated by the United States' refusal to participate in the Kyoto Protocol on climate change (see Chapter 5) and the proposed compliance protocol to the Biological Weapons Convention.

9.6.2 The state-centric, consent-based nature of international law

While non-state actors play important roles, international law remains largely state-centric—the dominant actors are states and the bulk of the duties generated by international legal activity target states. This reality means that the jealous guarding of sovereignty by states, which has long complicated and weakened international law, continues to cause problems for international cooperation. In the context of GPGH, the need to rely almost exclusively on the treaty as a source of international legal rules heightens the role sovereignty plays because treaty rules only bind when a state consents to be bound.

The "sovereignty problem" creates a general dynamic in international law on GPGH—the "inverse triangle effect"—that undermines the production of such goods. The dynamic works like this: the more superficial the international legal obligations, the greater the number of states joining the international legal regime. As the international legal obligations in the regime become more onerous, participation by states decreases. Figure 9.2 illustrates the inverse triangle effect using the four levels of international law discussed previously.

The inverse triangle effect also appears in specific areas of international law, such as international environmental law, where framework conventions establishing a procedural approach to a problem gain wide adherence but protocols to the conventions imposing very specific obligations do not attract as many state adherents (Fidler 2001). The layering of the international legal regime as designed by the framework-protocol strategy does not, therefore, necessarily achieve its objective.

The "sovereignty problem" is also apparent in international legal regimes that contain institutional, procedural, substantive, and enforcement elements. For example, the IHR contain all four elements, but WHO Member States have historically ignored the procedural and substantive duties as well as the enforcement mechanism. The unwillingness of states to comply with the IHR illustrates the

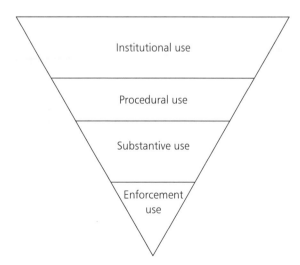

Fig. 9.2 The "inverse triangle effect"

vulnerability of international legal regimes on GPGH to the expedient preferences of sovereign states.

9.6.3 Priorities in the production of GPGs

Another factor that complicates the use of international law in the production of GPGH involves perceived conflicts between GPGH and other GPGs. These conflicts have arisen most famously in the context of international trade law. Many commentators have analyzed the question whether the GPG of trade liberalization, supported by the international trade law overseen by the WTO, trumps the GPG of better environmental protection pursued through international environmental law. Similar questions have arisen about whether trade liberalization takes priority over public health concerns and the improvement of international labor standards.

Non-state actors can also find themselves at loggerheads over priorities. In the dispute over compulsory licensing and parallel importing of HIV therapies in South Africa, MNCs and NGOs squared off in a bitter controversy about whether access to HIV therapies should take precedence over the protection of intellectual property rights. States can minimize such conflicts over priorities in the drafting of treaties, so international law can be used to finesse priority controversies. Whether the priorities are struck in a way that favors the production of GPGH is, however, not a legal but a political question determined by the give-and-take of diplomacy.

9.6.4 Financing international legal regimes

The production of GPGH requires resourcing. IGOs have to be funded. Diplomatic negotiations to adopt new procedures and rules are expensive endeavors. National laws and policies have to be changed in light of substantive duties contained in treaties. Developing countries require technical and financial assistance to participate effectively in regimes seeking to produce GPGH. Financial woes plague the use of international law to produce GPGH.

Member states chronically under-fund WHO. Developing countries complain that the cost of participating in negotiations for new regimes or the revision of existing regimes is prohibitive, leaving them voiceless as new procedures and rules are set. Developing countries also routinely complain that technical and financial assistance promised in some international legal regimes arrives in inadequate amounts, with too many strings attached, or not at all. As with priority setting, the use of international law for the production of GPGH is hostage to states deciding and agreeing to spend the financial sums necessary to sustain the international legal regime over the long-term.

9.6.5 Weaknesses of governments and national systems of law

Another limitation on the use of international law to produce GPGH relates to the interdependency between international and national law. The creation of international legal duties represents only the first legal step in producing GPGH. In virtually every case involving public health problems, states have to incorporate the international legal obligations into national law and policy. If the incorporation process breaks down, the entire international legal regime is jeopardized because states have not taken the necessary policy and legal measures domestically to attack the problem in question. Commentators have noted the weaknesses of many developing countries with respect to their national legal systems generally (Fox 1999) and domestic public health law specifically (L'hirondel and Yach 1998). Multiplying international legal regimes on GPGH does little to address the incorporation of international legal norms into domestic law and policy if states do not simultaneously improve the rule of law in developing countries.

9.7 Conclusion: The future of international law in producing GPGH

For the foreseeable future, humanity will remain divided into sovereign states interacting in a condition of anarchy. International cooperation on public health matters will continue to be practically and normatively necessary. International law will continue, therefore, to play a central role in the production of GPGH. There are some indications that the use of international law to achieve GPGH may increase as WHO and non-state actors push for specific international legal regimes on particular global public health problems and the global public health community becomes more sophisticated in understanding how international law affects the mission of global public health. Three trends will likely characterize the foreseeable future of international law's role in the production of GPGH.

First, the creation and refinement of traditional international legal instruments, namely treaties, on public health issues will continue. Within WHO, the role of international law will be defined by how Member States revise the IHR and develop the FCTC. Outside WHO, treaty making and refinement will also continue to occur, as evidenced in 2001 by the adoption of the Stockholm Convention on Persistent Organic Pollutants (UNEP 2001) and the revision of the Kyoto Protocol on climate change (United Nations Framework Convention on Climate Change 2001).

Second, public health controversies and conflicts will continue in many international legal regimes bearing on public health, such as international trade law and human rights. The global fight over access to essential drugs and vaccines pits intellectual property protection under the WTO agreements against claims that such access is a fundamental human right. The outcome of this dispute and other controversies surrounding the role of public health in international trade law, such as the public health impact in developing countries of liberalization in international trade in health services under the General Agreement on Trade in Services, will play a significant role in shaping international law's role on the production of GPGH in the future.

Third, new forms of governance regimes will appear that will present public health with institutions, rules, and procedures different from the traditional international legal model represented by treaties and IGOs. These new institutions, rules, and procedures will develop in initiatives such as the Global Fund to Fight AIDS, Tuberculosis and Malaria (G8 Genoa Communique 2001) and the public–private partnership to reduce the costs of second-line tuberculosis drugs and to ensure their proper use (Gupta 2001). The latter effort provides new institutions, procedures, and rules that differ markedly from traditional international legal approaches to the production of GPGH. Tuberculosis-control projects in affected countries are offered lower-priced second-line tuberculosis drugs obtained by the public–private partnership through negotiations with drug manufacturers, but access to such drugs is conditioned on the projects adhering to international recommendations for establishing DOTS-Plus projects (Gupta 2001).

A body known as the "Green Light Committee," consisting of representatives from the WHO, two national governments (Peru and the United States), and civil society groups (Royal Netherlands TB Association, Harvard Medical School, Médecins Sans Frontières), makes decisions about access to lower-priced tuberculosis drugs (Gupta 2001). The new institution, procedures, and rules attempt to make sure that cheap drugs are both available to treat tuberculosis and used properly to prevent the development of drug resistance. The institution, procedures, and rules are not, however, created through a treaty, rule of CIL, or general principle of law. Further, civil society participation seems as critical to the creation and implementation of the new regime as the involvement of WHO and representatives from states. The contribution of this and other novel governance regimes to the production of GPGH deserves close attention in the future, particularly in connection with their impact on public health in developing countries.

Whether the refinement of existing international legal regimes and the creation of new ones will constitute progress in the production of GPGH, especially for developing countries, is by no means certain. Framing global public health problems in terms of the production of GPGH does not shed radically new light on the role of international law in the world politics of public health. The protection of human health is present as an objective in many existing international legal regimes; but many public health officials fear global public health problems are growing worse, not better, in the developing world, despite all the relevant international law. The implication of the analysis presented in this chapter is that developing countries need to devote more attention to international law and public health, particularly as it relates to the three trends described above.

Obstacles stand, however, in the path of this recommendation. First, developing countries generally exhibit weak capabilities in international law (Gaubatz and MacArthur 2001). Second, capacity in national and international public health law is weak worldwide. Third, developing countries generally have weak public health systems; and some developing regions, such as Sub-Saharan Africa, are experiencing deterioration (Simms 2001). This situation provides difficult ground on which to try to improve the use of law in any form to produce public goods for health.

A strategy to improve the supply of GPGH that concentrates only on international law will, to paraphrase Edmund Burke, rely too heavily on the "instrumental part" of international relations, while ignoring the more fundamental problem that the protection of human health globally may not in fact be an "obligation written in the hearts" of developed and developing states in the international system (Burke 1796). The undersupply of GPGH can only be remedied when the *national* and *international* commitment of states to the interdependence of individual and population health in the global era becomes less superficial. The disappointing level of financial commitments made to date by developed countries to the Global Fund to Fight AIDS, Tuberculosis and Malaria ($1.5 billion committed by G8 countries (G8 Genoa Communique 2001)) against an estimated need of $7–10 billion *annually* just to fight HIV/AIDS (Annan 2001) indicates that commitment to producing GPGH among developed states remains shallow.

As suggested by constructivism, international law can prove useful in challenging states to re-conceptualize their approaches to global public health problems. But international law is, at the end of the day, merely a tool whose use and effectiveness is controlled and determined by the values and creativity of those sculpting the political, economic, and social fate of the human race.

References

Annan K. We can beat AIDS. *New York Times*, June 25, 2001.

Attaran A, Sachs J. Defining and refining international donor support for combating the AIDS pandemic. *Lancet* 2001; **357**: 57–61.

Barton J. Financing of vaccines, *Lancet* 2000; **355**: 1269–70.

Birnie PW, Boyle AE. *International Law and the Environment.* Oxford: Clarendon Press, 1992.

Brownlie I. Statute of the International Court of Justice, June 26, 1945. In: *Basic Documents in International Law*, 4th edn. Oxford: Clarendon Press, 1995, 438–55.

Brownlie I. *Principles of Public International Law*, 5th edn 1998, Oxford: Clarendon Press, 1998.

Bull H. *The Anarchical Society: A Study of Order in World Politics.* London: Macmillan, 1977.

Burke E. First letter on a regicide peace (1796). In: DP Fidler, JM Welsh (eds) *Empire & Community: Edmund Burke's Writings and Speeches on International Relations.* Boulder, CO: Westview Press, 1999, pp. 287–320.

Buse K ,Walt G. Global public–private partnerships: Part I—a new development in health? *Bull WHO* 2000*a*; **78**: 549–61.

Buse K, Walt G. Global public–private partnerships, Part II—What are the health issues for global governance? *Bull World Health Organ* 2000*b*; **78**: 699–709.

Charney J. The persistent objector rule and the development of customary international law. *Br Yearbook Int Law* 1985; **56**: 1–24.

Constitution of the World Health Organization (1946). In: *WHO. Basic Documents*, 40th edn. Geneva: World Health Organization, 1994, pp. 1–18.

Fidler DP. Challenging the classical concept of custom: Perspectives on the future of customary international law. *Germ Yearbook of Int Law* 1996; **39**: 198–248.

Fidler DP. The future of the World Health Organization: What role for international law? *Vanderbilt J Transnat Law* 1998; **31**: 1079–126.

Fidler DP. International law and global public health. *Univ Kansas Law Rev* 1999; **48**: 1–58.

Fidler DP. Challenges to humanity's health: The contributions of international environmental law to national and global public health. *Environ Law Report* 2001; **31**: 10048–78.

Fluss SS. World Health Organization. In: H Nys (ed.) *International Encyclopaedia of Laws: Medical Law*, Vol. 1. Boston: Kluwer, 1998, WHO/1-WHO/99.

Fox GH. Strengthening the state. *Indiana J Glob Legal Stud* 1999; **7**: 35–77.

G8 Genoa Communique. At http://www.genoa-g8.it/eng/attualita/primo_piano/ primo_piano_13.html, 2001.

Gaubatz KT, MacArthur M. How international is "international" law? *Mich J Int Law* 2001; **22**: 239–82.

Guerrant RL, Blackwood BL. Threats to global health and survival: The growing crises of tropical infectious diseases—our "unfinished agenda." *Clin Infect Dis* 1999; **28**: 966–986.

Gupta R. Responding to market failures in tuberculosis control, *Sciencexpress*, July 19, at www.sciencexpress.org, 2001.

Goodman NM. *International Health Organizations and Their Work*, 2nd edn. London: Churchill Livingstone, 1971.

Howard-Jones N. *The Scientific Background of the International Sanitary Conferences 1851–1938.* Geneva: World Health Organization, 1975.

ILO. C155 Occupational Safety and Health Convention, June 22. *United Nations Treaty Series* 279, 1981.

IHR. (1969). In: *WHO International Health Regulations*, 3rd Annu. edn. Geneva: World Health Organization, 1983.

International Covenant on Civil and Political Rights. *United Nations Treaty Series* 171, 1966.

International Covenant on Economic, Social, and Cultural Rights. *United Nations Treaty Series* 3, 1966.

Jernigan DH. Towards a global alcohol policy: Alcohol, public health and the role of WHO. *Bull WHO* 2000; **78**: 491–9.

Kaul I, Grunberg I, Stern MA. *Global Public Goods: International Cooperation in the 21st Century.* New York: Oxford University Press, 1999, pp. 2–19.

L'hirondel A, Yach D. Develop and strengthen public health law. *World Health Stat Q* 1998; **51**: 79–87.

Montreal Protocol on Substances that Deplete the Ozone Layer. *Int Legal Mater* 1987; **26**: 1550–61.

Pecoul B. *Priorities for Research and Development.* Paper presented at the International Conference on Infectious Diseases, Okinawa, Japan, December 7–8, 2000.

Shubber S. *The International Code of Marketing of Breast-milk Substitutes: An International Legal Measure to Protect and Promote Breast-Feeding*, Boston: Kluwer, 2000.

Simms C. *The Bitterest Pill of All: The Collapse of Africa's Health Systems*, London: Save the Children, 2001.

Taylor AL, Bettcher DW. WHO framework convention on tobacco control: A global "good" for public health. *Bull World Health Organ* 2000; **78**: 920–9.

Taylor AL. Making the World Health Organization work: A legal framework for universal access to the conditions for health. *Am J Law Med* 1992; **18**: 301–46.

Understanding on Rules and Procedures Governing the Settlement of Disputes (1993). In: JH Jackson *et al.* (eds) *1995 Documents Supplement to Legal Problems of International Economic Relations*, 3rd edn. Minneapolis, MN: West Publishing, 1995, pp. 366–90.

United Nations Convention against Torture and Other Cruel, Inhuman or Degrading Treatment or Punishment (1984). In: I Brownlie (ed.) *Basic Documents on Human Rights*, 3rd edn. Oxford: Oxford University Press, 1992, pp. 38–51.

UNEP. *Final Act of the Conference of Plenipotentiaries on the Stockholm Convention on Persistant Organic Pollutants*. UNEP Doc. UNEP/POPS/CONF/4, June 5, 2001.

United Nations Framework Convention on Climate Change. *Review of the Implementation of Commitments and Other Provisions of the Convention—Preparations for the First Session of the Conference of the Parties Serving as the Meeting of the Parties to the Kyoto Protocol (Decision 8/CP.4)*. UN Doc. FCCC/CP/2001/L.7, July 24, 2001.

Vienna Convention on the Law of Treaties. *United Nations Treaty Series* 331, 1969.

Watson A. European international society and its expansion. In: H Bull, A Watson (eds) *The Expansion of International Society*, Oxford: Oxford University Press, 1984, pp. 13–32.

World Health Organization (WHO). *Framework Convention on Tobacco Control*, at http://tobacco.who.int/en/fctc/index.html, 2000.

WHO. *Global Health Security—Epidemic Alert and Response: Report by the Secretariat*. WHO Doc. A54/9, April 2, 2001.

WHO. *Health and Environment in Sustainable Development: Five Years After the Earth Summit*, Geneva: World Health Organization, 1997.

WHO. *Raising Awareness, Fighting Stigma, Improving Care: Brundtland Unveils New WHO Global Strategies for Mental Health, Sees Poverty as Major Obstacle to Mental Well Being*. WHO Press Release WHO/67, November 12, 1999.

Chapter 10

International health regulations and epidemic control

Johan Giesecke

10.1 Introduction

The international spread of epidemics has been a constant companion of the movement of people, animals, and goods across borders, and control measures have mostly consisted in trying to close these borders to infection. However, in addition to responding to a real health threat, presumed risk of contagion has often served to justify barriers to traffic as a means of trade restriction, thus compromising epidemic control through fear of disproportionate economic losses due to other countries' protective measures.

The international health regulations (IHR) are the product of 150 years of international attempts to balance these two concerns, seeking to merge efficient infection control with as little trade restriction as possible. The Regulations fulfill this objective only to some extent, and they are presently being revised (WHA 1995). This revision will have to bring the two worlds of public health and trade together if it is to realize its potential of protecting the world's population from serious epidemics and pandemics without unnecessarily harming economies.

This chapter seeks to consider the role of the IHR in coordinating international action to control the spread of epidemics from one country to the next from the perspective of the "Global Public Goods for Health" (GPGH) concept. The reasoning throughout is that the ubiquitous freedom from epidemics is the *final* GPGH and that the surveillance and control mechanisms to achieve this constitute an *intermediate* GPGH. Thus, the legislation and administrative structures to support this, including the IHR, may be seen as an *enabling* GPGH.

Following this introduction, Section 10.2 discusses to what extent the early detection and elimination of epidemics could be seen as a GPGH. Section 10.3 describes the existing international agreement aimed at such control, the IHR, and covers some of the reasons for its present revision and the problems with this agreement. Section 10.4 follows by making some suggestions how these problems could be circumvented and the IHR strengthened, and Section 10.5 concludes with an assessment of the usefulness of the GPGH concept in this context.

10.2 **Epidemic control as a GPGH**

Before considering the role of the IHR, it is important to establish whether a coordinated international effort to control the spread of epidemics necessarily constitutes a *global* and/or *public* good for health. This is considered in this section.

10.2.1 **Epidemic control as a *public* good**

For epidemic control to be a *public* good it must be non-rivalrous (the protection offered to one country should not leave other countries more exposed) and non-excludable (it should be impossible, or very impracticable, to exclude countries from the protection offered).

Nationally, most regulatory measures applied by a state to protect its citizens from infection constitute clear *public* goods for health based on this definition. For example, providing clean water and sanitation will confer a good that is both non-excludable (it will benefit everyone, even those totally unaware of the risks eliminated), and non-rivalrous (my benefit will not preclude my neighbor's). Likewise, general rules for food hygiene control will benefit everyone who buys and consumes food. For example, many countries have now gone to enormous expenses to make certain that eating beef will not carry a risk of developing variant Creutzfeldt–Jakob's disease.

These are examples of classical public health measures, originating with the "hygiene movement" at the end of the nineteenth century: people are protected from infection risks in their normal, everyday lives, and do not have to consider the risk of becoming infected every time they drink a glass of water or travel on a bus. Matters become slightly more complex for risks that are coupled to certain behaviors; sexually transmitted diseases being a good example. Here, the national public health measures focus on informing the public rather than on laws and regulations. It is conceivable that such information will primarily reach the well-informed, excluding the illiterate and the socially disadvantaged. Although such public health measures may be excludable, they remain non-rivalrous (they will not leave those groups worse off than they would have been without the measures) and hence effectively form a "club good."

The most problematic infection control action as regards the definition of "public good" is represented by the *cordon sanitaire*: in an outbreak of dangerous disease, a police or military ring is drawn around the epicentre, preventing anyone from getting in or getting out. This decreases the risk of dissemination to the wider population, but also increases the risk of becoming infected for those still susceptible trapped inside the cordon. Such a public health measure is thus exclusive as well as rivalrous (whether or not it can be justified to sacrifice the few to save the many is outside the scope of this discussion).

National infection control therefore has two parts: the identification of a health problem, and the actions taken to control it. Most countries have legislation covering both parts: the continuing surveillance of infectious diseases, and the appointed agencies to deal with problems observed. In many developed countries, those mechanisms have now been progressively refined and extended to the point at which surveillance is more aimed at detecting the occasional breakdown in routine control procedures than at the discovery of completely new problems.

What should be clear from this example of national infection control is that responsibilities for surveillance and for control are clearly defined and delineated by *legislation*. Physicians are obliged to notify certain infectious diseases, and failure to do so may have repercussions. Water companies are under strict regulations for how, and how often, the purity of their water should be checked. In addition to such public health laws, there is an increasing tendency for individuals or groups to take legal action against a company whose products may have spread disease, and such disputes can also be handled by national legislation. Such "enabling" goods are generally lacking on the international level.

10.2.2 Epidemic control as a *global* public good

For epidemic control to be a (GPG) the benefits should extend to more than two non-neighboring countries, and to the entire populations of these countries, both present and future.

In order to examine whether international infection control constitutes a GPG then, it may be illuminating to reverse the question: are epidemics a *global* public bad? For those diseases that have the ability to spread rapidly from country to country, the answer is clearly "yes." This is especially true for pandemics such as the Black Death or the 1918/19 influenza, which hit indiscriminately. Outbreaks of dangerous contagious disease anywhere in the world are a threat to people everywhere.

Does this mean that attempts by the international community to stop such spread are always GPG? Not necessarily. The international situation obviously differs from the national one in that there is no legal structure—such as a public health law—that obliges countries to report outbreaks or to take measures to protect other countries from epidemics. It is, however, a *collective action* problem at the global level, which has two facets requiring international action to secure its provision.

First, if there were an international agreement to notify all dangerous outbreaks with a potential to spread internationally, it is easy to see that countries could "free ride." They would be alerted to all external outbreaks, and thus be able to take counter-measures, such as stopping travellers or goods from affected areas. However, a failure to notify internal problems would not leave their own populations worse off—at least not in developed countries that have the resources to control an epidemic internally—and it would not have negative consequences for their own export or tourist industry.

Second, countries face a "prisoner's dilemma." The strongest disincentive to international notification has little to do with public health, but rather with economics: countries know that if they report outbreaks, their economy will suffer. There is also a "temporal asymmetry," since other countries will be much quicker to impose trade sanctions against an affected country than to lift them when the problem is over. Ideally, before the international notification system comes into place, each country should be aware of the measures other countries intend to take to protect themselves from importation of disease.

Just as for national infection control, there are two primary parts to the process: the alert function and the control measures.

Alert function

The alert function builds on the principle that when a country discovers an outbreak that may spread to other countries, it immediately notifies these other countries. In this sense, the alert function is a non-rivalrous and non-excludable GPG. Other countries are forewarned and can take action to protect their citizens. Tourists can be warned not to travel to the affected area, and arrivals of people or goods from that area can be checked for disease—or even refused. In this example it is the information itself that should be an intermediate good, but it is easy to see that unless the process is totally transparent, some countries could be excluded from information, and it would thus become a "club good" among countries with sensitive international intelligence systems.

Also, just as in the example of the "cordon sanitaire" above, "global" may not include the affected country. In most instances this country has little to gain from an alert, and more often than not it will suffer—at least in the short run. Tourists will stop coming, its citizens will be subjected to checkups or quarantine when traveling abroad, and its exports may be stopped.

Control measures

Traditionally, the strategy to stop the international spread of infection has been nationalistic: each country attempting to prevent importation of disease into its territory by quarantine measures or trade barriers. With increasingly rapid movement of people and goods between countries, this strategy is becoming less and less effective. According to the International Air Travel Association (IATA) around 500 million international flights were made in 2000, and the annual increase during the 1990s was some 7 percent (IATA 2000).

From this aspect, it would almost always be preferable for the international community if outbreaks were discovered and reported early, so that they could be eliminated where they first appeared. This would require an international alert function, but also a willingness by the developed countries to rapidly assist the less developed when a problem emerges.

Evidently, however, such coordinated international assistance could be both excludable (some countries may not be eligible for support for political reasons), and rivalrous (assistance may not be offered first to those countries most in need, but to those where the epidemic poses the most urgent threat to developed countries).

10.2.3 Summary

There are a number of specific measures that may comprise epidemic alert and control functions, which will be too numerous to consider in detail here. However,

Table 10.1 Global public good characteristics of epidemic alert and control measures

	Rival	Excludable	Global/regional/national
Alert			
Surveillance	No	Potentially	All levels
Rapid information sharing	No	Potentially	All levels
Control			
Clean water	No (usually)	No (usually)	National/regional
Vaccination	Yes	Yes	All levels
Isolation	Yes	Yes	National

the GPG characteristics of some illustrative examples of alert and control measures are provided in Table 10.1.

From Table 10.1, it can be seen that achieving the GPG of freedom from epidemics has many problems, as measures which may comprise an alert and control function may often be private or club goods. The question is therefore to what extent the IHR can be a mechanism to solve some of the potential problems that may result in the widespread use of alert and control measures, and thus achieve the final GPG of epidemic control. Before moving on to explore the IHR in more detail, however, it may be instructive to consider a specific example of international coordination of alert and control measures.

10.2.4 International alert and control—the European Union example

The realization that outbreaks need to be detected and reported early is perhaps best illustrated by present developments within the European Union. The creation of its internal market requires free movement of people, animals, and goods between the Member States. From an infectious disease control perspective, this means that the Union is effectively becoming one country with no internal borders. The need for a common approach to surveillance and control was first recognized in the Maastricht Treaty from 1993, which gave the Union competency in the field of public health, and again in Article 153 of the Amsterdam treaty from 1998.

One practical consequence of these two Treaties was the decision to set up a network for surveillance and control of infectious diseases within the Union, EC 2119/98 (European Commission 1998). The events to be reported by each Member State are defined in a short list (European Commission 2000):

(1) outbreaks of communicable diseases extending to more than one Member State of the Community;

(2) spatial or temporal clustering of cases of disease of a similar type, if pathogenic agents are a possible cause and there is a risk of propagation between Member States of the Community; or

(3) spatial or temporal clustering of cases of disease of a similar type outside the Community, if pathogenic agents are a possible cause and there is a risk of propagation to the Community; or

(4) the appearance or resurgence of a communicable disease or an infectious agent that may require timely, coordinated Community action to contain it.

Decision 2119/98 also stipulates that Member States should coordinate their efforts in prevention and control, and that they should inform each other and the Commission in advance about control measures that they plan to adopt (Article 6).

A very readable account of benefits and problems in coordinating surveillance and response between Member States, which was based on five real-life case studies has been published as a Commission project (Maclehose *et al.* 2001; see also Maclehose *et al.* 1999 for the complete report).

Even if this example of the European Union applies to a limited number of countries at similar levels of economic development and with related public health agendas, it is still illustrative since it shows that when quarantine and border controls are no longer feasible options, an international surveillance system and harmonization of control measures becomes necessary.

It should be noted that this international system for surveillance (and, to a lesser degree, control) did not primarily grow out of the concerns of the public health professionals of Europe, but rather as a consequence of the trade demands from the open internal market: that there should be as little ground as possible for Member States to revert to the "shut-all-borders" reflex in the face of outbreaks or epidemics. However, there have been several instances when this collaboration within the European Union has had a clear public health benefit in preventing further spread of disease to the citizens of the Community (Pebody *et al.* 1999, Lever and Joseph 2001).

The problems of "free riding" and "prisoners' dilemma" are to some extent countered by a subcommittee of the Council of Ministers that meets regularly to review actions taken by Member States in recent outbreak situations.

10.3 **The IHR**

As mentioned, the classical way to stop the international spread of infectious disease is to erect border controls—for people as well as for goods. At the middle of the nineteenth century, such quarantine laws in the different European states had become so disparate—and seemed so inept at stopping the spread of cholera— that the First International Sanitary Conference was called in Paris in 1851 by the Foreign Ministers of 14 European countries. That it was the Foreign Ministers and not the Ministers of Health who met is important, since it demonstrates the appreciation that the issue of international infection control is inseparably connected to the issue of traffic. That is, that: the free movement of people and goods will increase the risk of cross-border transmission; quarantine is an impediment to free trade; and public health arguments can therefore be used to justify trade barriers.

Since 1950, the International Health Regulations (IHR) have been the responsibility of the World Health Organization (WHO). They are the only *binding* international agreement on public health, whereby all WHO Member States have agreed to notify cases of certain infectious diseases, and to abide by the limits of the allowed counter-measures laid out in the Regulations. The link between public health and trade is stressed by a sentence in the portal paragraph that gives as its purpose to *"ensure the maximum security against the international spread of disease with a minimum interference with world traffic"* (WHO 1969). Very briefly, the Regulations oblige Member States of WHO to notify cases of cholera, plague, and yellow fever to the Organization, and also state the maximum measures allowed by countries to protect themselves from importation of these diseases.

10.3.1 Problems with the IHR

The need for a revision of the IHR became increasingly evident during the 1990s. The main problems with the present version of the IHR are that: it only covers the three diseases mentioned, whilst well-known ones like meningococcal meningitis or hemorrhagic fevers, or new ones like avian influenza or Nipah virus, are not addressed at all; it contains no incentive for reporting an outbreak; WHO can only act on information officially given by a Member State; and it has been ineffective in controlling protectionist over-reaction to outbreaks.

However, perhaps most problematic is that even if giving WHO responsibility for the IHR may have secured a good scientific public health input to rules and procedures, it has estranged the people involved in agreements on international trade from the process; most of whom are now not even aware of the existence of this international legislation. Among other things, this has lead to the risk of international spread of disease through trade now being debated and assessed in committees of the World Trade Organization (WTO), an arena where public health experts have little influence. We are thus seeing a separation of the two worlds of public health and traffic, a movement counter to the spirit behind the International Sanitary Conferences of 150 years ago.

Ideally, the IHR should give WHO three main functions:

1. Alert the world of potentially dangerous outbreaks.

2. If needed, coordinate international action to control them early.

3. Restrain over-reaction in the form of quarantine rules or trade barriers that lack a scientific public health foundation.

However, there are severe restrictions on the capability of WHO to fulfil each of these functions, discussed in more detail below.

Alert function

There is, generally, a weak incentive for an affected country to notify WHO of its problems. It is also questionable whether the long-term goodwill from a reputation of always being open about infectious disease problems confers any advantage to a country.

The full potential of an alert function is further restricted by the short list of diseases reportable under the IHR, and by the fact that WHO can only act on official information from a national government. Even if there is clear evidence of a dangerous outbreak that is threatening other countries, the IHR gives no mandate for WHO to spread this information if the country affected does not report it.

The argument also presumes that it is the individual countries who are most apt to discover, or verify, outbreaks within their own territories. One alternative might be that one well-equipped, developed country assumed responsibility for global surveillance. Another route is indicated by the electronic forum ProMED (ProMED 2002), in which scientists and public health officials around the world exchange information on outbreaks daily. Both these options share the problem that national control of epidemics still remains a task for each country's government—with or without external assistance.

Early control

Many developed countries could probably manage to control most of their outbreaks themselves, without outside assistance, whereas most developing countries may not. Assurance that such assistance will be provided could even act as an incentive to notify the outside world of internal problems. Following the line of reasoning that it is better to eliminate epidemics early, it may also be a net saving for developed countries to provide assistance to a less-developed country immediately an outbreak situation occurs, rather than try to prevent importation or treatment of disease later.

Such an economic gain may be clearly visible when one country is directly threatened by an outbreak in another, but less so when there is a diffuse threat to a number of countries. In this case, some international mechanism is required to share the burden and coordinate the response for the public good of many. This view on concerted actions for the prevention of international outbreaks—led for example by WHO—is probably less prevalent than the purely humanitarian wish to save lives at an epicenter of an epidemic. Resources put into such an action could thus easily be regarded as *expenditure* rather than as *investment*, and the portions granted by individual countries would not automatically correspond to that country's share of the savings from the early control of an outbreak.

Also, by definition, outbreaks are rapid events. International assistance may be required urgently, and coordination is often a problem (Goma Epidemiology Group 1995). The IHR does not automatically give this coordination role to WHO, and, even if it did, this might not be recognized by NGOs and other organizations working in the field.

Restrain counter-measures

The major problem for the IHR lies in its portal paragraph: *"ensure the maximum security against the international spread of disease with a minimum interference with world traffic."* How can trade barriers be restrained to what is necessary and sufficient for public health, so that countries feel safe in reporting their epidemic problems? (Giesecke 2000).

Overall, the IHR has not been a very effective tool for WHO to temper protective national (over) reaction to outbreaks occurring in other countries. To some extent, this is due to ignorance: present-day civil servants working in Departments of Trade or Border Control may often be unaware of an international agreement brokered by people in another field more than a generation ago.

A serious hurdle for control through the IHR is the increasing acceptance of the so-called "precautionary principle" in international trade. Even the WTO, with its stringent demands on a scientific basis for any import restrictions based on health arguments, allows countries to *temporarily* raise their trade barriers in situations of uncertainty. In an outbreak, the use of this precautionary principle could always over-ride any public health-based attempts from WHO to issue directives on what would be necessary and sufficient to control international spread. Protectionist states are reluctant to let an international organization make any decisions on their behalf. It seems very natural for those states to demand that other—often much more economically vulnerable—countries should inform the world about potentially dangerous outbreaks, but much less natural to accept that this demand requires some assurance, for the country hit by an outbreak, that reporting will not be punished by over-reaction from the rest of the world.

If the IHR is to enable the final GPGH of lower risk from international epidemics, they thus have to deal both with the incentive problem involved in alert and control from free-riding (e.g. in the equal sharing of surveillance information), and with the prisoners' dilemma inherent in the application of the precautionary principle. Some of these problems of the present IHR have been well illuminated by, among others, Fidler (1996) and Zacher (1999).

10.3.2 Other international agreements on notification of sudden health hazards

It is clear that if the IHR is to reclaim its function to protect the world from epidemics it will have to be revised in several ways. One important input to this process would be to look at other, similar, international agreements that deal with the duty to report a sudden health hazard in one country that is threatening other countries.

There exist a surprisingly large number of international conventions, agreements, regulations, guidelines, and recommendations on cross-border health effects of contaminated food, infectious diseases, nuclear and industrial accidents, toxic waste, pharmaceuticals, biological and chemical weapons, sanitary and phyto-sanitary measures, and pollution. Although there is insufficient space in this chapter to consider in detail the experiences that could be drawn from each of these agreements, a list is given in Appendix 10.1. All of these are more recent than the IHR, and there are numerous lessons that could be drawn for the IHR revision process (e.g. several of these agreements contain rather elaborated dispute resolution processes, something that will probably have to be incorporated in a revised IHR).

One particular example in the list might be the program on the international reporting on adverse events to drugs, as this has interesting parallels to the IHR with respect to potentially sensitive information. It connects the formally recognized monitoring centers of some 60 countries in a network in which participants share reports on verified, and even suspected, adverse drug reactions. The principle is thus very similar to the reporting of national outbreaks of infectious diseases that could affect other countries. Such reports on adverse reactions could obviously be very damaging to producers, even if erroneous, and it is interesting to speculate why there seems to be less reluctance from countries to participate in this network than to report under the IHR. One reason may be that it is private companies rather than nations that would be hurt, another is that the network does not try to harmonize any response—it just provides information to all the monitoring centers for them to act on individually.

10.4 **Strengthening the role of the IHR**

As mentioned, several international agreements exist on urgent public health hazards that threaten to spread from one country to another. Sharing of experience between these agencies would enable a less successful international organization to learn from the work and experience of more successful ones. A more formalized cooperation between all agencies with a task to handle urgent international public health events could be considered, and a first step would be to arrange a meeting of them all: something that has never been tried.

Returning to the IHR proper, what more has to be changed to make it a better tool for achieving the final GPG of reduced epidemics? This question can be answered on two levels: one concerns the technical structure of the agreement, the other the process around the negotiations and the place for this agreement in the international community. The second level is of more interest here, but I will just first address some necessary changes to the technical structure.

10.4.1 **New operational directions**

There are at least five changes that need to be made to the way the Regulations operate:

Use of other information sources

News about outbreaks is generally spread to the world through media or electronic discussion sites much faster than through any official channels. Although WHO cannot act on rumors, the present obligation on countries to report cases of certain diseases should be extended to an obligation to rapidly respond to requests from WHO for more information based on unofficial reports. This extension of the reporting obligation is not without its political problems, since it shifts the initiative from the country to WHO.

Informal, confidential notification

Reporting could be made more acceptable by adding a proviso to the IHR that Member States could consult WHO about an outbreak that could possibly spread to other countries without this information being made public. The Organization and the country afflicted could then work together on assessing the problem, and when—as invariably happens—the news about the outbreak reaches the media, the country could gain much credibility by explaining that it is already cooperating with WHO.

A wider remit

It is impossible to foresee the emergence of new diseases that may have a global public health impact. Also, a case of a certain, known, disease does not in itself constitute an international problem, but rather the combination of circumstances around the case: how virulent is the disease, what are its routes of transmission, and how likely is it to spread to another country? There thus seems little value in having a list of notifiable diseases in the IHR. Instead, countries should notify "urgent international public health events," with a number of criteria to define this concept given in the IHR (somewhat like the list of criteria for the European Union Early Warning System cited above).

Guaranteed assistance

The obligation of WHO to rapidly assist countries in controlling outbreaks should be clearly spelt out in the IHR. This would be one of the most important factors to increase countries' propensity to report outbreaks. Part of this assistance would also be to, when appropriate, assure the rest of the world that the situation was under control. Even for developed countries, who would manage an outbreak on their own, such a WHO function, as independent, third-party assessor of the control measures taken, could probably be of value at times, as exemplified by the BSE situation in the United Kingdom in the mid-1990s, or the West Nile virus outbreak in north-eastern United States of America in 1999.

A rapid, transparent decision mechanism

With the widened scope of the IHR from a short list of diseases to "urgent international events" it follows that adequate international control measures cannot be listed beforehand. They need to be tailored to the actual epidemiological situation, and may change as this evolves. WHO must establish a mechanism to rapidly collect the best available data, and to turn this into a recommendation or a directive. The balance between speed and participation of recognized experts in as many Member States as possible is not easy, and some kind of electronic communication seems necessary.

10.4.2 **Achieving agreement on a revised IHR**

Below follow some suggestions for how an international agreement on a revised IHR could be achieved.

Strengthened national surveillance

The IHR builds on national surveillance, which needs to be improved in many countries. Events within a country are rarely visible from the outside. This is not a politically contentious issue, but it will require large amounts of funds, for epidemiology training and capacity building as well as for improved communications and laboratory resources. Such strengthening measures would, of course, not constitute a GPGH in itself, but rather act as an "access good" necessary to achieve the primary goal of the IHR in the alert and control of epidemics (e.g. see Chapter 8).

One problem is that such structural improvement has little discernible direct effect on morbidity compared to, for example, immunization campaigns, and may thus have difficulties in attracting the interest of the donor community. However, it might help funding if it was made clearer to donor countries that building better surveillance is not without self-advantage. The strong present Nordic initiative to improve surveillance in the north-west areas of the former Soviet Union builds on a political insight that this might also help protect health in the Nordic countries themselves (Council of the Baltic Sea States 2000).

It could also be envisaged that the revised IHR would include the minimum requirements for any national surveillance system, with a time plan for when these should be met. Similar provisos exist in several other international agreements (e.g. the SPS agreement of the WTO), and such a list of necessary capacities could be used by developing countries to secure outside funding.

Contemporary negotiation process

One reason to list earlier the other international treaties on health emergencies was to point out that most of them have constituted major undertakings of their respective parent organizations, with large resource input and a prolonged process of negotiation. Within WHO, the political impetus behind the IHR revision is minimal compared, for example, with that behind the Framework Convention on Tobacco Control—another binding international agreement on public health (see Chapter 11).

There has been a tendency within WHO to regard the IHR revision as a task for experts on public health and surveillance, but this view leaves out the equally, if not more, important aspect of traffic and trade. If Member States are to accept a revised set of Regulations that give the Organization mandate to coordinate international response to outbreaks, there must be a much broader consultation and participation, not only of the national Ministries of Health, but also of the Member States as such. If WHO wants its UN mandate to coordinate international public health to apply in the area of epidemics and pandemics, it will have to invest commitment, resources and time on a scale that has so far been lacking.

In comparison, for example, the EU Network Decision took at least three years of negotiation, being a recurring agenda item in the weekly preparatory Group Santé of the Council of Ministers for large part of that period, even though the Decision explicitly states that control measures follow the subsidiarity principle, and are thus up to each Member State, not to the Community.

Working with trade

As mentioned, the WTO and especially its SPS Committee, increasingly deals with issues of trade and health. Since the membership of the WTO and WHO largely coincide, there is a risk that countries will find themselves bound by two conflicting international agreements. The revision of the IHR therefore needs to proceed in close collaboration with the WTO. Indeed, since the IHR concerns traffic and trade just as much as public health, there has even been a serious suggestion by a group of British public health experts that the revision and future supervision of IHR should in fact be wholly taken over by the WTO (Palmer *et al.* 1999). They give as one reason that this organization is influential on national governments in a way that WHO is not.

An insurance solution?

If it is agreed that the early detection and control of epidemics is a GPG, but that the threat of economic repercussions prevent a global surveillance system from functioning, one could speculate how this hurdle could be removed. For example, power companies and oil companies can secure large insurance policies against a nuclear reactor meltdown or an offshore oil rig blow-out. In a similar fashion, an outbreak of serious infectious disease could be seen as a natural disaster, against the consequences of which it should be possible to obtain insurance. A pre-requisite for the refund of economic losses could then be that the country had followed the procedures laid down in the IHR.

Of course, even under such an insurance scheme, the developed countries would most likely have to pay for the less developed, but it would be evident that this premium was primarily for the protection of the own populations, which could make it more politically acceptable.

10.4.3 **IHR and national politics**

The greatest cost of building a functioning global surveillance system lies with strengthening national capacity in a large number of countries. There is also a need for a considerably stronger technical coordination team centrally at WHO, but this cost is many orders of magnitude lower.

It may not be easy to secure funds of the size required from national budgets in developed countries: the need to improve surveillance and control in developing countries on the other side of the globe will probably come low on the priority list. Also, the notion of the world as one single arena for epidemics is still not intuitive. Instead, the reflex to return to the closing of borders lies deep within us, however inefficient this may be. Therefore this consequence of globalization needs to be stressed repeatedly to policymakers.

Another aspect from the country perspective concerns the relations between public health and trade. An adoption of a more efficient IHR will lead to a stronger position for public health in matters of trade and trade sanctions. This may not be an easy shift of balance in several countries.

10.5 **Conclusion**

An open reporting and sharing of information on outbreaks, which makes it possible for the international community to eliminate them early is a clear GPGH. Many fatal diseases could spread from any place on the globe to any other place within one or two days, often by people who are unaware of their infection.

Such a free reporting requires that the protective counter-measures taken by other countries are just those necessary and sufficient for public health, so that the reporting country will not unduly suffer economically. It also requires assured international assistance in the control of the outbreak, if necessary.

In many countries, considerable resources are required to improve surveillance. These will have to come from more affluent countries, and in order to make such assistance more politically acceptable internally it should be underlined that the early detection and elimination of outbreaks in a distant country may often be cheaper than protection at the national border later.

But how, if at all, does the thinking and terminology around GPGs help in the analysis of the IHR process? To someone unfamiliar with the field, it could be tempting to regard the GPGH discussions as a somewhat elaborate attempt to put labels on rather obvious facts. However, there are elements of the GPGH concept that make for clearer thinking. For example, it is instructive to analyze the problems of global epidemic control in terms of the potential for, and possible solutions of, the "prisoners' dilemma" and "free-riding." The GPGH concept thus highlights the need for a new IHR to make all decisions on measures as transparent and predictable as possible, thus alleviating the dilemma for the prisoners.

The GPGH analysis also suggests that the final goal of the control of epidemics is only achievable by goods (e.g. surveillance and vaccination) that are largely private or club goods. It is therefore vital to understand the fundamental nature of "access goods" in supporting a GPGH such as the IHR: there is little point in having a binding international agreement if countries cannot physically comply with it through lack of infrastructure, personnel, or other resources. There are large costs coupled to a dependable global surveillance system.

Overall then, a functioning IHR should be seen as an *enabling good*, one that provides a foundation to solving the core GPGH problem of epidemic control.

Appendix 10.1 **International agreements that require reporting of health emergencies in one country that may affect other countries**

World Health Organization: *International Health Regulations*, Geneva 1969. http://policy. who.int/cgi-bin/om_isapi.dll?infobase=Ihreg&softpage=Browse_Frame_Pg42.

International Atomic Energy Agency: *Convention on Early Notification of a Nuclear Accident,* Vienna 1986; *Convention on Assistance in the Case of Nuclear Accident or Radiological Emergency,* Vienna 1986, both at: http://www.iaea.org/ worldatom/documents/ legal/ cenna.shtml.

Codex Alimentarius Commission: *Codex Guidelines for the Exchange of Information in Food Control Emergency Situations,* 1995.

United Nations Economic Commission for Europe: *Convention on the Transboundary Effects of Industrial Accidents,* Helsinki 1992, http://www.unece.org/ env/teia/english/home-page.html.

United Nations Economic Commission for Europe and WHO Office for Europe: *Protection and Use of Transboundary Watercourses and International Lakes,* Helsinki 1992, http://www.unece.org/env/water/text/water_convention/textll.toc.htm with a *Protocol on Water and Health to the 1992 Convention on the Protection and Use of Transboundary Watercourses and International Lakes,* London 1999, http://www. who.dk/London99/WelcomeE.htm.

World Health Organization: *Network Between the Medical Products Agencies of over 50 Countries to Report Adverse Events to a WHO Collaborating Centre,* http://www.who-umc.org/umc.html.

United Nations Environment Programme: *Convention on the Control of the Transboundary Movement of Hazardous Waste and Their Disposal, Basel 1989,* http://www.unep.org.

The Biological and Toxin Weapons Convention: *Convention on the Prohibition of the Development, Production and Stockpiling of Bacteriological (Biological) and Toxin Weapons and on their Destruction.* London, Moscow and Washington 1972, http://projects.sipri.se/ cbw/docs/bw-btwc-text.html.

References

Council of the Baltic Sea States. (2001). http://www.baltichealth.org accessed on May 25, 2002.

European Commission. Decision No. 2119/98/EC of the European Parliament and of the Council of 24 September 1998 setting up a network for the epidemiological surveillance and control of communicable diseases in the Community. *Official J Eur Commun* 1998; **C268**: 1–6.

European Commission. Commission decision of 22 December 1999 on the early warning and response system for the prevention and control of communicable diseases under Decision No. 2119/98, *Official J Eur Commun* 2000; **L21**: 32–5.

Fidler DP. Globalization, international law, and emerging infectious diseases. *Emerg Infect Dis* 1996; **2**: 77–84.

Goma Epidemiology Group. Public health impact of Rwandan refugee crisis: what happened in Goma, Zaire. *Lancet* 1995; **345**: 339–44.

Giesecke J. Prevention, not panic—epidemics and trade sanctions. *Lancet* 2000; 356: 588–89.

International Air Travel Association (IATA). *International Air Travel Report.* Montreal, Lever F, Joseph CA. Travel associated legionnaires' disease in Europe in 1999. *Eurosurveillance* 2001; **6**: 53–61.

Maclehose L, Reintjes R, Camaroni I *et al. An Evaluation of the Arrangements for Managing an Epidemiological Emergency Involving More than One EU Member State.* Nordrhein-Westfalen: Institute of Public Health, 1999, Wissenschaftliche Reihe, Band 8.

Maclehose L, Brand H, Camaroni I *et al.* Communicable disease outbreaks involving more than one country: Systems approach to evaluating the response. *BMJ* 2001; **323**: 861–3.

Palmer SR, Salmon RL, Thomas DR *et al. The Contribution of Global Health Policy to the Control of Emerging Infectious Diseases* 1999, The Nuffield Trust Series No. 7.

Pebody RG, Furtado C, Rojas A *et al.* An international outbreak of Vero cytotoxin-producing Escherichia coli O157 infection amongst tourists; a challenge for the European infectious disease surveillance network. *Epidemiol Infect* 1999; **123**: 217–23.

ProMED. www.healthnet.org, 2002.

World Health Organization (WHO). *International Health Regulations.* Geneva: 1969, http://policy.who.int/cgi-bin/om_isapi.dll?infobase=Ihreg&softpage= Browse_Frame_Pg42.

Zacher MW. Global epidemiological surveillance: International cooperation to monitor infectious diseases. In: I Kaul, I Grunberg, MA Stern (eds) *Global Public Goods: International Cooperation in the 21st Century.* New York: OUP, 1999, 266–83.

Chapter 11

International law and the international legislative process: The WHO framework convention on tobacco control

Allyn L Taylor, Douglas W Bettcher, and Richard Peck

11.1 Introduction

The planetary context of development has profound implications for public health and, concomitantly, the expansion of international health law. In the global village of the early twenty-first century it is evident that the health of populations is increasingly affected by transnational economic, social, scientific, technological, and cultural forces. As a result, domestic and international spheres of health policy are becoming more intertwined and inseparable.

Although public health protection has traditionally been viewed primarily as a realm of national concern, the globalizing world requires new frameworks for international collaboration to deal with global threats to, and opportunities for, health. Consequently, the codification and implementation of binding global health norms is becoming increasingly important as global health interdependence accelerates and nations increasingly recognize the need to cooperate to solve essential problems (Taylor 1992).

Despite the evolution of international lawmaking in health and related realms of international concern in the last few decades under the auspices of numerous intergovernmental organizations, the World Health Organization (WHO) has only recently utilized its constitutional authority to promote the development of a binding international convention in any field of global public health. In particular, in May 1999 the Member States of WHO adopted a resolution that accelerated the process for negotiating WHO's first convention under Article 19 of the WHO Constitution, the WHO Framework Convention on Tobacco Control (FCTC). The historic resolution was a landmark both for WHO and global tobacco control.

The globalization of public health provides a context in which the development and implementation of global norms and standards in some areas of public health concern is becoming increasingly relevant. As an integrated world economy emerges, the provision of global public goods (GPGs) is likely to become an increasingly important issue. A salient feature of a GPG is that its provision, at least at efficient levels, requires international cooperation. The negotiation of the WHO FCTC therefore provides a significant case study of how transnational public health problems can be addressed by an international approach, and also how scientific evidence, both in the spheres of public health and economics, have provided a foundation for the development of this agreement.

This chapter presents this case study. Following this introduction, Section 11.2 outlines the public health implications of globalization and briefly reviews the role of GPGs and international legal regimes within that context. Section 11.3 describes the impact of various aspects of globalization on tobacco consumption, Section 11.4 discusses the GPG features of tobacco control and Section 11.5 discusses the "intermediate" GPG features of international law. The FCTC is examined in detail as an intermediate global public good for health (GPGH) in Section 11.6. Section 11.7 concludes with a consideration of the importance of international law and the international legislative process, as evidenced by the FCTC, in promoting GPGH.

11.2 **Globalization, public health, and public goods**

11.2.1 **Globalization**

Globalization and integration of national economies is the preeminent economic phenomena of the late twentieth and early twenty-first centuries. The roots of globalization can be traced back to the industrial revolution and *laissez-faire* economic policies of the late nineteenth century. However, the globalization of the late twentieth century is assuming a magnitude—and taking on patterns—unprecedented in world history (Yach and Bettcher 1998).

Globalization means different things to different people. On the one hand, it can simply refer to increasing financial and trade interconnectedness between countries. Of course, trade between countries has been an important feature of economic life for centuries, but this process has accelerated dramatically in the last 30 years. On the other hand, globalization suggests a much broader and more complex process of increasing economic, political, and social interdependence which takes place as capital, traded goods, persons, concepts, images, ideas and values diffuse across states' boundaries (Hurrel and Woods 1995). Many health issues cannot be resolved by national policies alone since such issues do not respect the geographical confines of sovereign states. Increased attention is being provided negative effects of an increasingly globalized world such as environmental degradation, including ozone depletion and climate change, which have negative repercussions for public health. Major transnational determinants of ill health, which would qualify as global bads, include the spread of infectious diseases via the food trade, increased trade, marketing and promotion of harmful products such as tobacco, and increased illicit trade in other harmful drugs.

Therefore, the domain of globalization includes many interconnected risks and phenomena that affect the sustainability of health systems and the wellbeing of populations in rich and poor countries. It should not be assumed, however, that all the implications for public health are negative (Yach and Bettcher 1998). It is possible that some transnational health threats could be turned into opportunities for improving our global public health futures. For example, the globalization of modern information technologies carries the risk of advancing the worldwide trade and consumption of harmful commodities, such as tobacco, but also opens many opportunities for collaborative action (Taylor 1999).

Overall, it is becoming obvious that the "polarizing effects" of globalization pose major threats to public health, and at the same time offer major opportunities for improving our global public health future. It is widely recognized that the process of globalization is also marginalizing poorer populations both in rich and poor countries—the so-called losers of globalization. In the context of the FCTC, the globalization of the tobacco epidemic is particularly relevant. This aspect of the globalization of public health debate will be addressed in detail later in this paper.

11.2.2 Globalization of public health and public goods

An over-arching theme of this chapter is that the growing number of public health concerns that are bypassing or spilling over national boundaries has ushered in a new era of global public health policy. Although there is a long history of multilateral cooperation in some limited areas of public health policy, particularly infectious diseases, public health has traditionally been viewed as a realm of almost exclusive national concern. However, with global integration has come a paradigm shift in which public health is now recognized as a topic of global concern and that many issues directly related to public health form global public goods for health (GPGH) (Chen *et al.* 1999, Zacher 1999, Taylor and Bettcher 2000).

With ever-expanding multilateral interdependence and integration, many policy questions that were once considered purely national issues or national public goods have now transcended national boundaries, since they cannot be addressed by unilateral domestic action. Domestic policy goals, such as financial stability, human security, and the preservation of culture, are more and more subject to international forces. Consequently, in recent years the international aspects of public goods have received much attention. GPGs can be categorized into intermediate GPGs and final GPGs.

- "final GPGs are outcomes rather than 'goods' in the standard sense. They may be tangible (such as the environment, or the common heritage of mankind) or intangible (such as peace or financial stability)"

- "intermediate GPGs, such as international regimes, contribute toward the provision of final GPGs" (Kaul *et al.* 1999).

Particularly noteworthy in the GPGs literature is the growing recognition that many issues directly related to public health are GPGs (Chen *et al.* 1999). This chapter asserts that the proposed FCTC and its future-related protocols represent an "intermediate" GPGH, which will actively contribute toward the attainment of the ultimate GPG of reducing the burden of disease and death attributable to tobacco.

11.3 Globalization and the tobacco epidemic

The globalization of the tobacco epidemic represents a key rationale for the FCTC. It is therefore important to set the FCTC in this context.

11.3.1 Burden of disease

Tobacco is one of the major public health disasters of the twentieth century. In the early 1990s, an estimated 1.1 billion individuals used tobacco worldwide. If the prevalence rate for tobacco use remains the same as today, by 2025 or thereabouts, this is projected to increase to 1.5–1.6 billion due to natural population increase. This projection may change depending on the success of tobacco control efforts over the next 20 years or so. For example, according to a recent model developed by WHO, if it is assumed that the global prevalence decreases at an annual rate of 1 percent for the next 20 and 50 years, the total predicted number of smokers would stand at just over 1.3 billion in 2020 and 2050.

Tobacco use is the now the largest cause of preventable death worldwide and the leading cause of premature death in industrialized countries. In 1990, tobacco use was estimated to have caused 3 million deaths worldwide. By 1999, this death toll had risen to an estimated 4 million, and new estimates for 2000 put the figure at 4.9 million.

Moreover, the epidemic of tobacco addiction, disease and death is rapidly shifting to developing and transitional market countries. The majority of smokers today are in developing countries (800 million); most are men (700 million) and 300 million are Chinese. WHO has projected that in 2020, based on current trends, the disease burden attributable to tobacco will be nearly double its current levels. Of these projected deaths in 2020, 70 percent (from 50 percent in 2000) will occur in developing countries. Hence, if unchecked, within the next 30 years tobacco will not only be the leading cause of premature mortality in industrialized nations, but also the leading cause of premature death worldwide.

11.3.2 Globalized corporate activities

A distinctive feature of the globalization of the tobacco epidemic is the role of multinational corporations. Since early in the twentieth century, a few major corporations have controlled much of the world's cigarette market. Today, the world market for tobacco is dominated by a small number of American, British, and Japanese multinational conglomerates, which have a controlling presence not only in western countries but also throughout the developing world. China stands out as an exception with its large production of tobacco products mainly used in the domestic market.

A significant contributor to the increased risk of tobacco-related diseases worldwide is therefore the globalization of the tobacco epidemic through the successful efforts of the tobacco industry to expand global tobacco trade and to achieve market penetration in developing countries and transitional market economies. Major transnational tobacco companies have targeted growing markets in Latin America in the 1960s, the newly industrializing economies of Asia (Japan, South Korea, Taiwan, and Thailand) in the 1980s, and in the 1990s, and have moved into eastern Europe, China, and Africa, and are increasingly targeting young persons and women (Connolly 1992).

11.3.3 Trade liberalization, international investment, and increased tobacco consumption

The global reach of the transnational tobacco industry has been enhanced by the recent wave of international trade liberalization, particularly the Uruguay Round of trade negotiations, which included, for the first time, the liberalization of unmanufactured tobacco (Chaloupka and Corbett 1998, Taylor *et al.* 2000). The Uruguay Round, concluded in 1994, established the World Trade Organization (WTO) and brought about an overhaul of the international trade regime by the conclusion of a number of new Multilateral Agreements addressing contemporary trade issues, including tobacco.

These new Multilateral Agreements of the WTO have facilitated the expansion of trade in tobacco products through significant reductions in tariff and non-tariff barriers to trade. Regional trade agreements and associations, such as the North American Free Trade Agreement, the European Union, the Association of Southeast Asian Nations, the Common Market of East and Southern Africa, the Common Market of Western African States and the Organization of American States, have acted in synergy with the global level by mandating further trade liberalization in goods and services, including tobacco, at the regional level. Further, bilateral trade agreements, such as those negotiated in the 1980s by the United States Trade Representative under Section 301 of the revised 1974 US Trade Act with Japan, Taiwan, and South Korea, have also facilitated market penetration in developing countries.

Trade liberalization and market penetration have been linked to a greater risk of increased tobacco consumption, particularly in low- and middle-income countries. A recent study examined empirically the relationship between cigarette consumption and global trade in tobacco products, indicating that reduced trade barriers have had a large and significant impact on cigarette consumption in low-income countries, with a small but significant impact in middle-income countries (Taylor *et al.* 2000). In order to test the hypothesis that trade liberalization positively affects tobacco consumption, Perucic and Guindon employed a model using panel data similar to that used by Taylor *et al.* (2000), but with a larger dataset covering more than 80 countries for the period 1970–97. Import penetration was found to positively contribute to cigarette consumption in low- and low-middle-income countries. These results are in agreement with Taylor *et al.* (2000), who found that import penetration had a large and significant impact in low-income countries and a smaller but still important effect in middle-income countries. Generally similar results were obtained using share of trade in GDP as a measure of openness (Bettcher *et al.* 2001).

In addition to trade liberalization, the transnational tobacco industry has taken advantage of direct forms of market penetration in cash-hungry governments of poor countries via direct foreign investment, either by licensing with a domestic monopoly, joint ventures, or other strategic partnering with domestic companies (World Tobacco File 1998).

11.3.4 Other transnational factors: Illicit trade and advertising

The globalization of the tobacco epidemic is not limited to international trade and investment. The epidemic is being spread and reinforced worldwide through a complex mix of factors, including trade liberalization, foreign direct investment and other factors such as global marketing and communications. Processes and practices that transcend national boundaries are fueling numerous aspects of the tobacco epidemic. For example, an estimated 355,000 million cigarettes, or 33 percent of the world market for exported cigarettes, is smuggled each year in order to avoid taxes. As Luk Joossens has noted, "cigarette smuggling is now so widespread and well organized that it poses a serious threat to both public health and government treasuries, which are losing thousands of millions of dollars in revenue (Joosens 1999)." Smuggled cigarettes are sold at below market price, making top international Western brands available to young people in developing countries, thereby increasing consumption and undermining efforts to keep children from smoking. A further example is tobacco advertising and promotion. Tobacco advertising and promotion contributes to the global spread of tobacco use through worldwide media, such as cable and satellite television, the Internet and sponsorship of worldwide sports and entertainment events.

11.3.5 Globalization of consumer culture

Current research in tobacco control suggests that many factors affect the initiation of smoking. Commentators have emphasized the larger social system's role in promoting tobacco use, including sociodemographic factors, sociocultural factors, and socioeconomic factors (Aghi *et al.* 2001).

An important and understudied area of international tobacco control is the globalization of the consumer culture surrounding tobacco use, through the global integration of populations resulting from international travel, migration, and global advertising. As world income rises and transportation costs fall, the demand for travel rises. The percentage of the population that crosses international borders has steadily increased over the last 50 years. In 1950, the number of tourist arrivals was 25 million, in 1999 it was 664 million and its rate of growth is about 3.5 percent, indicating that the level will double about every 20 years. Travel is an important aspect of the global economy and signifies the emergence of a global culture. It also means that individuals are routinely exposed to advertising and behaviors that are different from that of their native countries.

A related aspect of increased globalization significant for global tobacco control is the internationalization of inputs. In particular, international flows of labour are an increasingly important aspect of the world economy. Individuals are continually moving from country to country. In Organization for Economic Cooperation and Development (OECD) countries, one in twenty workers is foreign born, but in particular sectors of the economy, for example construction, the foreign born percentage is much higher. Similarly, a related implication of such phenomena is that there are spillover effects of one country's tobacco control efforts. The impact of international travel, migration, and labor flows on smoking prevalence has not, however, been examined.

11.4 **Curbing the epidemic: Tobacco control as a "Global Public Good"**

The dramatic increase in tobacco consumption in the last couple of decades portends a public health and economic tragedy for nations worldwide in the twenty-first century. Much of the potential calamity can be averted, however, through effective implementation of national and international tobacco control strategies. In its recent report, *Curbing the Epidemic: Governments and the Economics of Tobacco Control*, The World Bank concluded that tobacco control is highly cost-effective as part of a basic public health package in all countries (World Bank 1999). The World Bank report supported global interventions such as harmonization of tax policies, elimination of tobacco smuggling, the banning of tobacco advertising, and the role that the FCTC may play in the promulgation and implementation of such measures.

Global tobacco control has significant GPG characteristics. The health effects of tobacco consumption have strong public characteristics because forced or passive smoking presents health risks to non-smokers. Further, the financial costs of treating tobacco-related diseases of smokers and non-smokers are passed onto the public in countries where health care is provided by the public sector. In industrialized countries alone, smoking-related health care accounts for between 6 and 15 percent of all annual health-care costs (World Bank 1999).

In the area of tobacco control, traditional research has been focused on the behavior of individual smokers; this research agenda focusing on the "individual free choice" of tobacco users has largely been driven by resources and groups associated with the tobacco industry. In contrast to this narrow focus, we contend that tobacco control measures satisfy the criteria of public goods, non-rivalry, non-excludability and non-rejectibility. For instance, a total ban on advertising as well as an increase in tobacco taxes, are public goods because, following the implementation of these policies, non-initiators will benefit from better health and more financial resources; all individuals (both smokers and non-smokers) will benefit indirectly from reduced exposure to secondhand smoke and may benefit from reduced government tobacco-related health-care costs. Similarly, any tobacco control intervention that induces cessation, encourages reduction in consumption or discourages initiation will have spin-off effects that will benefit all individuals in society.

In support of these arguments that tobacco control interventions are public goods the recent World Bank study shows how price and tax measures, non-price interventions, and efforts to eliminate smuggling provide spin-off benefits for the entire population in the form of decreased health-care costs, increased productivity and the better health of the population at large (World Bank 1999). Furthermore, as demonstrated in this chapter, globalization has blurred the traditional line between private and public in health and brought international tobacco control efforts within the domain of GPGs (Chen *et al.* 1999, Taylor and Bettcher 2000). Thus, as a consequence of globalization, international tobacco control has the characteristics of a GPG. Since many, if not all, of the challenges of tobacco control increasingly transcend national boundaries, stemming the growth of the tobacco epidemic requires global agreement and action. The globalization of the tobacco epidemic restricts the capacity of countries to unilaterally control tobacco within their sovereign borders (Taylor 1996). All tobacco control issues, including trade, smuggling, advertising, and sponsorship, prices and taxes, control of toxic substances, and tobacco package design and labeling, require multilateral cooperation and effective action at the global level. If not attended to, these global problems can threaten the best national tobacco control strategies.

11.5 International legal agreements: Intermediate GPGs

As there is no supra-national authority equivalent to a national government that can provide GPGs, the implications of globalization include the need for greater intersectoral action, as well as transnational cooperation and partnerships. It is widely recognized that there is "broad justification for a more systematic and integrated approach to international cooperation" as "improving international cooperation will strengthen the capacity of national governments to achieve their national policy objectives" (Kaul *et al.* 1999). A central component of enhanced multilateral cooperation in support of final GPGs is the expanded use of international instruments, including conventional international law, as intermediate GPGs. In order to obtain national objectives for the protection and promotion of public health, governments must increasingly turn to international cooperation to achieve some control over the transboundary forces that affect their people. As described below, many realms relevant to global public health support the expanded use of international law as well as international institutions, typically established under international agreements, as intermediate GPGs to promote or achieve a final global public health good.

International legal agreements are among the most important intermediate GPGs. As described further below, international agreements provide a legal foundation for many other intermediate products with global public benefits, including an institutionalized forum for global cooperation, research, surveillance, technical assistance programs, and information clearinghouses. However, not all treaties effectively function as intermediate GPGs. In particular, bilateral and regional treaties are not meant to have global scope, and it is therefore self-evident that they do not constitute, and indeed are not intended to lead to the attainment of, GPGH. In this respect, it could be argued that at least some of these agreements could be defined as intermediate "club" goods, in that states can be excluded from the benefits of a given agreement, but its use by one state that is a Party to a given bilateral or regional agreement does not detract from its use by another Party to these agreements.

In contrast to bilateral or regional treaties, many global treaties aspire to a universal reach. Global treaties, for example the Vienna Convention for the Protection of the Ozone Layer and the Framework Convention on Climate Change, were negotiated in order to secure global cooperation to address important environmental problems that transcend national boundaries. Therefore, we argue that some global multilateral treaties qualify as intermediate public goods on the following grounds:

(1) Non-rivalry in consumption, in that the use of by a given State generally does not prevent another State from using it;

(2) Non-excludability, for example global treaties negotiated under the auspices of public international organizations are generally open to adoption and ratification by at least all State Members of the organization, even though some may not decide to exercise their sovereign prerogative to ratify a given treaty.

(3) The aim of many global treaties is to facilitate international cooperation, commitment, and action toward the attainment of a final public good, for example the reduction of the burden of disease due to tobacco or the protection of the ozone layer.

It should be noted, however, that the free-rider problem also affects, or can affect, global treaties as it does with other public goods, both at the global and national levels. For instance, most States now belong to the ozone treaty regime. However, even those States that have not exercised their prerogative to ratify these instruments or changed national practice in accordance with the terms of such instruments, enjoy some of the benefits of the enhanced protection of the ozone layer even though they have not paid the price to maintain the legal regime through national action.

It must be kept in mind that many treaties do not enter into force or do so for only a limited number of states. Further, may treaties that have entered into force do not effectively promote implementation of the obligations that they establish. Indeed, a weak treaty regime may be worse than none at all since a weak international instrument can function to alleviate public and media pressure without nations resolving or committing to real action. Difficulties in encouraging implementation of existing treaties has become such a paramount concern that much of the attention of the international community has shifted from codifying new treaties to enhancing mechanisms to promote compliance with existing regimes.

The extent to which treaties are effective and under what conditions has been a continuing subject of theoretical fascination and dispute among scholars of international law and international relations. Whether governments obey the rule of law with respect to any international norm depends on a number of variables both within and outside the framework of the law (Schachter 1982). The sense of obligation to obey international law has been a subject of theoretical fascination because, among other things, the international legal system differs markedly from domestic law administration. For example, in international law there is no supranational authority that can enforce the law with sanctions against errant states (Henkin 1979).

International legal scholars have developed diverse theories to explain the "compliance pull" of international law. For example, the eminent scholar Louis Henkin has observed that nations will comply with international law only if it is in their best interests to do so; they will disregard law or obligation if the advantages of violation outweigh the advantages of observance (Henkin 1979). As Murphy has observed, the calculation of self-interest is highly complex because of the dynamic quality international relations in which states and other transnational actors operate as part of a transnational social structure, continuously interacting in ways that shape national interests and, thereby, the codification and implementation of international law (Murphy 2001).

Contemporary international scholars have posited various theories about how law is generated from such interactions between transnational actors. Thomas Franck, for example, argues that effective international lawmaking depends upon substantive and procedural fairness: that is, fairness in the law itself and the process by which it is created (Franck 1995). Policy oriented jurisprudence suggests that international law involves an ongoing process of authoritative and controlling decision which involves ascertaining the policy goals of the community that should be guided by normative values surrounding the notion of human dignity (Wiessner and Willard 1999, Murphy 2001). In an alternative vein, Chayes and Chayes depict international law as primarily a series of complex treaty-based regulatory regimes in which states create and abide by international law because it is efficient to do so, because it promotes the long-term interests of states and because states have a general propensity to comply with international obligations (Chayes and Chayes 1995); they note that in most cases the failure of nations to comply with international law does not reflect a lack of political will, but ambiguities present in the law, the inherent difficulties in applying rules to changing conditions and limitations of capacity. Hence these scholars advocate a "managerial model" of compliance emphasizing a cooperative, problem-solving approach.

Despite difficulties in promoting negotiation, codification and implementation of international norms, there has been a dramatic expansion in conventional international lawmaking in a wide variety of areas since the founding of the United Nations and treaties now serve as the primary vehicle for multilateral cooperation. The experience of international organizations in developing international environmental agreements, provides some useful insights regarding the beneficial impacts of international legal regimes. The global commitments to curb ozone depletion provide an example of a particularly effective international legal regime. Scientific findings led in the mid-1980s to the negotiation and adoption of a framework convention—protocol regime consisting of the Vienna Convention for the Protection of the Ozone Layer and the Montreal Protocol and amendments thereto (Taylor 1996). As a result of the implementation of the Montreal Ozone Protocol and Vienna Convention, the global consumption of CFCs between 1986 and 1996 declined by more than 70 percent, from 1.1 million tons worldwide to 160,000 tons. The agreement and effective collaboration by the international community to reduce CFC levels qualifies as an intermediate GPG, in that this international legal regime is contributing toward the attainment of a final GPG, namely the attainment of an intact ozone shield (Kaul *et al.* 1999*a*).

The principle of international environmental legal regimes as intermediate public goods provides a template for global social action for tobacco control and other public health concerns. As described further below, the growing significance of GPGs in health also creates a situation in which the codification and implementation of new international norms will become increasingly relevant as health interdependence accelerates.

11.6 **The FCTC**

The 1999 WHA resolution that accelerated the process of developing the Framework Convention established a two-step political process for negotiating the FCTC. First, it created a working group, open to all WHO Member States, to consider the potential technical foundation for the FCTC and related protocols. Second, it established an Intergovernmental Negotiating Body (INB) open to all Member States to formally draft and negotiate the FCTC.

The first stage of the process is complete. During the pre-negotiation period, a technical working group met twice between May 1999 and October 2000 to elaborate the scientific and policy foundation for the FCTC. This group agreed at is first meeting in October 1999 that substantive tobacco control obligations in the FCTC and related protocols should focus principally on empirically established demand-reduction strategies. Hence, starting in the initial phase in the FCTC process, WHO Member States emphasized that the FCTC should promote global agreement and action on the primary interventions on which there is overwhelming scientific support: tobacco taxes and prices, advertising and promotion, education, warning labels, clean indoor-air policies, and treatment of tobacco dependence. Consistent with The World Bank's recommendations on tobacco control, the working group supported coordinated action against smuggling as the one key supply-side area for global agreement and harmonization of policies.

Political negotiations on the FCTC commenced with the convening of the first session of the INB in Geneva in October 2000. At the time of writing, the FCTC INB has held six sessions. A major decision was taken in March 2002, during the fourth round of negotiations, for the new Chair of the Negotiating Body, Ambassador Seixas Correa of Brazil, to develop a new "Chair's Text" which would contain proposed provisions for all proposed articles of the treaty. The New Chair's Text was released in July 2002, and considered the full range of price, non-price, and supply factors that affect the prevalence of tobacco use worldwide. The draft treaty text also proposed institutional arrangements for the implementation and monitoring of the FCTC, the mobilization of financial resources for implementation of the treaty, as well as approaches for the establishment of a global surveillance system for tobacco control. This proposed new text was examined during the fifth session in October 2002. On the basis of these discussions, the chair released a revised text on 15 January 2003 for consideration by the sixth session of the Negotiating Body in February 2003. At the end of this sixth session, Member States agreed to transmit the final draft of the Convention to the World Health Assembly for consideration for adoption in May 2003.

The legal model being pursued in the tobacco negotiations is the framework convention—protocol approach proposed by Taylor and Roemer to WHO in 1995 (Taylor and Roemer 1996, Bodansky 1999). This model of international law-making has been applied extensively and, at times successfully, in the field of inter-national environmental law as well as other international concerns, including international protection of human rights. This approach to international law-making consists of two components: a framework convention, that establishes a general consensus about the relevant facts and an appropriate international response (some framework conventions contain only general obligations, while others may contain more specific commitments); and protocols that supplement, clarify, amend or qualify a framework convention and usually set forth more specific commitments or added institutional arrangements. This approach allows for the addition of protocols and annexes to the basic framework as improved scientific understanding is reached and/or political consensus for concrete action develops (Taylor 1996). The WHO FCTC process is being developed as a scientific, evidence based, approach to global tobacco control that, consequently, has the potential to significantly advance national and international efforts to curb the growth of the epidemic.

Evidence from other treaty-making processes establishes that the institutions and procedural mechanisms established by the FCTC can prompt timely consensus and action on cogent implementing protocols and, thus, contribute to the implemen-tation of the FCTC and the advancement of the GPG of international tobacco control (Taylor 1996). For example, environmental framework conventions, and protocols are often designed to encourage parties to adopt implementing proto-cols by mandating regular and institutionalized meetings of the parties. In the case of some framework conventions, the mandatory provisions for consultation "offer the prospect of a virtually continuous legislative enterprise" (Handl 1991).

Rapid implementation of the FCTC can also be encouraged by institutions and mechanisms that establish incentives for the parties, such as information, technology, training, and technical advice and assistance. The 1999 World Health Assembly Resolution accelerating the negotiation of the FCTC set the target date for the adoption of the treaty for May 2003. Upon entry into force, the FCTC and its potential protocols will be binding international law for those states that adopt and ratify these agreements.

Of course, the effective international lawmaking experiences achieved at times by other international organizations in other areas of international concern may not accurately reflect WHO's potential to garner broad support for the development and implementation of the FCTC and related protocols. Although it is beyond the scope of this article to detail the factors that may contribute to the effective adoption and implementation of the WHO Convention, it may be noted that tobacco control does share the characteristic of scientific certainty that has galvanized international action in some areas of international environmental law (Taylor 1996). Like the hole in the ozone layer above Antarctica leading to the conclusion of the Montreal Protocol, the health and economic consequences of tobacco consumption are empirically established. In addition, the use of the framework convention protocol approach will allow countries to undertake added substantive and/or institutional commitments as global consensus for concrete measures on tobacco control develops. Finally, evidence from other treaty making processes shows that a variety of institutional and procedural obligations potentially established by the FCTC can prompt timely consensus and action on cogent implementing protocols and, thus, contribute to the implementation of the Convention and the advancement of the GPG of international tobacco control.

11.6.1 The FCTC and conventional international law as "intermediate" GPGs

As a significant cause of death, disease and disability, tobacco use is a paramount public health priority in all countries. Consequently, in the literature on GPGs, global tobacco control can be classified as a pure GPG. "A pure GPG is marked by universality—that is, it benefits all countries, people and generations" (Kaul *et al.* 1999). The potential benefits of enhanced global tobacco control may reach a broad spectrum of countries and a broad spectrum of the population, rich and poor. As a rational, evidence-based approach, the FCTC holds the potential of significantly advancing global cooperation for tobacco control and, as outlined above, can be considered an intermediate GPGH.

It is important to recognize that the FCTC is not just *a* platform to develop comprehensive and binding global standards on tobacco control, but in fact, the *only* platform available to develop such international commitments and harmonize national policies. The principles, norms and standards ultimately codified in the FCTC may legally establish global priorities for national action and multisectoral cooperation on tobacco control. The institutions eventually established by the FCTC, including, potentially, a financial mechanism, technical advice, and assistance programs, a mechanism to monitor treaty compliance and provisions for ongoing consultation of the parties, may help contribute to the adoption of effective global tobacco control measures. Overall, by providing an ongoing and institutionalized platform for multilateral consultations on tobacco control, the WHO Convention may be able to promote adoption and implementation of effective tobacco control strategies worldwide.

Not previously examined in the literature of international public goods, the experience with the FCTC process also illustrates that the sheer process of negotiating and developing a global treaty can also be considered an intermediate public good. That is, WHO's efforts to achieve global public support for an international regulatory framework for tobacco control is stimulating national policy change and thus making an important, albeit limited, contribution to curtailing the epidemic well before global consensus on cogent tobacco norms is secured (Taylor 1996).

It is widely understood in international legal circles that the sheer process of international negotiation can promote global public opinion and stimulate national action long before a treaty is adopted and entered into force. The experience of treaty negotiations in other areas of international concern, such as climate change and ozone protection, illustrates the principle that the treaty-making process itself can make a difference in the provision of GPGs. Most recently, the negotiation of the Stockholm Convention on Persistent Organic Pollutants provided a platform that enabled the United Nations Environmental Programme (UNEP) to encourage and work with states to reduce production of such chemicals before the treaty was adopted in 2001.

Early in the negotiation process evidence began to accumulate on the ways in which the FCTC negotiations were already promoting global coordination and domestic action in support of tobacco control. For example, at the global level, the process has created an unprecedented opportunity to highlight tobacco control and educate and inform political leaders of the health and economic consequences of tobacco. Tobacco, of course, has long been a subject of concern of the World Health Assembly (WHA). However, the lawmaking process has created the opportunity to broaden the dialogue beyond the health ministers that typically comprise delegations to the WHA, to include ministries of foreign affairs, trade, customs and agriculture as well as others that are participating in the treaty negotiations. Consequently, the process is giving political leaders the world's first forum to learn about the health and economic consequences of tobacco, forge partnerships and implement solutions.

At the national level, the FCTC is facilitating domestic tobacco control action in various ways. For example, representatives from a number of states, including the Philippines, India, Ukraine, and Morocco, have reported that their governments are reviewing and strengthening tobacco control legislation in the process of participating in the FCTC negotiations. As a further example, the FCTC is promoting the creation of national tobacco control coalitions. States as diverse as Brazil, Thailand, Russia, Paraguay, South Africa, Trinidad and Tobago, and the United States of America have established formal FCTC multisectoral committees to enhance participation in treaty negotiations. In other states, such as China, these interministerial consultations are occurring at informal levels. Whether formal or informal, these committees are giving different ministries within national governments the opportunity, perhaps for the first time, to collectively discuss and address the domestic burden of tobacco.

In these and other ways the FCTC process is making a key contribution to the global political environment for strengthened tobacco control and can thus be considered an intermediate public good.

11.7 **WHO, international health lawmaking and GPGH**

As described above, the global context of development has profound implications for public health and, concomitantly, the expansion of international health law. New frameworks for international collaboration are needed to deal with global threats to, and opportunities for, health. Consequently, the codification and implementation of binding global health norms is becoming increasingly important as a supportive tool, as global health interdependence accelerates and nations increasingly recognize the need to cooperate to promote the attainment of GPGH. Of course, not all areas of international health concern will call for the gearing up of legal machinery or be politically ripe to do so. However, we are likely to see the expanded use of international public health law in this century to take advantage of the opportunities afforded by global change, to minimize the transnationalization of health risks and protect the health of populations who have not benefited from globalization.

Globalization has been a cardinal factor triggering the expansion of international health law. This emerging field of international legal cooperation now encompasses increasingly complex concerns, including aspects of human reproduction; biomedical science and human cloning; human organ transplantation and xenotransplantation; infectious diseases; international food trade and the control of the safety of health services; pharmaceuticals, and the control of addictive substances such as narcotics (Grad 1998). As a result of the new globality, international health law is now recognized as inextricably linked with other areas of international normative concern, including international environmental law, labour law, and arms control. The current configuration of international health law, and the contribution of intergovernmental organizations to its development, have recently been documented (Taylor *et al.* 2002).

One question that remains is what role WHO will serve as a center for international codification, to promote GPGH. A decade ago, Taylor described how, despite the proliferation of international law as a mechanism for global cooperation, since the founding of the United Nations, WHO had traditionally neglected the use of international legislative strategies to promote its public health policies. Among other things, it was noted that WHO had never utilized its constitutional authority to serve as a platform for any international convention to protect public health, and had otherwise neglected the role of law, national and international, in promoting the implementation of its public health goals. WHO's "traditional conservatism" was attributed, in large part, to the cultural predispositions—the organizational culture—of the institution (Taylor 1992).

Some observers continue to apply this concept of WHO's "traditional conservatism" and, thereby, appear to marginalize the present and future role of WHO in international health lawmaking and implementation. However, it is unclear whether this now decade old paradigm retains validity. A strong organizational culture can dominate an organization's behavior and constrain it from making needed changes. However, an organization's culture can evolve and develop (Taylor 2002a).

Patterns of organizational behavior that contradict WHO's traditional conservative culture are emerging. While evidence of the process of organizational adaptation or evolution has been accumulating for some time, most notably, of course, is the revitalization and the acceleration of WHO's process of negotiating the FCTC under the leadership of Dr Gro Harlem Brundtland.

The FCTC may signal a turning point in WHO's approach to international health lawmaking, and with it herald a new era in international health cooperation. In this globalizing world, health and, concomitantly, public goods for health are emerging as central issues of multilateralism. It may be that the forces of globalization at work in tobacco and other areas of international health are compelling WHO and the world community to think creatively and to develop new models of cooperation, including the expanded use of international health law, to protect and promote the health of populations worldwide. The FCTC is, in the last analysis, a critical test case of WHO's organizational and political capacity.

11.7.1 Conclusion

Tobacco control is one of the most rational, evidence-based policies in health care. As outlined in this article, the FCTC, the FCTC process itself and national tobacco control policies have important public goods aspects. Once adopted and entered into force, the FCTC may provide a mechanism to respond to the GPG aspects of tobacco control. The FCTC may facilitate the flow of information about tobacco control and serve as a mechanism to coordinate various transnational aspects of tobacco control, including smuggling, advertising, packaging, and labeling. In addition, the treaty may enhance global surveillance, information exchange, and international technical, legal, and financial cooperation in support of the GPG of tobacco control. Moreover, the sheer process of negotiating the FCTC is a GPG in that it is facilitating the development of tobacco control policies in countries throughout the world.

References

Aghi A, Asma S, Yeong CC, Vaithinathan R. *Initiation and Maintenance of Tobacco Use*. In: Woman and the Tobacco Epidemic. WHO/NMH/TFI/01.01.2001. Geneva: World Health Organization.

Bettcher D, Subramaniam C, Guindon E, Perucic AM, Soll L, Grabman G, Joossens L, WTO Secretariat, Taylor A. *Tobacco Control in an Era of Trade Liberalization*. WHO Document WHO/NMH/TFI/01.04.2001. Geneva: World Health Organization.

Bodansky D. *What Makes International Agreements Effective? Some Pointers for the WHO Framework Convention on Tobacco Control.* Framework Convention on Tobacco Control Technical Briefing Series: Paper 4. WHO/NCD/TFI/99.4, 1999. Geneva: World Health Organization.

Chaloupka F, Corbett M. Trade policy and tobacco: towards an optimal policy mix. In: I Abedian *et al.* (ed.) *The Economics of Tobacco Control: Towards an Optimal Policy Mix,* University of Cape Town, 1998, pp. 129–45.

Chayes A, Chayes AH. *The New Sovereignty: Compliance with International Regulatory Agreements.* Cambridge: Harvard University Press, 1995.

Chen LC, Evans TG, Cash RA. Health as a global public good. In: I Kaul, I Grundberg, MA Stern (ed.) *Global Public Goods,* New York: Oxford University Press, 1999, pp. 284–304.

Connoly GN. Worldwide expansion of the transnational tobacco industry. *J Natl Cancer Inst Monogr* 1992; **12**: 29–35.

Cornes R. Dyke maintenance and other stories: Some neglected types of public goods. *Quart J Econom* 1993; **108**: 159–271.

Franck TM. *Fairness in International Law and Institutions,* New York: Oxford University Press, 1995, pp. 1–536.

Grad FP. Public health law; its form, function, future, and ethical parameters. *Int Digest Health Legis* 1998; **49**(1): 19–39.

Handl G. Environmental security and global change: The challenge to international law. In: W Lang *et al.* (eds) *Environmental Protection and International Law.* London: Graham & Trotman/Martinus Nijhoff, 1991, pp. 59–87.

Henkin L. *How Nations Behave.* [NN PG NBRS].Columbia University Press, 2nd edn. 1979.

Hurrel A, Woods N. Globalization and inequality. *Millen J Int Stud* 1995; **24**(3): 447–70.

Joossens L. *Improving Public Health Through An International Framework Convention on Tobacco Control,* Geneva: World Health Organization, Framework Convention on Tobacco Control Briefing Series. WHO/NCD/TFI/99.2, 1999.

Kaul I, Grunberg I, Stern M. Defining global public goods. In: I Kaul, I Grundberg, MA Stern, (ed.) *Global Public Goods.* New York: Oxford University Press, 1999*a*, pp. 2–19.

Kaul I, Grunberg I, Stern M. Introduction. In: I Kaul, I Grundberg, MA Stern (eds) *Global Public Goods.* New York: Oxford University Press, 1999*b*, pp. xix–xxxviii.

McMichael AJ, Haines A, Sloof, R, Kovats S. (eds) *Climate Change and Human Health.* Geneva: World Health Organization, 1996, pp. 161–74.

Murphy S. Biotechnology and international law. *Harv Int Law J* 2001; **42**: 47–138.

Roemer R. *Legislative Action to Combat the World Tobacco Epidemic.* Geneva: World Health Organization, 1997.

Schachter O. *International Law in Theory and Practice: General Course in Public International Law.* Academy of International Law Offprint from the Collected Course, Vol. 178, 1982-V, 1982.

Taylor A. Making the World Health Organization work: a legal framework for universal access to the conditions for health. *Am J Law Med* 1992; **18**(4): 301–46.

Taylor A. An international regulatory strategy for global tobacco control. *Yale J Int Law* 1996; **21**(2): 257–304.

Taylor A. Globalization and Biotechnology: UNESCO and an International Strategy to Advance Human Rights and Public Health. *Am J Law Med* 1999; **25**(4): 479–541.

Taylor A, Bettcher D. A WHO framework convention on tobacco control: a global public good for public health. *Bull World Health Organ* 2000; **78**(7): 920–9.

Taylor AL, Chaloupka F, Guindon GE, Corbett M. Trade policy and tobacco control. In: P Jha, F Chaloupka (eds) *Tobacco Control in Developing Countries*. Oxford: Oxford University Press, 2000, pp. 343–64.

Taylor AL, Roemer R. *An International Strategy for Tobacco Control*. Geneva: World Health Organization, WHO/PSA/96.6, 1996.

Taylor AL, Bettcher D, Fluss SS, Deland K, Yach D. International Health Law Instruments: An Overview. In: Detels R, McEwen J, Beaglehole R, Tanaka H (eds) *Oxford Textbook of Public Health: The Scope of Public Health*. Oxford: Oxford University Press, 2002, pp. 359–86.

Taylor AL. Global Governance, International Health Law and WHO: Looking towards the future. *Bulletin of the World Health Organization* 2002*a*; **80**(12): 975–9.

World Bank. *Curbing the Epidemic: Governments and the Economics of Tobacco Control*. Washington, DC: The World Bank, 1999, pp. 1–129.

Wiessner S, Willard AR. A policy-oriented jurisprudence and human rights abuses in international conflict: Toward a world public order of human dignity. *Am J Int Law* 1999; **93**: 316–34.

Wilkinson R. *Unhealthy Societies: From Inequality to Well-Being*. London: Routledge, 1996, pp. 1–272.

World Tobacco File. London: International Trade Publications Ltd, 1998.

Yach D, Bettcher D. The globalization of public health, 1: Threats and opportunities. *Am J Public Health* 1998; **88**(5): 735–8

Yach D, Bettcher D. The globalization of public health, II: The convergence of self-interest and altruism. *Am J Public Health* 1998; **88**(5): 738–41.

Zacher MW. Global epidemiological surveillance: International cooperation to monitor infectious diseases. In: I Kaul, I Grundberg, MA Stern (eds) *Global Public Goods*. New York: Oxford University Press, 1999, pp. 266–83.

A critique of the global public goods for health concept and practice

Chapter 12

Global public goods for health: A flawed paradigm?

Gavin Mooney and Janet Dzator

12.1 Introduction

Many of today's health problems extend beyond national boundaries and raise questions of their management internationally. Examples include the emergence of new infectious diseases that can affect people across the globe. While such diseases and their effects may be difficult to contain, there could be few more challenging tasks than determining how best to design and finance relevant health intervention programs to deal with them. The question then becomes how resources can best be used, not only to maximize the outcomes of specific health intervention programs but also to promote the health benefits of programs that are not necessarily first and foremost concerned with health.[1] In the context of this chapter that question can be narrowed down to asking whether the "Global Public Goods for Health" (GPGH) concept is the best way forward.

Given that the poor bear the greatest burden of disease, it then becomes equitable for health care projects, and health projects more generally for the indigent, to be supported by governments, and/or to appeal to donors and/or philanthropists to support projects, at least up to some basic threshhold or other. Donors, for example, could finance inputs targeted at the health of the indigent and they themselves may derive some satisfaction from doing so. Although the benefits of such programs are private to the recipients, in so far as the donors also obtain benefits, there is a positive externality. Again, if the consumption of the service (by the recipient) were also to prevent the spread of an infectious disease to the community, then the reduction in the level of carriers for that disease would also constitute a form of external benefit. In most cases of government intervention, the motivation is to achieve levels of consumption in keeping with what is deemed socially desirable. While the goal relates to consumption, this can be

---

[1] The production of health even at the microlevel clearly can involve more than goods which are first and foremost concerned with health.

achieved either by governments altering in some way the level of production, and thereby altering the level of consumption which would otherwise have prevailed, or by more direct intervention on consumption. Goods of this ilk mostly fall into those known as public goods.

This chapter examines critically the concept and implications of GPGH, concluding that to attempt to build an approach to international health based on GPGH is likely to be less than ideal, not least because of the welfarist base of GPGH and the lack of concern for altruism (see Section 2). We accept that one could accommodate various potential problems that arise within the GPGH concept, and retain the nomenclature. We do not, however, favor that approach as it ends up distorting the notion of GPGH to such an extent as to make it almost unrecognizable, and at the same time constrains it in ways that we see as being unhelpful. That is why we argue that GPGH is a flawed paradigm and seek to replace it with one that we believe is better, based on the notion of "communitarian claims" (Mooney 1998, 2001; see Section 3).

12.2 Global public goods for health revisited

The concept of "Global Public Goods" (GPGs) has been outlined earlier in this volume by Woodward and Smith (Chapter 1), who suggest a revision of the definitions provided by Kaul *et al.* (1999*a*). In that chapter the authors suggest that "health" itself cannot be considered a public good (and, we would argue, cannot be considered a "good" as such), but that there may be "public goods" at the global level which contribute to improved health. Here we present a fuller examination of the flaws that we believe exist within both the concept of GPGH and its suggested application in generating a transfer of resources from wealthy to poor nations for the improvement of global health. These flaws encompass four areas, each of which is explored in more detail below: the philosophy behind the GPG concept; the welfarist nature of the GPG concept; the inability to reflect "caring"; and the determination of what is defined as a GPG.

First, the philosophy allegedly behind the global agenda is to promote health intervention programs that will result in economic and social benefits to all humanity at the global level. That is: to identify potential GPGHs of particular importance to poor people in developing countries which might also provide more general benefits at a global level; to outline how they could be provided and financed; and to gauge their economic merits and political feasibility. The successes of multicountry and multiregional health initiatives, compared with less remarkable country-to-country (bilateral) health projects, indicate that the recognition of common risks and attempts to cope with them at the "global" level could result in health improvements for all or most people. For example, it can be argued that smallpox was eradicated only when both developed and developing countries united altruistically in the control and prevention process, as will polio (see Chapter 2).

Global governance in the case of producing global public goods appears to be one of the difficult issues. Such governance is defined to involve the interaction of states, international organizations, and non-state actors to shape values, policies and rules, and is perceived to be different from international governance, defined as intergovernmental cooperation (Fidler 2001). The globalization of public health, as indicated by Fidler (2001), is not a new phenomenon but has characterized the human struggle against infectious diseases, opium, pollution, etc. for about one and a half centuries. It has been dominated by challenges for global governance that led to the development of international health diplomacy and regimes resulting in many treaties with the aim of making the world a better place for all. The establishment of institutions such as the World Health Organization (WHO) and the Pan American Health Organization (PAHO) were the result of international efforts to persuade individual states to cooperate with each other and build partnerships with non-state actors, such as multinational corporations and nongovernmental organizations, in order to develop global governance. The challenge of realizing such visions is still haunting humanity today. The difficulties exhibited in defining what constitute GPGH, which sort of global government should produce them and how, as well as for which global public, mimic Samuelson's discussions of public expenditure theories with their focus on welfarism (Samuelson 1954, 1955, 1958). Having drawn attention to the nature of difficulties in moving from theory to empiricism, Samuelson concluded "the theory of public finance [and we would argue also for GPG] is but part of the general theory of government. And at this frontier, the easy formulas of classical economics no longer light our way" (Samuelson 1958).

Current discussions about producing GPGH, such as research into diseases of the poor, strengthening global surveillance, as well as capacity for prevention and control anytime anywhere, could be targeted mostly for their expected positive effects on health. Intermediate goods such as computers and the software required for establishing communication networks, vaccines and drugs that may be involved in producing the GPGH are, however, predominantly private. There is a need to pay special attention to the production and transfer of these resources to the "public domain," especially of the poor. Recent debates on alternative pathways to improve health in developing countries highlight issues such as the use of subsidies, including guarantees of markets, for industries operating in developing markets, and emphasize the need for policies that could enhance the level of integration of those left behind in the globalization process (Dollar 2001, Drager and Beaglehole 2001). The treatment of these goods as "public goods" for the sake of the GPGH concept is rather confusing. More importantly, the targeted problems should be relevant and beneficial to people in their natural locations.

Even though proponents of GPGH could argue that the poor will benefit from improved health, the question to be asked is: at what cost? In developing countries, cost considerations are crucial to the success of most programs. For example, there is evidence that people are more concerned about the cost than nutritional value, or even personal preferences, when they shop for food (Evans *et al.* 2001). As a result, policies that aim at promoting global health should ensure that the principles underlying GPGH do not encourage "socialization of costs and privatization of benefits" (see Korten 2001). What this means is that individual nations should not be coerced into, for example, obtaining loans that have stringent binding conditions (which is a public bad for future generations) in order to participate in the GPGH program and then miss out on having their immediate health concerns addressed because it is thereafter considered as a regional issue.

The second flaw concerns the nature of GPGH, which remains essentially welfarist in nature. It is relevant therefore to think through some of the implications that may be ascribed to welfarism. For example it is normally assumed *inter alia* in welfarism that only individuals' values are relevant and not community values, that there is no allowance for commitment (Sen 1977), and that all that is in the objective function is assumed to be both measurable and commensurable (again an issue criticized by Sen 1992).

In discussing distributive justice in the context of welfarism, Sumner (1996) poses the question: "What is the good of which citizens are to be assured equal shares?." He goes on: "Does welfarism suggest an answer to this question? . . . . On a subjective account, some aspects of our wellbeing (our aversion to pain, for instance) are relatively unaffected by our idiosyncrasies of taste or our freely chosen projects. But others are not: what counts as the best life for you will be strongly influenced by your particular constellation of personal values or aspirations. Suppose that, having convinced yourself that you are the sort of person who deserves the best, you are unable to be satisfied with less than the fastest cars, the flashiest clothes, and the best cosmetic surgery, while your more modest neighbors are able to achieve the same level of well being with much more limited resources. A theory of justice which requires that resources be distributed so as to ensure equality of welfare will, in effect, enable you to tax your neighbors for the maintenance of your expensive life style. And that seems unfair, not least because . . . . you too could have chosen to cultivate more humble tastes."

Sumner then argues that "most theories will . . . counsel the adoption of a strategy consisting of whatever set of rules or dispositions is calculated, given realistic assumptions about the nature of human agents and their circumstances, to increase the likelihood of success in making the right decisions." The GPGH concept inadequately addresses the problems, particularly the equity problems, but also the valuation problems, that bedevil welfarism. Since GPGH rest on welfarism, these problems need to be addressed.

These issues lead our thinking directly to Sen's (1992) capabilities, and also his critique of utilitarianism and welfarism more generally in his wonderfully insightful comment that damns utilitarianism in this context to a timely death— that "an overdependence on what people 'manage to desire' is one of the limiting aspects of utilitarian ethics."

A major problem with globalization, and we would submit with GPGH, is this: the terms of trade, whether it be in goods or in benefits (health and other) from GPGH, are set in a world of very unequal power or, what is the same thing, where the distribution of property rights is very firmly skewed in favor of rich countries. This is the key argument against free trade where free trade only equals fair trade if it is between more or less equal powers, or if there is altruism present in the negotiations. What happens in reality is that the more powerful (i.e. richer) nations can ensure that the terms of trade work much more in their favor than can the poor—unless the rich are affected by altruism. Let us explain more.

Rich countries—having more power and greater ability to pay in the market—largely dictate the "terms of trade." (This situation is exacerbated for poor countries in which a single product dominates their export markets e.g. coffee or copper.) Let us say that, in terms of exchange, 5 tonnes of Kenyan coffee = 1 Australian mobile phone rather than 4 or 5 mobile phones. Now the point here is that it is clearly better (in market terms) that Kenya produces coffee and Australia produces mobile phones (just as it is better that the plumber does the electrician's plumbing and the electrician does the plumber's electrical work).

Kenya locally could produce say 50 tonnes of coffee for the same local costs as those they would require for the production of 1 mobile phone. Australia could produce say 50 mobile phones for 1 tonne of coffee. In getting to the "terms of trade" for coffee/mobile phones, the bargaining power of the rich is so much greater than that of the poor, the result is that the poor are not treated equitably. So instead of 50/1 and 1/50 giving some reasonable compromise at around 1 : 1, it ends up as 5/1 against the Kenyans. That is the law of welfarism, of the market place. This is what happens when caring and commitment are absent.

Given the extent to which the distribution of power across the globe is entrenched with respect to not only income and wealth but also health, there would seem to be poor prospects for improving that distribution. We will thus have to rely on caring and commitment if we are to advance the health of poor countries. Our concern is that the GPGH concept not only does not rely on caring and commitment, but is likely to regress rather than advance these.

It is worthy of note in the work of Kaul *et al.* (1999*b*) how they grapple with very similar issues in assessing how to finance GPGH. Again, given the distribution of property rights between rich and poor countries, we have a parallel situation. A fair outcome would be for the rich to take the greatest majority of the burden of finance. In practice however, as Kaul *et al.* (1999*b*) identify, they will not without some sort of incentive. They suggest that a global participation fund be established. They argue that participation is a useful starting point for equity and suggest that "equity in participation should be embedded in the structures of international governance." If one were drawing up a manual on how to make free trade fair, one might well have a central clause which read: "equity in participation should be embedded in the structures of international governance." As explained above, given the distribution of property rights between rich and poor in terms of the terms of trade, *free* trade does not end up as *fair* trade. No global participation fund for free trade has been set up. Why would we expect more success with GPGH?

It is also a concern that the GPGH paradigm excludes "caring." There is no thought of duty, or commitment or variations in the ability of different peoples to manage to desire. The concept of caring is absent. As identified above, the way forward is to build a caring world, and especially caring governments and caring institutions. This point is made by Sen (2001). He argues that while economic progress can yield health benefits to a population "much depends on how the income generated by economic growth is used," and even in poor economies "major health improvements can be achieved through using the available resources in a socially productive way." Sen's message is, as ever, optimistic, but what it does require is that governments be good, caring, compassionate; believing that they can be a force for building a better society for the poor and not just a facilitator for market forces to hold sway or a mediator for the worst excesses of modern capitalism.

A related, although slightly separate point, at more of a national rather than international level, is reflected in some work by Navarro (2000) in the context of globalization in European countries. The point here relates to whether any benefits, if they do accrue to a country through globalization, will only accrue to the rich or will "trickle down" to the poor. Navarro (2000) shows that in the European Union it has been possible for some governments to "throw off" some of the potentially bad distributional impacts of globalization and follow their own chosen road. The notion that globalization must result in increasingly neoclassical markets is shown by Navarro to be not proven, and in some cases false. Thus what he labels the "social democratic countries" (which are primarily Scandinavian), which were the most globally integrated of all the European countries (according to the measures he uses), were also in the period from 1960 to the mid 1970s the ones where the growth in public expenditures was greatest and hence in redistribution to the less well off. Navarro's hypothesis that it is possible to "buck the globalization trend" seems to be borne out in Europe.

What is crucial, however, in Navarro's analysis is that where this has happened there have been correspondingly strong institutions that have provided the framework to allow this to happen. He writes that, on the basis of this evidence, despite globalization, in some countries it has remained possible to follow social democratic, redistributive policies in the European Union. He states: "Whether a country follows these policies depends on the correlation of forces within a country . . . and *the presence of political and social institutions that enable the development of such policies.*" (emphasis added). He continues that among these institutions "a key element is the existence of a social pact between employers and unions and the government" where a central part of that pact is a commitment to "full-employment and expansionist policies."

It is worthy of note how this theme is picked up, seemingly independently, by Dreze and Sen (1989) in their book on hunger. They emphasize there the concept of "capability." The problem of hunger, they suggest, is about more than simply food intake. With respect to overcoming hunger they write that "a more reasoned goal [than concentrating solely on food intake] would be to make it possible for all to have the capability to avoid undernourishment and to escape deprivation associated with hunger." They then argue that avoiding hunger requires analysis not just of food intake but also "the person's access to health care, medical facilities, elementary education, drinking water, and sanitary facilities." While again it would be possible to see these purely in resource terms, or to "commodify" them, the whole argument here comes back to the need to have or to create the social institutions to allow these other aspects to be present, and indeed to allow such a philosophy to underpin public policy. Again we see here the emphasis on social institutions.

A final problem relates to who decides on the GPGH. What is potentially problematical with respect to this view of the possible road to avoiding the neoclassical stringencies of the market forces of globalization, and we would submit the breakdown of genuine scope for cooperation on a global scale (i.e. neoclassical market forces driving a wedge between rich and poor), is that many, if not most, developing countries tend to be weak in terms of these social institutions. Nonetheless the links between poverty and infectious diseases, and the other chain of links between market economics, globalization, increased poverty, and worsening distribution of income, are such that the very recognition that there is a way out is important. What perhaps merits yet more attention in the fight against the contagion of neoclassical economics through globalization is the building of solid democratic institutions where the power of unions is not only present but accepted as a key factor in pacts with government and industry in deciding how the resources of a country—including clearly for health—are to be used. The alternative is to let neoliberal economic forces not only determine the shape of the national economy but the shape of the society.

The solution does not lie in leaving solutions to "market forces." Nor does it rest in hoping that GPGH might come to the rescue. Indeed these two—the power of neoclassicism in world markets at present and the potential futility of GPGH—are linked. As Sutherland (1998) argues on trade (but we could substitute relevant terminology for the sentiment to be true of health as well): "Global trade negotiations could offer a partial solution to marginalization, but low income countries are not well equipped to drive a hard bargain, and, indeed, progress on opening markets to their important agricultural and textile exports has been slow." He continues: "Poverty remains the world's most urgent moral challenge . . . . Eliminating poverty is not only the right thing to do; it is essential to fulfilling the world's growth potential." It is not only, however, poverty that remains a problem in its own right, but "rich" (as in rich nations) has become synonymous with "powerful" (as in powerful nations). There is nothing in the GPGH paradigm that explicitly addresses this issue.

It follows that there needs to be a much greater recognition of a world autonomy where the rich are willing and able to allow the weaker nations of the world to have not just their token sovereignty, but genuine autonomy in their own affairs. Tolerance is needed but is not always available in abundant supply. Despite the success, and maybe because of the success, of Cuba in its health-care system, and indeed in improving the health of its population, the United States of America has seen fit to tighten the screw on its neighbor with yet more stringent sanctions. As a result some medicines are now much less accessible and cannot be obtained from

US suppliers. There is clear evidence that health is suffering (Garfield and Santana 1997). A "caring globalization" is needed which puts human freedom and development above economic market forces in any ideological competition. It is these aspects that GPGH seem not to be addressing, and indeed the worry is that they act as negative influences and disincentives in developing a more caring world.

The essence of GPGH is that they are produced with important externalities, not deliberately, but rather that when these characteristics are present they are taken into account in assessing the costs and the benefits involved. Now that is acceptable up to a point, but two things remain worrying. First, at a more technical level, whose values are brought to bear on the valuation of the benefits associated with the externalities? The values of producers, or the values of "external consumers"? If it is not the producers' values, then how are the external consumers' values to be obtained? Given that often the willingness to pay of these external consumers, who will tend to be poor, will be constrained by their ability to pay, what technique is to be used to assess value in this context? Add in Sen's concerns about the inability of many of these external consumers to manage to desire adequately (Sen 1992), and there are potentially serious problems within this essentially welfarist model of under provision of GPGH.

Second, and our greatest concern regarding GPGH, is that placing these centre stage, or even paying any sort of attention to them, is likely to inhibit rather than enhance any feelings of international caring and altruism. The whole emphasis of GPGH is in essence that if by chance good can be done for others, then let us take into account these benefits to others in deciding whether or not and at what level to produce these goods. There is no appeal to a wider concern for the welfare of others. There is no value attached to caring or compassion. There is more a view that even without such caring we can do more for the poor of this world. The argument from Sen (1999) that when we fully seize our most basic identity of being human beings we broaden our viewpoint, and the imperatives that we may associate with our shared humanity may not be mediated by our membership in collectives such as "nations" or "peoples," supports our position. In GPGH, it is not only Sen's concept of commitment that is absent, but also his concept of sympathy (Sen 1977).

Globalization, if it is seen purely in economic or economic market terms, will almost certainly lead to resource allocation in individual countries being dominated by the laws of the neoclassical market place. This, in turn, is most likely to result in a continuing lack of commitment to doing anything about the standard of living of the world's poor. Factors other than market economics need to prevail. The same arguments, even if from a somewhat different standpoint, can be put forward against GPGH. The base of GPGH remains welfarist and does not adequately address problems of values, especially those surrounding caring and compassion. We would postulate that GPGH may even *inhibit* the fostering of caring and compassion. The freedom that Sen recognizes in his analysis of human, rather than economic, development (Sen 1999) has to be the way forward.

The emphasis on capabilities and on building strong democratic institutions can mean that the benefits from globalization can be both obtained and distributed fairly across all, especially given an emphasis on vertical equity (Mooney 1996) with positive pro-poor policies being the way to reduce poverty and thereby infectious diseases.

12.3 **An alternative paradigm**

It appears to be the case that to attempt to build an approach to international health based solely on, or even just largely on, the GPGH paradigm is less than ideal. We have tried to show that since GPGH are both welfarist and seem to ignore, and even act against, more altruistic endeavors, they are in that context a flawed paradigm. If the goal is to seek some construct that will allow a fostering of attempts to improve the health of poor populations then again, being lacking in altruism, GPGH are likely to fail. A non-consequentialist approach is needed in reappraising the relevant value base. Various possibilities are available but it is proposed that the notion of a constitution for health services might be useful in this context, even if until now this has been seen purely in terms of individual countries' health services rather than internationally, and has not been restricted to issues of poverty in either income or health. Such a constitution represents the value base on which the services might be built rather than the goals or objectives of the system (Vanberg 1994). Leading into this, we propose, is best done through "communitarian claims" (Mooney 1998), although other routes are possible.

Communitarians, not surprisingly, place the community at the centre of their analyses and their value system. Community can be defined in various different ways, but perhaps most satisfactorily as a group of people with some common life through reciprocal relationships. Communitarians emphasize the social and community aspects of life, arguing in essence that life, identity and relationships are all communally based. Communitarianism is at odds with the atomism of modern liberalism, and the idea therein of a disembodied self. There is a value to the community *per se*, and a value in being a part of—being embodied in—the community. It allows clearly for altruism and caring between individuals, but also between different groups within a community (Sen 1992). While we are not aware that it has previously been considered in the context of the "global community," there is nothing within the construct of communitarian claims to stop it being asked to address issues at that level.

Communitarianism can be both prescriptive and descriptive. It is prescriptive in that it assumes that life will be better if we allow communitarian and public values to guide our lives. It is descriptive in the sense that communitarians believe that this social self is a truer reflection of how individuals actually are. Communitarians reject both a bottom up approach to the construction of society—an aggregation of atomistic discrete individuals—and a top down one—an imposed authoritarian regime. Social institutions can be valued for themselves and not just for what they produce as outcomes or consequences. With respect to the notion of claims, Broome (1989) has proposed that a claim to a good involves a duty that a candidate for that good should in fact have it. His analysis concentrates on claims as a basis for fairness. One of us has previously suggested that this notion can be extended to include concerns for both efficiency and fairness, and that the concept of "communitarian claims" may be helpful in deciding how best to allocate society's scarce resources in the specific context of health care (Mooney 1998). Such communitarian claims "recognise first that the duty is owed by the community [i.e. in this context the 'global, international' community] of which the candidate [citizens of countries, geographic regions, health professionals, philanthropists, other funders of health care, etc.] is a member and secondly that the carrying out of this duty is not just instrumental but is good in itself" (Mooney 1998a, 2001).

This construct of communitarian claims avoids the problems of GPGH both in that it allows altruism to be present, indeed fosters it, and does not rely necessarily on a welfarist base. It is, we would argue, therefore much better suited to act as a paradigm for the enhancing of the health of poor populations.

Four particular advantages that we see for communitarian claims are as follows. First, they do not require that the basis for allocation is consequentialist. They can thus extend beyond welfarism. Second, the values adopted in their application can be those of the overall community in the way that resources are allocated between different groups (e.g. cultures or countries). To this extent, since welfarism is based on individuals' values, communitarian claims represent a second extension or critique of welfarism. Third, it is these different groups' values that are applied when deciding *how* to use the resources. Fourth, while not guaranteeing it, communitarian claims are more encouraging of commitment, and in turn altruism, than a welfarist GPGH approach.

When one begins to think through the global nature of what the underlying concern is in this attempt to embrace GPGH, it becomes significant that both the construct of health and the values surrounding it are likely to vary from country to country and culture to culture. Even within countries this can happen—for example, Aborigines in Australia have a different construct of health than do non-Aboriginal Australians (see e.g. Houston 2001). We would add to this the important criticism that Sen (1992) makes of welfarism that not everyone will have the same ability to manage to desire. At the same time there is a desire to recognize the need to avoid paternalism, to respect different cultures' values and thereby to promote self-esteem and, in turn, health.

The effect of all of this is that we cannot use a single set of values in setting objectives or weights, which is what WHO currently does in its World Health Report (WHO 2000) and which GPGH are in danger of doing. Communitarian claims would suggest that it is for the community as a whole to decide on what basis, and according to that what weights, resources for health should be allocated to different groups. Once such allocations are made, it would then be for the different subcommunities, cultures or countries to decide how to use the resources that have been allocated to them and to do this according to their values and to their construct of health.

This process relies very explicitly on a form of altruism across different sub-communities, cultures and countries in how claims are determined and weighted. It is to be noted, however, that it is not strictly the altruism associated with a clear demarcation between donors and recipients, us and them. It is also the case that being involved in the process of establishing and weighting claims is considered to have potential value to those who perform this role (i.e. "the carrying out of the duty . . . is good in itself," Mooney 1998). At the same time it gives each "local" grouping the opportunity to determine how it wants "its" resources spent.

Relevant to this, there is some limited evidence in Australia that society is prepared to be altruistic toward Aborigines. This is reflected in some tentative findings favouring positive discrimination toward Aboriginal people's health (Mooney 2001), and in turn weighting health benefits to Aboriginal people more highly than is currently reflected in the allocation of health-care resources (Deeble *et al.* 1998). This is seen, however, in terms of not just of supporting Aboriginal people, but promoting a more decent society as a whole, which is a community benefit and one that is not restricted to Aboriginal people.

It is also possible to use the example of Australia to argue that "local" preferences and different constructs of health need to be respected. The history of Aboriginal health in Australia has been marred by an assumption that non-Aboriginal Australians knew better than did Aborigines how resources for Aboriginal health should be used (Houston 2001). It is only more recently that Aboriginal-controlled health services have begun to reflect such "local" preferences better. Australian Aborigines, in their under-valuation of their health problems (Wiseman 1999), also lend support to Sen's (1992) argument about deprivation leading to an inability to manage to desire adequately.

It is not argued that the paradigm of communitarian claims can resolve all the issues involved in providing and allocating resources more equitably for global health. Our submission is, however, that such a paradigm is more likely to succeed than the GPGH paradigm. At the same time, it overcomes the risks we foresee in attempting to get the concept of GPGH to cover issues that it is not designed or defined originally to cover. This is not intended as a purist argument, although we do not object to readers interpreting it in that way. What drives us to suggest this new paradigm is that we think that conceptually GPGH are flawed, and to make them less flawed creates too much distortion of the original meaning. Others of course may prefer to continue to work within an amended GPGH paradigm.

We believe that the idea of a "world community" attempting to establish a "world constitution" for health, which sets the value base for resource allocation globally, and which at the same time respects and reflects local values in how health is constructed and delivered at an operational level, is a step forward. That at least creates a forum for establishing Kaul *et al.*'s (1999*b*) "global participation fund." It is also in a way a new version of the old slogan of "think globally; act locally," but expanded to "think globally according to global preferences; act locally according to local preferences."

We would submit that GPGH do nothing to encourage altruism and are more likely, we believe, to inhibit it. Whatever, we still need Sen's caring governments. The paradigm of communitarian claims represents an attempt to encourage such caring.

12.4 **Conclusion**

There is a need to rethink the GPGH concept, and very definitely a need to rethink it in terms of economic terminology. We suggest stepping back to think through again what is being attempted in this literature on GPGH and the desire to use this entity as a base for international health; to attempt to describe what is being formulated and/or explained; and to recognize that providers of public goods sometimes fail too. Lifting the masses from disease is great propaganda, but such an analogy heightens doubts as to whether WHO is genuinely engaged in that noble purpose or is simply throwing its weight behind the global market to the detriment of the health of the poor. Put more bluntly: endorsing GPGH suggests that WHO is settling for attempting to lessen the worst vicissitudes of the global market rather than seeking to change it.

If WHO does genuinely seek to improve the health of poor populations, then this is better achieved through a paradigm built on communitarian claims than on GPGH.

References

Broome J. *Weighing Goods*. Oxford: Blackwell, 1989.

Deeble J, Mathers C, Smith L, Goss J, Webb R, Smith V. *Expenditures on Health Services for Aboriginal and Torres Strait Islander People*. Canberra: Commonwealth Department of Health and Family Services, 1998.

Dollar D. Is globalization good for your health? *Bull World Health Organ* 2001; **79**(9): 827–33.

Drager N, Beaglehole R. Globalization: Changing the public health landscape. *Bull World Health Organ* 2001; **79**(9): 803.

Dreze J, Sen A. *Hunger and Public Action*. Oxford: Oxford University Press, 1989.

Evans M, Sinclair RC, Fusimalohi C, Liava'a V. Globalization, diet, and health: an example from Tonga. *Bull World Health Organ* 2001; **79**(9): 856–62.

Fidler DP. The globalization of public health: The first 100 years of international health diplomacy. *Bull World Health Organ* 2001; **79**(9): 842–9.

Garfield R, Santana S. The impact of the economic crisis and the US embargo on health in Cuba. *Am J Public Health* 1997; **87**(1): 15–20.

Houston S. *Cultural Security*. Perth: Health Department of Western Australia, 2001, Occasional Paper.

Kaul I, Grunberg I, Stern MA. Defining global public goods. In: I Kaul, I Grunberg, MA Stern (eds) *Global Public goods: International Cooperation in the 21st Century*. New York: Oxford University Press, 1999a, pp. 2–19.

Kaul I, Grunberg I, Stern MA. Global public goods: concepts, policies and strategies. In: I Kaul, I Grunberg, and MA Stern (eds) *Global Public Goods: International Cooperation in the 21st Century*. New York: Oxford University Press, 1999b, pp. 2–19.

Korten DC. *For the Love of Money: When Corporations Rule the World*, 2nd edn. http://.iisd1.iisd.ca/pcdf/corprule/failure.htm, 2001.

Mooney G. And now for vertical equity: some concerns arising from Aboriginal health in Australia. *Health Econom* 1996; **5**(2): 99–104.

Mooney G. Economics, communitarianism and health care. In: M Barer, T Getzen, G Stoddart (eds) *Health, Health care and Health Economics: Perspectives on Distribution.* London: Wiley, 1998, pp. 397–413.

Mooney G. Communitarian claims as an ethical basis for resource allocation in health care. *Soc Sci Med* 1998*a*; **47**(9): 1171–80.

Mooney G. A communitarian road to health care? In: J Davis (ed.) *Social Economics of Health Care,* London: Routledge, 2001, pp. 40–60.

Navarro V. Are pro-welfare state and full-employment policies possible in the era of globalization? *Int J Health Services* 2000; **30**(2): 231–51.

Samuelson PA. The pure theory of public expenditure. *Rev Econom Stat* 1954; **36**: 387–9.

Samuelson PA. Diagrammatic exposition of a theory of public expenditure. *Rev Econom Stat* 1955; **37**: 350–6.

Samuelson PA. Aspects of public expenditure theories. *Rev Econom Stat* 1958; **40**: 332–8.

Sen A. Rational fools. *Philos Public Aff* 1977; **6**: 317–44.

Sen A. *Inequality Re-examined.* Oxford: Clarendon Press, 1992.

Sen A. *Development as Freedom.* Oxford: Oxford University Press, 1999.

Sen A. Economic progress in health. In: D Leon, G Walt (eds) *Poverty, Inequality and Health. An International Perspective.* Oxford: Oxford Medical Publications, 2001, pp. 334–47.

Sumner LW. *Welfare, Happiness and Ethics.* Oxford: Clarendon Press, 1996.

Sutherland PD. *The 1998 Per Jacobsson Lecture: Managing the International Economy in an Age of Globalisation.* London: Overseas Development Council, 1998.

Vanberg VJ. *Rules and Choice in Economics.* London: Routledge, 1994.

WHO. *World Health Report,* Geneva: WHO, 2000.

Wiseman V. Culture, self-rated health and resource allocation decision-making. *Health Care Anal* 1999; **7**(3): 207–23.

Chapter 13

Global public goods for health: Use and limitations

Richard D Smith and David Woodward

13.1 Introduction

A considerable body of expert opinion and knowledge has been brought together in this volume to assess the relevance and implications of the global public good (GPG) concept as applied to health. Although each chapter has been written independently, there is a surprising amount of consensus on aspects of the GPG concept that are of value, and also those that present possible dangers.

Our purpose here is to draw together the main messages and lessons that arise from these chapters, in order to draw some conclusions concerning the usefulness and limitations of the GPG concept in the context of health. The final chapter, Chapter 14, will then reflect back on the purpose of the book, as indicated in the foreword, and attempt to address directly the questions raised there, and consider more specifically the next steps for the GPG concept in health.

Following this introduction, Section 13.2 considers the primary importance of correctly identifying a global public good for health (GPGH). Section 13.3 details aspects of the "production" of a GPGH, focusing on the need for a "champion" to lobby for the GPGH in question, and the importance of knowledge, international legislation, and access goods in securing a GPGH. Section 13.4 reflects on the means by which the costs and benefits of GPGH can be assessed. Section 13.5 outlines briefly the relationship between GPGH and wider issues of human rights and equity, with Section 13.6 considering the relationship between GPGH and non-health GPGs. Section 13.7 focuses upon the funding of GPGH, and Section 13.8 offers some conclusions on the applicability and usefulness of the GPG concept in health.

13.2 Correct identification of a GPGH

As indicated in Chapter 1, the identification of a possible GPGH is critical. However, defining a GPGH is not as obvious as it first appears, since the core characteristics of non-rivalry and non-excludability are somewhat "elastic." This creates a danger, highlighted in several chapters, of the concept being applied to more and more tangential (i.e. "nonpublic") "goods." In fact, as indicated in Chapter 1, there are likely to be very few "pure" GPGH: largely some communicable disease control/eradication (but by no means all) and some environmental preservation measures. Important "intermediate" GPG will be knowledge and international legislation, with a key "access good" being health systems and infrastructure. While there is room for discussion concerning the appropriateness of classing goods as "intermediate" or "access" goods, and the extent to which they then may be treated as if they were GPGH, it is clear that the final GPG of interest are likely to be few.

If the GPG concept is seen as a means to ensure greater funding, or even just protection of current funding from "other" claims, then the temptation will be to use the "elasticity" of the concept to create "one size fits all." This danger was highlighted both in a conceptual sense by Mooney and Dzator (Chapter 12), and in a practical sense by Aylward et al (Chapter 2) with respect to their experience of the use of the concept to advance polio eradication. Yet, as the GPG concept becomes "fashionable," it faces the real possibility of becoming over-exposed, and even abused (in a manner, perhaps, similar to the fate of "public–private partnerships"), with the natural result that the concept becomes devalued, treated with skepticism and, eventually, with cynicism. The concept at this point will lose all value, and unfortunately this will apply even to those cases of "true" GPGH.

This highlights the fundamental dilemma faced by GPGH as an advocacy tool. If it is used strictly, in the traditional sense of non-rivalry and non-excludability, it will be more robust and convincing to policymakers, but the scope of GPGH will then be very limited. If, on the other hand, the strict definition is relaxed, in order to be inclusive of a wider range of health activities and programs, it loses its policy relevance, and therefore its effectiveness.

A framework is therefore needed to identify possible GPGs more systematically. A useful starting point for this may be to distinguish between problems conducive to GPG-type solutions, and GPG-based means of resolving problems. This suggests viewing possible GPGs for health in two dimensions: the type of problem they address; and the type of solution they offer. GPG-type solutions include those in the areas of global governance (international institutions and rules which could provide benefits by improving health); knowledge (basic epidemiological research, the development of medical technologies, and dissemination of information); and interventions (international support to specific health programs at the national level). This category might also be considered to include national access goods to widen access to a range of potential GPGs—principally support to national health systems.

Problems conducive to such solutions can be broadly divided between those addressing within-country health problems with cross-country externalities (primarily infectious disease control, but also noncommunicable disease control to the extent that it has economic effects), and those addressing the cross-border transmission of factors influencing health risks (such as tobacco marketing).

Figure 13.1 illustrates a possible framework for the identification of candidate GPGs according to these criteria, with columns indicating problems, and rows

Solutions proposed	In-country health problems with cross-border externalities			Cross-border transmission of and influences on risk factors, etc						
	Prevention	Treatment	Control of cross-border transmission of infection	Food-borne risks	Marketing of unhealthy products	Narcotics	Disease vectors	Chemical pollutants	Incomes and prices	Health system costs
Global governance and regional arrangements										
Institutions										
Rules										
Standards										
Coordination										
Information sharing										
Knowledge										
Basic research										
Product development										
Information sharing										
Policy research										
Best practice dissemination										
Interventions										
Health systems										
Other										

Fig. 13.1 A checklist to identify possible health GPGs, by problems addressed and solutions proposed

indicating potential solutions. This provides a checklist for possible GPGs. However, this is merely a starting point for discussion, as alternative frameworks may be more appropriate or feasible, and thus work is clearly required in the development of an appropriate framework to identify GPGH.

13.3 **The "production" of a GPGH**

The production of a GPGH, as indicated in Chapter 1, will require a wide range of inputs. Some may themselves be global (or regional) public goods, others national public goods, club goods, or private goods. Some will be specific to a particular disease, while others will confer broader benefits to other (health or non-health) national and international public goods. Some may be essential to produce the GPG, whilst others may only make its attainment more likely, easier, cheaper or faster, affecting its economic viability or political feasibility. But all inputs together will determine whether or not the GPG will be produced. Of particular import-ance is the degree to which these goods may be considered as "intermediate" GPG or "access" goods. There is also, in addition to actual inputs to the production process, the political process of ensuring that production is undertaken.

The four case studies in Section 2 of this volume (Chapters 2–5) were concerned not only to establishing the GPG characteristics of the topic area, but also to out-line key issues in the production of the GPGH. From these studies, several themes of importance emerge if production is to be secured: the need for a GPGH "cham-pion"; the importance of knowledge; the importance of international legislation; and the need for "access goods". These are considered in more detail below.

13.3.1 **The GPGH "champion"**

First and foremost, a GPGH such as polio eradication or tuberculosis (TB) control needs a "champion"—that is, a person and/or institution who will be the driving force behind the GPGH in question. Given the inherent potential for a country to "free-ride" on the efforts of others to produce a GPGH, production of a GPGH will not be spontaneous or achieved through the "invisible hand" of the market. Rather, someone—a group or institution—needs to be the focus for the coordina-tion of efforts to achieve the production of the GPGH, to persuade relevant parties to cooperate, to act as a "clearing house" for coordination and information man-agement (to avoid the "prisoners dilemma") and to lobby for funding. This was well illustrated in the case of polio eradication (Chapter 2), but also emerged as key in TB control (Chapter 3) and is highlighted as important in several other chapters.

13.3.2 **Knowledge**

All the case studies in Section 2 of this volume discussed, to a greater or lesser degree, the importance of knowledge in the provision of the GPGH of interest. Many of the GPGH considered there rely heavily, for example, on the generation and transmission of knowledge about the incidence of disease (surveillance) and the means of its control (e.g. pharmaceutical and other technologies, and best practice for prevention and treatment). Section 3 of this volume (Chapters 6–8) looked at issues of knowledge more specifically, with respect to medical knowledge generally, and then specifically at genomics and public health as specific types of knowledge.

Interestingly, all three chapters in Section 3 highlighted the *conceptual* rather than *practical* nature of the status of knowledge as a GPGH. Although in principle knowledge is totally non-rival and non-excludable, in practice there are myriad ways in which knowledge may be excludable (and possibly rival). The single word "knowledge" actually encompasses three quite different and distinct processes: the production of knowledge, its dissemination, and its use. Exclusion may occur in each of these processes; for example, due to "artificial" legislative exclusion (typically some form of intellectual property protection), physical inability to "access" the knowledge (e.g. through printed media), or the inability to "consume" a product which is the final embodiment of that knowledge, and thus to benefit from its use. Chapter 6 illustrated this well, highlighting that although medical (e.g. pharmaceutical) technologies are GPGH *in principle*, the use of this knowledge is made private through patent régimes, transforming technologies into "club goods," limited to those who can afford to purchase the products that embody them. Nonetheless, these goods may be necessary to produce GPGH, just as private goods are needed for the production of national public goods (e.g. bricks and labor in the classic case of the lighthouse). It will therefore be necessary to ensure access to them in order for many GPGH to be produced, as indicated in Section 13.3.4. below.

In highlighting this distinction, the GPG concept is therefore seen to be of value in two ways. First, it highlights the tension that exists between ensuring that knowledge is *produced* in the first place, through measures such as intellectual property (IP) protection, and the subsequent *distribution* and *use* of that knowledge. If one accepts that the value of knowledge lies in its use, not its mere existence, this raises the question of how to optimize the combination of the production of knowledge and its dissemination and use. All three chapters on knowledge in this volume make this point very clearly. IP protection is used to exclude access to knowledge, or to restrict its use artificially. Where use is non-rival (as in the case of GPGH), this will lead to a suboptimal use of that knowledge. International rules (e.g. on patents) and finance programmes (e.g. subsidies and public purchases) must therefore be explicitly designed to provide an optimal balance between incentives for the development of medical technologies of public health priority and access to them.

The GPG concept thus indicates the need for the current IP protection system to be redesigned, to optimize this balance, since knowledge use, and indeed production, are currently strongly skewed toward the developed nations and rich populations. This might, for example, entail a stronger focus on the use of pre-purchase agreements, public finance or the "Global Fund," and less reliance on legislating "monopolies" for patent holders.

Second, in considering how and why some elements of knowledge production, dissemination and use may be excludable, the GPG concept highlights once more the importance of access goods—that the ability to use knowledge depends on national public/private/club goods. For knowledge to contribute effectively it must be *applied*, which requires effective health systems and infrastructures, as indicated in Chapter 8. For example, the knowledge yielded by surveillance requires countries both to produce information and to act on it, and thus requires an effective health infrastructure and appropriate technical expertise at the national level. Similarly, knowledge of best practice and medical technologies depend on effective health services for their application.

13.3.3 International legislation

Appropriate legislation, policies, and regulations, and their coordination nationally, regionally and globally, varying according to the disease concerned, will be required to facilitate the production of GPGH. Law, especially international law, creates the "rules" that will govern the collective action being required to ensure the finance and production of the GPGH in question. This was highlighted by several of the case studies, and Section 4 of this volume is devoted to consideration of three aspects of legislation as it relates to GPGH. From these case studies, three issues emerge as important in facilitating the production of GPGH.

First, the GPG concept highlights the need for a change in the role of international institutions, which have historically been reluctant to engage in the development of international law. This is especially true of the World Health Organization (WHO), as highlighted by all three chapters in Section 4. WHO has not historically invoked its powers to create international law, especially treaties. However, developments in globalization, and in the field of GPGH, suggest that this needs to change, as such law is essential to achieving GPG production. Both the International Health Regulations (IHR) and Framework Convention on Tobacco Control (FCTC) (Chapters 10 and 11) are moves in this direction. Hopefully, as both Fidler (Chapter 9) and Taylor *et al.* (Chapter 11) suggest, this signals a change in role of WHO away from its "traditional" role to a more central role as inter-national broker of politico-legal and econo-legal treaties to ensure the production of key GPGH.

Second, the GPG concept highlights the need to be aware of trade-offs that may be required. In the case of IHR, for example, there is a trade-off between epidemic control and trade, which the GPG framework can assist in tying together. The potential importance of such trade-offs—and the health implications of apparently "non-health" GPGs, such as trade in some contexts—is highlighted by recent research on European Union (EU) food safety standards. It estimates that a proposed increase in EU aflatoxin standards, which would save one life per two years in the EU would cost African exporters some $700 million per year in lost incomes and foreign exchange earnings. There can be little doubt that the health effects of such losses would be far greater than the lives saved.

It is important, therefore, that public health considerations are fully and effectively taken into consideration in non-health fora where decisions have potential effects on health, either directly (e.g. international agreements concerning pharmaceutical patents or trade in health services) or indirectly (e.g. agreements concerning trade on which poor countries and low-income producers depend). This issue is dealt with in more detail in Section 13.6.

Third, there will be a danger in international legislation as long as powerful countries and interests are still able to set the agenda and disproportionately influence the outcome of negotiations. The prospect of securing a favorable international policy and regulatory environment therefore depends on decision-making processes in the international bodies that develop international policies and regulatory régimes being fully representative of developing countries and their populations.

13.3.4 Access goods

Perhaps the most central, yet potentially the most controversial, issue to be addressed in the production of GPGH is that of "access goods." In Chapter 1, the importance of access goods, and the debate about their being treated as if they were GPG, was foreshadowed. While this controversy cannot be resolved here, the uniformity of comment on the importance of access goods—across all chapters—means that it will have to be addressed more thoroughly.

All of the case studies in Section 2 of this book highlight the importance of those private goods and services required to produce the GPG of their specific interest. After all, the production or availability of a GPG is of no relevance to those who do not have the means to benefit from it. For example, in the case of TB control (Chapter 3), there is a need to access the drugs. Consequently, like much of infectious disease control, TB control is a "club good"—that is, it is open only to those with the wealth to afford treatments. However, this produces a global under-supply of control, and is seen as especially short-sighted in view of its implications for antimicrobial resistance (AMR) (Chapter 4). The single most important access good raised by the chapters in this volume was that of access to adequate health systems and public health infrastructure, in terms of knowledge, institutions, and commodities. The importance of the role of public health infrastructure was addressed directly by Powles and Comim in Chapter 8.

The success of the polio eradication initiative (PEI) demonstrates that at least some GPGs can be delivered without effective health systems in *all* countries (e.g. in conflict areas) by operating through parallel systems. However, this and other chapters suggest that the absence of functioning health systems in some countries is an important constraint on GPG provision, rendering production of some GPGH impossible, increasing the cost and/or reducing the benefits of others, increasing the likelihood of under-provision, or preventing benefits from being universal. The result is to reduce the number of GPGs that could be provided in two ways.

First, inadequate health services in many low-income countries would severely limit the ability of much of their populations to *benefit* from many potential GPGH (e.g. best practices in treatment, and medical technologies) if they were provided. This not only affects the cost–benefit calculus for their provision, but may also bring into serious question their status as GPGs in terms of the universality of benefits.

By excluding those in greatest need, the absence of effective health systems also heightens the tension between the GPGH approach and equity considerations. Where the benefits of a GPGH are purely private (e.g. knowledge of best practice in palliative care for noncommunicable disease), this represents a prima facie case against prioritizing its subsidization over alternative uses of funds—although this may be overridden by other policy considerations (e.g. human rights, if there were considered to be a *right* to the (private) benefit which could be derived from the GPGH). Alternatives might include converting the good into a club good by administrative exclusion and/or by technological means. The issue of equity is dealt with in more detail in Section 13.5 of this chapter.

Notwithstanding the issue of equity, however, since those in greatest need are, in many contexts, also those for whom the potential benefits of GPGH provision are greatest, exclusion through lack of adequate health services may also have a disproportionate effect on the potential benefits of the GPGH, thus reducing the *efficiency* of its provision through perverse targeting of the public resources used.

Second, accessible and effective health services are essential to the *production* of GPGH such as disease eradication and communicable disease control, and may thus represent a critical constraint on their provision. Their absence in many low-income countries may thus limit the scope of GPGH whose provision is economically viable. There is little question, for example, that polio eradication could have been achieved more easily, quickly and cheaply had strong health services existed in all countries, or that this would have a similar effect on AMR control.

Equally, the role of health services in GPGH provision means that there are important opportunity costs that need to be taken into account in assessing their costs and benefits. Using resource-constrained health services in developing countries for the provision of GPGH may divert resources away from alternative uses that are of greater priority locally—for example, the control of diseases which represent a greater health problem locally, but which have smaller cross-border externalities. To the extent that different GPGH depend on the same (limited) health sector resources for their production, they may in practice be competitive in their production.

Most, if not all, potential GPGH will be affected by the existence or otherwise of effective and accessible health systems through one or other of these mechanisms. As discussed in Chapter 8, health services may therefore be considered as "access goods," necessary to the production and enjoyment of GPGH, as the cost of providing health services to those who do not have them may be no greater than the externalities arising from their use. Support to the development or restoration of adequate health services in countries where they do not currently exist may therefore be justified on GPG grounds, particularly where universal or near-universal coverage is necessary to ensure GPGH production, as in the case of disease eradication. This represents a strong case for the provision of free health services as a public good at the national level, and for external subsidies to achieve this.

The likelihood of health system support being justified on GPG grounds is greatly increased by the disparity in resources available for health between rich and poor countries. For the cost of a 1 percent increase in total health spending for the 860 million people living in the developed countries, public expenditure on health could be increased by 90 percent for four times as many people living in low-income countries. It is by no means inconceivable that the cross-border health and economic externalities to developed countries of this improvement could be greater than that of the lowest priority use of public funds in the developed countries, particularly if additional resources were focused on health services with the greatest potential cross-border impacts, in countries where the needs and potential benefits were greatest. Had additional resources on this scale been allocated to activities designed to slow the spread of HIV/AIDS in countries at highest risk early in the epidemic, for example, the number of cases in developed countries might have been substantially reduced. Given the high cost of treatment for HIV/AIDS in developed countries, the financial savings to their health systems alone could well have been greater than the costs.

Overall, analysis provided by the authors in this volume suggests that decisions concerning which GPGs should be provided should take account of the implications of the absence of functioning health systems in some countries (and the possibility of future health system failure) for the feasibility and cost of their production, and the extent and universality of their benefits. As an extension of this, international support for health systems in countries where they are critically weak would be required for the efficient provision of at least some, if not all, GPGH. A long-term view is required of GPG provision, taking account of the potential for health system strengthening to contribute to *future* provision as well as the direct benefits of *immediate* provision.

13.4 **Assessment of costs and benefits of GPGH**

The case studies presented in this volume all reaffirm the need to assess, not only the costs and benefits relating to the GPGH in question, but also, critically, their distribution and timing. This is important, both to consider the desirability of GPGH provision, and because the "collective action" problem underlying the GPG concept makes the *incentives* to different players, including the costs and benefits they face, critical to the provision of a GPGH.

There are three key questions in considering how to analyze the costs and benefits of GPGH: which costs and benefits to measure; how to compare or aggregate health benefits with financial costs and benefits; and how to aggregate financial costs and benefits at different income levels in such a way as to reflect their welfare effects.

Irrespective of whether a potential GPGH is provided internationally, it may be at least partly provided through national actions in some countries. In the case of polio eradication, for example, almost all countries had polio prevention or control programs before the decision to aim for global eradication of the disease. However, few had programs aimed at its *elimination* at the national level, because it was not a high enough priority in terms of their own public health needs. Eradication entails a strengthening of these programs, and it is this strengthening that constitutes the difference between national provision and provision as a GPGH.

From a GPG perspective, the relevant questions are then what *additional* action is required beyond autonomous national activities, what benefits this would bring and how much it would cost. This means that the calculus of costs and benefits for analysis will vary considerably between different GPGH, according to variations in their excludability characteristics, in the balance between expenses incurred at the national and international levels, in the current levels of provision in different countries and in the balance between benefits within each country as a result of its own contribution to providing the GPG, and cross-border benefits to other countries.

Comparing financial costs or benefits with health benefits is a long-standing problem in cost–benefit analysis. There are essentially three possible approaches: cost-effectiveness methodologies, opportunity cost, and traditional cost–benefit analysis. These are all outlined in more detail in Appendix 13.1. While all raise problems in the comparison of health and financial costs and benefits, and the treatment of the latter at different income levels, we propose a modified version of cost–benefit analysis to resolve this problem (see Appendix 13.1 for more detail). Specifically, this entails replacing absolute financial costs and benefits with multiples of per capita household income (for private costs and benefits) or Gross National Product (GNP) per capita (for public sector costs and benefits), and then valuing life, ill health, and disability as multiples of income on the basis of "willingness-to-pay" for reductions in risk. In effect, this assumes that it is a one *per cent* change in income that has an equivalent effect on welfare at all levels of income, rather than a one *dollar* change, as in conventional cost–benefit analysis.

It also has to be recognized that there is a potential danger in the assessment of the *pattern* of expected costs and benefits. In the case of polio, for example, establishment of costs and benefits was useful, but largely because it demonstrated that the rich stood to benefit if they helped the poor in eradicating polio. However, this may not always be the case—it could be that in some cases the costs considerably outweigh the benefits for the rich, which will likely then militate against their cooperation in assisting the poor. The reluctance of the United States of America to sign up to the Kyoto agreement concerning environmental pollution is a clear illustration. Even if the overall benefit is greater than the cost, if the reverse is the case for a specific country this will influence their willingness to cooperate. This is likely to be a significant problem if the country concerned is a major potential source of financing.

13.5 **GPGH and wider issues of human rights and equity**

The GPG concept is fundamentally concerned with improving efficiency, and is in principle "neutral" with respect to equity: whether something is or is not a GPG provides no indication as to whether its benefits are, or should be, distributed equitably. The case studies, however, highlight three possible implications for equity from the GPG concept.

(1) If the "GPG agenda" is set by the rich without regard for the priorities of the poor, the existing imbalance of power between rich and poor nations may be reinforced, and the poor may be made worse off.

(2) Poor nations may incur significant opportunity costs in the pursuit of the GPG agenda (which may, as indicated above, not be set by the poor themselves), also potentially making them unable or unwilling to cooperate in the provision of the GPG.

(3) There may be a conflict with other frameworks, such as human rights.

Here some initial thoughts concerning the interaction between the GPG framework and human rights and equity are outlined; however, this is an important and extensive area, and we do not address all the relevant issues comprehensively. Rather, we aim to provide a background to where the GPG concept may lie in relation to concerns for human rights and equity.

The status of some health-related goods and services as public goods is not the only justification for public action to ensure their provision. In particular, it is internationally recognized that the highest attainable standard of physical and mental health is a human right—not only on a philosophical level, but also as a legal claim of people toward their governments. This extends to the underlying determinants of health, including a wide range of socioeconomic factors that promote health, as well as health services. Governments have a responsibility to ensure that goods, services and living conditions necessary to health are available, accessible, acceptable and of good quality, and are provided in accordance with the principles of respect for individual rights, dignity, and autonomy.

The public goods approach and the rights approach are different in nature: the rights approach is fundamentally *normative*, asserting what *should* be the case, while the concept of public goods is a *positive* one, describing the *nature* of goods. However, while there is no inherent conflict between the rights approach and the public goods approach, there are major differences in their scope. While it would not be untenable to argue that people have a right to public goods, this would extend rights to some unconventional areas (e.g. radio broadcasts and lighthouses). Equally, the right to health clearly implies ensuring access to goods and services necessary to health irrespective of whether they constitute public goods, or even whether they have positive externalities.

An intermediate position between the rights approach and the public goods approach is the view of health (or of goods and services required for health) as "merit goods"—that is, as goods to which people *should* have access, irrespective of their circumstances or their ability or willingness to pay, because they have positive externalities in consumption. It should be noted, however, that this has a more limited scope than the rights view, in that not all aspects of health or health interventions have externalities, or can therefore be considered to be merit goods.

While they are not coextensive, however, the concepts of public goods for health, the right to health and health as a merit good overlap in some areas, and are complementary rather than conflicting: some prescriptions are common to all three, and none obviously precludes the prescriptions of the others.

The same applies in principle to GPGH and equity. The equity approach suggests that efforts to improve health should focus on the most disadvantaged groups. Some GPGs (e.g. prevention of most infectious diseases) will indeed benefit these groups disproportionately; but many would not be provided on the basis of equity considerations, as some are likely to benefit primarily more advantaged groups and/or countries (e.g. disease eradication).

This does not, in itself, imply that GPGs should not be provided, although it is important to ensure that they do not worsen the situation of disadvantaged groups. However, the requirement (in the UNDP definition, at least) that GPGs should benefit all countries and population groups suggests a shift away from those programs that provide the greatest benefits to those in greatest need, and toward those programs that benefit them less, but also provide some benefit to those in less need.

This problem is seriously compounded by the financial and political dimensions of GPG provision. Given the limited capacity at present of international decision-making processes, the disproportionate influence of better-off countries and population groups, and the limited resources available for activities at the international level, there is a real risk that the provision of GPGs will in practice be skewed away from the provision of GPGs which could most benefit disadvantaged groups. This could bring the GPG approach into direct conflict with the equity approach, and in this respect we support the concern raised in the case studies that the existing imbalance of power between rich and poor nations may be perpetuated.

It is therefore essential that decision-making processes concerning GPGH ensure full, effective and equal representation of poorer countries, with the opportunity for well-informed decisions, in their political dynamics as well as their formal structures. The agenda will otherwise be skewed toward those with greatest power, rather than those with greatest needs, and the incentives for global participation and collective action will therefore be limited.

13.6 **GPGH and non-health GPGs**

Several case studies raised the issue of the interface between GPGs *for health*, and other, *non-health-related*, GPGs. It is clear that the role of health as a receptor of externalities means that health is likely to be a significant dimension of the benefits of many public goods in other sectors or with other primary objectives.

Pollution control, for example, may be primarily motivated by environmental objectives (e.g. conservation of biodiversity, or climate change), but, as indicated in Chapter 5, it is also likely to have significant health benefits. Similarly, education may be directed in part toward improving overall productivity and economic performance, but health-related behavioral changes are also a significant positive externality, as indicated in Chapter 8, as are the health benefits of the increased incomes associated with education, and the increased supply of health professionals.

Conversely, health improvements may have positive effects that extend beyond health status—in particular, they increase productivity and improve economic performance. This not only extends the externalities associated with health improvement, but may also facilitate the provision of other public goods, by increasing the productivity of the personnel involved and reducing the costs of staff turnover associated with chronic morbidity and mortality (discontinuity, recruitment, training, health insurance, pensions, etc). Other linkages may also be relevant; for example, improved health status improves educational performance by reducing non-attendance due to ill health and improving performance while in school, adding to the positive externalities of education.

This suggests that there is a significant degree of synergy between health-related and non-health public goods, so that the costs, benefits and appropriate design of a GPG may depend significantly on which other GPGs are provided. For example, the level of education will influence the effectiveness of health information campaigns, the nature and extent of the behavioral problems they address, the appropriate means of delivery (e.g. written versus non-written) and the availability (and potentially the cost) of educated and skilled personnel.

Clearly there is a need for *collective action* between international agencies, as well as between countries, in the provision of health- and non-health-related GPGs. This could be a first major step in advancing the GPG agenda, with international bodies, such as WHO, United Nations, World Bank, and World Trade Organization *together* establishing the range of possible GPGs of interest, and *together* seeking to set the agenda for action.

13.7 **Funding GPGH**

Global public good provision, in health as elsewhere, requires funding. Where this funding is to be found is therefore a key issue. Although the case studies presented in this volume identified a variety of sources of funding, from public and private, charitable and commercial, sectors, and a variety of means to obtain this funding, the majority of funding is likely to come directly or indirectly from the (national) government sector. In an ideal world, the cost of providing GPGs would then be allocated between countries in proportion to their benefits. However, resource constraints (as well as differential welfare effects at different levels of income) will limit the ability of poorer countries to contribute to GPGH provision. This both undermines the political will to cooperate and limits effective participation, impeding effective global action. Even the creation of a legal *duty* does not ensure *compliance*, as this depends on having adequate resources to fulfill such obligations. Circumventing this problem requires that financial and other contributions reflect each country's *ability* to contribute, as well as its potential benefits from the GPG. In practice, this means that much of the cost—including costs *within* developing countries—would therefore need to be borne by developed countries (although even then developing countries would face major opportunity costs, for example of health workers' time, diverting resources from national priorities).

However, a common concern in the case studies is that the GPG concept might prove *substitutive* rather than *complementary*, leading to a diversion of existing overseas development assistance (ODA) monies rather than providing additional funding. If funds were diverted from existing projects to the provision of GPGH, this might arguably represent an overall improvement in efficiency. However, assuming that current aid monies are invested wisely, if the GPG concept simply led to a "changing of the share" rather than an "increasing of the size" of the cake, it would therefore fail in its core role to liberate additional funding for projects on a basis separate to that of ODA.

The GPG concept is "designed" to highlight the need for the provision of certain goods because of their current under-supply from a global perspective. This is predicated on self-interest—that we would all be better off if collective action could be orchestrated to produce a particular good, such as polio eradication. Thus, if some countries are unable to finance their "part" of this collective action, the benefits to others of their involvement, or the lack of cost of their involvement, make it irrational to exclude them, and in many cases make it rational to fund their activity (see our modified definition of GPGH in Chapter 1). The GPG concept implies that supporting other countries' GPGH strategies is not a question of humanitarian aid, but a self-interested investment in domestic health: while recipient countries also benefit, the *primary* objective for the developed countries is to improve *their own* health. This suggests that national health (or other) budgets are a more appropriate source of funding, leaving existing aid monies unaffected, and increasing total funding to developing countries rather than merely reallocating it between uses.

Resources to cross-subsidize GPGH should therefore *not* come from current aid resources, but primarily from developed countries' domestic budgets, as their support is, as indicated, a matter of self-interest. Where the benefits of a GPGH to developed countries are financial, rather than in terms of health (e.g. savings on polio immunization after eradication, and on treatment costs with effective AMR control), savings in principle provide a basis for estimating the appropriate contribution from domestic budgets (although this may be complex in practice, due to uncertainty and long time-lags).

13.8 Conclusion

The chapters in this book suggest that there are several areas where the GPGH concept is of value, as well as noting several limitations to the use of the concept. This chapter has attempted to bring most of these together in a series of important "lessons" on the uses and limitations of the GPGH concept. However, it is clear from the case studies that the primary value of the GPGH concept is as an *advocacy tool*—a coherent framework which may be understood by many different audiences. This is important in two key respects.

First, it highlights the global nature of many problems, and the need for global solutions to some problems that may appear local—global problems are local problems and global solutions are local solutions—and that cooperation will yield greater benefit overall to all than operating alone in isolation. It thus increases awareness of the interdependency of nations in several areas to be raised. The production of GPGH relies heavily on national legislation, regulation, and health systems; but these also have the potential to produce negative externalities impacting on other countries.

Equally, conflicts or synergies between strategies pursued by different (e.g. neighboring) countries in the health arena may increase or reduce their effectiveness. Such positive and negative spillovers are becoming ever stronger as the process of globalization progresses, and the cost to health of failing to address them effectively in national policies will grow commensurately. The GPG concept, by its very nature, stresses the *global* aspect of health and health issues and thus the need for collective action to solve these problems—not just that global problems need local action, but also that local problems need global action. The GPG concept can therefore play a crucial role in raising the awareness, and facilitating the lobbying, of governments about the importance of this interdependence, as well as in policy coordination.

Interestingly, this seems to counter a key concern raised by Mooney and Dzator, in Chapter 12, that the GPG concept is in some way "atomistic," devaluing the community (which they place at the center of their alternative "communitarian claims" paradigm). From the studies presented in this volume, it would appear that the value placed on the GPG concept is actually that it *also* places the community (of nations, as defined in Chapter 1) at the center of the analysis, seeking the means to secure effective cooperation between nations rather than leaving their activities self-centered. Admittedly the reason for cooperation may differ (self-interest rather than altruism or "caring") but the outcome may be effectively the same. Mooney and Dzator argue that the outcome is not the same, as the GPG concept is consequentialist, while communitarian claims are not. However, the "outcome" could possibly be one of increasing caring and altruism. That is, through "forcing" collaboration and collective action for self-interested purposes, the very interaction involved may generate sympathy and understanding and lead to the caring and altruism that Mooney and Dzator seek. Their paradigm may possibly only differ in this respect, therefore, in requiring this caring altruism to enable the achievement of their goals, whereas the GPG concept does not, but sees them as perhaps an outcome in themselves. While it is accepted that such "caring" would be a secondary and not a primary effect of the GPG concept, the two paradigms may not be as opposed as Mooney and Dzator suggest.

Second, the GPG concept may be used to highlight the shortcomings in the current international decision-making, and legislative, process. While the process of *producing* GPGs occurs primarily at the national level, the key determinant of the under-provision of GPGs is the existence of collective action problems at the international level, and the absence of effective (largely legal) mechanisms to resolve them. Only when international decision-making mechanisms are effective in representing the collective interests of the population of the world as a whole will the systematic under-provision of GPGs be overcome, and the GPGs provided be appropriately prioritized. The benefits forgone by all countries as a result of the non- and skewed provision of GPGs is a partial measure of the costs of this failure of global governance, both within the health sector and more generally.

However, it is also clear that the pursuit of the GPG concept needs to be undertaken with caution. There is a danger that focusing excessively on the provision of GPGs as an objective of development policy will skew global policy further toward developed country and commercial interests, and away from low-income country interests and poverty reduction. This would not necessarily have a negative impact if GPG provision were *additional* to other developmental activities, but in practice this is unlikely to be the case. The capacity of the international system to take decisions at the global level is limited, due to the combination of institutional weaknesses and time constraints on national and international policymakers and the staff of international agencies; and considerable time and effort is required to develop an international consensus on a particular issue. In practice, deciding to provide GPGs is likely to mean slower progress in some other areas of international activity, and, given the current international decision-making process, it is unlikely to be activities that serve the interests of developed countries or transnational corporations which suffer. This problem would be accentuated to the extent that developed countries' contributions to the provision of GPGs were funded from aid budgets.

If our primary purpose is the improvement of health, then it would be inappropriate to use the GPG concept as an organizing principle,[1] or as a tool for setting international priorities. On the one hand, applying a strict definition would exclude or de-prioritize many activities that are of critical importance to health (e.g. malaria control and urban environmental improvement), as motivated, for example, by the right to health, social justice, equity, or altruism. On the other hand, relaxing the definition to include such priority issues would mean stretching the concept so far that it would cease to have any coherence or usefulness (a danger identified and discussed earlier in this chapter). The concept should not then be used as a criterion for the prioritization or financing of policies and programs. Rather, decisions on prioritization and financing should be based on the relative contributions of alternative policies and programs to meeting the greatest and most urgent health needs from a global perspective.

---

[1] Indeed, GPG theory is defined by consumption rather than production characteristics, and as such provides no organizational basis for the provision or financing of such goods.

There are limits to the GPG concept's effectiveness as a means of identifying international objectives. It is not *necessarily* appropriate to provide *everything* that can be considered a GPG: from a strictly economic perspective, if the cost outweighs the potential benefits for technical or economic reasons, non-GPGs may be a better use of funds. It may therefore be more appropriate to focus primarily on the *failure of collective action* as an organizing principle, and on the development of effective and representative mechanisms for international decision-making as the primary means of developing appropriate priorities, policies and programs for health at the global level.

Where the concept of GPGs may nonetheless be useful is in informing the process of achieving such policies and programs at the international level—for example, by identifying goods which are non-rival in consumption, and therefore candidates for international provision, and opportunities for the promotion of "clubs" to broaden access to those that are excludable. The GPG concept may also, as indicated above, be useful as an advocacy tool, to appeal to the self-interest of potential funders (primarily developed country governments) and thus "sell" the program of concern. However, the usefulness of the concept in this context depends on an increased awareness and understanding of it; and it may be preferable to use the idea of collective action problems at the international level impeding the development of programs and policies that would be in the collective interest. The latter has the advantages of being less complex conceptually, more intuitive, more clearly defined, and more inclusive.

What, then, is the role of the GPG concept in a health context? The discussion provided in this chapter suggests that it provides a useful framework to:

(1) raise additional funds from developed countries' domestic budgets to supplement aid funds;

(2) promote investment by developed countries in the health systems of developing countries, as "access goods";

(3) promote strategic partnerships between developed and developing countries; and

(4) guide the political process of establishing, and mechanisms for providing and financing, global programs with GPG characteristics.

In short, the GPG concept is not a reliable guide for the global community in deciding *what* to do, but it may, in some areas, be more useful in guiding their decisions about *how* it might be done.

Appendix 13.1 **Comparing costs and benefits**

Three approaches to comparing financial costs or benefits with health benefits are possible. The most straightforward solution would be to adapt the conventional cost effectiveness methodology, developed to compare health interventions in response to the problems associated with cost–benefit analysis, for the evaluation of candidate GPGs. This could be done by deducting the economic benefits of a GPG from the costs of providing it, and dividing the resulting net costs by the health benefits (e.g. in disability-adjusted life years (DALYs)) to generate a figure for the *net cost per DALY saved*.

However, this approach has three serious drawbacks.

(1) It treats financial benefits to anyone as though they accrued to the financiers of the GPG.

(2) The results may be very sensitive to the estimation of economic benefits, which will at best be very approximate.

(3) For a given level of overall (i.e. health and economic) benefits, it skews the results toward GPGs with primarily economic benefits.

Also, the results would not be directly comparable with others generated by cost-effectiveness methods, which take account only of health benefits, and not economic benefits, limiting the scope for comparing expenditure on at least some GPGH with other health expenditures.

Alternatively, funding for a GPGH could be valued at its *opportunity cost* in terms of health-related spending, again measured, for example, in DALYs. However, the appropriate "exchange rate" is problematic: the interventions for which public subsides are provided cover a vast range of cost-effectiveness, and the least cost-effective are not necessarily the first to make way for other spending. This applies even at the national level, and much more so globally, because of the disparities in the resources available in different countries. Moreover, the alternative uses of funds might well lie outside the health sector, in which case cost-effectiveness measures cannot be used. A more realistic approach would be to use an average figure for the cost-effectiveness of funds currently used in the health sector globally. However, this would still be arbitrary. The size of the disparities make the calculation of the average problematic, and the results very sensitive to the measure chosen (e.g. mean or median) and, if the funds used were provided disproportionately from developing countries or aid budgets, the opportunity cost could be substantially understated. Equally, valuing economic benefits (and losses) in this way would, in effect, value changes in private incomes as if they had health effects equivalent to public spending on health. This is unrealistic, particularly at higher income levels.

A third approach is provided by *cost–benefit analysis*. This is the orthodox approach for evaluating projects and policies with diverse benefits. However, the valuation of health (and other non-financial benefits) is problematic, and while methodologies exist for such valuation, their results are not consistent.

Whichever of these approaches is used, a further problem arises in the valuation of financial benefits. The problem is that simply adding together the dollar amounts of financial benefits distorts the measurement of welfare benefits, because the same absolute change in income has a very different impact at different income levels. The welfare gain associated with a $1 gain in income for a major shareholder in a transnational company, for example, is much smaller than that of a $1 increase in income for a poor rural farmer in a low-income country. Equally, the impact of a $1 contribution to the provision of a GPG will be much greater for a poor country than for a rich country.

One possible approach would be to assume that a 1 percent change, rather than a $1 change, in income has an equal effect on welfare at all income levels (mathematically, that welfare is proportional to the logarithm of income). This would imply replacing *absolute* changes in income or expenditure in the calculation with changes in income and costs *relative to (per capita household) income*. The financial benefits of a GPG in a particular year would then be measured as a number of annual per capita household incomes.

Financial costs can be valued in the same way as income, and non-financial costs (primarily the time spent receiving treatment, waiting to receive it and traveling to and from the health facility) can be valued similarly, using hourly income as a proxy for the opportunity cost of time (although this approach also raises some problems, despite its widespread use). Costs to public and other subsidized providers might be valued on the basis of GNP per capita.

This offers a resolution to the problem of comparing or aggregating health and financial benefits. Methodologies based on the willingness to pay for reductions in the risk of death have typically found that the valuation of life varies broadly in line with income. This suggests that the value of life to the individual might, in principle, be stated as a multiple of income. This could be directly added to the financial benefits, measured as described above.

The benefits of escaping illness or disability through the provision of a GPG could be valued using the weightings for illness and disability used in the calculation of DALYs for cost-effectiveness calculations, or based on local surveys of the valuation of different types of illness and disability relative to death—local, because they are, to a significant extent, socially determined by local conditions (e.g. access to, and quality of, health care, facilities for people with disabilities, social attitudes and culture, etc).

This approach would provide a means of aggregating health and non-health benefits, generating a result measured in annual per capita incomes. While some aspects of this methodology are somewhat arbitrary, they should at least be less systematically skewed against those on low incomes than more conventional approaches.

Another issue is the aggregation of benefits over time. Both health and economic externalities are likely to be spread over a long period, possibly with a complex lag structure. In the latter case especially, there may be a combination of positive and negative effects in different areas and for different countries (e.g. increased production of primary commodities for export is likely to reduce world prices, imposing costs on other producers, but benefiting consumers).

Discounting future costs and benefits using the market interest rate as a discount rate may not be appropriate for use in conjunction with the proposed welfare function. This is because part of the market interest rate may arise from the expectation of higher incomes in the future, both at the individual level (for life-cycle reasons) and in aggregate (due to economic growth). Consideration should be given to making an adjustment for this factor.

This issue is all the more important because *the results of the present value calculation will be particularly sensitive to the discount rate used*, because of the very long-term nature of the benefits entailed (particularly if the GPG is to be provided for an extended period), and the potentially long time lags between provision and some of the health effects (especially intergenerational effects).

An additional problem is that converting health benefits into financial terms, amalgamating them with economic costs and benefits, and discounting the results means, in effect, discounting health benefits. While there is a sound basis for the discounting of financial costs and benefits (because saving and borrowing can be used to rephase consumption over time), there is no such consensus in the discounting of health benefits—particularly years of life, which by definition cannot be substituted over time. It may therefore be appropriate to use different discount rates for financial costs/benefits and effects on health status.

Section 6

Global public goods for health: the future

Chapter 14

Global public goods for health: From theory to policy

Richard D Smith, Robert Beaglehole, David Woodward, and Nick Drager

14.1 Introduction

As indicated in the foreword to this book, writing on global public goods (GPGs) has been mostly broad-based and multisectoral; consideration of GPGs with specific respect to health has been brief and largely focused on medical technologies. This book brings together a series of papers exploring whether, and how best, the GPG concept may be used to advance global health, and especially the health of poor populations and countries, in a broader sense.

In the foreword we proposed a series of questions to be addressed. These were to:

(1) examine the validity of health *as* a GPG, and which elements, if any, of health may be considered as GPGs *for* health (GPGH);

(2) clarify whether the topics covered as case studies could be classified as GPGH, or have GPG aspects;

(3) consider the usefulness of the GPG concept in improving health as illustrated by the case studies; and

(4) present a policy and research agenda for the implementation and development of the GPGH concept in such a way as to optimize its health effects.

These questions form the basis for this chapter, which outlines conclusions, recommendations and possible next steps in the GPGH field.

14.2 Health as a GPG?

In Chapter 1, we argued that health could not be seen as a GPG, at the individual, national, or international level, as individuals and countries are the primary beneficiaries of their own health status. However, two important *externality* aspects of health are amenable to conceptualization as having GPG properties.

The first is the *prevention or control of communicable disease*. As outlined in Chapter 1, and by the case studies in later chapters, preventing one person from getting a communicable disease (or treating it successfully) provides a significant positive externality to people other than the individual concerned by reducing their risk of infection. Similarly, the reduction of communicable disease within one country reduces the probability of cross-border transmission to other countries. However, while communicable disease control is non-rival and non-excludable in its *effect* (one person's lower risk of contracting a disease does not limit the benefits of that lower risk to others), its *production* requires a mix of both excludable and non-excludable inputs. In this sense, it may therefore be considered a "club good" (non-rival but excludable), although its non-rival effect does imply that even if it is feasible to exclude people this may not be desirable, as the marginal effect on the health of others may outweigh the marginal savings from exclusion.

The second aspect of health amenable to conceptualization as having GPG properties is that of *economic externality effects*. The economic effects of ill health on households may be considerable. While these effects might appear to be essentially private, the cumulative effect on the national/regional economy of the resulting loss of production and income, and thus the potential gain from health improvement, may be substantial. If export markets or the profitability of foreign investments are affected, such economic externalities may spread across borders.

However, while a lower incidence of communicable disease may be considered as a public good, good health more generally is better viewed as a private good, although one which may provide substantial positive (health and economic) externalities. In this respect, the conclusion from Chapter 1 is that it is more appropriate to consider improvements in health as the *goal* of policy, and *interventions to improve health internationally* as possible GPGs *for* health. The majority of this book focuses on such possible GPGH, exploring their status as GPGH and then the usefulness of the concept in enhancing the finance and/or provision of the GPGH in question.

14.3 **What are GPGs for health?**

According to the United Nations Development Programme (UNDP) definition, global public goods *for health* are defined as public goods yielding improvements in health globally, across countries, people, and generations. In Chapter 1 of this book, we proposed a modified definition: that a GPG be considered as

> a good which it is rational, from the perspective of a group of nations collectively, to produce for universal consumption, and for which it is irrational to exclude an individual nation from its consumption, irrespective of whether that nation contributes to its financing.

As indicated in Chapter 1, while the scope of *potential* GPGs for health is wide, it may be narrowed to three broad areas: the production, dissemination and use of knowledge; policy and regulatory regimes; and health systems, which are key *access goods*. Chapters 6–11 explored these three areas in more detail.

As highlighted in Chapter 13, the correct identification of potential, or existing, GPGH is of fundamental importance. If goods are classified incorrectly, either deliberately or accidentally, then the concept risks becoming discredited and losing value even for those goods which are correctly identified as GPGH. A proposed framework for classifying goods as potential GPGH was also offered in Chapter 13, although further work is required to establish a more systematic framework.

As discussed in Chapter 1, health is important as a receptor of externalities. As a result, it is not only GPGs specifically aimed at health improvement that are of relevance; there are many other GPGs outside the health sector for which health is also an important component of the benefits. Other GPGs, which are oriented toward non-health objectives (e.g. international trade agreements) may also have potentially important effects on health, which may be positive, negative, or neutral. If the GPG agenda is to develop in a direction favorable to health, it is important to ensure that the health perspective is effectively taken into account in decision-making, not only in GPGH, but also in what might be considered "non-health" GPGs.

14.4 The "added value" of the GPG concept

But is it worth developing the type of identification framework proposed in Section 14.3? What is the value of identifying something as a GPGH? Chapter 13 brought together several areas where the case study authors felt that the GPGH concept offered something in their specific area, and these do not need to be repeated here.

Overall, we suggest that the primary value of the GPG concept is that the GPG "lens" frames issues and the objectives of public policy, in ways that make explicit the inputs needed to produce the final product. The GPG perspective demonstrates that today's global health challenges require not just good national policies, but also strong global responses, the focal point thus being *international collective action*. Policymakers and their constituencies need to recognize existing interdependencies and the futility and inefficiency of attempts to go it alone. Globalization and increasingly porous borders have globalized aspects of health; international cooperation in health has become a matter of self-interest as well as humanitarian concern.

This cooperation requires a framework for analysis and implementation. The GPG concept, defined in economic terms, provides a distinctive framework for analyzing the financing and provision of specific (global public) goods to improve health. Treating a GPGH as a "good" in the economic sense which has to be produced, rather than as a policy objective, focuses attention on the "production function"; this in turn facilitates the analysis of who benefits and who loses from its production and whether it is a priority within the overall basket of (health and non-health) public goods that could be produced and financed. In today's political and economic climate, an "economic" argument is required, at least as much as a humanitarian one, to secure investment. The stark realities of resource constraints, and the plethora of goods, services and causes that they can be used for, mean that economic considerations are more important than ever in establishing why one thing should be pursued over another. The GPGH framework, as an economic approach, focuses explicitly upon the costs and benefits of possible courses of action. Identification of these costs and benefits, in conjunction with analysis of the mix of public *and* private goods required and domestic or international inputs, then facilitate consideration of the incentives that are needed to produce and disseminate the final good. For example, approaching "free riding" with a set of political and economic "intellectual tools" may generate alternative methods of funding to "solve" the problem.

The GPG concept provides a rationale for investment by developed countries in resolving developing country health problems and supporting their health systems. It may also help to facilitate strategic partnerships between developed and developing countries in the production of goods which will enhance global health and wealth. By considering explicitly and systematically issues in the production and financing of GPGH, the concept prompts new thinking in the realm of finance arrangements. For example, it has been argued that the financing of GPGH should be additional to overseas development assistance (ODA), and countries may begin to allocate resources through two ODA accounts: one for "humanitarian" development aid and one for "GPG" funding. Similarly, to ensure that "free-riding" is minimized, there may be support for the creation of focused GPG funds, or a global participation fund, with contributions mandated such as for current organizations like WHO, with these funds independently managed to support GPGH.

14.4.1 GPGH and poverty reduction

But does the GPG concept help the poor? This is a key aspect in assessing the value of the GPGH concept from the perspective of WHO's Corporate Strategy, which identifies, as the first of four "Strategic Directions" for the Organization, "reducing excess mortality, morbidity, and disability, *especially among poor populations*" (WHO 1999).

Clearly, health and wealth are mutually dependent: investment in poverty reduction is critical to improving health, and investment in health critical to alleviating poverty. To the extent to which they improve the health of the poor, GPGs for health can be seen as an instrument for poverty reduction. Such GPGs for health may also act as inputs to other, non-health, global public goods that are important for alleviating poverty. However, as discussed in Chapter 13, in the context of equity, there are tensions between the GPG concept and a focus on the health needs of the poor. Specifically, the GPG approach implies the prioritization of programs which benefit all over those which offer the greatest benefit to those in greatest need, including the poor.

At the same time, there is a danger that there will, in practice, be a trade-off between alternative GPGH and between GPGH and other health programs in developing countries, as the political and financial capacity of the international system to produce, or to promote the production, of GPGs is considered limited.

This has two important implications. First, it means that the prioritization of possible GPGH is critical. If the net effect on those in greatest need is to be positive, it is imperative to ensure that those GPGH that are produced are those that benefit them most. This means that the decision-making processes through which GPGH are prioritized must represent the poor fully and effectively.

Second, it means that financial support for GPGs (including support for GPG-related activities in developing countries) should not be seen as part of aid or a substitute for it, but rather as a *complement* to aid—the concept represents a reason for *additional* international cooperation and assistance, not for a *reorientation* of that which already exists. Developed countries benefit from GPGH, but their provision is rooted at the national level, and often disproportionately in developing countries. It is therefore in the *self-interest* of wealthy nations to assist poorer nations in contributing to their production. Thus the GPG concept encourages—and in practice is likely to require—extra financial assistance to poor countries, not because they are poor *per se*, as in the case of development assistance, but to enable them to make their contribution to GPGs which benefit developed countries.

However, provision of GPGs depends on the ability to create arrangements that account for the differing incentives facing different countries, and not least the differing means of developed and developing countries. In this context, financial assistance for GPG production may have three key roles.

First, where developed countries have the incentives to produce the GPG and developing countries do not, but where the participation of the developing country is vital, financial assistance can offset the costs to developing countries of participating in the production of the good. This applies particularly to "*weak link*" GPGH, such as disease eradication where efforts to eradicate a disease are only as effective as those in the country exercising the least effort. More generally, financing the production of GPGs from developed country sources rather than developing countries or aid budgets reduces their opportunity cost, and shifts the financial burden to higher levels of income, where its welfare costs are smaller. This increases both the scope of GPGs that are potentially beneficial, and the net benefits of those that are produced.

Second, when incentives exist for developing countries, but not for developed countries (e.g. where diseases are disproportionately incident in poor countries, such as HIV/AIDS, or only incident in poor countries, such as onchocerciasis), financial assistance can help create incentives for the commercial sector ("push-and-pull" mechanisms, such as subsidization for research, advance purchase commitments, and expansion of orphan drug laws) or facilitate market access.

Third, financial support is needed for institutions (or GPG-related activities within institutions) at the global level.

14.5 **Toward a research and policy agenda**

Each of the chapters within this book highlights specific areas for further work in research and/or policy terms. We do not repeat these here, but rather draw together some common themes that form the basis for discussion of future research and policy agendas in the area of GPGH.

14.5.1 **Research**

First, more work is needed to establish a framework for the systematic and appropriate identification of possible GPGH. As indicated, the identification of a possible GPGH is critical; but this is by no means straightforward due to the "elastic" nature of the criteria of rivalry and excludability in consumption. Without an accepted and accurate classification system, the *ad hoc* or opportunistic classification of patently non-GPGs as GPGs will merely lead to the concept becoming devalued, treated with skepticism and, eventually, with cynicism. This will render the concept useless, even to those cases that are "true" GPGH.

The most fundamental research would therefore seem to be the construction of a universally agreed framework. A potential starting point for discussion in this area was illustrated in Chapter 13, but other systems have also been proposed (Sagasti and Bezanson 2001) and a "team" to work on this, encompassing agencies such as the WHO, UNDP, and the World Bank, would clearly be the preferred approach (see also point 5 under Section 14.5.2).

Further, the development of a framework to systematically identify appropriate GPGH could be the foundational element in the development of a more responsive global health architecture. As indicated in the foreword to this book, health is rising rapidly up the global agenda, and globalization has highlighted the ever-closer relationships between countries in securing the health of their population. However, the global health architecture, or policy coherence, has not kept pace and, as indicated in various chapters in this book, has led to inability to address adequately many of today's health problems. The GPGH framework could therefore be of use in focusing attention on the need to draw a more overarching global approach, and the identification of appropriate GPGH to be tackled is a key first task.

Second, an agreed system for the measurement and valuation of the potential costs and benefits of the GPGH needs to be identified consistent with the agreed framework. Accurate assessment of the extent and distribution of costs and benefits expected from the production of a GPGH, have repeatedly been identified within this book as a fundamental prerequisite for the progression of that GPGH. However, there is no clear guidance concerning, for example, which costs and benefits should be included in an analysis of GPGs (especially "indirect" costs and benefits); whether they should be assessed on the basis of health outcome, monetary, or other measures; or how the different welfare effects of financial costs and benefits at different levels of income can satisfactorily be taken into account. Work on a set of "standards" in this area is urgently required.

Third, "access goods" have been repeatedly raised as vital in enabling countries to produce, and populations to enjoy the benefits of, GPGH. However, this may be one area where the GPGH concept risks becoming too "elastic." There is therefore a need to establish the appropriate role and status of "access goods" in the production of GPGH—whether, as we have suggested, they can legitimately be treated *as if* they were GPGs, or whether they are better viewed as a prerequisite for GPGH production, or as synergetic with a GPG approach.

Fourth, there should be a more systematic analysis of the relationship between health and non-health GPGs. Important here will be identifying and quantifying the proximal and distal synergies and contextual determinants of each GPG. For example, water, education and peace/security may all be contextual features within which the GPGH is to operate. In a similar manner, the health-care system and health of the population may be contextual features within which GPGs for education have to operate. It is likely, therefore, that a combined approach may make the production and/or finance of each GPG (health and non-health) more effective than pursuing each alone. What is important here is that the health sector does not focus solely on health-related GPGs, but considers the impact of other GPGs.

Fifth, there is a need for further work on the conceptual and practical relationship between the GPGH framework and other frameworks for international development, such as equity, human rights and "communitarian claims." This is required to secure the appropriate role, or "*niche*" for the GPGH concept, as discussed in Chapter 13, to ensure that it is complementary, rather than competitive or substitutive, with these other frameworks.

Sixth, there is little systematic evidence concerning the appropriate financing systems for GPGH provision in different contexts. Although this has been covered in a broad fashion (e.g. in work conducted for the Swedish Ministry of Foreign Affairs (Sagasti and Bezanson 2001), and the Commission on Macroeconomics and Health (2001)), work is still required to determine what works best in what circumstances. Progress could be made here through the construction of an economic/policy model of GPGH provision and finance, using the research suggested in point 2 above.

Finally, political processes are central both to decision-making on GPGH and to their production, and understanding of them is therefore of critical importance to making the GPG concept work for health. This indicates a need for research on the political opportunities for, and constraints to, effective collective action in the collective interest at the international level, in terms both of formal political structures and processes, and the political dynamics of interactions between countries within such processes.

14.5.2 Policy

First, since it appears that GPGH, once identified, progress only if they are supported by a "champion," it would be appropriate for a lead person or team to be appointed to "manage" the process of ensuring the production of the GPGH identified in this book. This has already been suggested elsewhere with respect to specific disease areas and GPGH (Kaul and Faust 2001). It is also important to establish effective mechanisms for collaboration and coordination between these issue leaders, and to ensure that they are accountable and responsive to potential beneficiaries.

Second, aspects of knowledge that are clear GPGH should be actively pursued. One element of this will be to further the global system and integration of surveillance of communicable disease, including, especially, antimicrobial resistance (AMR) disease. Another critical element will be to redress the balance between the production of knowledge and its dissemination and use, particularly in the case of "intellectual property rights" (IPR) and patent legislation. Specifically, there is an urgent need for revision of the WTO TRIPS Agreement, orphan drug legislation, and other rules affecting IPR relating to medical technologies. The GPG concept clearly indicates the need for the current IPR system to be a redesigned, to optimize the balance between the *production* of knowledge and its *use*, and its alignment with public health priorities, in terms of its effect on health outcomes. This is especially important in ensuring *access* to knowledge that is produced, either in terms of basic R&D results or embodied in products or services.

Third, as indicated in Section 14.6, there is a need for a change in the role of international institutions, and specifically WHO, which have historically been reluctant to engage in developments of international law.

Fourth, there is a desperate need for support to develop national health systems in countries where they are critically weak. As is clear from this book, health systems are the foundation of the efficient provision of most GPGH, and a key constraint to their production. Without such support much of the discussion of GPGH will be in vain, and progress toward their production limited.

Fifth, an inter-agency "GPG task force" should be established to facilitate inter-agency dialogue and coordination concerning GPGH and non-health GPGs, informed by the research agenda outlined above. This would allow international bodies, such as the UN, WHO, the World Bank, and WTO, *together* to establish the range of possible GPGs of interest, and *together* to set the agenda for action. This would be a major first step in advancing the GPG agenda in a favourable direction.

Finally, as a long-term objective, the importance of political processes to the appropriate selection, prioritization and production of GPGH suggests a need to make international fora in which decisions are taken on GPGs more representative, democratic, accountable, and transparent.

14.6 **Next steps for WHO, other health-related agencies and interested parties**

The central role of collective action at the global level makes international organizations an obvious locus for activities related to decision-making on, and the production of, GPGs. The first function of WHO listed in its constitution is to "act as the directing and coordinating authority on international health work" (WHO Constitution Article 2a). This clearly mandates the Organization to adopt a leadership role, in relation both to GPGH and to health dimensions of "non-health" GPGs.

The policy and research agenda outlined above also ties in closely with WHO's corporate strategy, adopted by its Executive Board in 1999. This identifies as "new ways of working":

> playing a greater role in establishing wider national and international consensus on health policy, strategies and standards by managing the generation and application of knowledge and expertise; triggering more effective action to improve health, and to decrease inequities in health outcomes by carefully negotiating partnerships and catalysing action on the part of others; [and] creating an organizational culture that encourages strategic thinking, global influence, prompt action, creative networking, and innovation. (WHO 1999)

Further, the WHO Director General's Annual Report for 2001 reported the planned development of

> new mechanisms to implement the lines set out in the corporate strategy, such as a broad approach to health, poverty reduction, international trade arrangements that do not undermine public health, health within the context of sustainable development and macroeconomic processes, and health and human rights. (WHO 2001)

This implies a focus on several areas of relevance to, and which may be informed by, the GPGH concept. For example, the GPGH concept clearly implies a *broad approach to health*, encompassing the environmental, economic, social and behavioral determinants of health as well as health systems and services; it has potentially important implications for *poverty reduction*, through its potential implications for pro-poor targeting of health programs; it overlaps substantially with *international trade* in areas such as IPR and food safety; and *sustainable development* and *macroeconomic processes* are closely linked to non-health GPGs, such as international financial stability, international trade rules, and international environmental agreements. Clearly, the appropriate application of the GPGH concept is important to the fulfilment of the aspirations embodied in WHO's corporate strategy, and should therefore form an integral part of these proposed "new mechanisms."

How should WHO (especially, but not uniquely) progress work in the area of GPGs and health? Clearly, a major part of its role is to lead the implementation of the policy and research agenda outlined above. Actions are also required in four other areas. First, providing coordination between "vertical" programs for the production of GPGH, and ensuring that efforts to deal with particular diseases contribute to the strengthening of overall health systems rather than skewing resource allocation within them. In particular, WHO should be seen to be actively encouraging and facilitating collaboration and coordination between vertical programs, and support governments in their coordination role at the national level.

Second, WHO could usefully pursue more rigorously the development of model legislation necessary for the production of the GPGH discussed in this book, such as in the fields of intellectual property rights and tobacco control. In particular, there is a need to coordinate both economic and political analyses of various potential legislative options to ensure that the most feasible option is pursued. WHO should therefore be engaged in politico-legal and econo-legal "brokerage" to ensure GPGH production.

Third, WHO could act as a "clearing house" for the information required to produce and finance GPGH. The key issue of the "prisoners' dilemma" results from a lack of information—WHO is perfectly placed to provide a central repository and channel for the transmission of key information relating to specific GPGH, for example, surveillance information for AMR. More broadly it could be involved in collecting and synthesizing information on the experience of GPGH production and finance elsewhere to inform future activities.

Fourth, WHO could raise the profile of the GPG concept to aid understanding of its purpose and relevance to health. This could be extended to provide technical support, guidance, and capacity-building to others working on GPGs and health, nationally and internationally.

These elements chime well with the recent recommendations of WHO's Commission on Macroeconomics and Health (2001), which stated that "an effective assault on the diseases of the poor will require substantial investments in global public goods, including increased collection and analysis of epidemiological data, surveillance of infectious diseases, and research and development into diseases that are concentrated in poor countries" (page 17). It was, further, recommended that "the supply of Global Public Goods (GPGs) should be bolstered through additional financing of relevant international agencies such as the World Health Organization and World Bank by $1 billion per year as of 2007 and $2 billion per year as of 2015" (page 19). The Commission proposed that financing be further supported through two specific routes: the Global Fund to Fight AIDS, Tuberculosis and Malaria ($8 billion per year by 2007) and the Global Health Research fund ($1.5 billion per year by 2007).

The Commission was especially concerned with the strengthening of health systems as a fundamental basis for activities to improve the health of poorer nations and populations. There was also support for the investment in knowledge, and reform to legislation to ensure that pharmaceuticals and other medical technologies are made affordable and available to the poor. The central role of international organizations, such as WHO, was emphasized, especially in the coordination of activities and dissemination of information concerning these activities, such as best practice. Finally, the link between health and non-health GPGs was highlighted.

14.7 Conclusion

The core feature of the GPG concept is recognition of the interdependency of national health and health systems and its focus on international collective action.

From this basis, the GPG concept provides a distinctive framework for analyzing the finance and provision of specific (global public) goods to improve health. This provides a new rationale for investment by developed countries in resolving developing countries' health problems and strengthening their health systems. Development of the concept could also facilitate strategic partnerships between developed and developing countries in the production of goods which will enhance global health, and may in some cases contribute to poverty reduction.

The GPG concept is an economic concept. It therefore frames the issues and objectives of public policy to make explicit the inputs needed to produce the final good, quantify the benefits resulting from that good, and examine the collective action problem in achieving a socially optimal production of that good. Key in this examination is identification of the mix of public and private goods required, what domestic and international inputs are required, and what incentives are needed to produce and disseminate the final "good."

Definition of health-promoting goods along a continuum from pure private to pure public goods, and from purely local to purely global, allows the application of economic theory and methods to the public policy issue of collective action in their production and finance. It may thus help in the development of collective global action in the collective global interest in the field of health. However, it is important also to recognize the limitations of the concept, and the potential dangers of its application.

First, it is not appropriate as an organizing principle or a prioritization mechanism—while it can tell us how to achieve desired outcomes in particular areas, it cannot, by itself, tell us what we should do. It must be seen as a complement to, and not a substitute for, other considerations, including the right to health and equity.

Second, it is essential to avoid stretching the term to include programs that do not constitute GPGs in an economic sense. This would do little to guide their provision, and would merely devalue the concept in contexts where it is more appropriate.

Third, it is important to ensure that GPG provision is additional to, and not a substitute for, development assistance.

Fourth, effective health systems in developing countries are essential to the effective provision of GPGH, without which the range of feasible GPGH will be limited and their provision unnecessarily complex and expensive.

Finally, it should be remembered that collective action—whether in the production of GPGH or in other areas—will be in the collective interest only to the extent that decision-making bodies represent effectively and *equally* the interests of the populations affected. This is as true at the global level as at the national level.

Provided these limitations are taken into account, the GPG concept has the potential to make an important contribution to the promotion of health at the global level.

References

Commission on Macroeconomics and Health. *Macroeconomics and Health: Investing in Health for Economic Development.* Geneva: World Health Organization, http://www.cmhealth.org/, 2001.

Kaul I, Faust M. Global public goods and health: taking the agenda forward. *Bull World Health Organ;* 2001; **79**: 869–74.

Sagasti F, Bezanson. *Financing and providing global public goods: expectations and prospects.* Developing Financing 2000, study 2001:2. Prepared for the Ministry for Foreign Affairs, Sweden, www.utrikes.regeringen.se/inenglish/policy/devcoop/financing.htm, 2001.

WHO. *A Corporate Strategy for the WHO Secretariat: Report by the Director-General,* EB105/3, http://www.who.int/gb/EB_WHA/PDF/ EB105/ee3.pdf, 1999.

WHO. Director General's Annual Report. www.who.int/gb/EB_WHO/PDF/WHA55/ DRPTanglais.pdf (paragraph 137), 2001.

WHO. *Constitution of the World Health Organization,* http://policy.who.int/ cgibin/om_isapi.dll?infobase=basicdoc&softpage=Doc_Frame_Pg42; Article 2(a).

Index